FIGURING
THE SACRED

FIGURING THE SACRED

Religion, Narrative, and Imagination

❋

Paul Ricoeur

Translated by David Pellauer
Edited by Mark I. Wallace

Fortress Press   Minneapolis

FIGURING THE SACRED
Religion, Narrative, and Imagination

Copyright © 1995 Augsburg Fortress. All rights reserved. Except for brief quotations in critical articles or reviews, no part of this book may be reproduced in any manner without prior written permission from the publisher.
Write: Permissions, Augsburg Fortress, 426 S. Fifth St., Box 1209, Minneapolis, MN 55440.

Biblical quotations, unless adapted or translated from the original by the author, are from either the New Revised Standard Version Bible (copyright © 1989 by the Division of Christian Education of the National Council of the Churches of Christ in the United States of America) or the Revised Standard Version of the Bible (copyright © 1946, 1952, and 1971 by the Division of Christian Education of the National Council of Churches).

Interior design: ediType
Cover design: Cheryl Watson, Graphiculture

Library of Congress Cataloging-in-Publication Data

Ricoeur, Paul.
    [Essays. English. Selections]
    Figuring the sacred : religion, narrative, and imagination / Paul
Ricoeur ; translated by David Pellauer ; edited by Mark I. Wallace.
      p. cm.
    Includes bibliographical references.
    ISBN 0-8006-2894-2 (alk. paper)
    1. Religion—Philosophy. 2. Storytelling. 3. Storytelling—
Religious aspects—Christianity. 4. Hermeneutics. 5. Bible—
Criticism, interpretation, etc. 6. Theology. I. Wallace, Mark
I., 1956- . II. Title.
BL51.R43225 1995
200—dc20   95-5454
                                         CIP

The paper used in this publication meets the minimum requirements of American National Standard for Information Sciences—Permanence of Paper for Printed Library Materials, ANSI Z329.48-1984. ∞™

Manufactured in the U.S.A.   AF 1–2894

99   98   97   96   95   1   2   3   4   5   6   7   8   9   10

Contents

Preface

There has long been a need for a systematic collection of Paul Ricoeur's important writings in religious studies. This volume is the most comprehensive anthology of Ricoeur's work in the related fields of history of religions, philosophy of religion, biblical studies, theology, and practical theology. I have included here twenty-one of his most representative articles in religion, beginning with his early biblical and theological writings of the 1970s to his more recent studies on such topics as Emmanuel Levinas's notion of testimony, the identity of Jesus in the Gospel of Mark, and the meaning of suffering in theology after the Holocaust. The collection includes theological articles, philosophical essays, exegetical papers, and sermons, and many of these pieces have been expressly translated for this volume. The book is organized topically and chronologically to aid the reader's critical appreciation of the full scope of Ricoeur's religious thought.

I am deeply grateful to numerous individuals who assisted in the completion of this project. My student research assistants at Swarthmore College—Alex Vishio, Erin Sawyer, Sean Latham, and Ben Bryson—prepared chapter drafts and helped with bibliographical work. They were joined at Swarthmore by Steven Sowards, humanities librarian, and Eileen McElrone, administrative assistant, in the laborious task of securing permissions for the book's contents. Kenner Swain and Eric Crump, faithful friends from the University of Chicago, shared with me some of Ricoeur's unpublished manuscripts and made helpful suggestions as to the final shape of the book's contents. John van den Hengel regularly kept me up-to-date regarding Ricoeur's oeuvre, helping me with the task of organizing an anthology around a thinker whose published work is always expanding. Tim Staveteig and Michael West at Fortress Press provided careful oversight of the project from start to finish. David Pellauer expertly translated the many texts included here, and together we mapped out the original vision for this project and the final composition of the volume. Paul Ricoeur generously gave his permission to publish some of the unpublished material in his possession, as well as his overall authorization to collect his writings in this format. Ellen Ross reviewed drafts of the manuscript and provided friendship and support that helped to make the dream of this project a reality. Finally, I am grateful to Swarthmore College, the National Endowment for the Humanities, and the American Academy of Religion for providing fellowship support that funded release time for the completion of this collection.

MARK I. WALLACE
Swarthmore College

FIGURING
THE SACRED

Introduction

Paul Ricoeur is one of the most original and provocative philosophers writing today. He is best known for his work in philosophy of language, psychology, historiography, social science method, literary theory, and religious studies. At a time when the usefulness of disciplinary boundaries is being questioned, Ricoeur's prodigious oeuvre is animated by a spirit of interdisciplinary interrogation that generates original insights into many of the most challenging intellectual and cultural issues we currently face. His wide-ranging studies bridge modes of inquiry that have long existed in isolation from one another, making his work field-encompassing without lacking depth, rigorously argued without being hegemonistic.

Ricoeur is a philosopher of conversation and mediation. He embodies the Socratic dictum that truth is a dialogic event as he seeks maieutically to bring forth a variety of possible perspectives on the questions under discussion. His charitable interpretations of diverse positions reflect a wide and generous philosophical style that allows him to uncover the often hidden middle ground between the factions that characterize contemporary intellectual life. But his attempts at rapprochement never purchase mediation at the price of ignoring important differences. Rather, Ricoeur's aim is patiently to track the topography of a particular debate in order to articulate a *via media* (often unseen by the disputants) by which one can negotiate the questions at hand. Truth—or better, deeper insight into hitherto unforeseen possibilities—emerges as a result of this careful tracking process. Truth happens in the space opened up in the conversation between newly found dialogue partners—whether those dialogue partners be human interrogators, literary texts, works of art, or cultural artifacts.

"Beyond the desert of criticism we wish to be called again."[1] In spite of (or to spite?) the death of God and the demystification of the cosmos, Ricoeur's dialogic thought echoes with a longing for spiritual values and forces once felt by primordial peoples but now forgotten in a technological age. An authentic response to the question Who am I? is founded, in part, on a recovery of the sacred by taking up residence in the worlds of

---

1. Paul Ricoeur, *The Symbolism of Evil,* trans. Emerson Buchanan (Boston: Beacon Press, 1967), 349.

mythopoetic literature, such as the Bible. Ricoeur well knows that a simple return path back to the powers of traditional religions is no longer tenable. But his writing is characterized, nevertheless, by a fragile hope that in the borderlands beyond calculative reason there might be a world of transcendent possibilities (mediated through the text) that can refigure and remake the world of the reader. The recovery of the power of myth and symbol is possible only through a self-critical, always revisable, and never certain hermeneutical wager. By risking this wager, the interpreter advances, even perhaps realizes, the task of becoming an integrated self. The *first naïveté* of primordial openness to religious symbolism has long been lost to modern people, but a *second naïveté* of belief founded on the traces of the sacred in the world of the text is possible.

In the first half of this introduction I offer a chronological reading of Ricoeur's intellectual biography with special reference to his work in religious studies. In the second half I conclude with comments concerning the scope and rationale of this anthology. I unify my exposition around a distinctively Ricoeurian thesis: the journey to selfhood is made possible by the subject's willingness to receive new ways of being through its interactions with the text-worlds of literature, myth, and religion.

Intellectual Biography

Early Development

Paul Ricoeur was born in Valence, France, on February 27, 1913, and raised by his grandparents in Brittany in the minority tradition of the Protestant Huguenots. He graduated with the *Agrégation de Philosophie* from the Sorbonne in 1935 and attended seminars conducted by Gabriel Marcel. From 1940 to 1945 he was interned in a German POW camp, where he was allowed to study German philosophy and theology, including the works of Immanuel Kant, G. W. F. Hegel, Edmund Husserl, Martin Heidegger, Karl Jaspers, Rudolf Bultmann, and Karl Barth. After the war he taught the history of philosophy at the University of Strasbourg (1948–57) and returned to the Sorbonne to occupy the chair of metaphysics (1956–1967). He was active in the Parisian socialist movement and the promotion of social democracy against the threat of market-driven capitalism. He wrote numerous articles for France's left-wing Christian journals—in particular, *Esprit* and *Le Christianisme social*—on the power of religious socialism to engender community and solidarity and overcome the alienation of modern urban life.[2] In the 1940s and 1950s he became especially well known for

---

2. Some of this material is in English translation. See Paul Ricoeur, *History and Truth,* trans. Charles A. Kelbley (Evanston, Ill.: Northwestern Univ. Press, 1965), and *Political and Social Essays,* ed. David Stewart and Joseph Bien (Athens: Ohio Univ. Press, 1974).

his writings in existential phenomenology and as both a translator of and commentator upon Husserl's thought.[3]

In these early studies Ricoeur argues for Husserl's methodologically controlled reflection in the *Logical Investigations* as a more rigorous extension of Marcel's existentialism. He agrees with Husserl that the value of phenomenological method lies in its description of consciousness to be a consciousness *of* something, a moving outside of oneself to the object or phenomenon intended. He avers, however, that Husserl's later work replaces the description of phenomena given to consciousness with the elevation of the transcendental ego's powers of unmediated perception of the world. Because all understanding is determined by one's historically situated presuppositions concerning the external world, Ricoeur maintains that Husserl's idealizing tendencies must be resisted by a philosophy that grafts the hermeneutics of signs and symbols onto the trunk of the phenomenological description of intentional objects.

This movement toward a "hermeneutical phenomenology" is anticipated in the second installment of a tripartite series by Ricoeur on the philosophy of the will. The first part consists of the volume *Freedom and Nature: The Voluntary and the Involuntary* (1950; Eng. trans. 1966), in which Ricoeur utilizes phenomenological method to describe the volitional and nonvolitional structures of the will. The second part consists of two separate books, *Fallible Man* (1960; Eng. trans. 1965) and *The Symbolism of Evil* (1960; Eng. trans. 1967), and the third part, now permanently suspended, was intended to be a poetics of the will. Although this third volume is technically in abeyance, the goal of this book—to develop a hermeneutical philosophical anthropology beyond the confines of phenomenology—has been realized by Ricoeur's subsequent writings, especially his most recent *Oneself as Another* (1990; Eng. trans. 1992). His many "detours," as he calls them, since the 1950s into psychoanalysis, structuralism, analytic philosophy, social theory, discourse analysis, narratology, and deconstruction have left him uninterested in formally completing the projected poetics of the will. The value of these detours, however, is that they have enabled Ricoeur to articulate a more complicated discordant-concordant understanding of human being than was available to him at the time he had projected finishing his trilogy.

All his early writings on the structure of the will make the same claim: human beings are tethered between freedom and nature, between the self-

---

3. See *inter alia* Paul Ricoeur and Michel Dufrenne, *Karl Jaspers et la philosophie de l'existence* (Paris: Seuil, 1947), and Paul Ricoeur, *Gabriel Marcel et Karl Jaspers* (Paris: Temps Présent, 1948). Ricoeur translated into French with commentary volume 1 of Husserl's *Ideas* in 1950; also see Paul Ricoeur, *Husserl: An Analysis of His Phenomenology,* ed. and trans. Edward G. Ballard and Lester E. Embree (Evanston, Ill.: Northwestern Univ. Press, 1967).

transcending powers of the imagination and the always limiting character of perspectival, fragmented experience. The possibility of an undivided self, the task of becoming a "whole soul," begins with reflective analysis on these two poles. Through this analysis, a self in possession of itself is "won" by a fragile mediation of the consciousness of freedom and the brokenness of unfulfilled desire. Selfhood is a *task* to be performed, not a *given* that awaits passive reception by the subject.

Fallible Man maintains that the always already disproportion between freedom and finitude is the constitutional weakness that makes evil possible. Content with an exposition of the limit-concept of fallibility, this study does not push forward to an analysis of the concrete manifestations of fault in the human condition. This further analysis is deployed in *The Symbolism of Evil,* the companion volume to *Fallible Man,* where the turn is accomplished from a phenomenological (eidetic) description of the faulted disproportion in human being to an interpretation (hermeneutic) of symbols and myths concerning actual evil. "First of all, my investigation into the *Symbolism of Evil,* which followed upon the *Voluntary and the Involuntary* and *Fallible Man,* carried me to the heart of the hermeneutical tradition. For in the case of evil there is no direct concept but, to begin with, symbols, narratives, myths, instead."[4] In *The Symbolism of Evil* Ricoeur takes up his central question, "What is the meaning of human being?" by submerging his analysis in the opaque worlds of story and symbol. The problem of noncoincidence with oneself is again manifest, but now in a mythological register: to be human is to be estranged from oneself because all humans, though destined for fulfillment, are inevitably captive to an "adversary" greater than themselves. The bitter irony of this predicament is most effectively symbolized by the myth of Adam's fall. Though the story is putatively about historical origins, it functions as an etiological myth about a cosmic battle between good and evil already anterior to Adam's decision. Adam is figured as alternately responsible for his own free decision and yet in bondage to an evil power outside of himself. Thus as both free and determined, human beings, like Adam, are "responsible and captive, or rather . . . responsible for being captive."[5]

The Symbolism of Evil brings religious studies to the threshold of a new methodology as a hermeneutical, rather than a strictly philosophical or dogmatic, discipline. Religious studies is a public inquiry into the meaning of symbolic discourses, not a rationalist justification of religious beliefs or a confessionalist defense of traditional doctrines. Ricoeur argues for the premier value of mythopoetic forms of expression, rather than purely philo-

---

4. Paul Ricoeur, "My Relation to the History of Philosophy," *The Iliff Review* 35 (1978): 9.

5. Ricoeur, *Symbolism of Evil,* 101.

sophical or theological modes of discourse, for understanding the meaning of human being in a world charged with the presence and absence of the sacred. The relative superiority of myth over philosophy—or "fiction" over "reason"—is manifest in the power of religious creation stories to uncover the structural disparity in human beings between their fractured nature and their destinies as integrated selves. This disparity can be imagined only indirectly on the basis of mythical imagery; it cannot be studied directly through a rationalist analysis of human history and culture. The myths of the Hebrews and Greeks concerning primordial chaos, primeval fall, original defilement, exile from paradise, tragic fate, and the servile will contain a surplus of meaning hostile to modes of intellectual inquiry that a priori deny to myths and symbols any truth-value concerning the nature of the human condition. The point is not that religious symbolism is irrational or unamenable to philosophical inquiry, but that the rationality of the symbol is available only to the theorist who values the efficacy of mythical literatures.

"The symbol gives rise to thought, and thought returns to the symbol."[6] Ricoeur defines the symbol as a multiple-meaning expression characterized by a hidden logic of double reference. Symbols are like signs in that they intend something beyond themselves. But whereas the sign possesses a relatively obvious and conventional set of denotations, the symbol's meanings are polysemic, difficult to discern, and virtually inexhaustible in depth. Ricoeur uses the example of the symbol "defilement" to make this point. "Defilement" is a double-meaning expression in which the clear, literal meaning stands for the state of physical uncleanliness, while the opaque, figurative meaning "points beyond itself to something that is *like* a stain or spot,"[7] as when one refers to ritual impurity or moral evil as a "stain" or "blemish" on one's character. Because the symbol possesses a figurative reference, it demands interpretation in a way that the transparent sign does not.

Ricoeur maintains that human beings enter consciousness as prior denizens of a world of symbols and myths. Figurative language first interprets us before we interpret it. Since there are no "shortcuts" to selfhood, only when the subject traverses a hermeneutical "long route" through the revealing power of the symbol can she or he enlarge and empower a fuller and more satisfying understanding of the self. This route follows a path from the loss of original belief in the sacred to a critical recovery of the power of myth in a world empty of meaning and hope. "Does that mean that we could go back to a primitive naïveté? Not at all. In every way, something has been lost, irremediably lost: immediacy of belief. But if we can

---

6. Ibid., 347–57.
7. Ibid., 15.

no longer live the great symbolisms of the sacred in accordance with the original belief in them, we can, we modern men, aim at a second naïveté in and through criticism. In short, it is by *interpreting* that we can *hear* again. Thus it is in hermeneutics that the symbol's gift of meaning and the endeavor to understand by deciphering are knotted together."[8] A critical consciousness needs the complement of a mature openness to the symbolic world; a hermeneutic of suspicion operates in productive tension with a hermeneutic of restoration. In this dialectic the voice of the sacred can be heard again, not in the mode of a precritical naïveté but by an interpretive gesture, a second naïveté, that wagers on the power of myth and symbol to elucidate the nature of human being.

The Hermeneutical Turn

In 1967 Ricoeur left the Sorbonne and joined the faculty of the University of Paris at Nanterre, where he was later appointed dean in 1969. At Nanterre he was instrumental in mediating the conflicts between faculty and students over the cries for reform in the French university system during the Paris uprisings of 1968. He did collaborative work with Emmanuel Levinas and was one of Jacques Derrida's teachers. At this time he also became a permanent faculty member of the University of Chicago with appointments in the Divinity School, the Department of Philosophy, and the Committee on Social Thought. He resigned from Nanterre in 1980 and continues as professor emeritus at Chicago.

After the appearance of *The Symbolism of Evil,* Ricoeur has published only one book-length project primarily devoted to the study of religion.[9] Rather, the 1960s and 1970s witnessed his attempts systematically to work out a general theory of interpretation (with regional application to religious studies) in the light of the "hermeneutical turn" in his thought. Three books (*Freud and Philosophy: An Essay on Interpretation* [1965; Eng. trans. 1970], *The Rule of Metaphor* [1975; Eng. trans. 1978], and *Interpretation Theory: Discourse and the Surplus of Meaning* [1976]) and as many collections of essays (*History and Truth* [1955, 1964; Eng. trans. 1965], *The Conflict of Interpretations* [1969; Eng. trans. 1974], and *The Philosophy of Paul Ricoeur: An Anthology of His Work* [1978]) develop

---

8. Ibid., 351.

9. See Paul Ricoeur, "Biblical Hermeneutics," *Semeia* 4 (1975): 29–148, where Ricoeur analyzes the parables of Jesus as refigurations of time at its limits; the parables display before the imagination the eternal and extravagant in the midst of the everyday. For another large-scale writing in religion, there is also his unpublished Sarum Lectures from Oxford University, 1980, on the topic of biblical interpretation and narrative theology. A small section of this manuscript, roughly pages 8–36, is included below in a revised form in "Biblical Time."

further theories of the imagination and the text beyond his earlier concern with myth and symbol.

These studies begin with a detour through psychoanalysis over the question of whether a restorative hermeneutics is possible after Freud's reconstruction of the human as a source of conflicted desires and unresolved forces. Earlier Ricoeur had written that the subject can construct a new identity through its commerce with self-generated figures of the imagination. The subject can experience "redemption through imagination" because in "imagining his possibilities, man can act as a prophet of his own existence."[10] But now Ricoeur follows Freud's description of the imagination, or consciousness, as a projection of unconscious distortions and impulses, or false consciousness. The subject who thinks and feels and dreams is a "wounded cogito" riddled with illusions of freedom and self-sufficiency. Nevertheless, Freud's location of the origins of the subject in false consciousness must be positioned against a similar projection of symbols and figures of a new humanity. In the dialectical spirit of his aborted poetics of the will, Ricoeur contends that an *archaeology* of the decentered subject should stand in tension with a *teleology* of the fulfilled subject that takes seriously, though not literally, childhood dreams, works of art, and religious symbols as lived possibilities for a transformative future. In spite of its overdetermined origins, the imagination can activate these possibilities and offer the broken subject new modes of being in the world.

Ricoeur's work from this period makes three points concerning the relationship between philosophical inquiry and religious faith. First, authentic faith emerges by way of its circuitous travels through a sustained hermeneutics of suspicion. What a Marx or a Nietzsche or a Freud offers the believing community is a panoply of iconoclastic devices for smashing the idols of belief naively unaware of its origins in certain systemic distortions—be those distortions economic, philosophical, or psychodynamic. But "to smash the idols is also to let the symbols speak."[11] In the tension between iconoclasm and belief—or distanciation and appropriation, as Ricoeur sometimes puts it—the believer's presuppositions are productively challenged even as the critic's assumptions are put to the test. Since the acid bath of criticism is mutually purifying for both modes of inquiry, neither the critic nor the believer emerges unscathed from this dialectical encounter. "The faith of the believer cannot emerge intact from this confrontation, but neither can the Freudian conception of reality."[12] The burden of faith is to

10. Paul Ricoeur, "The Image of God and the Epic of Man," in *History and Truth,* 127.

11. Paul Ricoeur, "The Critique of Religion," in *The Philosophy of Paul Ricoeur: An Anthology of His Work,* ed. Charles E. Reagan and David Stewart (Boston: Beacon Press, 1978), 219.

12. Paul Ricoeur, *Freud and Philosophy,* trans. Denis Savage (New Haven: Yale Univ. Press, 1970), 551.

evoke a refined passion for the possible by way of an excavation of the distortions at the base of its origins.

Second, the metaphorical imagination is an ally for the understanding and articulation of faith. In its essence, faith is a living out of the figures of hope unleashed by the imagination. Glossing Kant, Ricoeur argues for the power of the productive imagination to "schematize" novel relationships between the data of experience and the figures of the imagination even though both realms of understanding seem initially unrelated to one another. The imagination generates new metaphors for synthesizing disparate aspects of reality that burst conventional assumptions about the nature of things. Figurative discourses *suspend* first-order references to literal objects and events in order to *liberate* second-order references to a more basic and nonliteral world of unimagined possibilities. The role of the living metaphor is to juxtapose two dissimilar forms of articulation in order to bring to language dimensions and values of reality that have been previously hidden by straightforward, descriptive discourse. "[M]etaphor is the rhetorical process by which discourse unleashes the power that certain fictions have to redescribe reality."[13] "Lamb" and "God," for example, are two distinct terms that resist combination. But the union of both terms in the metaphor "lamb of God" sets free a new understanding of the divine life—as bloody and innocent salvation-bringer—hitherto unavailable to the interpreter apart from this metaphorical innovation.

Third, the power of the text to disclose new possibilities offers the reader an expanded view of the world and a deeper capacity for selfhood. "It is the text, with its universal power of world disclosure, which gives a self to the ego."[14] On this point Ricoeur's lively dialogue with his critics comes to the fore. As he counters some analytic philosophers' arguments against the truth-value of poetic texts, he also disagrees with certain literary theorists' contention that such texts operate within a self-enclosed, private universe that makes no purchase on everyday experience. His point is that the vast majority of poetic texts do refer to the world, though not the world accessible to thoroughgoing positivism and aestheticism, but the world now refigured under the tutelage of the imaginary and the possible. Poetic language does intend reality—it is not a language unto itself divorced from any referential function—but its power of reference is the power to set forth novel *ontologies* that disorient readers in order to reorient them by way of an ever-expanding vision of the whole.

In theological parlance, Ricoeur maintains that a variety of nonreligious and religious fictions (including the Bible) are potentially revelatory—not

---

13. Paul Ricoeur, *The Rule of Metaphor,* trans. Robert Czerny with Kathleen McLaughlin and John Costello (Toronto: Univ. of Toronto Press, 1977), 7.

14. Paul Ricoeur, *Interpretation Theory: Discourse and the Interpretation of Meaning* (Fort Worth: Texas Christian Univ. Press, 1976), 95.

in the sense that they are *deposits* of divinely inspired truths but because they faithfully *enact* a productive clash, and sometimes a fusion, between their world and the world of the reader. Ricoeur understands *revelation* in performative, not propositional, terms: it is an event of new meaning between text and interpreter, rather than a body of received doctrines under the control of a particular magisterium. He refers to the disclosive power of figurative (including sacred) texts as an "areligious sense of revelation" just insofar as any poetic text—by virtue of its powers of metaphorical reference—can become a world that I inhabit and within which I project my innermost possibilities. The world of the text can figure the identity of the sacred and reveal dimensions of the human condition as such for any reader who risks her own self-understanding in the process.[15]

Ricoeur's analysis of the referential function of literary works is an extension and correction of the hermeneutics of Heidegger and Hans-Georg Gadamer. Heidegger maintains that works of art reveal the character of reality by disclosing to the observer the "world" depicted in the art work. Vincent van Gogh's paintings of peasant shoes, for example—with their separated soles, frayed threads, and protruding nails—distill the very essence of working-class life in late nineteenth-century France. "The art work opens up in its own way the Being of beings."[16] Aesthetic objects offer direct access to the nature of Being. With some qualifications Gadamer agrees with Heidegger's thesis concerning the truth of art; he further specifies its application in terms of a "fusion of horizons" between the world of the reader and the world of the text.[17] Understanding occurs in the to-and-fro dialogue between text and interpreter whenever the interpreter is willing to be put into question by the text and risk openness to the world of possibilities the text projects.

While Ricoeur consistently appropriates these insights into the truth-value of art and the dynamics of horizon-fusion, he enters a caveat against a certain romanticist bias against *explanation* in the German hermeneutical tradition from Friedrich Schleiermacher and Wilhelm Dilthey to Heidegger and Gadamer. This tradition has labored against the importation of reductionist methods from nonhumanistic disciplines for the understanding of literary texts and other works of art. While this prohibition has rightly preserved the truth-bearing integrity of creative works, it has wrongly insulated the interpretation of these works from a full and critical evaluation of their origins and interactions with structures of domination and

---

15. Paul Ricoeur, "Toward a Hermeneutic of the Idea of Revelation," *Harvard Theological Review* 70 (1977): 26.

16. Martin Heidegger, "The Origin of the Work of Art," in *Basic Writings*, ed. David Farrell Krell (New York: Harper and Row, 1977), 166.

17. Hans-Georg Gadamer, *Truth and Method*, rev. ed., trans. Joel Weinsheimer and Donald G. Marshall (New York: Crossroad, 1989), 300–311.

oppression. Ricoeur has learned from Jürgen Habermas that a pure conversational model for textual understanding is not enough in the face of the systematic distortions that undermine open dialogue and understanding. Here again Ricoeur articulates the need for both rehabilitative and critical interpretive gestures: no text is free from ideological distortion, and a romantic hermeneutic that blunts the uncovering of such bias is dangerously short-sighted.[18] In order for a fusion between text-world and the reader's world to be efficacious, no critical explanatory device should be excluded from the interpretation process as long as that device does not in principle deny the ontological potential of the work in question. Ricoeur's consistent motto, succinctly expressed in his recent work, is "[T]o explain more is to understand better."[19] Though mindful of the hermeneutical tradition's truth-claims concerning aesthetic media, Ricoeur replaces their "short route" of direct access to Being with his "long detours" of successive methodological requirements for understanding works of art.

The Recovery of Narrative

I have suggested that *The Symbolism of Evil* (as well as other works from the 1950s and early 1960s) inaugurates an expansion beyond the analysis of the structure of the divided will so characteristic of Ricoeur's immediate postwar writings: a hermeneutic of opaque symbols is now grafted onto the phenomenological method. Likewise, *The Rule of Metaphor* marks a shift from Ricoeur's earlier depth readings of myth and symbol to a general interpretation theory that presses a variety of reductive hermeneutics into the service of a more complicated philosophical anthropology. "Today I should be less inclined to limit hermeneutics to the discovery of hidden meanings in symbolic language and would prefer to link hermeneutics to the more general problem of written language and texts."[20] Ricoeur's writings from the 1980s to the present signify still a third stage in his itinerary: the challenge of narratology and deconstruction. The current major texts include *Time and Narrative* (3 vols., 1983–85; Eng. trans. 1984–88), *Lectures on Ideology and Utopia* (1986), and *Oneself as Another* (1990; Eng. trans. 1992). He has also authored papers that have been collected as *Essays on Biblical Interpretation* (1980), *Hermeneutics and the Human Sciences* (1981), *From Text to Action* (1986; Eng. trans. 1991), *A Ricoeur Reader: Reflection and*

---

18. See Ricoeur's mediation of the debate between Gadamer's use of German romanticism and Habermas's critical philosophy in "Hermeneutics and the Critique of Ideology," in *Paul Ricoeur: Hermeneutics and the Human Sciences,* ed. and trans. John B. Thompson (Cambridge: Cambridge Univ. Press, 1981), 63–100.

19. Paul Ricoeur, *Time and Narrative,* 3 vols., trans. Kathleen McLaughlin and David Pellauer (Chicago: Univ. of Chicago Press, 1984–88), 2:32.

20. Ricoeur, *Rule of Metaphor,* 317.

Imagination (1991), and *Lectures* (3 vols., 1991–1994). With these recent works in mind a distinctive pattern can be traced in Ricoeur's oeuvre. His thought has followed a trajectory from his initial analysis of the bad will and the power of symbolic language to a comprehensive hermeneutical model now complemented by an emerging theory concerning the role of narrative in the formation of subjectivity.

"[T]ime becomes human time to the extent that it is organized after the manner of a narrative; narrative, in turn, is meaningful to the extent that it portrays the features of temporal experience."[21] The importance of narrative in understanding human temporality is the leitmotif of Ricoeur's recent thought. His previous work had spoken to the power of myths, symbols, and other figurative discourses in the mediation of consciousness; his current work argues that the desire to be, the task of existence, is inseparable from the scripting of an individual story that gathers together the untold and sometimes repressed narrative fragments constitutive of personal identity. Everyone needs a story to live by in order to make sense of the pastiche of one's life. Without a narrative a person's life is merely a random sequence of unrelated events: birth and death are inscrutable, temporality is a terror and a burden, and suffering and loss remain mute and unintelligible.

Ricoeur's use of narrative as a solution to the problem of identity is founded on the dialectic between history and fiction analyzed in *Time and Narrative*. While he recognizes the differences between history and fiction, he argues that both forms of writing are united by their common reference to the fundamentally historical and temporal character of human existence. One may think of history and fiction as presenting opposing referential claims: history intends a lawlike description of past events, while fiction refers to the unrealities of the imagination that bear little relationship to everyday life. Ricoeur rejects this dichotomy and argues instead that "in spite of the evident differences in the way that history and fiction are related to 'reality'—in whatever sense of the word—they refer nonetheless, each in its own way, to the same fundamental feature of our individual and social existence. This feature is characterized in very different philosophies by the term 'historicity,' which signifies the fundamental and radical fact that we make history, that we are immersed in history, that we are historical beings."[22] He continues that history and fiction share a common *narrative structure* with a shared reference to the field of human action. The concept of plot—or rather "emplotment," as he prefers—is the linking idea that holds together both forms of writing. Emplotment is the art

---

21. Ricoeur, *Time and Narrative,* 1:3.
22. Paul Ricoeur, "The Narrative Function," in *Hermeneutics and the Human Sciences,* 274.

of "eliciting a pattern from a succession";[23] it is the ability to configure episodic and unrelated temporal events into a meaningful totality. The plot sets up a sequence of events and characters, whether real or imaginary, in a certain directed movement under the control of a particular point of view. Emplotment is a historical or literary text's capacity to set forth a *story* that combines the *givens* of contingent historical existence with the *possibilities* of a meaningful interpretation of the whole.

Ricoeur's thesis concerning the role of emplotment as the underlying principle of both history and fiction challenges some fundamental assumptions. First, history contains more "fiction" than a positivist model of history would allow. Insofar as history is a form of *writing* that seeks coherence in the chaos of real events, and not simply a disconnected recounting of these events, history, like fiction, is governed by a wide variety of different aesthetic strategies for organizing past events into a narrative whole. "In other words, history is both a literary *artefact* (and in this sense a fiction) and a representation of *reality*."[24] Historical events are recounted in many different forms—from relatively objective annals and chronicles to full-fledged narratives and highly embellished stories—all of which, by definition, emplot what is recounted according to a certain viewpoint as to the proper configuration, or "meaning," of the events in question.

Second, as history is, in a manner of speaking, "fictional," so fiction is more "real" than is often recognized. Fictional narratives on the order of a novel or play have the capacity to redescribe features of human historicity by bracketing ordinary descriptions of reality. The aim of an imaginative text is the creative imitation of human action—even as the purpose of metaphor, as we saw above, is to redescribe the actual world in terms of possibility. Yet while narrative fiction's mimetic capacities are creative—they do not offer slavish copies of the ordinary world—they remain historically rooted in the common world of human action. Ricoeur paradoxically writes that "because history is tied to the contingent it misses the essential, whereas poetry, not being the slave of the real event, can address itself directly to the universal, i.e., to what a certain kind of person would likely or necessarily say or do."[25] Narrative fictions do have a certain truth-value by virtue of their claim to *assert* something about reality—even if this assertion is on the order of an imaginative variation on the possibilities of everyday existence. Thus both history and fiction (as ideal types) share a

---

23. Paul Ricoeur, "Narrative and Hermeneutics," in *Essays on Aesthetics: Perspectives on the Work of Monroe C. Beardsley,* ed. John Fisher (Philadelphia: Temple Univ. Press, 1983), 153.

24. Ricoeur, "The Narrative Function," 291. See also Ricoeur's qualified endorsement of different narrativist models of history in *Time and Narrative,* 1:121–74.

25. Paul Ricoeur, "Can Fictional Narratives Be True?" *Analecta Husserliana* 14 (1983): 16.

common narrative interest in *describing* what reality *is* (so history) or in *re-describing* what reality is *like* (so fiction) to the end that our being-in-time and being-in-history might be rendered meaningful.

Analogously, Ricoeur maintains in *Oneself as Another* that the construction of a life-story is necessary to give shape and meaning to one's existence. Storytelling helps make sense of the disparate parts of one's experience. Each life is a medley of inchoate events waiting to be told in a comprehensive format; each life is an incipient story waiting to be rendered intelligible by a narrator. In scripting a life-story as one's own, a *self* is born in possession of a refigured identity. To write a life, or to tell a life, is to wager that an exegesis of the self's untold story will pay rich dividends in one's quest for authenticity and integrity.

According to Ricoeur, the solution to the problem of personal identity rests in the distinction between identity as sameness (or idem-identity) and identity as selfhood (or ipse-identity). Idem signifies identity as self-subsisting *permanence* and uninterrupted *continuity* over the span of one's life. Ipse stands for the struggle to faithfully *interpret* one's life by a subject that is continually *refiguring* itself through the stories it appropriates as its own. In the first case, identity is a fait accompli; in the second, a hermeneutical process with no a priori resolution. Generally, however, the notion of identity is used equivocatively, or with primary reference to identity as sameness, with the result that the self is understood foundationally in terms of the Cartesian cogito, a fixed substratum that perdures over time.[26] This entitative notion of the self generates both historicist and physicalist criticisms, neither of which is finally satisfactory according to Ricoeur. Some anticogito thinkers (for example, Michel Foucault) contend that insofar as there is no nonverbal core self, then the subject is nothing other than the sum total of the discourses practiced by its particular culture. Similarly, some analytic philosophers (for example, Derek Parfit), who also criticize Cartesian essentialism, argue that the subject is reducible (without remainder) to its brain states and bodily functions. Ricoeur rejects all three options—foundationalist, historicist, and physicalist—in favor of a narrative hermeneutic of the subject. The self, as neither a fixed entity, cultural cipher, nor biochemical remainder cobbles together its identity by constructing a life-story that uses the resources of various narrative fragments. In the narrative interpretation of a life both history and fiction are borrowed from; and since the references of both genres crisscross the plane of human historicity, a life mediated by stories is a "fictive history, or if one prefers, an historic fiction."[27] We have seen that because narrative fic-

---

26. Paul Ricoeur, *Oneself as Another,* trans. Kathleen Blamey (Chicago: Univ. of Chicago Press, 1992), 1–39 and passim. For a summary of the argument, see Paul Ricoeur, "Narrative Identity," *Philosophy Today* 35 (1991): 73–81.

27. Ricoeur, *Oneself as Another,* 114.

tions are imitations of human action, they can be relied upon as paradigms for answering the question, Who am I? The "who" who asks this question must take the long route to selfhood through the "vast laboratory of thought experiments" available to the subject in cultural stories and symbols.[28]

Is there a religious subtext to this argument? Ricoeur says "no" in the interest of preserving the autonomy and integrity of both philosophy and theology: just as he does not want *Oneself as Another* to be accused of cryptotheology, he does not want theology founded on biblical faith to ground itself on any cryptophilosophy. With this "conflict of the faculties" proviso stated, however, he then teases the reader, as he often does, by going on to adumbrate what a theology of the narrative self would look like given his thesis. In the manner of Levinas, for example, he suggests that such a theology would articulate the ways in which the self is *summoned* by the other (be it the divine or human other) to realize its desire to be by responding to the voice of the other.[29] The call of the human other, the neighbor, for justice and compassion secures the ethical and political aspects of forging a narrative identity. This prescriptive dimension of selfhood brings to light one of the many valences of the book's title: my self is constituted by the other who calls me to responsibility.

In analyzing how the self hears and responds to this call, however, a theology of the refigured self should not take false refuge in any putative metaphysical certainties concerning the nature of the "self" who is addressed. Rather, such a theology would rely on the fragile testimonies to divine graciousness within the biblical literatures and eschew the pseudo-security provided by attempts to prove the reality of God, or found the self, on the basis of some onto-theological amalgam. "The dependence of the self on a word that strips it of its glory, all the while comforting its courage to be, delivers biblical faith from the temptation, which I am here calling cryptophilosophical, of taking over the henceforth vacant role of ultimate foundation."[30] Thus the theology briefly sketched out in *Oneself as Another* is a theology of the summoned self—the self that relies on the self-divesting word of the other in order to repossess itself by following the "true fictions" biblical faith offers to the reader-disciple.

The role of figurative texts in the formation of human subjectivity is the unifying theme that underlies Ricoeur's writing. In this vein, he envisions religious studies as a hermeneutical inquiry into the imaginative potential of myth, symbol, and story to aid our efforts to exist with integrity. Religious

---

28. Ibid., 148.

29. For the role of the other in identity formation, see Emmanuel Levinas, *Totality and Infinity*, trans. Alphonso Lingis (Pittsburgh: Duquesne Univ. Press, 1969). Ricoeur's use of Levinas is developed in *Oneself as Another*, 188–90 and 335–56.

30. Ricoeur, *Oneself as Another*, 25.

traditions use ontologically potent language and imagery to illuminate all that ultimately concerns human beings—our questions about life's meaning, our confrontations with death, our struggles to be at home in the universe. Our individual and corporate worlds remain underdeveloped and impoverished because we no longer have a public symbolic language that speaks both to the brokenness and the intimations of transcendence in our lives. Through hermeneutics of reduction and retrieval, Ricoeur shows how the world's cultural classics (including the Bible) can expansively figure rich and full projections of another way of being in the world that liberates what is *essential* by suggesting what is *possible*.

Outline of This Anthology

The essays collected in this volume comprise the most comprehensive overview of Ricoeur's writings in religion. Most of these essays have not been previously anthologized in a volume devoted to Ricoeur's work. While perhaps a few of the essays will be familiar to readers, the bulk of this collection is not well known in the English-speaking world. David Pellauer has translated many of the essays included here expressly for this volume. The anthology consists of writings from 1970 to the present; except in Part Two, the essays in each section are arranged in chronological order. Though the collection focuses on the religious aspects of Ricoeur's recent thought, it also serves as an introduction to many of his other interests because his religious writings are always situated in close relation to the wide variety of general philosophical topics that occupy his inquiries. These collected essays constitute a rich and diverse body of thought that complements Ricoeur's writings in a variety of other fields, including philosophy, psychology, literary criticism, and historiography. As such this collection fills a lacuna in Ricoeur scholarship in particular, and contemporary religious and philosophical thought in general, by surveying the full range of Ricoeur's recent religious writings in chronological and thematic fashion. This approach allows the reader to trace the development of his thought from his midcareer use of discourse analysis for understanding religious language, to his subsequent concern with the role of narrative in the study of biblical genres, to his more recent inquiries into models of personal identity and the relevance of continental philosophers such as Rosenzweig and Levinas to the contemporary task of theological reflection.

To speak of "development" in Ricoeur's thought is to speak of extensions of, rather than fundamental breaks with, the themes and concerns of his previous writings. I have suggested one such recurrent emphasis in his overall philosophical project: the power of religious language to metamorphize the world of the reader by opening up new possibilities of being-in-the-world. What is distinctive about his specifically religious writings is the regional application of this theme to the role of scriptural discourses—including narratives, laws, prophecies, wisdom writings, and hymns—as occasions for challenging the reader to alternative forms of existence.

In this vein, the particular genre that Ricoeur returns to again and again in these essays is biblical *narrative* by way of his studies of narratology in general. Yet he uses and understands narrative differently from the way many theologians use and understand narrative in the contemporary setting. His concern is to show how the stories of the Bible are not one-dimensional exercises in concordance and triumph but rather multivalent points of intersection for a variety of discourses and their contrasting theological itineraries. He demonstrates how much of the Bible's narrative and nonnarrative material speaks as readily to the ambiguity and futility of existence as it does to the providence of God within covenant and history. Ricoeur's use of—and caution against—narrative for theological reflection places him on the fringes of the camp of narrative theology per se, if by that phrase we mean the privileging of biblical narrative as *the* means to redescribing "reality within the scriptural framework rather than translating Scripture into extrascriptural categories."[31] Ricoeur is wary of assigning final priority to any one particular construal of reality because all forms of literary discourse (and not only biblical narrative discourse) can potentially refigure one's experience and offer new possibilities for understanding. Any genred text that works figurative variations on reality by proposing an imaginative "world" that the reader might inhabit can be said to be "revealed." While the biblical stories are a medium of revelation, they are a species of a wider revelatory function that can be participated in by any text (biblical or otherwise) that unleashes novel alternatives for the reader.

Part One

The first part consists of Ricoeur's general explorations into the nature of religion. He uses methodological tools from history of religions and literary criticism to analyze the articulations of religious belief through symbol and discourse. While he does not go so far as to argue that religion is a sui generis phenomenon, he does maintain that religious beliefs have their own integrity and should not be reduced to explanatory schemas that fail to account for the self-understandings of religious communities. To facilitate the understanding of religion "on its own terms" Ricoeur argues, in a manner similar to Ludwig Wittgenstein, that just insofar as religious be-

---

31. George Lindbeck, *The Nature of Doctrine: Religion and Theology in a Postliberal Age* (Philadelphia: Westminster Press, 1984), 118.

lief and experience are primarily expressed through various discourses, the study of religion should begin with analyzing these modes of articulation. "[W]hatever ultimately may be the nature of the so-called religious experience, it comes to language, it is articulated in a language, and the most appropriate place to interpret it on its own terms is to inquire into its linguistic expression."[32]

In one of the articles collected here, "Philosophy and Religious Language," Ricoeur shows how different modes of signification—symbols, myths, narratives, metaphors, and models—generate a surplus of meaning in the study of religious texts. These literary forms of articulation are not simply taxonomic devices for categorizing discourse but rather the means by which theological meaning is produced. These forms are not merely "decorative [with] an emotional value but no informative value."[33] Modes of discourse, then, are more than just classificatory codes or ornamental trappings because the *content* of religious discourse is determined by the literary *forms* employed to mediate particular theological understandings. The scriptural figuration of the divine life, for example, is radically problematized by attention to the mixed genres employed by the biblical writers. "Throughout these discourses, God appears differently each time: sometimes as the hero of the saving act, sometimes as wrathful and compassionate, sometimes as the one to whom one can speak in a relation of an I-Thou type, or sometimes as the one whom I meet only in a cosmic order that ignores me."[34] The advantage of using discourse analysis for understanding religious texts is that it renders more complicated and heterogeneous the interpretation of biblical faith. In this approach the Bible emerges as an asymmetrical intertext of oppositional genres—genres that alternately complement and conflict with one another—rather than a stable book unified by a particular discourse or singular perspective.

While discourse analysis aids the interpretation of biblical literature, comparative history of religions enables a broader understanding of religious phenomena that includes textual as well as nontextual modes of experience. In "Manifestation and Proclamation" and "The 'Sacred' Text and the Community," Ricoeur takes up the dialectic between the phenomenology of the sacred and the hermeneutic of the word in world spirituality. Primordial religious communities are founded on numinous, preverbal experiences of the sacred in nature and the cosmos, while latter-day, book-centered traditions are formed by belief in an intratribal deity and subscription to a body of iconoclastic teachings. In manifestation communities, religious truth and meaning are universally rooted in the

---

32. Ricoeur, "Philosophy and Religious Language," below, 35.

33. Paul Ricoeur, "Poétique et symbolique," in *Initiation a la pratique de la théologie,* vol. 1: *Introduction,* ed. Bernard Lauret and François Refoulé (Paris: Cerf, 1982), 48.

34. Ricoeur, "Philosophy and Religious Language," below, 41.

correspondences between agricultural cycles and divine power, while in proclamation traditions truth and meaning are authoritatively defined by revealed texts that warn against any manifestation of the Wholly Other through nature and the image.

Equally important are the distinctive temporalities characteristic of the two types. This is the difference between backward-looking archaic time as repetitive of the original cosmogony, and forward-oriented historical time as the progressive anticipation of a better future. Ricoeur argues that if these two notions of time are bifurcated into ideal types, then the one is aesthetic, generic, cyclical, and nature-bound while the other is ethical, particular, interruptive, and history-based. Lest this opposition harden into a false dichotomy, however, Ricoeur avers that biblical religion is actually a recombination of both temporalities: it oscillates between the celebration of "cyclical" festivals and seasons and the testimony of the word in "linear" history. One of the themes, then, of Part One is the need for biblical religion continually to combine the clarifying precision of the *word* in history and the cyclical modalities of the *sacred* in nature. Moreover, unless proclamation traditions reactualize the rootedness of all life in sacred patterns and symbols, these traditions will be empty of the power and mystery that primordial people experienced in their recurring encounters with the numinous. "In truth, without the support and renewing power of the sacred cosmos and the sacredness of vital nature, the word itself becomes abstract and cerebral."[35]

These initial articles highlight Ricoeur's intensive debate with Mircea Eliade on the question of the phenomenology of comparative religions. Ricoeur was a colleague of Eliade's at the University of Chicago Divinity School until Eliade's death in 1984. While Ricoeur is greatly indebted to Eliade for his perspicacious studies of primordial traditions, he questions his lack of attention to the primacy of proclamation in religions founded on a revealed scripture. "In Christianity there is a polarity of proclamation and manifestation, which Mircea Eliade does not recognize in his homogeneous concept of manifestation, epiphany, and so forth.... I think there is something specific in the Hebraic and Christian traditions that gives a kind of privilege to the word."[36] Ricoeur borrows from Eliade (as well as from Rudolf Otto and others) the notion that the universe is charged with the power of the sacred; the universe signifies the numinous through symbols and myths rooted in the depth structures of reality itself. But he takes issue with the deployment of Eliadean analysis at the expense of an equally powerful hermeneutic of the capacity of scriptural texts to open up new dimensions of reality that often challenge the established patterns of

---

35. Ricoeur, "Manifestation and Proclamation," below, 67.
36. Ricoeur, "The 'Sacred' Text and the Community," below, 71.

the sacred universe. While canonical texts need the sustenance of primordial symbolism, the power of such texts cannot be sufficiently accounted for by a comparative phenomenology inattentive to the distinctiveness of word-based religious traditions.

Part Two

The three essays selected for this part represent Ricoeur's close readings of the important works about religion by Kant, Rosenzweig, and Levinas. These essays are not freestanding position papers by Ricoeur but rather critical engagements with different philosophical approaches to religion according to their major practitioners. Ricoeur's own constructive position on various questions is painstakingly worked out by way of expositing each thinker's approach and usually is explicitly delineated only toward the end of each essay.

The essay on Kant forms a natural pair with an earlier essay on Hegel. The two articles give alternative answers to the question of whether the proper aim of philosophy of religion is to secure the idea of God as a *speculative* concept free of figurative thought, or whether its aim is to avoid speculative theorizing in order to enable the *practical* realization of human freedom. For Hegel, the inner dynamism of thought concerning the figures and symbols of religion leads to a sublation (*Aufhebung*) of such figures in pure conceptual thought where Spirit is self-conscious to itself. For Kant, on the other hand, the final absorption of figurative religious thought into speculation is not the dialectical realization of reason's inner directionality but rather a transcendental illusion that should be vigorously resisted. Such an illusion is a violation of the boundaries of reason within the confines of conceptually mediated sense experience. Insofar as Ricoeur upholds the integrity of figurative modes of religious discourse against attempts to translate such discourse into a speculative metalanguage, his sympathies lie more with Kant's philosophy of limits than with Hegel's system of absolute knowledge.[37]

In the essay on Hegel, Ricoeur's purpose is to examine both the evolution of the role of figurative thinking (*Vorstellung*) in Hegel's religious thought and to establish whether such thinking is finally dissolved into conceptual thought (*Begriff*) devoid of pictorial imagery. In the *Phenomenology of Spirit,* Hegel puts the stress on the inadequacy of religious *Vorstellung* to apprehend its subject matter; for this reason religious picture-thinking must endure a continual process of self-realization until it reaches its final

---

37. See Paul Ricoeur, "The Status of 'Vorstellung' in Hegel's Philosophy of Religion," in *Meaning, Truth, and God,* ed. Leroy S. Rouner (Notre Dame, Ind.: Univ. of Notre Dame Press, 1982), 70–88. On Ricoeur's dialogue with Kant and Hegel, see also his argument for a "post-Hegelian return to Kant" in "Biblical Hermeneutics," 136–45.

consummation in conceptual thought. Prior to its final realization, this dynamic inner process reaches its *religious* climax in Christianity just insofar as Christ is the perfect symbol of the self-consciousness of Spirit in and through its other. But because thought about this symbol remains rooted in historical imagery, it is only partially aware of the meaning of the Spirit in and for itself, and so it must be sublated by conceptual thought.

Ricoeur argues, however, that in spite of Hegel's generally negative evaluation of religious *Vorstellung* in the *Phenomenology*, figurative thinking carries a more positive valence in Hegel's later Berlin *Lectures on the Philosophy of Religion*. The reason for this change is that the subject matter of the *Vorstellung* in question changes: the focus on biblical and christological imagery in the earlier work gives way to a valorization of the doctrine of the Trinity in the later work as a more adequate (albeit religious) form of speculation about Spirit. The idea of the Trinity—the interrelationship of Father, Son, and Spirit in and for each—discloses the dynamic nature of reality itself. Thus in the Berlin *Lectures* this idea mediates between the inadequacy of religious pictorial thinking and the superiority of conceptual thought. "Between the trinitarian expression of Christian thought and the high dialectic of conceptual thinking there is a homology that exceeds the shortcomings of pictorial thinking."[38] Ricoeur ends the essay by arguing for the importance of conceptual rigor in philosophy of religion, but without disparaging (as Hegel often does, and especially in the *Phenomenology*) the narrative and figurative dimensions of religious discourses that have founded communities of faith and hope. As Hegel seems to call for at the end of his Berlin *Lectures*, Ricoeur says that only when philosophy is nourished by the figurative ideals of a culture's sacred texts can it fulfill its destiny as a medium for insight and understanding.

In the essay on Kant included here, Ricoeur maintains that Kant's philosophy of religion is a hermeneutic of symbols exercised outside the parameters of his critical philosophy. The reason for the exteriority of religion to philosophy stems from the problem of the "bound will," a problem that is not approachable on the basis of the methodology in the three *Critiques*. Kant argues that while an originary disposition to evil is basic to the human condition, this disposition can only be indirectly "thought" by interrogating the figures and myths of religious belief; it cannot be directly "known" as an element of objective knowledge and experience.

Ricoeur's analysis of Kant's fundamental anthropology in *Religion within the Limits of Reason Alone* hews to the line of Ricoeur's own discussion of the innately faulted character of human volition in his earlier poetics of the will. Humans suffer from the loss of free will—from a propensity to evil even though the actual performance of evil is a result of free choice

---

38. Ibid., 85.

rather than "original sin." Evil, then, is our predilection but also our responsibility; we are both victimized by it and culpable for it. "We might say, supporting Kant, that he has identified what is so upsetting in the confession of evil—I do not say the experience of evil—namely, the following paradox: in each instance, we do evil; but evil was already there.... [Kant] caught sight of the paradox of something that has always been there and yet for which we ourselves are responsible."[39] Kant's response to this paradox is drawn from what Ricoeur aptly calls the "dramaturgy" of biblical Christology where Christ, as the supreme archetype of a person who fully lives the moral law, is pictured as victorious over a cosmically evil antagonist. The value of this archetype lies in its ability to figure the will (and thereby liberate it from its predisposition to evil), not in its reference to the life of the historical Jesus. In this sense we should say that the origin of the Christ symbol is not in a historical event but in the figurative powers of the moral imagination. The archetype is generated by a "schematism of hope" in which the rational *concept* of a will no longer bound by evil inclinations is rendered intelligible and applicable to experience by the concrete *example* of an individual who singularly embodies the autonomy of a rational will. Again, however, Ricoeur is quick to underscore that this archetype in Kant is a figure of the imagination and not an extension of objective knowledge into the inner workings of Reality itself (contra Hegel). "The archetype of a humanity well pleasing to God can be admitted only as a practical ideal, not as a reflective moment of the absolute itself."[40]

Kant frankly admits that the *origin* of evil is inscrutable and that only the *infusion* of supernatural grace (figured by the Christ symbol) can free the bad will. While Kant insists on the importance of these two affirmations for liberating the will, he does not try to *reconcile* them to his earlier critical philosophy. By the same token, such confessionalist statements do not *contradict* the critical philosophy since they clearly fall outside the boundaries of critical reason. Ricoeur concludes that Kant's adroit use of a variety of religious figures (*Vorstellung*) to interrogate the nature of human volition is the key to the success of his project. Whereas Hegel argues that *Vorstellung* in religion is inadequate to the concept of pure Spirit, Kant maintains that the more limited task of interpreting the rich imagery of religious faith has potential for enabling the practical realization of human freedom. Ricoeur argues that this is the burden that should be carried by all philosophy of religion: the explication of figures of hope as a response to the avowal of radical evil.

The essay on Rosenzweig and that on Levinas can also be read in association with each other. In the Rosenzweig essay, Ricoeur's basic interest is

---

39. Ricoeur, "A Philosophical Hermeneutics of Religion: Kant," below, 79.
40. Ibid., 85.

in the meaning of the rhetorical figures that underpin Rosenzweig's philosophy of Judaism in *The Star of Redemption*. For Ricoeur the book's central figure is the six-pointed Star of David. This figure generates a wide range of significations: its upward triangle stands for God at its peak with the world and humanity at its lower angles, while its downward triangle connects the modalities of creation, revelation, and redemption—the central themes that form the structure of the book's first and second parts. But the star is also a figure of the face, both the face of humanity and the face of God. (Here Ricoeur notes in French the affinity between *figure*, or form, and *visage*, or face.) Insofar as the "physiognomy" of the six-pointed star can be understood analogically in relation to a "face" with forehead, eyes, nose, mouth, and so on, and insofar as the face makes an absolute demand on one's ethical obligations, Ricoeur regards the figure/face of the star in Rosenzweig as the master trope for understanding both the interhuman as well as the God-human relationship.

Ricoeur argues that the centrality of the figure of the star in Rosenzweig positions Rosenzweig's project closer to Levinas than Hegel. Ricoeur reads the *Star* as an extended metaphor where *figuration* (rather than *speculation*, as in Hegel) is privileged as the primary medium for philosophical insight. "It might even be more fruitful to compare the tie between figure and speculation for Rosenzweig to the relation of *Vorstellung* (representation) and *Begriff* (concept) for Hegel. We might then see that the relation is something quite other than what Hegel meant. With Rosenzweig we would have a speculation that is metaphorical throughout, a metaphorics that is speculative throughout."[41] In the register of a sustained "metaphorics," Ricoeur highlights two concepts that tie together Rosenzweig's and Levinas's thought: the epiphany of the face and the criticism of totality. On the one hand, both thinkers maintain that the other's face generates within the subject a compelling sense of responsibility for the other's welfare; on the other, they criticize the penchant of Western philosophers for subordinating all experience to absolute reason. Ricoeur concludes by noting, however, that while Levinas appears successful at escaping the sirens of totalizing philosophy, it is less clear whether Rosenzweig, with his facility for system building as demonstrated by the architectonic elegance of the *Star*, has completely abandoned the all-encompassing idealism he purports to have disavowed.

In the final essay of this section, Ricoeur considers the notion of "testimony" in Levinas's thought in relation to the themes of height and exteriority in Heidegger, Jean Nabert, and Levinas. He argues that a "reading together" of these three thinkers shows an increasing reliance on the dimensions of height and exteriority culminating in Levinas's philosophy of the other. At first glance Heidegger seems to assign importance to these

---

41. Ricoeur, "The 'Figure' in Rosenzweig's *The Star of Redemption*," below, 97.

two elements. The subject is never coincident with itself and must rely on a voice "beyond itself" in order to be itself; but this is the voice of conscience *within* the subject and is not finally *exterior* to the subject. Likewise, Heidegger's reference to the value of others exterior to oneself is ultimately subsumed by the notion of the uncanny and the pernicious effects of being in relation to the "they." Ricoeur criticizes Heidegger's philosophy as characterized by an "exteriority without otherness [that] corresponds to this height without transcendence."[42] Nabert fares better than Heidegger in Ricoeur's analysis because Nabert argues for a self-divested subject who testifies to the absolute beyond itself and who can recover its own dignity and identity only by means of this exterior testimony. Ricoeur then analyzes Levinas's full turn to the transcendence and alterity of the other in relation to the subject. For Levinas, subjectivity consists in existing through the other and for the other. To take responsibility for the other, even hostage oneself to the other, is the vocation of true selfhood. In the end, however, Ricoeur returns to Nabert's philosophy of consciousness as a needed counterpart to Levinas's thoroughgoing stress on responsibility for the other. Ricoeur avers that self-identity is not merely a *result* of one's response to the call of the other; it is also what must be *presupposed* for the call to be heard and understood in the first place.

Part Three

Even though Parts Three and Four announce two sometimes unrelated topics—exegesis and theology—both of these sections form a coherent whole in Ricoeur's development of a biblically informed theology. I have divided the parts for heuristic purposes, but the interests of each part constitute the dual foci of a single ellipse. For Ricoeur the disciplines of biblical interpretation and theological reflection operate within the same gravitational space: the complementary and contrasting genres of Hebrew and Christian Scriptures. Theology, first and foremost, is a hermeneutical exercise at work upon the multiple modes of discourse within the Bible. Closer to exegesis than philosophy, theology is a nonspeculative interpretation of the founding discourses of Jewish and Christian faith without the benefit of any rational foundation upon which to base such an enterprise. The temptation of theology has always been to ignore its rootedness in the originary—albeit provincial—languages of biblical religion in favor of a more philosophical orientation. As rational thought-about-God, theology would then be able to justify itself as an independent exercise in reason and argument and go beyond its provenance in the peculiar imagery and language of religious

---

42. Ricoeur, "Emmanuel Levinas: Thinker of Testimony," below, 110.

faith. Ricoeur, however, rejects this homology between theology and philosophy and argues instead for the reinvigoration of theological discourse on the basis of biblical hermeneutics. Theology, then, is *biblical theology*— but not in the sense that that phrase is often understood with reference to neoorthodox thought, as we will see below.

Part 3 brings together Ricoeur's various exegetical writings. The four essays that have been selected are examples of his theory of biblical hermeneutics as well as case studies of his actual readings of biblical texts. Though a philosopher, Ricoeur seeks to avoid theory-heavy methods of biblical reading in favor of a text-immanent approach that projects possibilities of meaning occasioned by the texts themselves. "The question is rather whether there is, before the philosophical-theological interpretation, an interpretation that would not be an interpretation *of* the text or an interpretation *about* the text, but an interpretation *in* the text and *through* the text."[43] This intrinsic approach is governed by sensitivity to the traditions of interpretation already at work within the texts under consideration. The Bible for Ricoeur is a multilayered mass of disparate literary traditions; a successful hermeneutic plumbs the depths of these textual strata and brings to light dimensions of sedimented meaning previously hidden and opaque. He alternately refers to this excavation process as a "depth semantics,"[44] a "semiotics of texts,"[45] or a "synchronic reading [that] complete[s] the diachronic approach of the historical-critical method."[46] Whatever the status of the recounted events in the Bible as historical occurrences, these events now enjoy a textual existence at some remove from their antecedent origins. Their meaning is now a product of their inscription within a network of texts that alternately support and displace one another in an intertextual whole. Whatever their original *Sitz-im-Leben,* it is now the mediation of these events through the *Sitz-im-Wort* of various literary genres that constitutes their present-day significance. Historical criticism can helpfully reconstruct the probable historical "occasions" that generated later literary traditions, but only a synchronic study of the interanimating conjunctions and dislocations between various modes of discourse can explain the complexities of meaning within the Bible.

In conversation with both structuralist (Vladimir Propp) and formalist (A.-J. Greimas) analysts, Ricoeur's semiotic approach considers the codes and oppositions that govern the transformations at work in the biblical texts. In "On the Exegesis of Genesis 1:1—2:4a," he isolates the theme of *separation* as the literary convention that structures the opening creation hymn into a series of dynamic oppositions: order and chaos, night and

---

43. Ricoeur, "On the Exegesis of Genesis 1:1—2:4a," below, 140.
44. Ibid.
45. Ricoeur, "The Bible and the Imagination," below, 148.
46. Ricoeur, "Biblical Time," below, 171.

day, plants and animals. This approach sets up a nature-centered rather than human-centered reading of the Genesis story. Such an interpretation clashes with the historical approach of the neoorthodox biblical theology movement (inspired by thinkers such as Karl Barth and Gerhard von Rad) that subordinated the creation account to the role of a prologue within the overall narrative space of the Hexateuch. Apropos to this *Heilsgeschichte* orientation, the creation of humankind is the crowning high point of the creation story. Ricoeur disagrees with the neoorthodox approach, however, and argues instead for a literary interpretation of the Priestly creation story that construes the story as an ecological text. Thus Genesis 1 is best read as a nonanthropocentric ordering of all life-forms into a cosmic biosphere that precedes and envelops the salvation-history account of the Yahwist redactors.

At stake in this recovery of the syntactical patterns that govern the song of creation in Genesis is the preservation of the integrity of nonnarrative sensibilities vis-à-vis the overall narrative shape of the Hebrew and Christian Scriptures. While narrative constitutes the "most visible framework" for biblical understanding, it is always balanced by its deep connections with other modes of articulation.[47] In "Biblical Time" Ricoeur argues that the biblical message may appear to be moderated by an extended and coherent unilinearity; in fact, however, progressive time is consistently fractured by nonlinear modes of scriptural temporality. Indeed, the biblical time line of a sometimes facile covenantal history is continuously interrupted by the ethical demands of legal discourse, the radically open and eschatological character of prophetic discourse, the cyclical and immemorial nature of wisdom writings, and so forth. The same point is made in this section's other essays. Ricoeur demonstrates in his reading of the Synoptic parables of the wicked husbandmen and the sower and the seed in "The Bible and the Imagination," and in his hermeneutic of the Gospel of Mark in "Interpretive Narrative," that the promise of a historical master story to explain all experience is a chimera. Both the parables and Mark's Gospel function as cautionary tales against naive trust in the power of narrative emplotment to render intelligible the aporetic nature of experience.

This collection of Ricoeur's essays concerning the theory and practice of biblical hermeneutics reflects both stability and change in his exegetical work over the past twenty-five years. All these works are characterized by the use of literary analysis over and against the regnant forms of historical criticism practiced then and now. But the most recent piece, entitled "Interpretive Narrative," reflects the progression in Ricoeur's hermeneutics from structuralism (so characteristic of his Genesis exegesis) to poststructuralism (especially through his current use of the work of Frank Kermode and

---

47. Ibid., 179.

John Dominic Crossan). Now not only does narrative *create* meaning in recombinations with other modes of discourse, but, moreover, in its cross-pollinations with the counternarrative stress on secrecy and futility, it also *subverts* straight-ahead literary and theological coherence by obfuscating what it purports to elucidate. "Is it not the case that we must say that the narrative not so much elucidates things as obscures them in the sense that its manner of narratively interpreting the kerygma is to reinforce the enigmatic aspect of the events themselves?"[48] In a postmodern culture, the pathos and promise of a Ricoeurian depth semiotics are its ability to bring to light the darkness and opacity that shadow even our most prized sacred stories.

Part Four

The essays in this section bring together Ricoeur's theological writings with reference to his literary analysis of the Bible's disparate modes of discourse. The irony of this collection is that while Ricoeur is well known for his theological writings, he has always been uncomfortable with being labeled a theologian. The reason for this discomfort is his suspicion that theologians (as well as philosophers) often fall prey to the tendency to homogenize the Bible's semantic polyphony by way of articulating a body of speculative concepts divorced from the originary discourses of Jewish and Christian Scripture. Two of the essays in this section—"Naming God" and "Toward a Narrative Theology: Its Necessity, Its Resources, Its Difficulties"—stress how attention to biblical genre diversity is necessary for a multifaceted understanding of the divine life. Again the focus falls on the confluence of narrative and nonnarrative discourses, but now with reference to an enriched understanding of God. Before God is defined in univocal terms as Being under the control of a particular metaphysical system, Ricoeur maintains that God is first "named" polyphonically in the medley of diverse biblical genres. "The naming of God, in the originary expressions of faith, is not simple but multiple. It is not a single tone, but polyphonic. The originary expressions of faith are complex forms of discourse as diverse as narratives, prophecies, laws, proverbs, prayers, hymns, liturgical formulas, and wisdom writings. As a whole, these forms of discourse name God. But they do so in various ways."[49] Reflection alongside, not away from, this polyphony should be the presupposition and telos of all theological work.

The use of discourse analysis sensitizes thought about God to the zones of indeterminacy and irruptions of radical discontinuity within the texts that first "name" God for the believing community. Unfortunately, how-

---

48. Ricoeur, "Interpretive Narrative," below, 199.
49. Ricoeur, "Naming God," below, 224.

ever, theology often proceeds as if the salvation-history paradigm it has created—that is, the enclosure of all reality within the creation and eschaton of biblical history—is exhaustive of the full meaning of the Scriptures. While the Bible can be read as a seamless exercise in narrative coherence, an extended "Christian pattern," such an interpretation ignores the Bible's *fête du sens* (festival of meaning) by suppressing the disjunctions that contradict the seeming unity of the all-encompassing plot.[50] "[T]his 'Christian pattern' tends to abolish the peripeties, dangers, failures, and horrors of history for the sake of a consoling overview provided by the providential schema of this grandiose narrative. Concordance finally conquers discordance."[51] Ricoeur's point, as we saw in his papers in Part Three, is that there is more than narrative coherence at work in the biblical naming of God—or, better, that it is only as narrative is interanimated by its cross-fertilizations with other modes of discourse that it can effectively make meaning.

This recurrent emphasis on the interplay between narrative and non-narrative echoes a theme that appears almost as an aside at the conclusion of Ricoeur's multivolume *Time and Narrative*. The book's working thesis concerning the potential of narrative to humanize time is problematized by a final reflection on the temporality of wisdom discourse. The sapiential literature of Proverbs, Job, Ecclesiastes, and Lamentations challenges the totalizing impulses of narrative literatures that purport to emplot all experience on a time line with a clear beginning, middle, and end. Wisdom contends that life in *media res* is riddled with such brokenness and "vanity" that it can never be subsumed under the hegemony of the supreme plot— even the plot of the Deuteronomic History. In the contest between narrative and wisdom, new possibilities of being-in-time are unleashed that question easy resolutions of the problem of existence according to the symmetry of the master story. We need stories in order to make sense of temporal existence, but stories unaided by the tonic of wisdom degenerate into simplifying life's insoluble ambiguities. Wisdom is attuned to the fragility and suffering of existence in a way that narrative is not. "It is not for narrative to deplore the brevity of life, the conflict between love and death, the vastness of a universe that pays no attention to our lament."[52] Without wisdom, narrative inevitably drifts toward a triumphalism insensitive to the power of time to rewrite one's personal plots—and even destroy the putative narrative coherence of one's life.

The two essays on hope and evil in this section make a similar point.

---

50. Paul Ricoeur, "Contribution d'une réflexion sur le langage à une théologie de la parole," in *Exégèse et herméneutique: Parole de Dieu,* ed. Xavier Léon Dufour (Paris: Seuil, 1971), 315.

51. Ricoeur, "Toward a Narrative Theology: Its Necessity, Its Resources, Its Difficulties," below, 238.

52. Ricoeur, *Time and Narrative,* 3:273.

Both essays take their point of departure in the failure of Hegel's dialectic to subsume negativity under the optimism of absolute knowledge. Anachronistically, Ricoeur highlights the value of Kant's attempt to break open Hegel's closed system by arguing for Kant's extension of thought beyond the limits of what can be known with rational certitude. It is not possible to know with finality whether one's hopes are ultimately illusory or in fact grounded in a final resolution of life's aporias, but the wager of religious hope (without the benefit of final certainty) can nevertheless be satisfying for the one who suffers the vagaries of aporetic existence. Correspondingly, this tack spells new directions for the question of theodicy; Ricoeur proposes a practical response to the problem of evil, rather than a theoretical solution. While the "false clarity of an apparently rational explanation"[53] for unmerited suffering and evil is the standard approach to theodicy, Ricoeur argues that only an affective or performative confrontation of evil is adequate to the problem. Returning again to the power of sapiential literature he argues that wisdom is the right source for a theodicy in the mode of feelings and catharsis. Thus a theology in a practical register—consisting of mourning, complaint against God, and the exercise of faith in spite of evil— is the best hope for the sufferer who has moved beyond the pseudosecurity of onto-theological optimism and speculation.

In "The Summoned Subject in the School of the Narratives of the Prophetic Vocation," Ricoeur again takes up the question of selfhood that underpins the bulk of his philosophical writing. This essay is the companion piece to the unpublished paper entitled "The Self in the Mirror of Scripture," which is not included here.[54] Together these two pieces were part of Ricoeur's Gifford Lectures of 1986 that formed the basis of *Oneself as Another*. Ricoeur says that he has not included these essays in the larger volume because he wants to preserve the autonomy and integrity of two related, but distinctive, modes of discourse: theology and philosophy. Thus the "Summoned Subject" essay and its unpublished counterpart provide a revealing angle of vision into the religious import of the larger project of *Oneself as Another*.

The connection between *Oneself as Another* and the essay included here is most obvious in the final chapter of *Oneself as Another*, "What Ontology in View?" In this chapter Ricoeur identifies conscience as the place where selfhood is constituted: in the interior voice of obligation each person is called into responsibility for oneself and the other. Conscience is a formal feature of existence; it is the generic capacity to discriminate between competing values in one's relations to others. In the "Summoned Subject" this

---

53. Ricoeur, "Evil, a Challenge to Philosophy and Theology," below, 254.
54. See also the related essay, "Pastoral Praxeology, Hermeneutics, and Identity," below, which examines the problem of self-identity in the context of practical theology.

moral capacity is examined through the different registries of the prophetic vocation in the Scriptures. The prophet is the model of the "mandated subject" who works for the health of the community by responding to the call to withdraw from the community in order to be sent back to the same. Ricoeur continues that the power of conscience has other theological implications as well. Indeed, conscience is now valorized as the contact point between the word of God and human beings. "Conscience is thus the anthropological presupposition without which 'justification by faith' would remain an event marked by radical extrinsicness. In this sense, conscience becomes the organ of the reception of the kerygma, in a perspective that remains profoundly Pauline."[55] Without conscience, the voice that summons the self to its responsibilities falls on deaf ears. In Ricoeur's earlier writings the imagination played the role of a sort of *praeparatio evangelica* for the reception of the divine word.[56] While not denying this previous emphasis, the focus is now on the subject's *moral* capacity to select which figures of the imagination best enable the subject's care and concern for the other. The work of imagination and the testimony of conscience together empower the subject to appropriate the command to take responsibility for the other's welfare.

The emphasis on the summoned self marks a return to—and extension beyond—Ricoeur's formative anthropological concerns in his unfinished trilogy on the will, but the stress now falls on the specific language of conscience rather than on the structures of volition in general. Perhaps we could say that his Gifford Lectures now complete his earlier poetics of the will. Again as before, the human as moral agent is both *free* and *determined*: free to exercise the autonomy of conscience but delimited since the subject is able to do so only within the confines of the symbolic matrixes that dispose the subject prior to entering consciousness. The resumption of the dialectic between freedom and finitude, so critical to Ricoeur's earlier trilogy, as well as the more recent analysis of conscience, reflects the lifelong impact of Levinas on Ricoeur's thought. For Levinas authentic selfhood is constituted by the self's response to its being summoned—indeed, determined—by the call of the other. "But responsibility for another comes from what is prior to my freedom.... It does not allow me to constitute myself as an *I think*, substantial like a stone, or, like a heart of stone, existing in and for oneself."[57] While Ricoeur makes clear his disagreements with Levinas in "Emmanuel Levinas: Thinker of Testimony" and the final chapter of *Oneself as Another*, he agrees with Levinas that the recovery of

---

55. Ricoeur, "The Summoned Subject in the School of the Narratives of the Prophetic Vocation," below, 272, and "The Logic of Jesus, the Logic of God," below.

56. See, for example, Ricoeur, "Toward a Narrative Theology," below.

57. Emmanuel Levinas, "God and Philosophy," in *The Levinas Reader*, ed. Seán Hand (Oxford: Basil Blackwell, 1989), 180.

the phenomenon of moral agency as care for another is the fundamental task in the journey toward selfhood. Without the assurance of an ultimate foundation (religious or otherwise) upon which to found oneself, the self, summoned by the divine entreaty mediated by conscience, wagers that fidelity to this entreaty will open out to a future of expansive possibilities for itself and others.

Part Five

The essays in this final section consist of sermons and writings in moral theology; they represent the practical extension of Ricoeur's religious thought into the areas of theological ethics, interreligious dialogue, and pastoral care. As with his other writings, these occasional pieces set out a counter-metaphysical approach to religious thought and praxis grounded in the diversity of biblical discourses. Ricoeur argues that theological ethics must begin with the complicated—even contradictory—expressions of virtue and morality within a religious tradition's founding texts before it turns to a conceptual analysis of the meaning of these expressions. He criticizes analytic moral philosophers—from Gene Outka to John Rawls—for systematically "leveling off" the oddities and discontinuities within the Bible's ethical teachings in order to iterate coherent philosophical theories of the good. His point is that general theoretical approaches to ethics both (1) ignore biblical polysemy and (2) offer solutions to the aporetics of moral philosophy that are insensitive to the practical difficulties of crafting an ethical existence. As we saw in the previous sections, Ricoeur is consistently wary of overarching theological systems that operate independently from their base in the primary documents of religious faith because such systems are ultimately false to the fractured character of human experience.

Two of the essays collected here ("Ethical and Theological Considerations on the Golden Rule" and "Love and Justice") and one of the sermons ("The Logic of Jesus, the Logic of God") analyze the biblical aporia between the extravagant commandment of Jesus to *love* one's enemies and give to the other whatever is asked for, and the rule of reciprocal *justice* that seeks to balance the other's needs against the subject's own welfare. Understood oppositionally, the gospel command to love the enemy is extravagant, unilateral, asymmetric, and excessively other-directed, while the biblical ideal of justice is rule-governed, bilateral, reciprocal, and thoughtfully self-reflexive. Ricoeur, however, argues against allowing this polarity to harden into an absolute antinomy and suggests instead the need for an "unstable equilibrium"[58] between the nonutilitarian demand to love at all

---

58. Ricoeur, "Love and Justice," below, 324.

costs and the practical efficacy of adjudicating competing interests in societies governed by the rule of law. This mediation allows for a mutual interpretation of each enterprise in the light of the other, so that the impossible command to practice pure altruism can be reintegrated, but never subsumed, into the reciprocal codes of social justice and penal law that order modern life.

The biblical teaching that forms the background of this dialectic between love and justice is that all human beings are codependent members of an originary and ongoing creation that is nurturing and benevolent. Drawing from the Reformed tradition the idea of a power over all greater than ourselves, Ricoeur maintains that the goodness of creation under divine governance teaches us to be good to one another. "[W]e set in the foremost place the sense of our radical dependence on a power that precedes us, envelops us, and supports us.... Each of us is not left face-to-face with another human being, as the principle of morality taken in isolation seems to imply. Rather nature is between us, around us—not just as something to exploit but as an object of solicitude, respect, and admiration. The sense of our radical dependence on a higher power thus may be reflected in a love for the creature."[59] Ricoeur's creation-centered approach to the tension between love and justice harks back to his earlier ecological exegesis of Gen. 1:1—2:4a. Creation precedes law, and practitioners of the law are reminded that the divine legislation is a *gift* like the creation itself. Understanding the gifted character of biblical obligation ensures that the performance of justice will not degenerate into calculative self-interest, on the one hand, and that the commandment to love the enemy will not slide into allowing oneself to become a victim of the other, on the other hand.

Two of the shorter pieces in this section, "Whoever Loses Their Life for My Sake Will Find It" and "The Memory of Suffering," reprise the role of wisdom discourse to illuminate the nature of the human condition. The first essay uses a wisdom interpretation of the gospel paradox that losing one's life is tantamount to finding one's life. The paradox teaches humility and warns against the pride of false security, even the security of religious knowledge, as a foundation for discipleship. Ricoeur says the gospel paradox only makes sense as an invitation to give up one's trust in God as the guarantor of absolute knowledge and instead trust in the weakness of the cross as the key to a meaningful existence.

The question of trust without security is a theme in the second essay as well. This paper was first delivered in Chicago to commemorate the Holocaust on Yom Ha-Shoah, 1989; it reads as a pastoral response to the wisdom theodicy adumbrated in "Evil, a Challenge to Philosophy and Theology" and the discussion of victimage in chapter 9 of *Time and Nar-*

---

59. Ricoeur, "Ethical and Theological Considerations on the Golden Rule," below, 297.

rative, volume 3. Ricoeur suggests that retelling the stories of the victims of the Shoah is a moral duty that gives a voice to those who were denied their voices. This retelling should avoid, however, the temptation of an explanatory system that would try to make theological sense out of the death camps. While the Bible does offer a theodicy of retribution in which the victims, because of their faithlessness, are held responsible for the violence inflicted upon them, Ricoeur argues instead for a wisdom theodicy of lamentation and anger where the perennial cries of Why me? and How long? are seen as the most adequate responses to unmitigated evil. "Whereas the theory of retribution makes victims and murderers equally guilty, the lamentation reveals the murderers as murderers and victims as victims. Then we may remember the victims for what they are: namely, the bearers of a lamentation that no explanation is able to mitigate."[60] The link between punishment and sin in a retribution theodicy animates a monstrous logic that holds victims and victimizers together as responsible for the Shoah. As we saw in Part Four, Ricoeur offers the alternative of a theodicy of complaint, nourished by biblical wisdom, as the most promising response to events that crush the human spirit and defy final explanation.

The essays in this volume demonstrate the value of Ricoeur's wager on the power of the founding myths and discourses of Western culture to enable the task of existence. In particular, Ricoeur's religious writings suggest that a contrapuntal reading of Judaism's and Christianity's originary scriptural texts offers the best hope for attuning oneself to the different, sometimes irreconcilable, "worlds" one might inhabit in the journey toward selfhood. Nuanced readings of these texts enable one to become an apprentice to the various forms of identity-formation within the Bible that can empower the move from being a nomad without hope to a storyteller of one's own life. This journey to selfhood demands that one compose several autobiographical plots and counterplots, in conversation with different literary genres, in order to make sense of the origin and destiny of one's personal odyssey. While narrative discourse offers the reader the promise of a stable and seamless self emplotted by the Bible's master stories, non-narrative biblical discourse reminds one that the scripturally refigured self can never escape the aporias and discordances of daily existence. We are readers and writers of our own lives, subjects and authors of our own biographies, and our solace is in being able to weave, with freedom and imagination, our fragmented selves into the wider cloth of the biblical tapestry.

MARK I. WALLACE

---

60. Ricoeur, "The Memory of Suffering," below, 291.

Part One

The Study of Religion:
Problems and Issues

Philosophy and
Religious Language

My title expresses in a few words a certain number of assumptions that it will be my task to clarify as far as is possible in the space allotted me.

The first assumption is that, for a philosophical inquiry, a religious faith may be identified through its language, or, to speak more accurately, as a kind of discourse. This first contention does not say that language, that linguistic expression, is the only dimension of the religious phenomenon; nothing is said—either pro or con—concerning the controversial notion of religious experience, whether we understand experience in a cognitive, a practical, or an emotional sense. What is said is only this: whatever ultimately may be the nature of the so-called religious experience, it comes to language, it is articulated in a language, and the most appropriate place to interpret it on its own terms is to inquire into its linguistic expression.

The second assumption is that this kind of discourse is not senseless, that it is worthwhile to analyze it, because something is said that is not said by other kinds of discourse—ordinary, scientific, or poetic—or, to put into more positive terms, that it is meaningful at least for the community of faith that uses it either for the sake of self-understanding or for the sake of communication with others exterior to the faith community.

My third presupposition is that philosophy is implied in this inquiry because this kind of discourse does not merely claim to be meaningful, but also to be true. This claim must be understood on its own terms. It implies that we do not yet recognize the truth value of this kind of language if we do not put in question the criteria of truth that are borrowed from other spheres of discourse, mainly the scientific one, whether we invoke a criterion of verification or a criterion of falsification. The presupposition here is that philosophy is confronted by a mode of discourse that displays

Reprinted with permission from *Journal of Religion* 54 (1974): 71–85. The essay was first presented as a lecture under the auspices of the John Nuveen Chair of Philosophical Theology.

claims both to meaningfulness and to fulfillment such that new dimensions of reality and truth are disclosed, and that a new formulation of truth is required.

Such are the main presuppositions implied in my title, "Philosophy and Religious Language" (or discourse).

My intention is to clarify these presuppositions one after the other by using the specific approach of a theory of interpretation, or, in more technical terms, of a philosophical hermeneutics.

Let me introduce this method by contrasting it with Anglo-American linguistic analysis on the issues raised by the three assumptions I just outlined.

I should say that hermeneutics and linguistic analysis equally share the first assumption, namely, that religious faith or experience may be identified on the basis of the language used. We shall see later, however, that hermeneutics qualifies this first assumption in a way that is proper to it. Nevertheless, this first assumption furnishes the common basis for a fruitful dialogue between the two approaches.

The second assumption, it seems to me, is common to a certain extent to both hermeneutics and linguistic analysis, at least to that brand of linguistic analysis that, with Austin and Wittgenstein, does not want to measure meaningfulness by the canons of artificial languages or of ordinary language as reformulated according to logical rules, but which rather seeks to analyze the functioning of the different language games according to their own rules. Here too we shall see how hermeneutics understands this methodological principle, that is, the requirement that the meaningfulness of a kind of discourse be measured by its own criteria of meaningfulness.

The main discrepancy between linguistic analysis and hermeneutics concerns without a doubt the third assumption. Linguistic analysis is so heavily determined by the history of the principles of verification and falsification that it is very difficult for this school of thought to conceive of a concept of truth that would not be taken for granted and defined a priori as *adequation*. The idea that each mode of fulfillment develops its own criteria of truth and that truth may mean not *adequation* but *manifestation* seems to be alien to the main thesis of linguistic analysis and more typical of hermeneutics, more or less influenced by Heideggerian philosophy. Nevertheless, there are hints of this feeling concerning a necessary revision of the basic concept of truth in the work of Ian Ramsey and Frederick Ferré. But whatever may be the difference in approach, I do not think that it is too inaccurate to say that even this third assumption may become, if not a common presupposition, at least a common issue.

My purpose is not to refute the methodology of linguistic analysis but merely to *clarify* the three assumptions of a philosophy of religious language following a hermeneutical method.

I

As I just said, the first assumption is common both to linguistic analysis and to hermeneutics. Both approach religious faith as *expressed in language.* But the difference of approach starts already at this level. Linguistic analysis readily starts with *statements* such as "God exists," or "God is immutable, all-powerful," and so forth—that is, from statements that clearly constitute a very sophisticated type of expression and that belong to a second-order discourse, that of theology. At this level religious discourse is reinterpreted in conceptual terms with the help of speculative philosophy. A hermeneutical philosophy, on the contrary, will try to get as close as possible to the most *originary* expressions of a community of faith, to those expressions through which the members of this community have interpreted their experience for the sake of themselves or for others' sake.

These documents of faith do not primarily contain theological statements, in the sense of metaphysical speculative theology, but expressions embedded in such modes of discourse as narratives, prophecies, legislative texts, proverbs and wisdom sayings, hymns, prayers, and liturgical formulas. These are the ordinary expressions of religious faith. The first task of any hermeneutic is to identify these originary modes of discourse through which the religious faith of a community comes to language.

To serve this purpose a philosophical hermeneutics will provide certain specific methodological tools, aimed at the clarification of the notion of *modes* of discourse. It will first consider discourse as such and describe its main traits, at least those that undergo a specific change when they are resumed and reshaped by the modes of discourse that we describe as narratives, proverbs, hymns, and so forth. Among these main traits the first feature to consider is the relation between the speech-act and its content, because this relation implies the most primitive dialectics of exteriorization and objectification on which the different modes of discourse will build the autonomy of the corresponding literary forms. What is said is already at a distance from the very act or event of saying. But a similar primary distance may be noticed between the discourse and its speaker, the inner structure and the outer referent, the discourse and its initial situation, and the discourse and its first audience. The problem of interpretation is already started. It does not begin with written texts but with all these subtle dialectics of oral language that give a basis to the concept of modes of discourse.

The decisive step, however, occurs with the consideration of these modes of discourse themselves. Literary criticism calls them "literary genres." I prefer to speak of modes of discourse, in order to emphasize their function in the production of discourse. By "genres," literary criticism designates *class*ificatory devices that help critics to orient themselves in the immense variety of individual works. The modes of discourse are more than means of classification—as the word "genre" seems to say; they are means of production—by this I mean instruments for producing discourse as a *work*. This aspect of discourse has not been considered enough by philosophers because it introduces categories into the field of language that belong to the field of practice, production, work. This, however, is precisely the case. Discourse as a work is organized in wholes of a second order, when compared to the sentence, which is the minimal unit of discourse. In the *Rhetoric,* Aristotle calls this fundamental category *taxis* (composition), which he places in the second place after the "invention of arguments" (*heuresis*) and before "diction" (*lexis*). Thanks to this *taxis,* to this "composition," a text, whether oral or written, presents a texture and calls for an interpretation of its inner organization. Understanding a text is always something more than the summation of its partial meanings; the text as a whole has to be considered as a hierarchy of topics.

It is to this notion of a text as a work that I should relate the function of literary genres, or better, modes of discourse—narratives, proverbs, and so forth. In the same way as the grammatical codes have a *generative* function, to help generate discourse as a sentence, the literary codes too have a generative function. They serve to generate discourse as a narrative, a proverb, and so forth. In this sense, we need a generative poetics that would correspond at the level of the composition of discourse—of the Aristotelian *taxis*—to the generative grammar in Chomsky's sense.

The main implication of this for hermeneutics would concern the new specific kinds of *distanciation* linked to the production of discourse as a work. A poem is a good example. But a narrative would serve the same purpose. A work of discourse, as a work of art, is an autonomous object at a distance from the authorial intention, from its initial situation (its *Sitz-im-Leben*), and from its primitive audience. For this very reason it is open to an infinite range of interpretations. There is room for interpretation because the recovery of the initial event of discourse takes the form of a reconstruction starting from the structure and the inner organization of the specific modes of discourse. In other words, if hermeneutics is always an attempt to overcome a distance, it has to use distanciation as both the obstacle and the instrument in order to reenact the initial event of discourse in a new event of discourse that will claim to be both faithful and creative.

Such is the hermeneutical way of treating our first assumption, namely, that the religious faith of a community has to be identified through its language. In hermeneutical terms this means that the first task of a biblical hermeneut is to identify the different modes of discourse that, taken together, constitute the finite field of interpretation within the boundaries of which religious language may be understood. This task precedes that of a linguistic analysis applied to theological statements that have lost their rooting in these primary expressions of religious faith and that proceed from a reformulation of these primary expressions in a conceptual language of the same order as that of a speculative philosophy.

II

If we assume the hermeneutical formulation of our first thesis—namely that religious experience comes to language through specific modes of discourse—we are prepared to clarify our second thesis according to the same line of thought.

It is not enough to say that religious language is meaningful, that it is not senseless, that it makes sense, that it has a meaning of its own, and so forth. We have to say that its meanings are ruled and guided by the modes of articulation specific to each mode of discourse. Here I reach the fundamental point of my essay, which I will formulate in the following way.

The "confession of faith" that is expressed in the biblical documents is inseparable from the *forms* of discourse, by which I mean the narrative structure: for example, the Pentateuch and the Gospels, the oracular structure of the prophecies, the parables, the hymn, and so forth. Not only does each form of discourse give rise to a style of confession of faith, but also the confrontation of these forms of discourse gives rise to tensions and contrasts, within the confession of faith itself, that are theologically significant. The opposition between narration and prophecy, so fundamental for the mentality of the Old Testament, is perhaps only one of the pairs of structures whose opposition contributes to engendering the global shape of its meaning. We shall speak later of other contrasting pairs at the level of literary genres. Perhaps we should even go so far as to consider the closing of the canon as a fundamental structural act that delimits the space for the interplay of forms of discourse and determines the finite configuration within which each form and each pair of forms unfolds its signifying function.

There are thus three problems to consider under the aegis of forms of biblical discourse: (1) the affinity between a form of discourse and a certain modality of the confession of faith; (2) the relation between a certain pair of structures (for example, narration and prophecy) and the corresponding tension in the theological message; and finally (3) the relation between the configuration of the whole of the literary corpus and what one might correlatively call the space of interpretation opened by all the forms of discourse taken together.

I should say here that I am particularly indebted to Gerhard von Rad for the understanding of this relation between the form of discourse and the theological content and that I find a confirmation of his method of correlation in similar works applied to the New Testament, especially those of Amos Wilder and William A. Beardslee.

The example of narration is perhaps the most striking since it is also in the domain of narrative forms and structures that structural analysis has had its most brilliant success. This example, systematically developed, no longer allows us to construct theologies of the Old or New Testaments that understand the narrative category to be a rhetorical procedure alien to the content it carries. It seems, on the contrary, that something specific, something unique, is said about Yahweh and about Yahweh's relations with the people Israel because it is said in the form of a narrative, of a story that recounts the events of deliverance in the past. The very concept of a "theology of traditions," which provides the title for the first volume of von Rad's *Theology of the Old Testament,* expresses the indissoluble solidarity of the confession of faith and the story. Nothing is said about God or about humankind or about their relations that does not first of all reassemble legends and isolated sagas and rearrange them in meaningful sequences so as to constitute a unique story, centered upon a kernel-event, that has both a historical import and a kerygmatic dimension. It is well known that Gerhard von Rad organizes the whole story from the basis of the primitive creed of Deuteronomy 26. This way of tying together the narrative dimension and the kerygmatic dimension is, for me, of the greatest importance.

On the one hand, taking the narrative structure into consideration in effect permits us to extend structural methods into the domain of exegesis. A comparison between von Rad and the structuralists trained in the school of Russian formalism and post-Saussurian semiology would be very interesting in this respect.

On the other hand, the relation between these two hermeneutics begins to reverse itself once we begin to consider the other side of the narrative, namely, the confession of faith. But this other dimension remains inseparable from the structure of the story. Not just any theology whatsoever can be tied to the narrative form, but only a theology that proclaims Yahweh to be the grand actor of a history of deliverance. Without a doubt it is this point that forms the greatest contrast between the God of Israel and the God of Greek philosophy. The theology of traditions knows nothing of concepts of cause, foundation, or essence. It speaks of God in accord with the historical drama instituted by the acts of deliverance reported in the story. This manner of speaking of God is no less meaningful than that of the Greeks. It is a theology homogeneous with the narrative structure itself, a theology in the form of *Heilsgeschichte.*

I have developed here to some extent a single example, that of the narrative structure and the theological significations that correspond to it. The same should be done with the other literary forms in order to bring to light in theological discourse itself the tensions that correspond to the confrontation of the structures. The tension between narrative and prophecy is exemplary in this respect. The opposition of two literary forms—that of the chronicle and that of the oracle—is extended even to the perception of time, which the one consolidates and the other dislocates, and even to the meaning of the divine, which alternatively seems to have the stability of the founding events of the history of the people and to unfold the menace of deadly events. With prophecy, the creative dimension can only be attained beyond the valley of shadows: the God of the exodus has to become the God of the exile in order to remain the God of the future and not only the God of memory.

I will not say more about this in the limited framework of this essay. It would be necessary to explore other forms of discourse and perhaps other significant contrasts, for example, that of legislation and wisdom or that of the hymn and the proverb. Throughout these discourses, God appears differently each time: sometimes as the hero of the saving act, sometimes as wrathful and compassionate, sometimes as the one to whom one can speak in a relation of an I-Thou type, or sometimes as the one whom I meet only in a cosmic order that ignores me.

Perhaps an exhaustive inquiry, if one were possible, would disclose that all these forms of discourse together constitute a circular system and that the theological content of each one of them receives its signification from the total constellation of forms of discourse. Religious language would then appear as a polyphonic language sustained by the circularity of the forms. But perhaps this hypothesis is unverifiable and confers on the closing of the canon a sort of necessity that would not be appropriate to what should perhaps remain a historical accident of the text. At least this hypothesis is coherent with the central theme of this analysis, that the finished work that we call the Bible is a limited space for interpretation in which the theological significations are correlatives of forms of disclosure. It is no longer possible to interpret the significations without making the long detour through a structural explication of the forms.

III

Let me now say something about the third presupposition of a philosophy of religious language, namely, that it develops specific claims to truth measured by *criteria* appropriate to this kind of discourse. Here too a philosophical hermeneutics paves the way to a more specific treatment of religious expressions, documents, and texts.

The category that has to be introduced here is that of *the world of the text*. This notion prolongs—but at the level of complex works of discourse—what I earlier called the reference of discourse. Let me remind you of the distinction introduced by Gottlob Frege at the level of simple propositions between the sense and the reference. The sense of the meaning is the ideal object that is intended. This meaning is purely immanent to discourse. The reference is the truth value of the proposition, its claim to reach reality. Through this character discourse is opposed to language that has no relationship with reality. Words refer to other words in the round without end of the dictionary. Only discourse, we say, intends things, is applied to reality, expresses the world.

The new question that arises is the following: What happens to the reference when discourse becomes a text? It is here that writing and above all the structure of the work alter the reference to the point of rendering it entirely problematic. In oral discourse the problem is ultimately resolved by the ostensive function of discourse. In other words, the reference is resolved by the power of showing a reality common to the interlocutors. Or if we cannot show the thing being talked about, at least we can situate it in relation to a unique spatial-temporal network to which the interlocutors also belong. It is this network, here and now determined by the discourse situation, that furnishes the ultimate reference of all discourse.

With writing, things begin to change. There is no longer a common situation between the writer and the reader. And at the same time, the concrete conditions for the act of pointing something out no longer exist. Without a doubt it is this abolition of the demonstrative or denotative characteristics of reference that makes possible the phenomenon that we call literature, where every reference to the given reality may be abolished. But it is essentially with the appearance of certain literary genres, generally tied to writing, but not necessarily so, that this abolition of reference to the given world is led to its most extreme conditions. It is the role of most of our literature, it would seem, to destroy this world. This is true of fictional literature—fairy tales, myths, novels, drama—but also of all literature that we can call poetic literature, where the language seems to glorify itself without depending on the referential function of ordinary discourse.

And yet if such fictional discourse does not rejoin ordinary reality, it still refers to another more fundamental level than that attained by descriptive, assertive, or didactic discourse that we call ordinary language. My thesis here is that the abolition of first-order reference, an abolition accomplished by fiction and poetry, is the condition of possibility for the liberation of a second order of reference that reaches the world not only at the level of manipulable objects but at the level Husserl designated by the expression *Lebenswelt,* and which Heidegger calls being-in-the-world.

It is this referential dimension that is absolutely original with fictional and poetic works that, for me, poses the most fundamental hermeneutical problem. If we can no longer define hermeneutics as the search for another person and psychological intentions that hide behind the text, and if we do not want to reduce interpretation to the identification of structures, what remains to be interpreted? My response is that to interpret is to explicate the sort of being-in-the-world unfolded in front of the text.

Here we rejoin Heidegger's suggestion about the meaning of *Verstehen.* It will be remembered that, in *Being and Time,* the theory of understanding is not tied to the comprehension of others but becomes a structure of being-in-the-world. More precisely, it is a structure that is examined after the structure of *Befindlichkeit,* state of mind, has been introduced. The moment of understanding responds dialectically to being in a situation, as the projection of our "ownmost" possibilities in those situations where we find ourselves. I want to take this idea of the "projection of our ownmost possibilities" from his analysis and apply it to the theory of the text. In effect, what is to be interpreted in a text is a proposed world, a world that I might inhabit and wherein I might project my ownmost possibilities. This is what I call the world of the text, the world probably belonging to this unique text.

The world of the text of which we are speaking is not therefore the world of everyday language. In this sense it constitutes a new sort of distanciation that we can call a distanciation of the real from itself. It is this distanciation that fiction introduces into our apprehension of reality. A story, a fairy tale, or a poem does not lack a referent. Through fiction and poetry new possibilities of being-in-the-world are opened up within everyday reality. Fiction and poetry intend being, but not through the modality of givenness, but rather through the modality of possibility. And in this way everyday reality is metamorphosed by means of what we would call the imaginative variations that literature works on the real.

Among other poetical expression, fiction is the privileged path to the redescription of reality, and poetic language is that language that above all effects what Aristotle, in his consideration of tragedy, called the *mimesis* of reality. Tragedy, in effect, only imitates reality because it re-creates it by means of a *mythos,* a fable that reaches its deepest essence.

Now let us apply this notion of a world of the text to some specific religious texts, say biblical texts. In doing so, I propose to say that, for a philosophical approach, religious texts are kinds of poetic texts: they offer modes of redescribing life, but in such a way that they are differentiated from other forms of poetic texts.

Let me follow the route of what must appear at first sight to be a simple "application" to biblical texts of a hermeneutic of poetic texts. This "application," far from submitting biblical hermeneutics to an alien law, restores it to itself and delivers it from several illusions. First, it delivers us from the temptation of prematurely introducing existential categories of understanding to counterbalance the eventual excesses of structural analysis. Our general hermeneutics invites us to say that the necessary stage between structural explanation and self-understanding is the unfolding of the world of the text. It is this latter that finally forms and transforms the selfhood of the reader according to its intention. The theological implications here are considerable: the first task of hermeneutics is not to give rise to a decision on the part of the reader but to allow the world of being that is the "issue" of the biblical text to unfold. Thus, above and beyond emotions, disposition, belief, or nonbelief, is the proposition of a world that in the biblical language is called a new world, a new covenant, the kingdom of God, a new birth. These are the realities unfolded before the text, which are certainly for us, but which begin from the text. This is what one might call the "objectivity" of the new being projected by the text.

A second implication is this: to put the "issue" of the text before everything else is to cease to ask the question of the inspiration of the writings in the psychologizing terms of an insufflation of meaning to an author that projects itself into the text. If the Bible can be said to be revealed, this ought to be said of the "issue" that it speaks of—the new being that is displayed there. I would go so far as to say that the Bible is revealed to the extent that the new being unfolded there is itself revelatory with respect to the world, to all of reality, including my existence and my history. In other words, revelation, if the expression is meaningful, is a trait of the biblical *world*.

Now this world is not immediately carried by psychological intentions, but mediately by the structures of the work. All that we have said above about the relations between, for example, the narrative form of the signification of Yahweh as the actor, or about relations of the form of prophecy with the signification of the Lord as menace and promise beyond destruction, constitutes the sole possible introduction to what we are now calling the biblical world. The power of the most powerful revelation is born in the contrast and the convergence of all the forms of discourse taken together.

A third theological implication of the category of the world of the text: because it is here a question of a world, in the sense of a global horizon, of a totality of meanings, there is no privilege whatsoever for an instruction addressed to the individual person and in general none for personal aspects, in the form of I-Thou or in general in the relation of humankind to God. The biblical world has aspects that are cosmic (it is a creation), that are communitarian (it speaks of a people), that are historical and cultural (it speaks of Israel and the kingdom of God), and that are personal. Humankind is reached through a multiplicity of dimensions that are as much cosmological and historical and worldly as they are anthropological, ethical, and personal.

The fourth theological application of the category of the world of the text: we have said above that the world of the "literary" text is a projected world that is poetically distant from our everyday reality. Is not the new being projected and proposed by the Bible a case par excellence of this trait? Does not the new being make its journey through the world of ordinary experience and in spite of the closedness of this experience? Is not the force of this projected world a force of rupture and of opening? If this is so, must we not accord to this projected world the *poetic* dimension, in the strong sense of the word, the poetic dimension that we have acknowledged of the issue of the text?

Pursuing this line of reasoning to its logical conclusions, must we not say that what is thus opened up in everyday reality is another reality, the reality of the *possible?* Let us recall at this point one of Heidegger's most valuable remarks on *Verstehen:* for him *Verstehen* is diametrically opposed to *Befindlichkeit* in the measure that *Verstehen* is addressed to our ownmost possibilities and deciphers them in a situation that cannot be projected because we are already thrown into it. In theological language this means that "the kingdom of God is coming": that is, it appeals to our ownmost possibilities beginning from the very meaning of this kingdom, which does not come from us.

The route that we have followed thus far is that of the application of a general hermeneutical category to the biblical hermeneutic seen as a regional hermeneutic. My thesis is that this route is the only one at whose end we can recognize the specificity of the biblical "issue." In this Gerhard Ebeling is correct: it is only in listening to this book to the very end, as one book among many, that we can encounter it as the word of God. But once again, this recognition does not appeal to a psychological concept of inspiration, as though its authors repeated a word that was whispered in their ears. This recognition is addressed to the quality of the new being as it announces itself.

One of the traits that makes for the specificity of the biblical discourse, as we all know, is the central place of God-reference in it. The result of our earlier analysis is that the signification of this reference of biblical discourse is implicated, in a special way that we have yet to describe, in the multiple unified significations of the literary forms of narration, prophecy, hymn, wisdom, and so forth. "God-talk," to use John Macquarrie's phrase, proceeds from the concurrence and convergence of these partial discourses. The God-referent is at once the coordinator of these varied discourses and the index of their incompleteness, the point at which something escapes them.

In this sense, the word "God" does not function as a philosophical concept, whether this be being either in the medieval or in the Heideggerian sense of being. Even if one is tempted to say—in the theological metalanguage of all these pretheological languages—that "God" is the religious name for being, still the word "God" says more: it presupposes the total context constituted by the whole space of gravitation of stories, prophecies, laws, hymns, and so forth. To understand the word "God" is to follow the direction of the meaning of the word. By the direction of the meaning I mean its double power to gather all the significations that issue from the partial discourses and to open up a horizon that escapes from the closure of discourse.

I would say the same thing about the word "Christ." To the double function that I have described for the word "God," this word "Christ" adds the power of incarnating all the religious significations in a fundamental symbol, the symbol of a sacrificial love, of a love stronger than death. It is the function of the preaching of the cross and resurrection to give to the word "God" a *density* that the word "being" does not possess. In its meaning is contained the notion of *its* relation to us as gracious and of *our* relation to it as "ultimately concerned" and as fully "recognizant" of it.

It will thus be the task of biblical hermeneutics to unfold all these implications of this constitution and of this articulation of God-talk.

We can now see in what sense this biblical hermeneutics is at once a particular case of the sort of general hermeneutics described here and at the same time a unique case. It is a particular case of a more general enterprise because the new being of which the Bible speaks is not to be sought anywhere but in the word of this text that is one text among others. It is a unique case because all the partial discourses are referred to a name that is the point of intersection and the index of incompleteness of all our discourse about God, and because this name has become bound up with the *meaning-event* preached as resurrection. But biblical hermeneutics can claim to say something unique only if this unique thing speaks as the world of the text that is addressed to us, as the issue of the text.

To conclude this essay I should like to make a suggestion concerning the concept of religious faith that we have not considered in itself but through its linguistic and literary expressions. For a hermeneutical philosophy, faith never appears as an immediate experience but always as mediated by a certain language that articulates it. For my part I should link the concept of faith to that of *self-understanding* in the face of the text. Faith is the attitude of one who accepts being interpreted at the same time that he or she interprets the world of the text. Such is the hermeneutical constitution of the biblical faith.

In thus recognizing the hermeneutical constitution of the biblical faith, we are resisting all psychologizing reductions of faith. This is not to say that faith is not authentically an *act* that cannot be reduced to linguistic treatment. In this sense, faith is the limit of all hermeneutics and the nonhermeneutical origin of all interpretation. The ceaseless movement of interpretation begins and ends in the risk of a response that is neither engendered nor exhausted by commentary. It is in taking account of this prelinguistic or hyperlinguistic characteristic that faith could be called "ultimate concern," which speaks of the laying hold of the necessary and unique thing from whose basis I orient myself in all my choices. It has also been called a "feeling of absolute dependence" to underscore the fact that it responds to an initiative that always precedes me. Or it could be called "unconditional trust" to say that it is inseparable from a movement of hope that makes its way in spite of the contradictions of experience and that turns reasons for despair into reasons for hope according to the paradoxical laws of a logic of superabundance. In all these traits the thematic of faith escapes from hermeneutics and testifies to the fact that the latter is neither the first nor the last word.

But hermeneutics reminds us that biblical faith cannot be separated from the movement of interpretation that elevates it into language. "Ultimate concern" would remain mute if it did not receive the power of a word of interpretation ceaselessly renewed by signs and symbols that have, we might say, educated and formed this concern over the centuries. The feeling of absolute dependence would remain a weak and inarticulated sentiment if it were not the response to the proposition of a new being that opens new possibilities of existence for me. Hope, unconditional trust, would be empty if it did not rely on a constantly renewed interpretation of sign-events reported by the writings, such as the exodus in the Old Testament and the resurrection in the New Testament. These are the events of deliverance that open and disclose the utmost possibilities of my own freedom and thus become for me the word of God. Such is the properly hermeneutical constitution of faith.

– 2 –

Manifestation and Proclamation

This essay will deal with the study of a polarity or tension that I wish neither to see disappear into a simple identity, nor to allow to harden into a sterile antinomy, or still less an unmediated dichotomy. Its two poles arise out of a concern for the hermeneutics of religious language, especially as this problem has been shaped by the question of demythologization in recent biblical theology, and the phenomenology of the sacred arising out the comparative history of religions. By a hermeneutic of religious language I understand that work of interpretation and reinterpretation by which a group or an individual appropriates the meaning content of speech-acts and writings that found the group's and the individual's existence as a community and as a person.

There is such a hermeneutic, therefore, where the accent is placed on speech and writing and generally on the word of God. This is particularly true of Judaism, Christianity, and Islam. Furthermore, there is such a concern for hermeneutics where the accent is placed upon the historicity of the transmission of the founding tradition and where this activity of interpretation is incorporated into the very constitution of that tradition. I will gather these three traits together under the common term "proclamation," and I wish to oppose the phenomenology of the sacred to such a hermeneutic of proclamation.

The first part of my essay will be devoted to an investigation of those traits of the sacred that, in my opinion, do not enter into a hermeneutic of proclamation and that give rise therefore to a phenomenology of manifestation. Then in my second part I want to accentuate those traits of a hermeneutic of proclamation that are either virtually or in fact destructive of the sacred. Finally, I want to pose the question that constitutes the horizon of this whole inquiry, namely: Can a hermeneutic of proclamation extricate itself from a phenomenology of the sacred? Or, to put it more bluntly, can the kerygma annihilate the sacred? Can the meaning of the word be constituted without in some way taking up into itself the signs of the sacred?

Reprinted with permission from *Blaisdell Institute Journal* 11 (1978): 13–35.

Let me repeat that I do not wish to harden our opposition into something insignificant because it is dichotomous. I wish instead to firmly establish this opposition in order to make more significant the exchanges that do take place between the two poles.

I. Phenomenology of Manifestation

I will begin by organizing the phenomenology of the sacred around five traits that I will accentuate in order to emphasize its antihermeneutical side. In so doing, I must acknowledge my debt to the work of Mircea Eliade, my colleague at the University of Chicago.

The first trait was brought to light by Rudolf Otto in his well-known book *The Idea of the Holy*. The sacred is experienced as awesome, as powerful, as overwhelming. Whatever objections one might address to this description of the sacred, especially against Otto's insistence upon the irrationality of the sacred, its character of being "shaking" (*tremendum*) and "fascinating" (*fascinosum*), it is appropriate that our study should begin at the heart of an experience that does not inscribe itself within the categories of the Logos of proclamation and its transmission and interpretation. The "numinous" element of the sacred is not first of all something to do with language, even if it may become so to a certain extent subsequently. To speak of "power" is to speak of something other than "speech," even if the power of speaking is thereby implied. It is a power that does not pass over completely into articulation since it is the experience of efficacy par excellence.

The second trait is one by which Mircea Eliade introduces his work. It concerns the central notion of a "hierophany." Eliade's insight is that although we cannot directly describe the numinous element as such, we can at least describe how it manifests itself. So anything by which the sacred shows itself is a hierophany. And at the same time, a phenomenology of the sacred is possible because these manifestations have a form, a structure, an articulation. However, and to me this is essential, this articulation is not originally a verbal one, even though the expressions "to manifest" or "to show" may suggest this. Here no privilege is conferred on speech. The sacred can manifest itself in rocks or in trees that the believer venerates; hence not just in speech, but also in cultural forms of behavior. (We will return to this point with our third criterion of the sacred.)

That a stone or a tree may manifest the sacred means that this profane reality becomes something other than itself while still remaining itself. It is transformed into something supernatural—or, to avoid using a theological term, we may say that it is transformed into something superreal (*surréel*), in the sense of being superefficacious while still remaining a part of common reality.

Now, that there are such things so saturated with efficacy is the primitive fact that does not simply get taken up into the element of proclamation. Here we must take into account not just the amplitude of the field of hierophanies but also its belonging to an aesthetic level of experience rather than to a verbal one. "Aesthetic," I use in the Kantian sense of articulation in space and time. What is most remarkable about the phenomenology of the sacred is that it can be described as a manner of inhabiting space and time. Thus we speak of sacred space to indicate the fact that space is not homogeneous but delimited—*templum*—and oriented around the "midpoint" of the sacred space. Innumerable figures, such as the circle, the square, the cross, the labyrinth, and the mandala, have the same spatializing power with respect to the sacred, thanks to the relations these figures establish between the center and its dimensions, horizons, intersections, and so on. All these phenomena and the related phenomena by which the passage from profane to sacred space is signified—thresholds, gates, bridges, pathways, ladders, ropes, and so on—attest to an inscription of the sacred in a level of experience beneath that of language.

The temporality of the sacred is no less preverbal than is its spatiality. The heterogeneity of time signifies something absolutely primitive in comparison to language. Certain founding events give time a center comparable to the omphalos of space. In sacred time there are strong and weak times. A festival interrupts profane time just as the temple interrupts space. So *tempus* and *templum* correspond to each other. The festival is that time when one lives closer to the gods, when the efficacy of being reveals itself within the density of time.

If it were a question of expressing this spatial-temporal constitution philosophically, it would be necessary to return to the categories of the imagination as they are presented in Kant's *Critique of Judgment*. There, in speaking of aesthetic ideas, Kant related them to the productive imagination that, he says, "gives us more to think about" (par. 49) because the capacity to determine an object by a concept is surpassed by the capacity to present the ideas of our reason in images. The sacred is in the same position in relation to its manifestations as the ideas of our reason are in Kant in relation to their presentation in the products of the imagination. Or, to use an expression of Henri Corbin, we could say that the sacred unfolds a space of manifestations that must be called imaginary (*imaginal*) rather than logical in nature.

A third trait of the sacred underscores its essential "nonlinguisticality." It concerns the close tie between the symbolism of the sacred and ritual. The sacred does not reveal itself just in signs that are to be contemplated, but also in significant behavior. The ritual is one modality of acting (*faire*). It is "to do something with this power or powers."

I do not mean by this just (or even essentially) those magical manipulations by which human beings attempt to dispel, appease, render favorable, or capture these powers, but rather every manner of practically signifying what is aesthetically signified in space and time. To see the world as sacred is at the same time to *make* it sacred, to consecrate it. Thus to every manifestation there corresponds a manner of being-in-the-world. For example, to the disposition of space around a center correspond the construction rituals that make that space inhabitable. Between the sacrality of space and the act of habitation subtle exchanges occur. The threshold of the temple or of the house, for example, is a visible expression of the discontinuity that occurs between the sacred interior and the profane exterior. This is also signified by acts of investiture that by means of a specific action maintain the opening of the profane domain toward the sacred. And in the same fashion, every human establishment practically reiterates this centrality: the village is constructed around an intersection oriented to the four horizons just as a square built around a central point is an *imago mundi*. *Roma quadrata* was installed at the center of the *orbis terrarum!*

The same correlation may be discerned between the sacrality of time and the rituals that make it sacred, the more so since rites practically organize the alternation of strong times and weak times, the rhythm of eating and drinking, of love and work, of the time for debate and the time of a festival. In this way not only the activities around the house or the temple are sacralized, but every act of life, especially the working of the ground that repeats the activity of the gods. The work of agriculture, in other words, more than any other expresses this relation between ritual and the cosmic paradigms.

Someone may object that there is no ritual or even any manifestation of the sacred without myth, that is, without a story about the beginning, hence without discourse. But precisely this correlation between myth and ritual— so abundantly demonstrated by the Scandinavian school of the history of religions for all the literature of the ancient Near East—attests to the nonautonomy of the linguistic element in the myth. The function of the myth is to fix the paradigms of the ritual that sacralize action. Today we read myths, transforming them into literature, but we have previously uprooted them from the act of recitation that had bound them to ritual action. Thus the creation myth *Enuma Elish* was a part of the great New Year's festival in Babylon where the whole ceremony was intended to reactualize the original combat between the god Marduk and the sea monster Tiamat; in short, the primordial cosmogonic act. Here speech is part of the ritual, and this in turn makes sense only as the actualization of the cosmogony. In this way myth as recited and inserted in the ritual of renewal makes *homo religiosus* participate in the efficacy of the sacred.

A fourth trait marks the distance between manifestation and proclamation in a still more decisive fashion. It concerns the role of nature, of the natural "elements"—sky, earth, air, water, fire—in hierophanies and in the phenomenology of the sacred. In his *Patterns in Comparative Religion*, Eliade has articulated the sacred as a function of certain great cosmic polarities. Thus the figure of the sky supports the symbolism of the Most High and generally of divine transcendence. And to this sky cycle are attached images of ascension, of mountains or ladders, those of flight and of levitation, as well as astral, solar, and lunar symbolism, along with uranian epiphanies such as thunder, lightning, storms, and meteors. This symbolism, in turn, refers back to the polarity of divine immanence that, in contrast to divine transcendence, is manifested in the hierophanies of life. This new symbolism, in a way, relieves the inaccessibility of the Most High, and Eliade in this regard speaks of myths of divine withdrawal, divine indifference and idleness, and of the retreat of the gods. The proximity of the gods is then attested to in the fertility of the soil, vegetative exuberance, the prosperity of the flocks, and the fecundity of the maternal womb. Nowhere else is the solidarity between the sacred and natural powers so well attested to. Nowhere else, either, may we apprehend the point of rupture between theologies of the word in battle with the sacredness of nature so clearly.

The sacred power of nature is first attested to by the fact that it is threatened and uncertain. The sacred universe, after all, is a universe that emerges out of chaos and that may at any instant return to it. The sky is ordered and life is blessed only because the chaotic depths have been and must unceasingly continue to be overcome. The sacred, in a word, is dramatic. This is well exemplified by water symbols. Their principal function is to evoke the universal source of potentialities from wherein existence emerges as both real and experienced. Through this power of water, as well as that of shadows, demons, and infernal regions, as well as in a multitude of other ways, nature speaks of the depth from which its order has emerged and toward which chaos it may always regress.

In their turn, the cults based on vegetation do nothing more than bring to the level of myth and ritual the primordial sacrality of life in its mysterious emergence into the world. In the sacred universe there are not a few living beings here and there, but life is a total and diffuse sacrality that may be seen in the cosmic rhythms, in the return of vegetation, and in the alternation of life and death. The symbol of the tree of life—or of knowledge, or immortality, or youth—in this respect is the highest figure of this fundamental sacrality of life.

And few images in this regard have marked religious humankind more than that of Mother Earth. One Homeric hymn celebrates her as follows: "Solid earth, beloved of the gods, who nourished everything in the world, ... you are the one who gives life to mortal beings and who takes it away again." It is also Mother Earth who is sung of by Aeschylus's Corephore: "You who have given birth to everything, raise them and receive them again into your womb." Even the Rig-Veda echoes this when in speaking of funerals it says: "You who are earth, I place on the earth." Here again what the myth says, ritual performs. When a woman, for example, gives birth while lying on the ground or when she places her newborn child on the ground, she is expressing the original pact between mortal life and the earth by means of a ritual gesture. So the sacrality of woman and of her fecundity is also inscribed within this immanence of the divine. And, to cite just one more example, in many cults marriage between two human beings imitates the cosmic hierogamy of the earth and the sky, which is once again to speak of the cosmogony.

Faced with these innumerable hierophanies of a natural character, the same objection mentioned earlier may again be raised: just as one cannot speak of ritual apart from myth, that is, without an element of linguisticality, so one may not speak of the sacredness of nature without the symbolism that expresses and articulates it and thereby brings it to language. This is quite true. But within the sacred universe, the symbolism is a *bound* symbolism, or, to speak like Kant when he speaks of independent beauty and adherent beauty, it is an adherent symbolism. Here, in my opinion, is the essential fact for the dialectic of manifestation and proclamation. Symbols come to language only to the extent that the elements of the world themselves become transparent, that is, when they allow the transcendent to appear through them. This "bound" character of symbolism—its adherence—makes all the difference between a symbol and a metaphor. A metaphor is a free invention of discourse, whereas a symbol is bound to the configurations of the cosmos. Thus we said above that water symbolizes something virtual or potential, but we are the ones who speak of virtuality and potentiality, yet it is the epiphanies of water itself that "bind" this discourse about virtuality, potentiality, the unformed, chaos.

Hereby saying this, I in no way mean to minimize the element of linguisticality inherent in the symbolism of the sacred. In particular, I repudiate entirely the idea that natural profane experience comes to be disguised in allegories based on nature, as though the reawakening of vegetation as a natural phenomenon were the ultimate meaning of vegetation cults. In this regard, Eliade is perfectly justified in saying that the experience of the renewal of the world precedes and justifies the valorization of spring as the resurrection of nature. Here language does not serve to disguise the profane within the sacred as with euhemerists or the Stoics. Rather, what I mean in speaking of the adherence of symbolism is that symbolism is significant only when borne by the sacred valences of the elements themselves. This adherence is not such that it does not call for a labor of speech and interpretation, as though it were a mute spectacle. However, this labor of speech and interpretation is not "free," but rather "bound" by the appearance of the elements and the appearance of the sacred in and through these elements.

Of course, something like a creation story is necessary if symbolism is to come to language, but the myth that recounts it returns in a way to nature through the symbolism of the ritual where the element becomes once again immediately meaningful, as may be seen in the rituals of immersion, emersion, ablution, libation, baptism, and so on.

We may also say that the innumerable particular revelations related to water form a system capable of integrating them and that this structuring and totalizing character, which the word "symbolism" itself suggests, brings into play a labor of language. This, too, is not false. We must even admit that a symbolism is operative only if its structure is interpreted—the case, for example, of the symbolism of the waters of death as interpreted by Eliade. And in this sense, any functioning of a symbolism requires a minimal hermeneutics. Yet this linguistic articulation does not suppress but rather presupposes what I have called the adherence of the symbolism that seems to me to characterize the sacred universe. The interpretation of this symbolism would not even get under way if its labor of mediation were not legitimated by the immediate liaison between the appearance and its meaning, as for example in the water hierophanies we have been considering. The sacredness of nature shows itself in symbolically saying itself. And the showing founds the saying, not vice versa. Its sacrality is immediate or it does not exist.

A final trait sums up the preceding ones. It concerns what we might call the logic of meaning in the sacred universe.

In their own way each of the four traits we have discussed so far concerned the discourse situation in the sacred universe. We noted, successively, the antecedence of the powerful over its meaning; the aesthetic, that is the spatial-temporal, level of manifestation; the correlation between myth and ritual; and, finally, and above all, the bound character, the adherence of natural symbolism. All these traits attest that in the sacred universe the capacity for saying is founded on the capacity of the cosmos to signify something other than itself. The logic of meaning here thus proceeds from the very structure of the sacred universe. Its law is a law of *correspondences*:

- the correspondence between creation *illo tempore* and the order of natural appearances and human actions—for example, the fact that the true temple always conforms to some celestial model;

- the correspondence between the macrocosm and the microcosm—for example, the hierogamy of earth and sky agrees with the union of male and female;

- the correspondence between the furrowed earth and the female genital organ, between the entrails of the earth and the maternal womb, between the sun and the eye, semen and seed grain, burial and the death of grain, between birth and the return of springtime;

- the correspondence in three registers of the body, the house, and the cosmos, which makes the pillars of a temple and the spinal column, the roof of a house and the skull, human breath and the wind, all mutually signify one another—and which makes thresholds, gates, bridges, and narrow pathways outlined by the act of inhabiting space correspond to homologous "passages" assisted by rites of initiation at the critical moments of the human peregrination, including birth, puberty, marriage, and death.

Such law of correspondence constitutes the logic of manifestation.

II. Hermeneutic of Proclamation

In my second part of this presentation I propose to sharpen the opposition between a hermeneutic of proclamation and a phenomenology of manifestation even further, in order to render even more fruitful the diverse mediations that are capable—up to a certain point—of mitigating an opposition that would be too curt and too little dialectical without such mediation.

The Judeo-Christian tradition, it seems to me, introduced a polarity into the religious sphere that we run the risk of misunderstanding if we purely and simply identify the religious and the sacred. It is perhaps on this point that I would stand at some distance from Mircea Eliade. Not that he is unaware of the difference, but he attempts to keep it within the sphere of the sacred as a divergence that does not really affect or alter the profound unity of the sacred universe.

We need to begin with the Hebraic domain. There, in effect, the rupture is consummated. Indeed, one cannot fail to be struck by the constant, obstinate struggle against the Canaanite cults—against the idols Baal and Astarte, against the myths about vegetation and agriculture, and in general against any natural and cosmic sacredness—as expressed in the writings of the Hebrew prophets. Nor can one fail to be bothered by this struggle if one thinks that these cults, idols, and myths illustrate exactly what we have described and, in a certain sense, celebrated as the sacred in the first part of our presentation. Considering our criteriology of the sacred once again, let us look for the reasons for such an unceasing combat against the sacred within the very strictures of the Hebraic faith.

I will say first of all that with the Hebraic faith the word outweighs the numinous. Of course, the numinous is not absent from, say, the burning bush or the revelation at Sinai. But the numinous is just the underlying canvas from which the word detaches itself. This emergence of the word from the numinous is, in my opinion, the primordial trait that rules all the other differences between the two poles of the religious. In this respect, the work of Gerhard von Rad is particularly illuminating. The whole of Israel's theology is organized around certain fundamental *discourses:* on the one hand, the story is the matrix of a theology of traditions, the instructions of the Torah being articulated in terms of the confession of the liberating acts for which the exodus is paradigmatic; on the other hand, there is prophecy, which goes so far as to overthrow the bases of certitude and confidence posited by the story of the founding events. Other forms of discourse—the hymn, wisdom, and so on—are grafted onto this polarity of tradition and prophecy. In every manner, the religious axis passes through such speech-acts.

As for hierophanies—where we saw the second criterion of the sacred—we may say that within the Hebraic domain they withdraw to the extent that the instruction through the Torah overcomes any manifestation through an image. A theology of the Name is opposed to any hierophany of an idol. Indeed, it is not by accident that the prohibition against graven images accompanies the speculation about Yahweh's name. Hearing the word has taken the place of a vision of signs. Certainly there is still a sacred space (a temple) and a sacred time (the festivals). But the general tendency, even though it did not entirely or enduringly prevail over its rival, is fundamentally ethical and not aesthetic. To meditate on the commandments wins out over venerating idols.

The third criterion of the sacred calls for similar remarks. If the Hebraic world is highly ritualized, the ritualization of life is no longer founded on the correlation between myth and ritual as in the sacred universe. In that universe, in effect, the correlation rests on the reactivation here and now of a theogonic act that serves as the paradigm for every sacred action. In Israel, on the contrary, a historical vector runs through the time of repetition and reactualization. No one has emphasized this capital difference between the ritual actualization of the cosmogony and a fundamentally historical vision of reality more than has André Neher in all his writings.

It is no surprise therefore that the sacredness of nature, which was our fourth criterion, generally withdraws before the element of the word, before the ethical element, and before the historical element. In particular, a theology of history could not accommodate a cosmic theology. The battle had to be merciless, without any concession. Listen, for example, to Second Isaiah: "You cut down a tree and cut it in two. With one half you make an idol, with the other a fire to warm yourselves!" Nothing could better express the Israelite refusal of a sacred environment. Yet this radical desacralization also turns back against everything that in a theology of traditions, even an Israelite theology, would give an assurance comparable to those given to the pagans by the paradigms that governed their myths. The perspective of the Day of Yahweh—a day of wrath, not of joy—opens up an abyss still to come, according to which every prior certitude must appear as derisory. Must we go so far as to say that prophecy unmakes the cosmos that ritual is employed to make sacred? Nostalgia for the "desert," the time of the betrothal of Yahweh and the people, is opposed polarly to the vision of a cosmos centered around a sacred place. The act of habitation is shaken to its depths. One day, another rabbi will say, "Follow me." "Yes, I come to separate the son from his father, the daughter from her mother-in-law. Your enemies will come from your own house." One does not become a disciple, in other words, without uprooting oneself.

This uprooting cannot finally fail to shake up what we called the logic of meaning of the sacred universe and its system of correspondences. I would now like to show this by dwelling upon the analysis of several modes of discourse that are quite characteristic of the teachings attributed to Jesus by the Synoptic Gospels. (I mean the parable, the proverb, and the eschatological saying.) I discern in them a radicalization of the antinomy of hierophany and proclamation by means of a new logic of meaning that is diametrically opposed to the logic of correspondences. This new logic is the logic of limit-expressions.

Considered in themselves, these modes of discourse are traditional. It is Jesus' use of them that is significant.

I will begin with the parables, for they offer a noteworthy starting point due to their essential profaneness. They are stories constructed around some predicament or plot, a *mythos,* to use Aristotle's language when he describes Greek tragedy in his *Poetics.* But the scenes in the parables are as unmythological as possible. We find in them landlords and sharecroppers, shepherds and their flocks, foreign princes or voyagers, tax collectors and extortioners, fathers and sons. As one contemporary commentator puts it, "A parable is a metaphor of normalcy." In turn, a predicament counts as a parable to the extent that its narrative form is animated by a metaphorical process that transfers its meaning in the direction of existential situations that constitute the parables' ultimate referent. Earlier we spoke of what this referent might be in a religious dimension that has nothing to do with the sacred. Let us for the moment confine ourselves to emphasizing the thoroughly linguistic character of this mode of discourse. Everything it contains is ordinary. On the one hand, the narrative plot lends itself to literary critical analyses based on the plot structure of the predicament. On the other hand, the metaphorical process that runs through the narrative structure may be entirely analyzed with the resources of a theory of metaphor close to model-theory in the philosophy of science. If a model is a heuristic fiction for redescribing reality, the parable is a fictive tale with a symbolic function. But here the symbolism is not bound to nature. It proceeds from the heuristic function of fiction. This function is heuristic inasmuch as it functions as an instrument of redescription.

By redescription, I mean that poetic language in the broad sense of the word abolishes the reference of ordinary language that is a first-order descriptive, didactic, and prosaic language, and by means of this epoché of natural reality it opens up a new dimension of reality that is signified by the plot. In a parable the fiction brings about this epoché that wipes out what I am calling the first-order descriptive reference in favor of the metaphorical reference that works here as a model does for scientific understanding. In saying this, I am really doing nothing more than rejuvenating Aristotle's analysis in his *Poetics*. Poetry is mimetic because it is mythic. It mimics reality because it creates a plot. In the same way, the parable redescribes life through the fiction of its story.

But, you may respond, what is religious in all this? You have described the parable in terms of a poetics in Aristotle's sense of this term, but what is specific about religious language with regard to poetic forms of language?

Here the comparison with the two other forms of discourse—the proverb and proclamatory discourse—will furnish the key to the difference of religious language within poetic language. This difference depends entirely on the logic of correspondences in the sacred universe. In his analysis of religious discourse, Ian Ramsey calls this language an "odd" or "bizarre" language, and he locates this oddness in the use of what he calls "qualifiers." These are modifiers that bring about a bursting of ordinary meaning as when we speak of the *omni*potence of God or of God as *first* cause. Yet, in my opinion, Ramsey was mistaken, like so many others in the school of linguistic analysis who have discussed the sense or nonsense of religious propositions, to attack assertions that were already highly elaborated from a theological point of view. In my opinion, we should consider the most originary, hence the most pretheological, level of religious discourse possible. The parables, proverbs, and eschatological sayings, for example. There we may grasp the working of Ramsey's "qualifers." It is, for example, noteworthy that the parables are parables *of* the kingdom of God. "To what shall we compare the kingdom? The kingdom is like a man who..." How does the expression "kingdom of God" work in the metaphorical movement that bears the plot toward redescription? We are unable to answer this question unless we bring the parable together with the other two modes of discourse. Then we see that the same process of "transgression" toward a limit-expression makes these three forms of discourse converge upon the signification "kingdom of God," which in a way may be said to constitute their vanishing point.

The logic of meaning at work in the proverbial formulas is in this regard extremely illuminating. Considered as a mode of discourse, the proverb is a traditional form of Oriental wisdom. In distinction from apocalyptic literature that emphasizes the uniqueness of the Hebraic tradition, the proverb intends to throw up a bridge between the point of view of faith and the experience of the person outside the faith circle. It is a maxim whose purpose is to further discernment and to orient a decision within the particular circumstances of existence. Yet, within the context of the Synoptic Gospels, this form of discourse is carried to its breaking point through a systematic usage of paradox and hyperbole that brings about what one contemporary critic has called an "intensification" in the use of the proverb. This intensification interests me because of the logic of meaning it implies. It is easy to discern the paradox, for instance, in those proverbs that, in a way, "abuse" the rhetorical figure known as a change of fate, as expressed in such antithetical formulas as "Whoever would save his life will lose it, and whoever loses his life for my sake will live." The reversal here is so sharp, says the same critic, that it dislocates our imagination and turns it away from its vision of a continuous sequence from one situation to another. Any project of making a continuous whole of one's existence is ruined, for what could it mean to formulate a coherent project on the basis of a maxim such as "Lose your life to find it"? And yet the same proverb implicitly affirms that, in spite of everything, life is reconciled and harmonious even through its paradoxical nature. If not, we would have here only a skeptical or ironical negation of the project of existing.

Hyperbole is another form of intensification: "Love your enemies, do good to them that hate you." Once again the hearer is dislocated in her or his life project. Still it is not a question here either of humor or detachment. Hyperbole, like paradox, leads us back to the heart of existence. The challenge posed to conventional wisdom is at the same time a way of life.

Such is the proverb's strategy; popular wisdom has achieved a first orientation, but the proverb in the Synoptic Gospels intends to reorient us by disorienting us. And the eschatological sayings function in the same way: "The kingdom of God will not come with signs that you can observe. Do not say, 'It is here; it is there.' Behold the kingdom of God is among you" (Luke 17:20-21). Here again a traditional form is submitted to use and abuse, and the language game of the eschatological saying is brought to its breaking point. Every literal temporal scheme capable of providing a framework to read the signs of the kingdom collapses. The apocalyptic practice of "seeking for signs" is overthrown, for the expression "The kingdom of God is among you" transcends all the classical interpretations of the kingdom—including Joachim Jeremias's self-realizing eschatology, Charles H. Dodd's realized eschatology, and Albert Schweitzer's consequent eschatology—in the direction of a completely new existential signification. And in this way the existential time so envisaged in relation to the mythic calculation of signs in traditional eschatology is analogous to the movement of disorientation and reorientation brought about by the proverb.

We can make the logic of meaning implicit in this use of limit-expression more precise if we return to the parable and discern there a trait that has not yet been emphasized, namely, the extravagance within the story. This extravagance, it seems to me, is homologous to the paradox and hyperbole of the proverb as well as to the rupturing of mythic time in the eschatological expressions. The parables recount stories that could happen and even that have happened. But it is precisely this realism of situations, characters, and predicaments that sets off the eccentricity of the behavior that the kingdom of God is compared to. The extraordinary within the ordinary, such is the logic of meaning in the parables. Consider, for example, the extravagance of the landlord in the parable of the evil tenants. After having sent his servants, he sends his son. What Palestinian landowner would act in such a foolish way? And what of the host in the parable of the great banquet who searches in the streets for guests to replace those who had been invited? Or the father in the parable of the prodigal son? Does he not exceed all the boundaries of complacency? The man who found a treasure in a field and sold everything he had to buy the field, is he not like the worst kind of real estate speculator or oil or coal baron? Where has anyone seen a small seed give rise to a tree so large that the birds may nest in it? Finally, think of the parables of crisis. Is ordinary life so avaricious, so cruel, that it really offers only *one* chance? Is life really so inexorable that there is *no* appeal against its condemnations? Extravagance—the extraordinary in the ordinary—does it not follow a logic highly similar to that of hyperbole and paradox?

I have said enough to suggest the idea that the logic of meaning in all these forms of discourse depends on the use of *limit-expressions* that bring about the rupturing of ordinary speech. This act of rupturing the ordinary is what I oppose to the logic of meaning of the sacred universe founded as it is on the correspondence of the macrocosmos and the microcosmos, of humankind, its dwelling place, and the universe, of our mother and the earth. The universe of the sacred, we said, is internally "bound." The paradoxical universe of the parable, the proverb, and the eschatological saying, on the contrary, is a "burst" or an "exploded" universe.

Exploded toward what? The Gospels say the kingdom of God. But what must be understood here is that this symbol entirely escapes from the circular symbolics of the cosmic interplay of correspondences. The kingdom of God is polarly opposed to paradise, not only as the future is opposed to the past but as every limit-expression is opposed to the whole of interplay of correspondences. And in this regard, the expression "kingdom of God" may be understood as the *index* that points limit-expressions in the direction of *limit-experiences* that are the ultimate referent of our modes of speaking.

Indeed, it seems to me that the final step that needs to be taken here is to say that religious language—at least *this* religious language—uses limit-expressions only to open up our very experience, to make it explode in the direction of experiences that themselves are limit-experiences. The parable, we said, redescribes experience. But it does not redescribe it in the fashion of one more poetic language among others, but according to its intending of the *extreme*. All discourse, including political and ethical speech, is touched by this demand for "something more" that is hinted at in the saying and in the extravagant life of the parable, in the paradox and hyperbole of the proverb, and in the announcement that the kingdom of God is present. These limit-experiences are not only experiences of crisis and decision, as in many theologies of crisis, nor just experiences of distress as in the thought of Karl Jaspers. They are also experiences of culmination, as in the parable of the pearl of great price where "finding the inestimable" constitutes the supreme joy.

III. Toward What Mediation?

I do not wish to conceal from you the work, even the adventure, involved in exploring the middle range of this powerful polarity, nor how incomplete this enterprise is at present. Hence I will confine myself to two forms of discourse, the first of which I will call iconoclastic discourse, and the other, discourse that would be a repetition or reenactment of the first. My preference is for the second form, but without forgetting the first one.

Iconoclastic discourse says something like the following.

First, one fact of our culture is that we live in a desacralized world. Our modernity is constituted as modern precisely by having moved beyond the sacred cosmos. Nature, for modern persons, is no longer a store of signs. Its great correspondences have become indecipherable to them. The cosmos is mute. Human beings no longer receive the meaning of their existence from their belonging to a cosmos itself saturated with meaning. Modern persons no longer have a sacred space, a center, a *templum,* a holy mountain, or an *axis mundi*. Their existence is decentered, eccentric, a-centered. They lack festivals, their time is homogeneous like their space. This is why we only speak of the sacred world today as something archaic. The sacred is the archaic. Furthermore, the beginning of the end of this archaism may be dated easily. Essentially, it was in adopting science and technology, not just as a form of knowledge, but as a means of dominating nature, that we left behind the logic of correspondences. Because of this we no longer participate in a cosmos, but we now have a universe as the object of thought and as matter to be exploited. This mutation is not something we could control; if the sacred constitutes a world of being, this mutation reveals a history of being. And we could follow Heidegger in his writings on technology in discussing this history of being.

Second, one can of course find remains of the sacred in our culture. They were even still quite perceptible just a few decades ago in the rural areas of Europe to the extent that agricultural existence was not fundamentally very far removed from the style of life of Paleolithic times. Even the industrialized world presents some traces of the sacred, but it is only a residue or, worse, a substitute sacred that does not merit survival. One cannot draw an argument, much less an apologetic, from the fact that the sacred is folded up in camouflaged myths or degenerate rituals, be it a question of our holidays, marriage ceremonies or funerals, the current interest in the occult, or attempts to transfer the sacred into the political sphere. Nor may one rejoice to see here or there theories of psychoanalysis invited to reap the heritage of the sacred, to mythologize the unconscious, or to develop the analytic experience into a form of initiation. The retreat of the sacred into the unconscious is no less a part of its being forgotten than is the elevation of science and technology to the rank of our dominant value. Indeed, this retreat is just the dark side of the same phenomenon, the counterpart of the Enlightenment. If only the person who dreams bears the sacred, this fate attests to the impotence of the sacred to furnish models of behavior for waking life or to transform reality in accordance with the paradigms that still haunt our sleep.

Third, since the sacred world is distanciated from us, or rather since we have distanciated ourselves from it, the only religion—be it Christianity or another form of religion—whose message may still be heard is the one that finds sufficient resources within itself not only to survive, but to accompany the decline of the sacred in a positive manner. Now as the whole prior analysis indicated, kerygmatic religion is virtually antisacral. So the argument would seem to require carrying this process through to free the kerygmatic kernel from its sacred husk. We need to do so in order to fulfill the innermost meaning of kerygmatic religion as inaugurated by the Yahwism of the Jewish prophets and confirmed in its profane sense by the teachings of Jesus. In this regard, the program of demythologizing the Christian message in the twentieth century may be understood as an attempt to radicalize a tendency already at work in primitive Christianity. Rudolf Bultmann, for example, has insisted that if demythologization is externally motivated by the destruction of the mythic universe under the blows of science, it is internally based on a dynamic of demythologization that is part of the kerygma itself and that can be documented by the exegesis of the New Testament. Christianity's response to desacralization therefore is not to submit to it as an unavoidable destiny but to carry it out as a task of faith. Or to put it another way, faith and religion must be separated, and we need to go so far as to conceive of an a-religious Christianity such as that spoken of by Dietrich Bonhoeffer in his later writings. The advent of this nonreligious religion is not just the work of exegetes interpreting texts; it is the work of the whole community dedicated to liquidating the sacred from its celebrations, its preaching, its ethics, and its political stance.

I want next to try to explain why I am not satisfied with such a program and why I am seeking instead for some mediation between the sacred and the kerygma.

The question is, Which mediation?

Reflecting upon the iconoclast's first argument, I have asked myself to what point the desacralization of the modern world is a *fact* that is simply to be noted. We are correct to assign its coming about to the advent of modern science and technology. But has not our identifying ourselves with the scientific ideal already become a problem for us? I am surprised to see how many critical thinkers, whose suspicious nature is elsewhere limitless, capitulate before what they take to be the verdict of modernity and adopt the ideology of science and technology in a most naive fashion. The discovery of the ideological function of science and technology as it may be found, from different yet convergent perspectives, in the work of such thinkers as Martin Heidegger, Herbert Marcuse, Jürgen Habermas, and Jacques Ellul constitutes a new starting point. That scientific ideal that earlier had served as an absolute measure for evaluating the overall progress of modernity has itself become problematic.

We might cite as an example the arguments advanced by Habermas that seek to tie empirical knowledge and the exploitation of nature to one limited interest, the interest in theoretically and practically controlling the human environment. Modernity then appears as the inordinate inflation of one interest at the expense of all others, especially of our interests for communication and emancipation. This leveling of the hierarchy of interests, and the one-dimensional person that results from it, are ideological phenomena to the extent that they serve to make every social agent accept the autonomous, devouring, and cancerous functioning of the industrial system given over to growth without limit or end beyond itself. Here is a consideration that may chill the zealots of modernity. And this same consideration ought to lead us to call into question the judgment modernity passes on what it makes appear as an archaism. This judgment in its turn has already begun to be judged itself. Modernity is neither a fact nor our destiny. It is henceforth an open question. At the same time, the opposition modernity/archaism is obscured, and a certain reevaluation of the sacred universe now seems tied to this reevaluation of our modernity.

This incipient reevaluation of the sacred, based on the very reevaluation of values in whose name judgment was originally passed on the sacred, invites us to completely call into question the iconoclast's second argument. What there are called "residues" or "traces" of the sacred may not be worthy of survival as such. Yet these degenerate and substitute expressions are the symptoms of something. What? I think it is the fact that the degenerate sacred and the scientific-technological ideology constitute a single cultural configuration. And this cultural configuration is that of nihilism. The scientist illusion and the retreat of the sacred into its own particular phantoms together belong to the forgetfulness of our roots. In two different yet convergent manners the desert is spreading. And what we are in the midst of discovering, contrary to the scientific-technological ideology, which is also the military-industrial ideology, is that humanity is simply not possible without the sacred.

Can we live without some originary orientation? Is it simply a residual phenomenon, or an existential protest arising out of the depths of our being, that sends us in search of privileged places, be they our birthplace, the scene of our first love, or the theater of some important historical occurrence—a battle, a revolution, the execution ground of patriots? We return to such places because *there* a more than everyday reality erupted and because the memory attached to what took place there preserves us from being simply errant vagrants in the world. Can the act of construction and of habitation be entirely desacralized without losing all significance? Can we abolish the symbolism of the threshold, the door, and the entrance, along with every ritual of entrance and of welcome? Can we completely desacralize birth (our coming into the world) and death (our passing to the place of rest)? Can we strip them of every rite of passage without completely degrading humankind into a utensil, without ceaselessly giving ourselves up to a manipulation that finds its conclusion in the liquidation of useless or worn-out people? Can we abolish all the other rites of initiation without life's "turning points" themselves becoming simple insignificant transitions? Does not sexuality become totally meaningless when every tie between it and the great interplay of cosmic unions is broken? Stripped of any ritualization, can the repetitive moments of life be anything other than an image of damnation? Is anything more paralyzing than the eternal return without regeneration? Is it possible to live in a time without festivals, according to a wholly profane calendar? Is it, finally, by chance that what you in the United States call "subcultures" should so almost despairingly be in search of festivals where, in communication with the forces of nature, one would once again begin to appreciate them without exploiting them?

Such are the new questions we are beginning to ask beyond the death of the sacred. Are we not on the verge of a renaissance of the sacred, at least if humankind itself is not to die?

At the same time, the iconoclast's third argument becomes just as problematic. Is Christianity without the sacred possible?

All the antinomies upon which our mediation has been based now need to be reconsidered. The word, we said, breaks away from the numinous. And this is true. But is it not so to the extent that the word takes over for itself the functions of the numinous? There would be no hermeneutic if there were no proclamation. But there would be no proclamation if the word, too, were not powerful; that is, if it did not have the power to set forth the new being it proclaims. A word that is addressed to us rather than our speaking it, a word that constitutes us rather than our articulating it—a word that speaks—does not such a word reaffirm the sacred just as much as abolish it? It does so if hearing this word is impossible without a transvaluation of the values *tremendum* and *fascinosum* into obedience and fervor. For my part, I cannot conceive of a religious attitude that did not proceed from "a feeling of absolute dependence." And is this not the essential relation of humankind to the sacred, transmuted into speech and, in this way, reaffirmed at the same time it is surpassed?

That word and manifestation can be reconciled is the central affirmation of the Prologue to John's Gospel:

> So the Word became flesh;
> he came to dwell among us,
> and we saw his glory,
> such glory as befits the Father's only Son,
> full of grace and truth. (John 1:14)

This identification of word and manifestation was the basis for the concept of revelation that from the Greek fathers to Hegel constituted the central category in terms of which thought about Christianity was organized. Indeed, for Hegel, Christ was the "absolute manifestation." He is God "being-there." And this philosopher did not hesitate to place the absolute manifestation as the prolongation of the archaic hierophanies, although, it is true, at the price of much suppression and transmutation. One need only recall here the magnificent pages in the *Phenomenology of Spirit* on the death of the pagan gods with their empty altars and overturned columns. In this way the manifestation of the sacred is dialectically reaffirmed and internalized into proclamation.

Next we said that the word opposed the teaching of the Torah to all hierophanies, the name of the Lord to idols, ethics to aesthetics, and history to nature. This too is true. But this truth is dialectical. It posits itself by implying its contrary. The question, in effect, is whether a faith without any sign is possible. Exegesis attests to a negative response to this question. It shows that the cosmic symbolism was not abolished but in a way reinterpreted according to the requirements of proclamation. For example, Yahweh is acclaimed the lord of the armies (which are no doubt heavenly bodies); Yahweh's face and glory conserve something of the solar majesty;

Yahweh is the Most High like the suprauranian gods. And the cosmogonic myths, held so long as untrustworthy, were adjusted to the essentially historical vision of the divine. Undoubtedly they lost their paradigmatic value for the cultus as well as for ritualized life, since life is ritualized in terms of the Torah, but they were not purely and simply abolished. They receive a new function in that henceforth they tell the "beginning" of a history that is through and through a history of deliverance. And the celebration of the great saving events does not hesitate to take up mythology's dramatic themes, especially that of victory over the powers of the waters and of chaos.

Everything indicates therefore that the cosmic symbolism does not die but is instead transformed in passing from the realm of the sacred to that of proclamation. The new Zion prophetically inverts the reminiscence of the sacred city, just as the Messiah who is to come projects into the eschatological future the glorious royal figures of divine unction. And for Christians, Golgotha becomes a new *axis mundi*. Every new language is also the reemployment of an ancient symbolism.

This reorientation of an archaic symbolism is fundamentally possible due to the labor of speaking that is already incorporated in it. We earlier insisted on this articulation of a variety of diverse symbols within a central symbolism that must always be reinterpreted. This is what we called the minimal hermeneutic implied in the functioning of any symbolism, inasmuch as an articulated system calls forth a reinterpretation, which as regards the kerygma takes the dramatic form of an inversion, not an abolition.

The forms of discourse we borrowed from the Synoptic tradition need to be reconsidered from this point of view. Their explicit structure is as we have already described it a transgressing of the traditional forms of the parable, proverb, and eschatological saying. But their implicit semantics remains that of the symbolism of the sacred.

This is especially evident in the case of the eschatological sayings that come to grips directly with the mythical depths of eschatology where an *Endzeit* responds to an *Urzeit*. But it is also not difficult to detect even in the profane language of the parables a reactivation of a primary symbolism. Shepherds, fathers, kings, and so on, are figures that are explicitly chosen for their familiar connotations, yet to the same extent these figures reactivate the ancestral symbols whose equivalents are to be found in every archaic culture. And as concerns the proverbs, the dramatic reversal they bring about—"the first being last, the last first"—only functions expressly because, at the same time, the proverb reawakens the latent values of the symbols of initiation: the narrow way, the narrow gate, call and election, and so on. Even Plato transposes—into philosophy, true—a central symbolism: "Many are the bearers of thyrses, few the bacchants." Thus in two different ways, philosophy and evangelical preaching give a second wind to archaic symbolism.

The most noteworthy example in this regard is the resumption of the symbolism of death and rebirth in the kerygmatic discourse concerning conversion. It is remarkable in two ways. On the one hand, it reveals the tie between the ancient symbolism and the word of faith; on the other, it has its counterpart in philosophy, since philosophy too in its fashion renovates the ancient myths. Conversion can thus be spoken of in several languages—in the profane language of limit-situations, conversion is nothing other than the decision to be made in the crisis situation redescribed by the parable and fictively signified by the metaphorical tale. This decision has ethical and political aspects that may be unfolded entirely within the a-religious dimension evoked by Bonhoeffer. Yet the existential breadth of this decision is preserved against all the insipidities and banalities that its profane transcription threatens to produce only if, at the same time, the older symbolic depths of death and resurrection, of the return to the maternal womb and rebirth, are reactualized. Would the word "conversion" continue to signify anything if we absolutely lost sight of what was expressed in these symbols of regeneration, new creation, and the advent of a new being and a new world? I think not.

This subtle equilibrium between the iconoclastic virtualities of proclamation and the symbolic resurgence of the sacred has expressed itself throughout the history of Christianity as a dialectic of preaching and sacraments. It is easy to see that in preaching the kerygmatic element carries the day with its concern to "apply" the word here and now both ethically and politically. In the sacrament, symbolism has the upper hand. We need only recall all the correspondences baptism awakens between the primordial waters, where all form is abolished, the flood, the water of death, and the water of purification; between immersion, nudity, and the grave; between emersion, the garments of light, and resurrection, to see that this is the case. The sacrament, we could say, is the mutation of sacred ritual into the kerygmatic realm.

In truth, without the support and renewing power of the sacred cosmos and the sacredness of vital nature, the word itself becomes abstract and cerebral. Only the incarnation of the ancient symbolism ceaselessly reinterpreted gives this word something to say, not only to our understanding and will but also to our imagination and our heart; in short, to the whole human being.

Must we not confess, therefore, that the hope to see faith in the word outlive the religion of the sacred is really vain and that the end of the word as well as of the hearing of the word is bound to some new birth of the sacred and its symbolism, beyond its death...?

3

The "Sacred" Text and the Community

I am intrigued by the question of the response of the community whose text has been "critically edited." Of course when this is done, it no longer *is* a sacred text, because it is no longer the text that the community has always regarded as sacred; it is a scholars' text. So, in a sense, there can *be* no such thing as the critical editing of sacred texts. It is true that, in the early history of the church, there were many communities, each with its own sacred text, and the church attempted to bring them together, to produce one sacred text. So there is the history of the canon, and therefore there is not "the" sacred text. But nevertheless, the critical act that we are committing is quite different from this gathering of texts from the Coptic and so on, when the community constituted its canon. The kind of biblical criticism that began in the eighteenth and nineteenth centuries was of quite a different nature, because now we may get texts that are not texts of *any* community, except perhaps of the community of the academic world.

Maybe in the case of Christianity there *is* no sacred text, because it is not the text that is sacred but the one about which it is spoken. For instance, there is no privilege of the language in which it was said for the first time; it is completely indifferent whether we read it in Greek or Hebrew or Aramaic, and so on. There is already something that allows the critical act; the critical act is not forbidden by the nature of the text, because it is not a sacred text in the sense in which the Qur'an is sacred (for a Muslim would say that to read the Qur'an in English is not to read the Qur'an; one must read it in Arabic). But in Christianity, translation is quite possible, for the Septuagint is a kind of desacralization of the original language, once one has admitted that the Bible could be set in Greek. And a certain critical activity was implied in this act of translation. Jerome was, for his time, a critical mind.

And so the nature of the text, at least in Christianity, is not completely hostile to the critical approach. And there is the fact that we have four

Reprinted with permission from *The Critical Study of Sacred Texts,* ed. Wendy D. O'Flaherty (Berkeley, Calif.: Graduate Theological Union, 1979), 271–76.

Gospels; we could imagine a church that would have said, "There is only one Gospel." But in Christianity all the discrepancies were preserved, and a certain equivocity of the texts was assumed at the beginning. No one said how many days the passion lasted; no one said how many days intervened between the crucifixion and the resurrection, and so on. Maybe the opaque notion of the sacred is shattered by this critical activity; it is really the concept of "sacred" that changes. The text becomes fundamental but no longer sacred in the sense that you have no right to touch and to change it. But what makes the Bible sacred in that sense? And for whom was it sacred? For all religious texts are not sacred in the same sense. We have to modulate the notion of sacredness not only according to different religions but also in the course of the history of these religions.

Maybe the notion of authoritative texts is different from that of sacred texts, because "authoritative" means that there is discrimination between the text that constitutes the founding act of the community and those who are excluded from this founding function. Even if they have a kind of kinship they may be excluded in this way; the *Gospel of Thomas* is very close, but it does not belong to the story of the way in which the community interpreted itself in the terms of those texts. This is what I should call authoritative but not necessarily sacred, because it is a hermeneutical act to recognize oneself as founded by a text and to read this text as founding. There is a reciprocity between the reading and the existing self-recognition of the identity of the community. There is a kind of reciprocity between the community and the text. There comes to mind the distinction that Augustine makes in *De christiana doctrina* between *signum* and *res*: we are aware that the *signum* is not the *res*, and there is a history of possible critical approaches to the *signum*. I wonder whether this actually implies a certain distance between the text and its reality, what it is about.

It is really important to say whether critical activity is assumed by the community that learns to read its text in a different way as a result. What happens to the reader and the community when critical activity is applied to the text? We might say that something arbitrary and uselessly compulsory is removed. I think that three relevant events took place in Christianity that were clearly distortions of the first situation: first, the text was frozen and the process of interpretation stopped because of the fight against heresies; this was, I think, a very destructive activity. This orthodox antiheresy may have started with the antignostic trend of the great church, and then the anti-Manichaean movement, and so on. And second, in the Middle Ages, an authoritarian interpretation was grafted onto the text; *one* philosophy was interpreting the text. But then the Protestants added to that, so that as the text was interpreted *per sui,* it became sacred as against the whole tradition. The text was then frozen, and you see the Protestants carrying their Bible, and their Bible is immutable against *the* tradition. And so the text is frozen *by* tradition, and it is frozen *against* tradition after it has been frozen against heresies. This may be seen as the third relevant event. And then we deconstruct these accretions, these sedimentations, merely to return to the fluidity of the hermeneutical situation of the precanonical period. The problem is whether there is a community to assume *that,* or whether it will remain only a kind of academic activity. So this is a critical situation: Will it kill the community or renew it? Or will they say, "You have no right to touch our book"?

The notion of sacredness becomes quite questionable. Dehomogenization has two effects, for a sacred text has two opposites: other sacred texts and nonsacred texts. And the two boundaries are more diffused now; for example, we know better that certain texts were not always in the canon, that other texts could have been and were not, by some historical accident, and therefore we have a kind of gradual continuum of several degrees between profane and sacred, not only massive opposition. And on the other hand, our tradition is more ambiguous, more complicated; and we see the other traditions also as more composite, and so you have more overlappings. It is a very complex situation in which to orient ourselves as individuals and as a community.

There is one act that continues, at least within Christianity, to preserve this double line of delineation, and this is preaching. You preach on canonical texts, but not on profane; the community would be completely changed if you chose a modern poet to do a sermon, or if you took the Bhagavad Gita into the church. This is a crisis of the community because its own identity relies on the identity of the text, as distinct both from nonsacred texts and from other sacred texts. If these two boundary lines should disappear, then the identity of the community would also disappear, and this is what happens: you have more intermediary cases between belonging to the church and not belonging to the church. In a sense you have several kernels but no boundary; the ecclesial community is a kind of series of centers without circles.

Preaching is the permanent reinterpretation of the text that is regarded as grounding the community; therefore, for the community to address itself to another text would be to make a decision concerning its social identity. A community that does that becomes another kind of community. I do not say that this is impossible, that it will never happen, but this would be a very important change in the continuity. Because in the notion of identity you have the community's capacity to situate itself as being this and not that, but also as having this past and not that past. This is a recognition of oneself in the process of history.

There is a kind of magisterium in Protestantism with the power to exclude noncanonical texts, but it functions (unlike the Catholic magisterium) by saying that the text interprets itself; you can criticize the Bible only by citing another text from the Bible. This leads to the reign of theologians. The Catholic church was not ruled by theologians, as the Protestant church was; to call oneself "Lutheran" is something very strange from a Catholic standpoint. But that Protestant magisterium consolidated the text, and in a sense it is for the Protestants that the Bible is more sacred, finally, more fundamental.

In Christianity there is a polarity of proclamation and manifestation, which Mircea Eliade does not recognize in his homogeneous concept of manifestation, epiphany, and so forth. I wonder whether there is not also, in the Hebraic and Christian traditions, a polarity of another kind, the charismatic, which is linked to language. For us, manifestation is not by necessity linked to language. The word "sacred" belongs to the side of manifestation, not to the side of proclamation, because many things may be sacred without being a text: a tree may be sacred, water may be sacred, and we read in Eliade that it is the cosmos that is sacred. And therefore if there is only the word to mediate this sacredness, it is precisely because it mediates something that is not of the nature of the word but of the nature of appearance. The manifestation is not verbal by origin. But I think that there is something specific in the Hebraic and Christian traditions that gives a kind of privilege to the word. You have the tradition that the word was created by the word; in the switch from the first narrative of creation to the second, God not only does but says. The notion of sacred text may have been alien to the Hebraic and pre-Christian tradition. We apply a category that belongs to this sacrality that is cosmic and then that is condensed, as it were, in a book and that thus changes its function as it becomes fundamental without being sacred. What Eliade shows is that the polarity sacred/profane is absolutely primitive in relation to this: this water is sacred but not that water; this tree and not that tree.

I wonder whether it does not belong to the nature of proclamation to be always brought back from the written to the oral; and it is the function of preaching to reverse the relation from written to spoken. In that sense preaching is more fundamental to Hebrew and Christian tradition because of the nature of the text that has to be reconverted to word, in contrast with Scripture; and therefore it is a kind of desacralization of the written as such, by the return to the spoken word. This is the impact of the fixation of liturgy, for in Christianity the liturgical kernel represents the Eucharist, as a kind of text that tells the story of the Last Supper; and it becomes a sacred text because it founds a sacred act, which is the Eucharist. What was the influence of the Eucharist in the sacralization of the text? For the word "sacrifice" used in this connection has to do with the sacred act.

I was very reluctant to use the word "sacred" in my essay on revelation.[1] I had to fight very hard to say finally what I believe, what I think, when I use the word "revelation." But to an extent I am prepared to say that I recognize something *revealing* that is not frozen in any ultimate or immutable text. Because the process of revelation is a permanent process of opening something that is closed, of making manifest something that was hidden. Revelation is a historical process, but the notion of sacred text is something antihistorical. I am frightened by this word "sacred."

---

1. See Paul Ricoeur, "Toward a Hermeneutic of the Idea of Revelation," in *Essays on Biblical Interpretation,* ed. Lewis S. Mudge (Philadelphia: Fortress Press, 1980), 73–118. ED.

Part Two

Philosophers of Religion: Mediation and Conflict

4

A Philosophical Hermeneutics
of Religion: Kant

Religion within the Limits of Reason Alone is certainly a philosophical work, an expression of philosophical reason. However, we should not see in it an extension of the perimeter of Kant's critical philosophy. Instead, I suggest that it should be called a "philosophical hermeneutics of religion."

The first reason for identifying it in this way is that this work does not take God as its object but rather religion. Indeed, it adds nothing to what had been said about God, either negatively in the "Dialectic of Pure Reason" or positively in the "Postulates of Practical Reason," in Kant's earlier work. And it deals with religion only in terms of the three aspects of representation, belief, and institution. These three themes form the framework for books 2, 3, and 4, although the division into books does not exactly overlap the division into themes. In fact, these three aspects of religion are not presented to philosophical reflection as facts whose objectivity would be completed by universality, as was the case with Newtonian nature (in the first *Critique*), the good will (in the second *Critique*), or even the teleological structure of the organism or the work of art at the level of reflective judgment (in the third *Critique*). Religion, owing to its historical, "positive" character, constitutes something specifically outside philosophy, an otherness that philosophy can take into account only as lying at its margin, at its boundaries, and, if I may put it this way, at the inner edge of the line that divides the ahistorical transcendental realm and the historical religious realm. Philosophical reflection will retain from this particular historical genre only what harmonizes with the transcendental realm, at the price of a rationalizing reinterpretation of the contents of the representation of belief and the structuring intentions of the institution of religion.

A second reason for classifying this work as philosophical hermeneutics has to do with the status of freedom in Kant's whole undertaking. Freedom

Originally published as "Une herméneutique philosophique de la religion: Kant," in *Interpréter: Mélanges offerts à Claude Geffré*, ed. Jean-Pierre Jossua and Nicholas-Jean Séd (Paris: Cerf, 1992), 25–47; printed with permission.

is no longer referred to the rational structure of the will (*Wille*) but to the idea of God. What sets the whole work in motion is the factual situation of free will (*Willkür*), its power to choose between obedience to the law and empirical desire. This factual situation, the *primum movens* of religion according to Kant, is the incapacity that originally afflicts our capacity for acting, and more specifically our capacity for doing what is good. To put it another way, that our actual will is a bound will is the enigma that sets in motion Kant's philosophical reflection on religion. This is a fact that we can call a historical fact, but we must do so in a sense different from the use of this term when applied to representations, beliefs, and institutions, all of which share the historicity of every cultural fact. It is a question of an existential historicity, for which there is no experience that is not mediated by narratives, symbols, and myths, all of which are also historical in the cultural sense of the term, as are the specific structures of any religion. All interpretation here has to take place within the limits of reason alone, yet the historical condition of captive freedom, which is the very fact of evil, finds its proper place outside the circle of the competence of transcendental philosophy, hence of critical philosophy.

A third motive for taking *Religion within the Limits of Reason Alone* as a philosophical hermeneutics has to do with the articulation of the thematics of evil, which inaugurates Kant's reflection on religion, and its relation to the threefold thematic constitutive of religion per se. In this respect, the existential-historical condition of evil constitutes the challenge to which religion brings the reply of an "in spite of...," an "even though...." This tie between challenge and reply is the tie of hope, concerning which one well-known text of the *Opus Posthumum* says that it can be formulated as a question—"What can I hope?"—that gives rise to the two questions that drive the first two *Critiques:* "What can I know?" and "What must I do?" So we can consider *Religion within the Limits of Reason Alone* as an attempted philosophical justification of hope, by means of a philosophical interpretation of the symbolics of evil and of the text of representations, beliefs, and institutions that delimit the religious per se.

If the question "What can I hope?" constitutes the central interrogation of the philosophy of religion, we can understand why the theory of radical evil, as a challenge, along with the theory of the means by which religion gives a reply to evil are so closely bound up with each other at one point that perhaps has not been sufficiently recognized. The theory of evil, it turns out, does not reach its completion in the famous essay, originally published separately, on radical evil, but rather accompanies the unfolding of religion in its triple texture as the specific perversion and, we may now say, as the increasing perversion that affects every religious mediation. Everything takes place as though the extreme of evil were attained only with the claim to totalization characteristic of religion at its institutional level. Yet the contrary is equally true: the restoration of the power to act, brought low by evil, does not start at the beginning of book 2; it is already anticipated in book 1 with the theme of a "disposition" toward the good that, in a sense I shall speak of more below, is more originary than evil is radical. The title of the first part of book 1 already indicates this: "Concerning the Indwelling of the Evil Principle with the Good, or, On the Radical Evil in Human Nature." Thus the motifs of radical evil and hope crisscross throughout this work, with evil affecting the process of religion from beginning to end, while hope is affirmed as strictly contemporaneous with the irruption of evil. For this reason, one of the major motifs of Kant's philosophical hermeneutics of religion is to give an account, within the limits of reason alone, of this interweaving of the confession of radical evil and the assumption of means of regeneration. And consequently, to the extent that this interweaving is constitutive of the motif of hope, we can say that hope is the specific object of this philosophical hermeneutics of religion. It is a hermeneutics, not a critique, because the interweaving of the signs of evil and the signs of regeneration is itself a second-degree "historical" phenomenon, one that combines the cultural historicity of positive religion and the existential historicity of the "propensity" to evil. It is in this complex sense that the Kantian philosophy of religion can be called a philosophical hermeneutics of hope.

Radical Evil

If we keep in mind the idea that the thematics of evil is not completed until we reach the end of this work, we see that book 1 has to do with the question of evil's intelligibility in principle, not with the question of its extent. Kant articulates this problematic in terms of three moments: the first has to do with the site of evil; the second with its radicality; the third with its origin. The intertwining of these three moments has to be reconstructed with care since Kant's text often conceals the back and forth movement that advances his reflections.

It is first of all a question of situating evil where it actually resides, namely, in the maxims of the will. The importance of this notion of a maxim in defining *Willkür* is well known. It is by formulating our projects in terms of maxims, that is, generalizable rules, that we make them suitable for the test of universalization constitutive of practical reason. If evil resides somewhere, it is surely in the maxims of our actions, by means of which we hierarchize our preferences, placing duty above desire, or desire above duty. Evil, in fact, consists in a reversal of priority, an inversion or subversion on the plane of the maxims of action. This way of entering into the problematic of evil is of great importance. However "rigorist" the Kantian doctrine of evil may later claim itself to be, it starts by setting aside two conceptions we might call "nihilistic." According to the first of these conceptions, evil would be identical with desire and pleasure as such. But Kant forcefully asserts that affects as such are innocent. According to the second conception, evil would consist in the corruption of reason. No, replies Kant, legislative reason is as innocent as is desire, which stands over against it. What remains is that evil consists in the perversion of a relation, namely, the relation of priority between law and desire. This is, Kant says, "a rule made by the will [*Willkür*]."[1] The evil person therefore is neither a beast nor a devil. The bad maxim is the opposite of respect, that is, "the real opposition, in time, of man's will to the law" (30–31). In its first moment, this reflection on evil preserves up to the existential plane a formal aspect, which dispenses with a material definition of evil through an enumeration of vices, as in an ethic of virtues. In this way, the field is left open for paradigmatic examples. We might even say that the figures of evil that best exhibit this characteristic of subversion in the maxim are also the most exemplary ones. This is the case with hypocrisy: "This dishonesty, by which we humbug ourselves and which thwarts the establishing of a true moral disposition in us, extends itself outwardly also to falsehood and the deception of others" (33). This form of deceit will be found in the representations, the beliefs, and especially in the institutions of religion in its privileged domain of expansion, as the bad faith of faith.

Second step: we pass from the still descriptive plane to the transcendental one by posing the question of the ground (*Grund*) of bad maxims. It ought to be possible if we are to call someone evil to "infer from several evil acts done with consciousness of their evil, or from one such act, an underlying evil maxim; and further from this maxim to infer the presence in the agent of an underlying common ground, itself a maxim, of all particular morally-evil maxims" (16). Here is an opportunity for us to observe at work the sort of hermeneutics Kant applies to one classical *topos* of theology, that of original sin. Within the limits of reason alone, this hermeneutics must consist in a deduction, in the transcendental sense of this term, that is, the positing by a regressive analysis of what has to be presupposed as the condition of possibility of some phenomenon. No inductive inference based on enumeration can lead to something like a "propensity" (*Hang*) to evil as the ground of all the maxims by means of which the will opposes the law in time. There is no experience of such a propensity. Therefore it is not an empirical concept. This propensity has to be apprehended a priori as a structure of the *Willkür*—experience, we read in one note, "can

---

1. Immanuel Kant, *Religion within the Limits of Reason Alone,* trans. Theodore M. Greene and Hoyt H. Hudson (New York: Harper and Brothers, 1960), 17; subsequent page numbers given in the text refer to this edition.

never reveal the root of evil in the supreme maxim of the free will relating to the law, a maxim which, as *intelligible act,* precedes all experience" (34). (By "intelligible," we are not to understand comprehensible, transparent to reason, but atemporal, nonempirical, as the third step will confirm.) The rational hermeneutics applied to the traditional concept of original sin leads to a difficult compromise, insofar as the classical vocabulary is preserved (human beings are evil "by nature" [*von Natur*]; evil is "rooted" [*gewurzelt*] in humanity; it is even said to be "innate," in the sense that it is not acquired in time; it is "present in man at birth—though birth need not be the cause of it"; etc.). It is rather a question of a kind of freedom coming from freedom. We might say, supporting Kant, that he has identified what is so upsetting in the confession of evil—I do not say the experience of evil— namely, the following paradox: in each instance, we do evil; but evil was already there. It is this unfathomable anteriority of evil that, in Kant, finds no other expression than nontemporality—Kant having no other temporal dimension at his disposal after the "transcendental aesthetics" than a successive time. At the very least, Kant, with the conceptuality at his disposal, caught sight of the paradox of something that has always been there and yet for which we ourselves are responsible.

This first-order paradox is doubled by a second-order one, namely, the coexistence of the propensity (*Hang*) to evil with the predisposition (*Anlage*) to good. The propensity to evil certainly constitutes "the subjective ground of the possibility of the deviation of the maxim from the moral law" (24). But it does not take the place of the disposition to good, which stems from a reflective judgment applied to the teleological structure of human destiny. In this regard, the predisposition to good is inscribed at the summit of the scale of ends constitutive of human destiny: above "the predisposition to animality in man, taken as a living being," above the "predisposition to humanity in man, taken as a living and at the same time a rational being," at the same rank as the predisposition "to personality in man, taken as a rational and at the same time an accountable being" (21). Here, the imputability of our acts is added to the independence of our free will with regard to every other motive. Our predisposition to good is summed up in these three predispositions. "All of these predispositions are not only *good* in negative fashion (in that they do not contradict the moral law); they are also predisposition *toward good* (they enjoin the observance of the law)" (23). Here we are at the threshold of the paradox. We have spoken of the propensity to radical evil. Now we are discussing the predisposition to an originary good—these three predispositions, in fact, are original because "they are bound up with the possibility of human nature" (23).

As we had anticipated above, the juxtaposition of good and bad principles, equally "inherent" in human nature, preserves the possibility of an initial step along the way of hope. But however radical evil may be as the a priori principle of every bad maxim, it does not occupy the originary place, which is that of the predisposition to good, the ultimate condition of respect for the law. Ought we not then to say that the recognition of this fundamental paradox works like a philosophical midrash with regard to the biblical narrative about the fall? This latter recounts as an event the passage from the innocence of the creature to guilt, and the antignostic gnosis of Augustine hardens this narrative into a kind of rationalized myth where the state of sin succeeds the state of innocence.[2] In Kant's philosophical midrash, this paradox is presented as a double inherence, as the sur-impression of the propensity on the predisposition. In this sense, radical evil is not original sin. Only beings who remain capable of respect can consciously do evil. However radical it may be, evil cannot bring it about that we cease being open to the appeal of conscience. In this sense, evil remains contingent, albeit always already there. This paradox could be called the paradox of the quasi-nature of evil.

Step three: we move up from the question of ground to that of the origin (*Ursprung*). A new occasion is offered for applying philosophical hermeneutics to Scripture. The basic gesture of this hermeneutics is to separate two meanings of the notion of "origin": an origin in time, which fits with the event of the fall in the biblical narrative, and a rational origin. To seek to situate the origin of evil in time is, in effect, to condemn oneself to applying the idea of a cause to a free act and thereby to fall into an infinite regression. In short, it means putting oneself back into the conditions of the third cosmological antinomy of pure reason. It is rather a matter, Kant says, of "the ground of the *exercise* of freedom," where "this ground (like the determining ground of the free will generally) must be sought in purely rational representations."[3] It is easy to see what is thereby excluded: Augustine's disastrous explanation in terms of heredity at the time of his quarrel with Pelagianism. "In the search for the rational origin of evil actions, every such action must be regarded as though the individual had fallen into it directly from a state of innocence. For whatever his previous deportment may have been, whatever natural causes may have been influencing him, and whether these causes were to be found within him or outside him, his action is yet free and determined by none of these causes; hence it can and must always be judged as *original* use of his *Willkür*" (36). It is worth noting that Kant takes his interpretation to be in agreement with the genre of representation Scripture uses to describe the origin of evil. Despite its narrative form, the event spoken of in the biblical narrative is not a unique event

2. See Paul Ricoeur, "Original Sin: A Study in Meaning," trans. Peter McCormick, in *The Conflict of Interpretations: Essays in Hermeneutics,* ed. Don Ihde (Evanston, Ill.: Northwestern Univ. Press, 1974), 269–86. TRANS.

3. Kant, *Religion within the Limits of Reason Alone,* 35.

whose trace we bear through heredity. "From all this it is clear that we daily act in the same way, and that therefore 'in Adam all have sinned' and still sin" (37). This is certainly a Pelagian interpretation of the phrase "in Adam," but it has as much right as does Augustine's in the conflict of interpretations. A difficulty remains, nevertheless, and it is a large one: How are we to think such an event that is both unique and multiple in a nontemporal—"rational"—way? We have given just a negative interpretation of the term "rational." What about its positive meaning? Here we have to admire Kant's intellectual honesty: "The rational origin of this perversion of our *Willkür* . . . remains inscrutable to us, because this propensity itself must be set down to our account and because, as a result, that ultimate ground of all maxims would in turn involve the adoption of an evil maxim [as its basis]. . . . There is then for us no conceivable ground from which the moral evil in us could originally have come" (38). Again, Kant can claim for his philosophical meditation a certain affinity with the biblical narrative in that it assigns the origin of the origin of evil to "a *spirit* of an originally loftier destiny" (39). "Thus is the *first* beginning of all evil represented as inconceivable by us (for whence came evil to that spirit?); but man is represented as having fallen into evil only *through seduction*" (39).

It is noteworthy that Kant glimpsed, beneath this theme of seduction, a connection between the hermeneutics of evil and that of hope. If humankind became evil through seduction, then it was not basically corrupt. In releasing humankind from the full weight of the origin of evil, the theme of seduction indicates the point where the culmination of radical evil coincides with the first glimmer of hope. "For man, therefore, who despite a corrupted heart yet possesses a good will, there remains hope of a return to the good from which he has strayed" (39). This "despite" is the "despite" of hope. And the concept of radical evil itself becomes the initial element of a *justified* hope.

Karl Jaspers has seen this in his wonderful essay "Le Mal radical chez Kant."[4] The inscrutable is the limit-experience of an impotence of our moral power: "[T]his is the factual situation. Beyond any knowledge we may acquire, we are finally forced to find our own way starting from a lack of knowledge that remains our actual origin. And there we become responsible, not just for this or that particular act, but for ourselves." We must go even further than this. "We would like instead of engendering our being through moral action to get out of this situation by a simple, superficial mastery of ourselves. We would like to cover up the original source, not hear the silence. Kant forces us to reach through thought the point where the origin has to speak in us, the point where thinking may flourish but not

---

4. Karl Jaspers, "Le Mal radical chez Kant," trans. Jeanne Hersch, *Deucalion* 4 (1952): 227–52.

be reduced to any one sure thing, and from which alone can spring a moral revolution."[5] In this sense, the confession of the inscrutability of evil closes the way of explanation only so as to hold open that of regeneration.

The Reply of Religion

Books 2 to 4 of *Religion within the Limits of Reason Alone* have as their theme the restoration of the lost power of our free will. (We may note in this regard the title of the "General Observation" that closes book 1: "Concerning the Restoration to Its Power of the Original Predisposition to Good." The titles of the following books also make use of this same vocabulary of power: "Concerning the Conflict of the Good with the Evil Principle for Sovereignty over Man," "The Victory of the Good over the Evil Principle, and the Founding of a Kingdom of God on Earth," "Concerning Service and Pseudoservice under the Sovereignty of the Good Principle; or, Concerning Religion and Clericalism.") This restoration constitutes a major paradox for philosophical reason. "How it is possible for a naturally evil man to make himself a good man wholly surpasses our comprehension," we read in the "General Observation" that closes book 1.[6] This is where religion presents itself as the great outside of philosophy. For it does not offer a comprehension but rather the very *operation* that is this revolution in human disposition. I said in beginning that the question here is not that of the existence of God, as the author or coauthor of this revolution, but rather that of the structure of religion; that is, of the ways it provides for this power of regeneration, namely, as we have already said, the triad of representation, belief, and an institution, a triad that structures the movement from book 2 to book 4.

Representation

Book 2 has for its theme the representation of the good principle in its struggle against the bad one. It brings on stage a dramaturgy whose protagonists are more than human. The good and bad principles are there represented, in a quasi-theatrical sense of this word, as personified hypostases of powers that fight one another in the human person's heart. On the one side is the archetype of the human being "as well pleasing to God," on the other side its antitype. If it is true that at the root of this dramatization we ought to be able to designate the existential conflict in which lies the reconquest of a lost power, it seems that we have no direct access

---

5. Ibid., 242.
6. Kant, *Religion within the Limits of Reason Alone*, 40.

to this existential conflict, except by way of the representation of a super-human conflict. The double possibility of human freedom opened through the inherence of the evil principle to "the side" of the good principle thus finds itself pictured, at the level of the representation and dramaturgy it brings about, as a battle between powers superior to us. We can speak of dramaturgy to the extent that it is not just the powers of good and evil that are depicted but the conflict itself, as stated in the title of section 2: "Concerning the Legal Claim of the Evil Principle to Sovereignty over Man, and the Conflict of the Two Principles with Each Other." Here Kant takes seriously the mythic structure of the cosmic process with its "legal" connotations. This imagery is appropriated for a gigantomachy where the stake is justification, a theme that Pauline theology, amplified by the Reformers, sets at the center of the problematic of the sovereignty of God. This hypostasis of great figures in conflict and the conflict itself constitute the given—the cultural given, if you will—that not only makes religion the other of philosophy but also confers on religion a historical dimension irreducible to politics or aesthetics, despite the connections that link religion to these other cultural dimensions, in particular at the levels of belief and of institutions.

For philosophical hermeneutics, the task is a double one: effectively recognize in religious representation the *other* of philosophical reflection and give it an interpretation that, without being derived from reflection, will be in agreement with such reflection. In the Christian tradition, the other of philosophy is the Christ figure. In this sense, book 2 offers us Kant's Christology, in the sense that we can speak of a Spinozist Christology in relation to Spinoza's "idea of God." Christ is the representation par excellence of the good principle, as the idea of a humanity agreeable to God: "This ideal of a humanity pleasing to God . . . we can represent to ourselves only as the idea of a person who would be willing not merely to discharge all human duties himself and to spread about him goodness as widely as possible by precept and example, but, even though tempted by the greatest allurements, to take upon himself every affliction, up to the most ignominious death, for the good of the world and even for his enemies" (55). We recognize here the confession of faith of the Letter to the Philippians (2:6f.). Two points need to be emphasized. First, Kant manifests no interest for the Jesus of history, as we would put it today. The only thing that is important philosophically is the Christ of faith elevated to an idea or an ideal. Second, Kant admits that, as regards this archetype of a good intention, "we are not the authors of this idea, . . . and it has established itself in man without our comprehending how human nature could have been capable of receiving it" (54). This is why "it is more appropriate to say that this archetype has *come down* to us from heaven and has assumed our humanity" (54). Joining these two points together, we can say the following: "[W]e need, therefore, no empirical example to make the idea of a person morally well-pleasing to God our archetype; this idea as an archetype is already present in our reason" (56).

Religion thus appears for the philosopher to be the depository and the guardian of this representation. But for the philosopher this paradoxical status of an idea both transcendent and immanent at the same time requires an interpretation that links it to the thematics of the transcendental dialectic, that is, to the theme of the highest good, no longer from the point of view of its transcendental function as a condition of possibility for the connection between virtue and goodness, but from the point of view of its capacity to regenerate a captive freedom, to make freedom free. The mediation of analogy, already anticipated in the idea of an archetype applied to the Christ figure, then presents itself. In this sense, Kant's Christology constitutes the second step of a hermeneutics that began with the reinterpretation of the biblical narrative of the fall. What remains to be done is to make more precise the epistemological status of such an analogy, where two factors—the alterity of the archetype inscribed in our moral constitution without our knowing how and its possible agreement with the philosophical principle of the autonomy of a rational will—will be respected. In an important note, Kant begins by setting us on guard against the temptation to place this work of analogy above reason: "It is indeed a limitation [Schrank] of human reason, and one which is ever inseparable from it, that we can conceive of no considerable moral worth in the actions of a personal being without representing that person, or his manifestation, in human guise. This is not to assert that such worth is in itself (kat'alêtheian) so conditioned, but merely that we must always resort to some analogy to natural existences to render supersensible qualities intelligible to ourselves" (58). And, in speaking of the sacrificial love of the Christ of the Gospels, Kant adds, "Such is the *schematism of analogy,* with which (as a means of explanation) we cannot dispense" (58). This note recalls the well-known section 59 of the *Critique of Judgment* on analogy. Analogy, we may recall, is a resemblance between relations, not between things that remain radically dissimilar. No similitude is established between the analogon and the analog. It is this highly restrictive doctrine that is recalled at the end of the note we are considering: "[B]etween the relation of a schema to its concept and the relation of this schema of a concept to the objective fact itself there is no analogy, but rather a mighty chasm, the overleaping of which (*metábasis eis állo génos*) leads at once to anthropomorphism" (59).

What is the result for the interpretation of the Christ figure? Two solutions are set aside. The first, clearly, is the treatment of the humiliation of the Suffering Servant as a historical event. "The presence of this archetype in the human soul is in itself sufficiently incomprehensible without our adding to its supernatural origin the assumption that it is hypostasized in a particular individual" (57). But there is also the conception that will be

Hegel's, that is, the inclusion of *kenosis* in the coming to be of God as absolute Spirit. Here the moral vision of the world reaches its limits. The archetype of a humanity well pleasing to God can be admitted only as a practical ideal, not as a reflective moment of the absolute itself. Nonetheless, we do not do justice to the idea of a schematism of analogy if we reduce this latter to a simple exemplification of what a human being must be who is said to be a saint. Practical reason has no need of religious symbolism to account for this exemplification. It does need religious symbolism, however, to designate the mediation between the confession of radical evil and the confidence in the triumph of the good principle. The Christ figure represents more than a mere hero of duty and less than an actual *kenosis* of the absolute itself; within the strict limits of the theory of analogy, it represents a genuine *schematism of hope*.

The transition from representation to *belief* is assured by critically taking up again the theology of expiation, classically associated with the Christ figure. This is a critical reprise that works in the first place to set us on guard against the idea that the sacrifice of the Suffering Servant might be substituted for a change of heart. Yet the philosophy of religion has to assume in its own way the paradox that this theology sharpens, the paradox that, on the one hand, human beings are incapable of doing the good, and, on the other hand, regeneration consists in the establishment of a new character. What is in question here is the idea of a "surplus," "over the profit from good works, and it is itself a profit which is reckoned to us *by grace*" (70). This "surplus" has to do with the efficacy of the Christ representation, which is the stake of religion in its dimension of belief.

Belief

The transition from representation to belief is implied in the very character of representation as dramaturgical or, to put it a better way, as agonistic. What is at stake in the whole process of religion, we need recall, is the effective liberation of the bound will. "To become free," it is recalled at the beginning of book 3—or, if we speak as Paul does in Romans 6: " 'to be freed from bondage under the law of sin, to live for righteousness'—this is the highest prize [man] can win" (85). Here representation must clothe itself in power. Belief is the dimension of the effectiveness of representation. The theological thematics with which the philosophical hermeneutics measures itself is the well-known one of justification by faith. For Kant, it constitutes the central stake of the great controversy that brings philosophy into an encounter with religion. It is not surprising, therefore, that here evil finds new resources for perverting the moral tenor that true religion has to preserve.

The quarrel over justification begins at the heart of book 2, inasmuch as it is on the representation that faith confers its efficacy, and it reappears in book 3, inasmuch as faith, as it is articulated in positive religion, is bound to the ecclesial institution and presented as a statutory faith. In this sense, belief indicates in the case of the religious person the turning point from the representation to the institution. The result is that it is not possible to speak of faith apart from its ecclesial dimension. This explains the conjunction set forth in the title to Part Three: "The Victory of the Good over the Evil Principle, and the Founding of a Kingdom of God on Earth."

The deduction of the idea of the justification of humankind is a deduction in the sense that it explores the conditions of possibility for the restoration of the originary disposition toward the good. The structure of religious belief brings it about that this deduction can be carried out only at the price of a fundamental antinomy. This antinomy affects the answers given to the question stemming from the confession of radical evil: namely, if human persons are radically evil, how can they do what they ought to do? The answer of religion seems to be univocally as follows: only a supernatural, external aid can return humankind's originary capacity to it, and this is because another has already paid for its sins. Kant adopts here, in order to test it, the most extreme version of the theology of expiation, that of vicarious sacrifice, of the substitute victim. Salvation is then conceived of as efficacious through faith in this extrinsic, or, as the theologians put it, forensic, expiation. This theology of expiation has to oppose, in terms of a relation of either/or, the thesis of justification by works that seems closest to the moral credo: "You can because you must." It is the confession of radical evil that makes this antinomy an obligatory place of passage in the deduction of the idea of justification. This is why, far from unequivocally assuming the side of the antithesis of vicarious expiation, Kant takes up the antinomy as constitutive of faith itself and as worthy of being philosophically interpreted. Something is retained from each of the theses, at the price, it is true, of a harsh correction of the first of them. On one side, faith in a forensic absolution cannot take its responsibility from the will; to believe in the effusion of a gift apart from every good intention is to corrupt the motives for morality. On the other side, a good disposition cannot proceed from a radically evil will. Without a gift, without some unfathomable aid, no change of heart would be possible. What remains is that the will turns toward this good coming from elsewhere than its disposition toward good that has not abolished its tendency toward evil. I will say that Kant has quite rightly transformed the antinomy into a paradox. This paradox becomes a structure of hope, as the paradox of our effort and the externality of a gift. This paradox prolongs, in fact, the very first paradox of book 1: the inherence of the evil principle alongside the good principle. Taken to its extreme, it consists in saying, on the one hand, that the reception of the gift counts as an injunction to mobilize the most repressed resources of the disposition toward good. On the other hand, and conversely, the recourse to these depths of the will, abetted by the very radicality of the confession of evil, counts as a disposition to accept this gift. It is as though, at an unsoundable depth, we can no longer distinguish, at the very heart of the disposition toward good, what is the identity of our effort and the alterity of the gift.

We need to acknowledge, nevertheless, that Kant is caught up in and blocked by this movement I have described as the passage from antinomy to paradox by the polemic that he carries out in book 3 against the statutory aspect of belief, which brings belief into the realm of the institution. With religion, faith always has to do with a statutory faith, where the accent is on those external events linked to the life of the historical Jesus and to the passion narratives. What is lost sight of in this objectifying of faith is the nonhistorical signification of the archetype of a humanity well pleasing to God, a signification regained earlier at the level of representation.

This intrusion of a relationship between authority and submission at the level of belief is responsible for the corruption of this representation itself. This explains in part why book 3 seems to take up once again the antinomy of justification (100ff.). If the antinomy persists, it is because the hypostasis of grace, understood in terms of a vicarious sacrifice, is consolidated by the statutory structure of faith. Kant's energetic battle against institutional religion is perhaps what prevents him from taking the full measure of the paradoxical character inherent in faith itself, just one side of which is in his eyes petrified through the authoritative teaching of the church. What is thereby lost sight of is the element of alterity that seems to be bound not just to the presence of the archetype at the heart of reason but more importantly to the efficacy of this representation, which is the very theme of faith. May we not say, in fact, that it is this factor of alterity that, in the final analysis, distinguishes hope itself from mere moral improvement? It is true that Kant is not far from recognizing the presence of this moment of passivity and alterity at the heart of conversion, despite his polemical posture against ecclesial faith, which increases from book 2 to book 4, when he allows that only those who sincerely wish to change the course of their lives are permitted to hope that an inscrutable aid will assist their effort and confer efficacy on it. Consequently, however inscrutable the origin of evil may be, the presence and efficacy of the archetype of a humanity well pleasing to God are even more inscrutable. If, nevertheless, Kant seems to concede, more than take up, this moment of alterity at the origin of the process of regeneration, then we may have to attribute this reticence not just to his hostility as regards ecclesial faith and in general as regards institutional religion, but rather to the absence in his work of a philosophy of the religious imagination (or, let us say, of the mythopoetic function of the imagination), which is just barely suggested by the ethics of the sublime and whose only trace in *Religion within the Limits of Reason Alone* is constituted by the schematism of analogy, referred to in regard to the presence of the archetype of good in the very constitution of reason. The influence of this archetype on our will seems to require that the accent be placed not just on the side of representation but also on that of the efficacy of this schematism. However, a mythopoetics of the imagination would violate the contract of agreement, of congruence, of mutual fit, that Kant attempts to establish and to preserve between philosophy and religion, on the frontier of reason alone. It leads from Kant's bounds to the vicinity of Schelling.

The Institution

The institutional dimension of religion was already taken into account in book 3, to the extent that faith is inseparably statutory, ecclesial faith. In this sense, the aim of the kingdom of God and the announcement of its establishment on earth through the figure of the church were already included in the structure of this faith. But it is with the question of worship and the conjoint question of ordination that the institutional aspect of religion passes to the first rank. Here representation makes itself belief, and belief is inscribed in practice.

It is at this stage that the confrontation with religious positivity is brought to its full height (already with the title of book 4, the expression "service and pseudoservice" indicates that a line has to be drawn). It is also at this stage that evil is going to find its most fertile ground of expression. Kant's position, however, cannot be reduced to a simple rejection as regards the institutional dimension of religion, to the extent that the question of the sovereignty of the good principle legitimately entails that of "true" service or worship. In this sense, we might speak of a Kantian ecclesiology or of a philosophical ecclesiology.

What the institution adds to belief is what Hannah Arendt will call a public space of appearance. What we must understand is that the "triumph of the good principle" (the title of the third part) becomes a sovereignty only on the condition of a public incarnation in an ecclesial body. Practical philosophy sets us on the way toward this decisive consideration. In its third formulation, the categorical imperative develops the demand for a realm of ends that would set the seal of totality on the plurality of moral persons announced in the second formulation of the imperative. (We recall how the *Groundwork of the Metaphysic of Morals* articulates the three formulations of the categorical imperative according to a progression from unity to plurality to totality.) Yet the realm of ends still designates only an ethical totality where the subjects are the legislators and reciprocally the legislators are the subjects. The kind of sovereignty implied by the triumph of the good principle stems from a distinct problematic, that of the regeneration of the will, which itself has its origin in the enigma of radical evil. Consequently, the ecclesial community cannot be reduced to the ethical expression of the kingdom of ends.

Nor can it be reduced to its political expression. The political order most certainly does contribute to this task of incarnation by giving a historical and institutional dimension to this bare idea of a realm of ends. In this regard, Kant's political writings constitute an important step from the *Critique of Practical Reason* to *Religion within the Limits of Reason Alone*. But no political institution can satisfy the requirements of a community devoted to the regeneration of the will. As the essay "Idea for a Universal History from a Cosmopolitan Point of View" suggests, historical action can engender only a relative state of public peace, motivated by the antagonism Kant calls our "unsociable sociability." The civil peace we call a state of law is not virtue, but rather an armistice in the war among interests. At most we can say that "the beginnings are laid for a way of thought which can in time convert the coarse, natural disposition for moral discrimination into definite practical principles, and thereby change a society of men driven together by their natural feelings into a moral whole."[7] At best, the citizens, as citizens, may act in conformity with duty but not necessarily out of duty. In this sense, a certain optimism at the level of the theory of political action is perfectly compatible with a radical pessimism at the level of ethical life. Kant even goes so far as to say in his essay "Perpetual Peace" that "the problem of organizing a state, however hard it may seem, can be solved even for a race of devils."[8] Establishing peace "does not require that we know how to attain the moral improvement of men but only that we should know the mechanism of nature in order to use it on men, organizing the conflict of the hostile intentions present in a people in such a way that they must compel themselves to submit to coercive laws. Thus a state of peace is established in which laws have force."[9] For this reason, no political philosophy, and more generally no philosophy of culture, can satisfy the requirement of a community that aims at the regeneration of the will through specific public means.

The question arises, therefore, whether the church is the community that the *sovereignty* of the principle of good requires. Here philosophical reason has to take into account the pure and simple existence of a community it has not engendered, which is a historical and cultural product, bound to historical events, to founders, to rules and customs, to professions of faith,

---

7. Immanuel Kant, "Idea for a Universal History from a Cosmopolitan Point of View," trans. Lewis White Beck, in *Kant on History*, ed. Lewis White Beck (Indianapolis: Bobbs-Merrill, 1963), 15.

8. Immanuel Kant, "Perpetual Peace," in *Kant on History*, ed. Beck, 112.

9. Ibid.

and to rites, which, taken together, admit to being contingent and in this sense irrational. All the evils that book 4 denounces with an ever-increasing irritation, under the general title of "false service," are grafted to this historical contingency: slavish submission, feigned veneration, hypocrisy; in a word, the bad faith of faith.

And yet Kant means to dissociate himself from the univocal condemnation of the *Aufklärer* of ecclesial rule. The patience with which he undertakes to disentangle the true figure of the church from its historical caricature merits our consideration and respect. Despite their notorious failings, churches, such as they are, constitute the already existing channels for the setting up of the reign of the good principle. Hence we must extend from the statutory aspect of belief to cultic practice the sort of hermeneutic effort found in the preceding books. A hermeneutics of the institution has to be joined to the hermeneutics of representation by way of the paradox of justification. Here once again the starting point is given: the churches already exist, in the same way that the human species is already evil and that the archetype of a humanity well pleasing to God is already inscribed in our hearts. It is not by chance that the notion of a schematism of an analogy reappears in book 4. The task here is to identify the "marks," the "traces" of the affinity between the historical institution and the sought for community. We ought to emphasize in this regard that Kant is not seeking an invisible church, but rather the signs of the genuine community to be found in the visible churches. And these signs are themselves visible.

The principle for such an analogy between the church and the idea of an ethical community lies in the assumed affinity—not to say the preestablished harmony—between historical Christianity and the true worship and service of true religion. Already in book 3, Kant had exclaimed: "How fortunate, when such a book fallen into men's hands, contains, along with its statutes, or laws of faith, the purest moral doctrine of religion in its completeness— a doctrine which can be brought into perfect harmony with such statutes ([which serve] as vehicles for its introduction). In this event, both because of the end thereby to be attained and because of the difficulty of rendering intelligible according to natural laws the origin of such enlightenment of the human race as proceeds from it, such a book can command an esteem like that accorded to revelation."[10] This proposition is held to be valid only through a militant hermeneutics: "If such an empirical faith, which chance, it would seem, has tossed into our hands, is to be united with the basis of a moral faith (be the first an end or merely a means), an exposition [*Auslegung*] of the revelation which has come into our possession is required, that is, a thoroughgoing interpretation [*Deutung*] of it in a sense agreeing with the universal practical rules of a religion of pure reason" (100). The

---

10. Kant, *Religion within the Limits of Reason Alone*, 98.

philosopher must therefore interpret as "allegories of practical reason" the narratives, teachings, and dogmas that Kant reviews in book 4. But there would be no respectable means of practicing this rationalizing interpretation of the classical dogmas of Christianity apart from a presumed affinity between an atemporal principle and a historical reality. What is more, such a hermeneutics would not be possible unless modernity had created the conditions for such an undertaking: "If one now asks, What period in the entire known history of the church up to now is the best? I have no scruple in answering, *the present*. And this, because, if the seed of the true religious faith, as it is now being publicly sown in Christendom, though only by a few, is allowed more and more to grow unhindered, we may look for a continuous approximation to that church, eternally uniting all men, which constitutes the visible representation (the schema) of an invisible kingdom of God on earth" (122). Hence it is only from Kant's day on that a philosopher can proclaim that "reason has freed itself, in matters which by their nature ought to be moral and soul-improving, from the weight of a faith forever dependent upon the arbitrary will of the expositors" (122).

Hence, whatever it may say against false worship and service, fanaticism, and clericalism (*Pfaffentum*), this philosophical hermeneutics it not just possible: it brings the intelligibility of hope to its fulfillment at the very moment when evil reaches its extreme point of perversity. At the last stage, evil is the origin of what we could call a pathology of totality, that is, the perversion of that impulse toward completeness that governs the movement from the "Analytic" to the "Dialectic of Practical Reason." Religious experience thereby becomes the occasion for a new sort of heteronomy, no longer affecting the principle of morality, but rather the goal of what the "Dialectic of Practical Reason" had called "the complete object of the will." Evil in religion in this way tends to become the evil of religion.

Let me offer the following remarks to conclude.

1. Philosophy has need of a hermeneutics of religion because the inscrutable character of the origin of evil, of the origin of the Christ representation implanted in our hearts, of the additional gift of grace to which belief confesses, and finally of the institution that gives visibility to the kingdom of God on earth, is inscribed *outside* the circumscription of reason.

2. This hermeneutics is, in any case, made possible by the presumed affinity between the requirements of philosophy and the reinterpreted contents of faith. The price of this agreement is thus a polemical relation, aggravated by the perverse effects of radical evil, which culminate in the heteronomous stance of false worship and service with their train of obsequity, hypocrisy, and fakers.

3. Owing to its mixed character, in its polemical moment as much as in its moment of agreement, the philosophical hermeneutics of religion cannot

be taken to be an extension of critical philosophy, in either its theoretical or its practical sense. If it has no place, if it is *a-topic*, this philosophical hermeneutics is not without a thematics: it gives embodiment to an understanding of hope as the unique kind of reply to the confession of radical evil.

5

The "Figure" in Rosenzweig's
The Star of Redemption

The remarks I wish to make in introducing *The Star of Redemption* have a didactic goal: to create a certain familiarity in the hearer or reader with the strange and unusual.[1] Stéphane Mosès's straightforward reading of *The Star* follows the main lines of a work consisting of three parts.[2] This obligates the author to confront head-on the most difficult of these three parts, the first one, concerning which we may say, broadly speaking, that it makes an irreducible plurality of the three objects that Kant placed under the titles of "rational psychology" (humankind and the soul), "rational cosmology" (the world), and "rational theology" (God) and that German idealism tried to reunite within the unity of a system. But this bursting apart of a totality is not comprehensible except to a reader already familiar with the philosophy that Rosenzweig submits to his forceful critique, in particular the later philosophy of Schelling, in his *Weltalter.*

For my part, I want to renounce taking up Rosenzweig's great book by entering into it from its beginning. Instead I have taken the risk of proposing a backward reading because such a reading offers an easier means of access to this work (at least in appearance): namely, the confrontation between Judaism and Christianity. I do not want to hide the mutilating character of such a reading, which I have sought to make as didactic as possible. This mutilation will already be apparent in my treatment of the closing pages of *The Star,* which call upon the esoterism of the cabala and the *Zohar* in exact symmetry to the discussion of Hegel and Schelling in Part One.

Originally published as "La 'Figure' dans 'L'Étoile de la redemption,'" *Esprit* 12 (1988): 131–46; printed with permission.

1. This essay was originally prepared as the introductory presentation to a conference held in Paris in 1987 to celebrate the centenary of the birth of Franz Rosenzweig. TRANS.

2. Stéphane Mosès, *L'Étoile: Système et révélation: La Philosophie de Franz Rosenzweig* (Paris: Seuil, 1982). See Franz Rosenzweig, *The Star of Redemption,* trans. William W. Hallo (New York: Holt, Rinehart and Winston, 1970); subsequent page numbers given in the text refer to this edition of *The Star of Redemption.*

In a word, I have chosen to follow the line of thought suggested by the title of Part Three: "The Configuration; or, The Eternal Hyper-Cosmos." In so doing, I want to take up the metaphorics of this work—and its subtle construction—as it finds fulfillment in the figure of the star. Hence we are going to trace out the six-pointed star, the star of David.

Life and Way

In choosing to begin at the end—or, rather, at those chapters that precede the end—I am choosing a theme that, despite its concrete character, already indicates the originality and oddness of *The Star*: namely, that it seeks to think together, as complementary and irreducible to each other, the postures of the Jew and the Christian in relation to the history of nations. I say the Jew and the Christian. It would have been better to say the Jewish people, as a "community of blood kinship," and the individual Christian, as a member of a missionary church. In Rosenzweig's metaphorical system the Jew is figured by "life" because the Jew exists and knows that he or she exists through the transmission from generation to generation. The Christian, on the other hand, is figured by the "way" because she or he is a pagan on route to becoming a Christian (something that is, we may note, completely in conformity with Tertullian's aphorism: one is not born a Christian, one becomes one). Doubling this metaphorics of life and way is another of fire and rays, metaphors that already point toward the form of the star. Life, the certitude of existing as a Jew, is in effect fire in relation to the way, which leads to the missionary conquest of the world starting from the fire held within its burning lamp.

This apparently simple symbolism conceals a richness of thinking that we need to begin to unfold. Indeed, Rosenzweig does not confine himself to holding Jewish existence and Christian existence in a kind of lover's quarrel. He wants to think through the reasons for their irreducible duality and their final, utopian convergence. These reasons are both speculative and existential (or, if you prefer, they are the reasons of a hitherto unknown genre of existential speculation), and they will constrain us below to return from the third part to the second, which joins together without reducing to unity creation, revelation, and redemption, and then from the second part to the first, which, in the subbasement of the nonunifying interconnections of the second part, uncovers the elementary, itself a product of the decomposition of systematic unity.

What is there, then, about the construction of the third part that constrains us to this walk backward? It may be found in the simple comprehension of the title of the third section of the third part, by which I will begin our didactic overview: "The Star, or Eternal Truth." Why eternal? Why truth? From one end to the other of *The Star,* eternity designates a quality of time bound to a limit-experience, that of a certain immobilization of time, contrary to that chronological time that succeeds itself without end. Judaism and Christianity are in this way reinterpreted as different and complementary ways of conquering time that simply passes, to the profit of a time that endures, in the sense of enduring as an indestructible stability. The Jew does this by withdrawing from the history of the nations, with their culture and their politics, in order to bear witness to his or her unique attachment to the immutable Torah, even at the price of a withdrawal into particularity. The Christian proceeds to this suspension of mutable time by working within the time of history, in order to elevate it above itself by propagating the Christian confession to the ends of the earth.

That eternity is in question in each instance is indicated by Rosenzweig when he writes of eternal life on the side of Jewish existence and eternal way on the side of Christian existence. And he confirms that such is the case by a comparative interpretation of the ritual calendar and the symbolism of the holidays in Judaism and Christianity, concerning which he shows the odd parallelism and the profound differences, especially in relation to the utopian aim he calls redemption, whose meaning we learn from Part Two. The idea, the great idea, the singular idea, the original idea of Rosenzweig is that these two manners of eternalizing concrete experience are incomplete, concurrent, and converging approaches to truth.

Let us next turn to this term "truth," as it appears in the title "The Star, or Eternal Truth." Here is where, with Stéphane Mosès, we plunge into Jewish esoterism and its speculation in order to comprehend in what sense Jewish and Christian existence are transcended by what Emmanuel Levinas characterizes as "otherwise than being." For here messianic utopianism is taken up in force into a type of discourse that while systematic (a point Mosès insists upon) is not like the Greek *theoria* stemming from Parmenides, nor is it like the speculative thought of German idealism. Refusing, for the reasons I have indicated, to enter into this final speculation, which is the exact counterpart of the decomposition of the system in Part One of Rosenzweig's book, I shall limit myself to indicating its place for a presentation that seeks to stay close to the metaphorics of the figure in *The Star.* Let me say, then, that for this metaphorics, eternal truth is the vanishing point toward which the two modes of eternalization, figured by life and way, and by fire and rays, converge. This is why Rosenzweig can decline eternity three times: eternal life, eternal way, eternal truth. In this sense, eternal truth is not an absolute Elsewhere but the common intention of Jewish life and the Christian way. This is why it can be figured, and figured precisely by the star.

The moment has come, in our didactic presentation, that seeks to remain close to Rosenzweig's metaphorics, to name the six points of the star. Doing so will lead us to return from the third part to the second and then to the first. The star is composed of two overlapping triangles, one of which points upward and the other downward. The first one is not really a triangle; it is just three points: God at the summit, the world and humanity at the two lower angles. These three discrete points figure the irreducible plurality in which the decomposition of the system in Part One ends up—"the impossible assemblage," as Levinas puts in his preface to Mosès's book. I will speak about this plurality only in concluding, leaving to Mosès the credit for having presented a thorough analysis of the philosophemes in Part One, as well as the care needed to justify the status of the "elements" of these three emblematic terms. (The extreme difficulty of Part One is accounted for by that which confers on these three leading words the status "elementary.")

As for the second triangle, which I shall speak of further in my backward march through *The Star*, it is essential that it overlap the first one, for it figures the three nonidentical connections that uproot the three philosophemes from their separation, their closure, their pure reference to themselves (the hidden God; the self-sufficient world; humankind closed in on itself, on the self [*Selbst*]). The three connections Rosenzweig names creation, revelation, and redemption are opposed to these three elements, and the exploration of the eminently relational status of these connections, opposed to the status of the elements identified in Part One, constitutes the exclusive object of Part Two.

In my backward reading, it is the third connection, redemption, figured by the point at the bottom of the second triangle, that provides the guideline to Part Three, the double eternalization through Jewish life and the Christian way expressing the double relation to historical, successive, and indefinite time of the utopian process in which redemption consists. This is why this third connection is the only one named in the title of the book: *The Star of Redemption*.

The Figure

Now we must return from the third part toward the second one. But before doing so, I would like to emphasize one last time the persistence of the figurative mode up to the speculation borrowed from Jewish esoterism, which gives a full sense to the expression "The Star, or Eternal Truth," the title of the final section of the book. In this regard, it would be useful I believe to compare the use of the term *Gestalt*—here translated as "figure"—with the tradition of *Figura*, as it has been presented by Erich Auerbach in his important essay "Figura."[3] Nor does *Gestalt* mean *Bild* (picture). How would this be possible for a tradition as iconoclastic as that of Judaism? Nor does it mean *typos,* as in Christian typological interpretation, which has often reduced Jewish existence to a shadowy state, denying it the aspect of a living, literal support, in the sense of being real in itself, in the transference of meaning from one economy to another. It might even be more fruitful to compare the tie between figure and speculation for Rosenzweig to the relation of *Vorstellung* (representation) and *Begriff* (concept) for Hegel. We might then see that the relation is something quite other than what Hegel meant. With Rosenzweig we would have a speculation that is metaphorical throughout, a metaphorics that is speculative throughout. Why then "figure"?

One key is given us by the marvelous encounter in French between the two words *figure* (figure, form, shape) and *visage* (face, countenance), which are two different words in German, but which Jewish speculation had already brought together starting from the biblical expression "the face of God." It is under the guidance of this expression and the speculation grafted to it that *The Star* reunites the two senses—of figure and face—into one figure, precisely that of the star. Readers will discover with astonishment—something that Mosès says was frequent in the cabala—that the figure of the star is itself a sort of face with ears, a nose, a right and a left eye, and a mouth. And Rosenzweig writes regarding Moses, who was not allowed to enter the promised land: "God sealed this completed life with a kiss of his mouth. Thus does God seal and so too does man."[4] The reader will, of course, have recognized the birth here of the theme of the face to which Emmanuel Levinas has given so much breadth and force.

The triad creation, revelation, redemption—or, it might better be said, the ternary rhythm—outlines what Maurice Merleau-Ponty would have called the membrane of the immense and sumptuous second part. In this brief introduction, I must limit myself to an overview, and I will say just two or three things concerning it. In the first place, what we have here is the discourse of faith, but as a discourse in which philosophy and theology are absolutely indistinguishable. This is a basic feature of the "new thinking" spoken of in *The Star* and even more so in Rosenzweig's correspondence. It is a discourse of faith, yes, but one that breaks away from the discourse of absolute knowledge that the first part had broken into pieces. To indicate this break with older forms of discourse, in his introduction to Part Two Rosenzweig uses the provocative heading "On the Possibility of

---

3. Erich Auerbach, "Figura," in *Scenes from the Drama of European Literature* (New York: Meridian Books, 1959), 11–76.
4. Rosenzweig, *The Star,* 423.

Experiencing Miracles." There is no clearer way of saying farewell to the *Aufklärung* and to absolute knowledge.

But we must not misunderstand what is meant here. The miracle is what the philosophical theologian calls "new thinking." We read: "The contact of revelation and redemption is of central importance to contemporary theology, which therefore, to put it theologically, calls upon philosophy to build a bridge from creation to revelation in which this contact can take place" (107). The philosophy left behind, in Part One, is ironically called, with a wink at Christians, theology's "old testament" (108). In fact, Part Two is like a new testament: it is the kerygma of the interconnections among three miracles—that there should be creation, revelation, redemption. Or, to put it another way, the miracle is that underlying the language of lived experience there are layers of ever-more fundamental language that precede the speaking subject, a language that Rosenzweig sees as already appearing and established in the biblical discourse made explicit through the Talmud. The miracle is that there should be a "speaking" of creation, of revelation, and of redemption. We are not the masters of this language, for it is this language that opens our most basic forms of experience to language. It is this language, again, that holds together metaphor and its speculative meaning. But this language has to be multiple. I have spoken of "layers of language" in order to emphasize that creation, revelation, and redemption do not succeed one another along the same line. It is rather a question of strata piled upon one another, with redemption—that is, utopia—constituting the highest stratum, revelation, the intermediary one, and creation, the bottom. Therefore it is not a question of some homogeneous triad.

The Beginning, Figure of Creation

In order to make sense of this layered structure of Part Two of *The Star,* I propose to follow two pathways that, we shall see, are really one, which will justify the title of Part Two, "The Course [or Way]; or, the Always-Renewed Cosmos." I shall begin with the pathway of the figure that is suggested by our backward reading, starting from the title of Part Three: "The Configuration; or, The Eternal Hyper-Cosmos." We can read the second part as a series of qualitative leaps within the order of the figure. What does creation mean? Creation, says Rosenzweig, is the beginning, the "in the beginning" of Genesis 1, of course, but also, in the philosophical-theological language that poses so many problems (in that we still hear in it Hegel and even more so the later Schelling), the beginning of the externalization of God. In this sense, it is power that is figured here (113–14), that is, that is given shape and visibility. Here, Rosenzweig draws upon

Maimonides: "[W]ith the utmost decisiveness, [Maimonides] asserted God's creativity as his essential attribute. He even developed the whole doctrine of the attributes of creative power in clear methodological assimilation to this attribute of creative power" (115). In other words, what has to be thought is a relational God, in terms of the very relation between creator and creature. Here being and being created overlap (see 131).

I shall say no more about creation, except to indicate the place for an important mediation on aesthetics, a meditation rooted in the "and God saw all that God had made, and indeed it was very good" of Genesis 1. This goodness that precedes the commandment and any obedience to the commandment incites beauty. Hence before leaving the section on creation, let me note again that a deliberately backward reading cannot fail to find its starting point in the admirable exegesis of Genesis 1, the poem of creation, that closes the section on creation. An aesthetics of creativity is implied there that springs from the confluence of Scripture and Rosenzweig's philosophical-theological reading of it. Genesis is the first appearance of the figure. The genesis of the figure in and through the figure of genesis...

The Soul, Figure of Revelation

The second setting forth of the figure comes with the theme of revelation. Under this title Rosenzweig has in mind a living relation between God and humanity that far surpasses revelation in the Mosaic sense, the revelation at Sinai, inasmuch as, as we shall see, this latter is contained in the former. We may put it as follows: revelation is the very opening of human experience to language on the model of a paradigmatic language that is precisely the language of the Bible. In this sense, Moses is not wrong in making revelation the central category of his study of Rosenzweig, as the title of his book indicates: *Système et révélation*. The language of revelation is, as we said above, the miracle of the setting up of a language on the basis of a model that undergirds it. However, Rosenzweig chose to title his book *The Star of Redemption*, and this was in order to indicate that the culminating category remains redemption, not revelation. Why? We shall understand this better in a while when we follow the path of temporality. But we can already understand why from following the path of figuration.

The figure of revelation, for Rosenzweig, is the soul and only the soul. It is important that the soul be solitary. The reception of a proper name takes place only in solitude before God, to speak like Kierkegaard. And in this way we learn that the individual is not some interchangeable unit of a genus, even if this be the human genus. But be that as it may, the figure of the soul lacks what is essential. It lacks the figure of the neighbor, who appears only in the third category, or, better, the third figurative layer. Why then do we have the soul and the soul alone? Essentially, in order to bring out the intimate character of one with another that constitutes love—that is, the unique power capable of making death fail, death that we shall say is what breaks the system into pieces. Love is strong as death (Song of Sol. 8:6). Indeed, this is the secret of the conversation between God and a solitary soul declared as love, a love "strong as death." The exemplary language that fits this conversation rests on the metaphorics of the lover and the beloved following the hermeneutical tradition of Jewish exegesis of the Song of Solomon. But Rosenzweig also makes use of Greek: Eros is as strong as Thanatos. For it is the universal language of the soul that is born here—that is, the self opened to language as dialogue through the paradigmatic dialogue, that of God and humanity. To the question posed to Adam, "Where are you?" only Abraham could answer, "Here am I." Therefore, if narrative was the appropriate literary form for creation, inasmuch as, according to Rosenzweig, the narrative takes place in terms of the third person (he), dialogue is the appropriate literary form for revelation, inasmuch as it brings together an "I" and a "Thou."

Allow me to add one more word concerning the figuration proper to revelation. To anyone who objects that we expected Sinai here and yet we get the Song of Solomon, two answers must be given. In the first place, the preference given to the Song of Solomon, beyond its justification in terms of Jewish ritual, immediately proposes a decisive correction to any overly narrow legalism. But we must not deduce from this a boundless anomism. Rosenzweig's genial insight is to have also caught sight of the birth of the commandment in the bond of love constituted by God's revelation to the solitary soul. The birth of the commandment—of the commandment that precedes every law—is the word that God addresses to the soul in saying to it: "Love me." It is the commandment of the lover, the "Love me" of the lover (176–77). Rosenzweig writes here: "[T]he sole commandment of love is simply incapable of being law; it can only be commandment. All other commandments can pour their content into the mold of the law as well. This one alone resists such recasting; its content tolerates only the one form of the commandment, of the immediate presentness and unity of consciousness, expression, and expectation of fulfillment" (177). This is the second moment of the figure.

The Kingdom, Figure of Redemption

The third moment is that of redemption. It comes third, but is first for a backward reading. And, indeed, it is this moment and this moment alone—apart from the two others—that is captured in the title *The*

Star of Redemption. It is also the moment most subject to equivocation, especially perhaps if we start from Christianity, which thinks of redemption in christological terms, hence as already accomplished or as partially accomplished.

The accent, here, is placed exclusively on the figure of the kingdom. This signifies several important things for the destiny of the figure of the star. First, it is only with redemption that the self has its Other, a fact that the category of revelation does not overlook but also does not emphasize. Figures of a new type follow—figures of community, where the kingdom is their fulfillment: "For God had, as long as He appeared to be merely creator, really become more amorphous than he had previously been in paganism, had, moreover, been in constant danger of slipping back into the night of a concealed God. Just so the soul, too, as long as she is only beloved soul, is now likewise still invisible and amorphous, more amorphous than in its time the self" (206). And again: "Only in the kingdom would the world be configuration as visible as had been the plastic world of paganism, the cosmos" (219). And again: "[T]his can only happen if the hand of the world-clock moves forward from revelation to redemption now, while the soul is taking form, as it moved from creation to revelation previously, while God was taking form" (211–12).

A history is thereby opened before us and for us. There is a neighbor and not just a lover and a beloved. There are also laws and not just a commandment, laws that develop the second commandment, the commandment to love one's neighbor as oneself. In this way, the grammar of pronouns unfolds: from the "he" of creation and narrative to the "I-Thou" of revelation and dialogue to the "we" of redemption and the kingdom. But at the same time we find ourselves amid the incomplete, amid becoming, whereas creation was presented as closed, or rather as sealed by God's Sabbath. We have entered the realm of growth. Rosenzweig says: the vitalization of existence (Dasein). The growth of life. Thus a correlation imposes itself for those who read backward, a correlation between the life of the Jew, from Part Three, and the growth of the kingdom, from Part Two. But this correlation is not spoken of in Part Two; hence it will not be perceptible to a progressive reading, a first reading. What we perceive in a first reading will be the constellation: the multiplicity of neighbors, the birth of history, the drive of this history toward the growing kingdom. There are new figures here: after the pair, the multiple, then the "we" of all of us. Retroactively, the self, at first closed in on itself, then opened by revelation, is definitively confirmed by the new commandment: not just "Love me," but "You shall love your neighbor." "Precisely here in the commandment to love one's neighbor, [man's] self is definitely confirmed in its place" (239). We have reached the realm of the ethical.

But for all that, the aesthetic is not lost sight of, as if it only applied to the realm of creation. The theme of growth is not just ethical; there is an aesthetic of growth: it is the "oeuvre," a word that has in both French and German a double allegiance—the poetic oeuvre and the practical one (191). The category of redemption is broad enough to encompass both wings of the oeuvre. This is confirmed by the text that closes the section on redemption and that, like every terminal text in Rosenzweig, is seminal: the exegesis of a hymn, Psalm 115, which Rosenzweig turns to because it is one of the "we" psalms, and moreover a psalm that denies the autonomy of this "we" and thus turns toward the kingdom: "Not to us, O Lord, not to us, but to your name give glory, for the sake of your steadfast love and faithfulness." (Let me note in passing the birth here of a grammatical dative starting from the biblical "to us.") If we are to stick with our meditation on the figure in Rosenzweig, we have to say that the figure, or the regime of the figure belonging to the third category, is being with the God who is with us and with the divine visibility. We have visibility precisely because of growth: "And thus the act of love, free as the world, comes upon the created world and its living growth" (253).

Temporality

I have followed one pathway, that of the figure. Now I propose to turn to the second, which redoubles the first one, that of temporality. We could have started here. But I have delayed turning to it for it is a way filled with many pitfalls. Indeed, it is too evident that the time of creation is the immemorial past, that of revelation the talk of the lover and the beloved today, that of the kingdom the time yet to come. And if we persist in our backward reading, it is the yet to come aspect of the kingdom that governs the copresence of one with another and the antiquity of creation. All this is too obvious, I have said. And also more troublesome than illuminating. For we cannot set the past of creation, the present of revelation, and the future of redemption on one line. It is a question, rather, of three levels of temporalization, of three layers with a different temporal quality, each of which, in its own way, contains a past, a present, and a future moment in the sense of linear succession. Thus there is, for example, a present and a future in the immemorial past of creation.

Rosenzweig is careful to emphasize this: "Creation; or, The Ever-Enduring Base of Things." The qualification "ever-enduring" announces the sovereign eternity of the third part, which was our first reference to temporality. In one sense, creation does not cease to lie behind us. The beginning is not a surpassed commencement but, in a sense, a unceasingly continued beginning. Otherwise, how are we to understand that creation was completed on the sixth day, that on the seventh day the Lord rested,

and yet that history according to the Bible unfolds "following" this beginning? In biblical language, in fact, the call of Abraham, in Genesis 12, does
not come after the sixth day, and even less after the seventh one. It is not
an eighth day. The immemorial past in some way underlies the present of
revelation and, if I may put it this way, the future of the expectation of the
kingdom, rather than being before the present of the one and the future of
the other. We move beyond all narrative linearity; or, if we can still speak of
narration, this would be a narration that will have broken with all chronology. As for the present of revelation, the today of the jubilation of the
lover and the beloved, the today of the commandment "Love me," is not
a present that passes, merely serving as a transition between the future of
expectation and the past of memory. The subtitle of book 2 of Part Two is
"Revelation; or, The Ever-Renewed Birth of the Soul." This "ever-renewed"
prolongs the "ever-enduring" base of things. Today does not signify now
but *Augenblick,* the blink of an eye, a term that, as Harald Weinrich makes
clear in his book on time, means *Plotzlichkeit,* suddenly.[5] In relation to
chronology, the moment or instant—in a quasi-Kierkegaardian sense of the
term—arrives at any moment; it is the occurring moment that opens toward
an ever-enduring.

"The power to change the color of created being, which is illuminated by
such a moment, from created 'thing' into a testimonial to occurred manifestation resides in the effulgence of this *coup d'oeil.*"[6] Let me note in passing
that many contemporary arguments about the present and presence could
be avoided if we stopped confusing presence in the optical sense and *Augenblick,* blink, glance, which applies to the voice, not to looking, to a voiced
profferation of the voice. This is why for Rosenzweig, the present does not
flee; the moment of revelation is the eternal "now" that prevents any flight
back into the past of the origin:

> Precisely as it is unconditionally product of the moment, revelation is
> thus the means for confirming creation structurally. The creator could
> still retreat behind creation into the darkness which is itself without
> structure just because so rich in structures. There always remained to
> him, so to speak, the flight into the past of "origin," where he "could
> modestly hide behind eternal laws." But the revealer in his all-time
> presentness can at every moment transfix him in the Bright, the Man-
> ifest, the Unconcealed, in short in the present. And by doing so, he
> lets God's concealedness sink into the past once and for all. Now God
> is present, present like the moment, like every moment, and therewith
> he proceeds to become a "matter of fact"—something which as cre-

5. Harald Weinrich, *Le Temps, le récit et le commentaire* (Paris: Seuil, 1973).
6. Rosenzweig, *The Star,* 161.

ator he had not yet truly been and which even now he only begins to become—like the gods of the heathen behind the ramparts of their mythology. (161–62)

(It looks as though there is a comparison to be made of Rosenzweig's "glance," not just with Kierkegaard's instant, but also with Heidegger's *Ereignis*. But I am deliberately abstaining here from all such comparisons.)

The Eternal Future

I would like to conclude these remarks devoted to the temporality of the way traced out in Part Two of *The Star of Redemption* with a few comments about the future, or better, the "coming" of the kingdom, under the sign of its third theme, redemption. Here once more the subtitle ought to alert us: "Redemption; or, the Eternal Future of the Kingdom." In what sense is it eternal? Let us recall what has been said about the incompleteness of the world in its becoming, which accounts for the fact that we can *erzählen* (count on or recount) what is yet to come, precisely the kingdom. Rosenzweig opposes the becoming kingdom to the moment of revelation. This point concerns both the figure and time: "[F]or creature to become structure, to be of the kingdom and not merely apparent existence tied to the moment, it must acquire essence, it must acquire durability for its momentariness, and for its existence—well, what?" (221). Well, the enduring reality of life.

There is no doubt that here once again Rosenzweig is thinking of the living endurance of the Jewish people. Yet Part Two maintains a calculated reserve regarding this and talks indistinctly of Jews and Christians, not yet having reached the great dialectic of Part Three. Thus Rosenzweig confines himself to such enigmatic expressions where "enduring," "structure," and "fixed" (223) are interchangeable. What gives stability is a necessity linked to growth: "Vitality, therefore, must increase; of an inner necessity it must increase. And this Must is likewise primordial. The world is created in the beginning not, it is true, perfect, but destined to have to be perfected" (224). And again: "[T]he kingdom, the vivification of existence, comes from the beginning on, it is always a-coming" (224). We cannot doubt that for Rosenzweig this eternalization of the moment has as its figure the visible perpetuation of the Jewish people. But, in Part Two, he systematically practices understatement. This is why the enigma of an anticipation that "endureth forever," an expression borrowed from Ps 136:1, is so carefully examined. Let us end with the words: "that which eternally cometh: the kingdom" (242).

Beyond Metaphysics?

I shall be brief as concerns Part One: "The Elements; or, The Ever-Enduring Proto-cosmos." This part expresses Rosenzweig's break with idealist philosophy, which makes use of all the self-destructive forces of that philosophy. To Rosenzweig, this is the collapse of paganism, already ironically named the "old testament" of the new thinking.

It is not a matter of indifference that we enter this first part with a reference to death, just as we left the second part with a reference to life and to growth: "All cognition of the All originates in death, in the fear of death" (3). Death is the prod of the *Thaumazein,* of philosophical wonder. Nothing resembles this first part so much as Kierkegaard's argument with Hegel in his *Concluding Unscientific Postscript to "Philosophical Fragments,"*[7] without forgetting Schopenhauer and Nietzsche, who are named in proximity to Kierkegaard. "He who denies the totality of being, as we do, thus denies the unity of reasoning. He throws down the gauntlet to the whole honorable company of philosophers from Ionia to Jena."[8] Levinas could not fail in his preface to Stéphane Mosès's book to call attention to this challenge, which is also that of his own *Totality and Infinity* and *Otherwise Than Being or Beyond Essence.*[9] But if for Levinas things have been judged, this is not the case for Rosenzweig, who uses the weapons of his adversary and gets caught in the snares of metalogic, metaethics, and metaphysics. Parting is not painless for a way of thinking whose strength is to have designated God, the world, and humanity as the primordial "elements," the wombs of the real, like those well-known Mothers of Plutarch in *Faust,* part 2. The elementary is the undergirding of our language, even when it is informed by revelation. This is the sense of the expression "the ever-enduring proto-cosmos." We live in the twilight of the gods—but this twilight persists in one sense. Even for Jews and, following them, Christians, the deficiency of this protoworld still speaks: "And the divine nowhere overflows the limits of its individuality. Antiquity arrived at monism, but no more. World and man have to become God's nature, have to submit to apotheosis, but God never lowers himself to them. He does not give of himself, does not love, does not have to love. For he keeps his *physis* to himself, and therefore remains what he is: the metaphysical."[10]

As for the world, the most self-evident of what is evident, well: "Of the world we know nothing" (42). And yet as regards this nothingness

---

7. Søren Kierkegaard, *Concluding Unscientific Postscript to "Philosophical Fragments,"* trans. Howard V. Hong and Edna H. Hong (Princeton, N.J.: Princeton Univ. Press, 1992).

8. Rosenzweig, *The Star,* 12.

9. Emmanuel Levinas, *Totality and Infinity,* trans. Alphonso Lingis (Dordrecht: Kluwer, 1980), and *Otherwise Than Being or Beyond Essence,* trans. Alphonso Lingis (Dordrecht: Kluwer, 1991).

10. Rosenzweig, *The Star,* 40.

of our knowledge, "Here, too, the original affirmation, the Yea of non-Nought, again wells forth, out of the Nought, just because it cannot remain Nought" (42). This is why the pagan "old testament" is not cut off. Rosenzweig is not a fanatic who would have burned the library of Alexandria because it did not speak like the Bible. The contest is endless, as the second part of the title of Part One conveys: "The Ever-Enduring Proto-cosmos." In the end, it is this latter that outlines the first triangle, onto which the second part places the second triangle that, with the first, forms the star.

As for humankind, in this first part, we know nothing of it either, except that the human person is already there as *Selbst,* as self. For "in him too the primeval words awaken: the Yea of creation, the Nay of generation, the And of configuration. And here too the Yea creates the true existence, the 'essence' in the infinite non-Nought" (63). None of this is revoked or abolished by the new thinking, the "new testament" to this "old testament." And this "old testament" extends indeed from Ionia to Jena. What Rosenzweig has to say about classical humankind in this respect is admirable: "Metaethical man too was a living configuration in antiquity, and again principally in the truly classical antiquity of the Greeks" (73). The figure of the self par excellence is that of the tragic hero "with the impetus of visibility" (ibid.). So we see how this theme can run through the whole book: from its *terminus ad quem,* the saint of the kingdom, to its *terminus a quo,* the tragic hero, following our backward reading: "The tragic hero of antiquity is nothing less than the metaethical self" (73). This hero is metaethical as the world is metalogical and God metaphysical. But notice: the metaethical self is closed in on itself, like the God who cannot love, and like the world that has no beyond, that is deaf and dumb, existing without God or the self. The metaethical self is "lord of its ethos" (82), with no outside, no exteriority.

The last words of Part One are: "[W]e hold the parts in our hand. Truly we have smashed the All" (83). "There is no fixed order among the three points God, world, and man" (84). Why, then, did Rosenzweig write this first part, why not start directly with Part Two? This is a question any reader of Rosenzweig must ask. Did Rosenzweig break with system building? Is it not necessary to first break a system before proposing what Stéphane Mosès calls *encore système?* I will not answer for you. I will end with one modest comment, however. One strange word emerges at the end of Part One, the word "perhaps." It assures the "transition" from Part One to Part Two: "the transition from the mystery into the miracle" (90). Perhaps the undergirding of paganism needed to be conserved so that its "perhaps" could give birth to the nostalgia of an absolute word.

In fact, this "perhaps" that gives the transition from Part One to Part Two corresponds to the "order of the route" that provides the "threshold" between Parts Two and Three, the threshold, it is said, that we cross in moving "from miracle to enlightenment" (261). And this threshold corresponds in turn to the "gate"—a kind of postface to *The Star*—that, we read on the last page of this work, "leads out of the mysterious-miraculous light of the divine sanctuary in which no man can remain. Whither, then, do the wings of the gate open? Thus knowest it not? INTO LIFE" (424). This "into life," the last words of the book, give its full weight, in a backward reading, to the opening sentence of *The Star*: "All cognition of the All originates in death, in the fear of death."

- 6 -

Emmanuel Levinas:
Thinker of Testimony

I have chosen as the theme for this essay the pages devoted to "witness" or "testimony" in chapter 5 of *Otherwise Than Being or Beyond Essence.*[1] Why this choice? It was motivated not just by the happy memory of having shared the hospitality of Enrico Castelli with Emmanuel Levinas at the Rome conference devoted to testimony in 1972, but even more by the occasion of trying to understand the originality of Levinas's treatment of this theme, especially as it relates to his discussion of substitution in chapter 4 of the same work, and to do this through a comparison of Levinas's thought with that of two other philosophers of testimony. The two other philosophers for whom testimony has been an important philosophical category are Martin Heidegger in the second chapter of Division Two of his *Being and Time,* under the title "Dasein's Attestation of an Authentic Potentiality-for-Being, and Resoluteness," and Jean Nabert in the third part of his *Le Désir de Dieu:* "Métaphysique du témoignage et herméneutique de l'absolu."[2] At first glance, there is something unexpected about putting these three works dealing with testimony together inasmuch as it initially seems to place, in a provocative way, Jean Nabert *between* Heidegger and Levinas. However, this order seemed justified to me by the fact that it underscores the increasing emergence from the first to the third of these thinkers by way of the second of two themes whose intersection seems to me to characterize a philosophy that merits the title "philosophy of testimony." These are the themes of "height" and "exteriority." Height is *Gewissen* (conscience) for Heidegger, originary affirmation for Nabert, and

Originally published as "Emmanuel Levinas, penseur du témoignage," in *Repondre d'autrui: Emmanuel Levinas* (Neuchatel: La Baconiere, 1989), 17–40; printed with permission.

1. Emmanuel Levinas, *Otherwise Than Being or Beyond Essence,* trans. Alphonso Lingis (Dordrecht: Kluwer, 1991).

2. Martin Heidegger, *Being and Time,* trans. John Macquarrie and Edward Robinson (New York: Harper and Brothers, 1962); Jean Nabert, *Le Désir de Dieu* (Paris: Aubier-Montaigne, 1966). All references to *Being and Time* are to the German pagination indicated in the margins of the English translation.

the glory of infinity for Levinas. Exteriority is expressed as the uncanny in *Being and Time,* by the mediation of other consciousnesses testifying absolutely to the absolute for Nabert, and, finally, for Levinas, by assigning to the other the responsibility for oneself in the extreme passivity of the condition of being a hostage to the other. Hence height and/or exteriority do not just constitute important features of these philosophies of testimony through their intersection; they also, as I shall demonstrate, provide the criterion for their differences, inasmuch as, from Heidegger to Nabert and from Nabert to Levinas, there is an increase in superiority that parallels the increase in exteriority.

I. Heidegger

The idea that there might be more kinship between Jean Nabert, who draws on Johann Fichte, and Levinas, who breaks with Heidegger, than between Heidegger and Levinas at first sight may seem somewhat shocking. However, I want to show how through the double criterion to which I have just referred, Heidegger is the one of these three who concedes the least to height and even less to exteriority in the case of attestation he considers.

It is not that Heidegger denies either of them. The element of verticality, to begin there, that separates philosophies of testimony from those that identify straightaway the self-attestation of the self with reflexive consciousness is not absent from *Being and Time.* It is represented by the *Gewissen,* the voice of conscience—or perhaps we should say the moral injunction, following Jean-Luc Marion?[3] However, as we shall see, for Heidegger *Gewissen* has little to do with morality—as little as possible!

The link to a hermeneutics of the self-attestation of the self is assured in *Being and Time* by the chain of "existentials" that, strengthened by the question "Who?" (§9 and §25), passes through the opposition between self (*Selbst*) and the "they" (§25), then through the conjunction between the problematic of care and that of the self (§41 and §64). The decisive pulling away from every merely reflexive philosophy takes place in the second division when the question is emphatically posed of what "assures" that the ontological characterization of Dasein as care constitutes an originary interpretation of this existent (see §45, p. 232).[4] This question finds its fullest formulation when it is said that "an authentic potentiality-for-

3. See his remarks in the issue of *Cahier de la nuit surveillée* devoted to Levinas, no. 3 (1984): 235.
4. The words "assurance" and "criterion" occur several times in this context. I shall return to them below.

Being is attested by the conscience" (p. 234).[5] Here is where the dimension of verticality intervenes. The voice of conscience hangs over me, calls me, calls me from on high. In this sense, conscience breaks apart any simple self-coincidence with oneself. But Heidegger's whole strategy is to draw something valuable from the superior force of attestation issuing from *Gewissen,* without according it the slightest status as transcendence. In this regard, Heidegger proceeds to a double reduction of transcendence: first on the side of the contents, the theme, the said—as Levinas would put it. What conscience attests to is the potentiality-for-being-oneself, both as an existential and as *existentiell,* not as some difference between good and evil. In this way, conscience is so to speak "demoralized." It is beyond good and evil. Here we come upon one of the effects of Heidegger's struggle against the value orientation of the neo-Kantians, and even more so of Max Scheler, in the name of fundamental ontology. The more emphasis we place on *sein* in Dasein, the less we are disposed to recognize any ethical force in the call of conscience. (Martineau, the French translator of *Being and Time,* even translates *Anruf* as *ad-vocation.*) I shall return to this below when I take up the status of the good and the bad conscience. On the side of the connotation of "call" there is nothing apart from what we have already named potentiality-for-being. Conscience says nothing, there is no uproar, no message, just a silent call. On the side of the caller, however, the reduction of transcendence is even more drastic. The caller is once again Dasein: "In conscience Dasein calls itself" (p. 275). This is undoubtedly the most surprising moment of Heidegger's analysis. It is within the integral immanence of Dasein to itself that Heidegger recognizes a certain dimension of height: "[T]he call undoubtedly does not come from someone else who is with me in the world. The call comes *from* me and yet *from beyond me* [*aus mir und doch über mich*]" (275).

This is the point where the interpretation of height catches up with that of exteriority. An exteriority without otherness corresponds to this height without transcendence. It is not that any reference to others is completely lacking. Rather the other is implied only in reference to the "they" and on the plane of the inauthentic mode of preoccupation: "The call reaches the they-self [*das Man-Selbst*] of concernful Being with Others" (p. 272).[6] However, the dominant tone remains pulling the self out of the "they": "Conscience summons Dasein's Self from its lostness in the 'they' " (p. 274). If exteriority is not otherness in an authentic relation to others, what is it? The uncanny takes the place here that is not filled by others. A subtle comparison is drawn between the uncanniness of the voice and the

---

5. One passage in §244 includes the whole series Dasein, who, self, care, potentiality-for-being-one's-self (p. 267).

6. Similarly at the beginning of §58 we have: "that is, as concernful Being-in-the-world and Being with Others" (p. 280).

fallen condition of being-thrown. Dasein has been thrown into existence. What alone can interrupt the familiarity of the "they" is an uncanniness, *a strangeness without a stranger*. This is the point where Heidegger and Levinas seem closest but in fact are farthest apart. They are close owing to this admission of passivity, of nonmastery, of the affection of being summoned. They are far apart in light of Heidegger's reduction of the stranger in parallel with his reduction of transcendence: "What could be more alien to the 'they,' lost in the manifold 'world' of its concern, than the Self which has been individualized down to itself in uncanniness and been thrown into the 'nothing'?" (p. 277).

Uncanniness is referred to a structure of being-in (the world) and dissociated from being-with (whose analysis is impoverished by the almost exclusive focus on the "they"). Whence Heidegger's recourse to the neuter: *es ruft* (it calls [p. 276]). It is strange that an analysis of care based on the question "Who?" ends up with the neuter and with "nothing." The caller in the end is no one, but rather the very uncanniness of the condition of thrownness and fallenness: "a call which comes *from* uncanniness," that is, from "thrown individualization" (p. 280).

The late introduction into this chapter of the notion of *Schuld* (guilt, debt) in no way restores any ethical or personal connotation to this height or this uncanniness. The accent is on the *sein* in *Schuldigsein*. What is essential here is that "being-guilty" (or "indebted") appears as a predicate of the "I am" (p. 283). Through this insistence on the ontology of guilt, Heidegger dissociates himself from what the ordinary meaning attaches to the idea of guilt: that we are guilty before or indebted to *someone*, that we are *responsible* as guilty (as in debt), finally that being with one another is *public*. And this is just what Heidegger intends to reduce to its barest allowance. Ontology guards the threshold of ethics. Heidegger hammers this point home: "[W]e first inquire in principle into Dasein's *Being*-guilty" (p. 283), then we inquire about this as a mode of being. In this way, the ordinary phenomena of guilt, of indebtedness, those that are related to "our concernful Being with Others" (p. 283), drop out. Being-guilty (*Schuldigsein*) therefore is not a result of indebtedness (*Verschuldung*), just the opposite (p. 284). If some fault is laid bare here, it is not evil—war, Levinas would say—but an ontological feature prior to all ethics: "*Being-the-basis of a nullity* [*Grundsein einer Nichtigkeit*]" (p. 283).[7] That Dasein is not the master of this basis that it however has to be is another proposition where the nearness and the distance between Heidegger and Levinas are apparent. Nearness: their common plea against any claim to self-mastery. Distance: the distance between, on the one hand, the nullity of being-a-basis and, on the other hand,

---

7. Heidegger also says: "*Dasein as such is guilty,* if our formally existential definition of 'guilt' as 'Being-the-basis of a nullity' is indeed correct" (p. 285).

being affected by the injunction of the other. With Heidegger, inquiry into guilt remains strictly oriented toward the ontological conditions of notness. There is no better way to get rid of ethics. "The primordial 'Being-guilty' cannot be defined by morality, since morality already presupposes it for itself" (p. 286).

Unfortunately, Heidegger does not show how we can travel this road in the opposite direction, from ontology toward ethics. This, however, is what he seems to promise in §59 where he takes up the discussion of "the way conscience is ordinarily interpreted." In this sense, his attestation does lead to a certain criteriology, at least as a critique of ordinary meaning.

It is first of all the notion of a "good" or a "bad" conscience that is labeled "ordinary." Bad conscience because it comes too late, after the fact—Nietzsche would say it is reactive. Therefore it lacks the *prospective* character inherent to care. There is nothing to be gained, then, from remorse or repentance. As for the good conscience, it is set aside as a "slave of Pharisaism" (p. 291), for who can say "I am good"? (But perhaps goodness is not what I glorify myself as having but that to which I am called?) Heidegger does not even want to hear any talk of conscience as admonition or warning, owing to the curious argument that conscience then once again becomes a prisoner of the "they" (p. 292). In all this, Heidegger's critique of ordinary meaning is manifestly to be compared to Nietzsche's *Genealogy of Morals*. Also rejected at the same time are Kant's deontological point of view, Scheler's theory of values, and, with them, the critical function of conscience. All this remains within the dimension of preoccupation, which misses the central phenomenon: the appeal to our ownmost possibilities. Attestation, then, is a kind of understanding, but one irreducible to knowing something. Its meaning is made clear: "calling forth and summoning us to Being-guilty" (p. 295).

It is true that the last word about this attestation has not yet been said. A comparison with Levinas requires that we question the fate of the self's responsibility, as it is solicited by the call coming from the basis of a nullity. For here again a significant proximity and distance between these two thinkers reveal themselves. The important point here has to do with the connection between attestation and resoluteness. The tie between resoluteness and being-for-death in Heidegger is well known. What resoluteness brings is, in effect, the aim of being-a-whole, sealed by being-for-death. The transition from the one to the other takes place in the expression: "wanting to have a conscience" (p. 295). Whence this last formulation: the "*reticent self-projection upon one's ownmost Being-guilty, in which one is ready for anxiety*—we call 'resoluteness'" (p. 297).

Note how Heidegger here avoids the vocabulary of acting, which to him seems to call for either an opposition to suffering that being thrown denies or an opposition to theory that would break up the total unity of Dasein into "distinct behaviors." On the other hand, attestation does get inscribed in the problematic of truth, as opening and uncovering: "In resoluteness, we have now arrived at that truth of Dasein which is most primordial because it is *authentic*" (p. 297).

But as cut off from the demand of the other and from every ethical determination, resoluteness remains as indeterminate as the call to which it responds. Thus comes the formula: " 'Resoluteness' signifies letting oneself be summoned out of one's lostness in the 'they' " (p. 299). As for any orientation as regards action, fundamental ontology refuses to make any proposals: "In resoluteness the issue for Dasein is its ownmost potentiality-for-Being, which, as something thrown, can project itself only upon definite factical possibilities" (p. 299).

Everything happens as though the philosopher sends his reader back to a moral situationalism destined to fill the silence of an indeterminate call. Indeed, this is what the following text seems to suggest, along with the note attached to it referring us to Karl Jaspers. "To present factical existentiell possibilities in their chief features and interconnections, and to interpret them according to their existential structure, falls among the tasks of a thematic existential anthropology" (p. 301). The note reads: "In the direction of such a problematic, Karl Jaspers is the first to have explicitly grasped the task of a doctrine of world-views and carried it through. Cf. his *Psychologie der Weltanschauungen.*"

II. Nabert

I have taken the risk of setting the philosophy of testimony of Jean Nabert between that of Heidegger and that of Levinas. I do not deny that there is something odd about this strategy. As far as I know, Levinas has never undertaken an extended discussion of Nabert, even though he does name him once in *Otherwise Than Being,* while his argument with Heidegger is a constant one. And we can understand why. Nabert belongs to that current of reflexive philosophy with which, in a way, Levinas broke by way of Heidegger, who himself confronted neo-Kantianism and Ernst Cassirer. The kind of height that reflexive philosophy confesses indicates the superiority of an originary affirmation that is not numerically distinct from empirical consciousness. The adequation of this empirical consciousness with the spiritual act that constitutes it even defines the itinerary for the liberation of freedom. Therefore, if there is verticality in Nabert, perhaps it is to be found elsewhere than within the very interior of the subject. And does not exteriority reduce to the succession of consciousnesses within the absolute, which includes the distance between subjects? If such were the case—or if this were the only case—my interposing of Nabert between Heidegger and

Levinas would be incongruous, even preposterous. Nonetheless, it imposes itself upon me due, on the one hand, to the ethical break (as we speak of an epistemological break) that Nabert's philosophy brings about in relation to ontology and, on the other hand, to the role of initiation that certain of Nabert's terms can play in regard to those formulas of Levinas that below I shall call "excessive," particularly among them: substitution. I would like to show that these two effects of a break and an approximation culminate in the philosophy of testimony to be found in Nabert's posthumous *Le Désir de Dieu*.

The ethical break brought about by Nabert, within the very framework of a reflexive philosophy, is consummated starting with his *Elements for an Ethics*.[8] This happens in two ways. First of all, it is affirmed that the "focal points of reflection" are multiple and irreducible to one another. The ethical sphere is thereby released from the subtle tutelage that the transcendental procedure of Kant's first *Critique* exercises on the second *Critique*. Above all, the entry into the ethical problematic occurs in experiences of passivity, gathered by *feeling*, before being taken up in reflection: fault, failure, solitude. The "pure consciousness" that these experiences deny is for all that brought to the forefront. However, it is in the protest against the "unjustifiable," with which Nabert's *Essai sur le mal* opens, that empirical consciousness takes the unmeasurable measure of the height of absolute consciousness.[9] The unjustifiable is what cannot be measured by the mere violation of those norms to which the moral conscience equates itself.

> In the presence of certain acts of cruelty, or of the abasement of certain men, or of the extreme inequality in the conditions of their existence, is it through the idea of a disagreement between these facts and our moral rules that we exhaust the reasons implied in our protest? When death, prematurely interrupting someone's destiny, strikes us dumb, or when it seems to us the ransom for a lofty spiritual ambition, is it through the idea of injustice that we evaluate such an event? Everything takes place as though, through the feeling of the unjustifiable, a more radical contradiction is laid bare to us, in certain cases, independent of those oppositions outlined by our norms, between the givens of human experience and a demand for justification that the mere transgression of these norms does not overthrow, that mere fidelity to these norms does not serve to satisfy. (p. 2)[10]

---

8. Jean Nabert, *Elements for an Ethics*, trans. William J. Petrek (Evanston, Ill.: Northwestern Univ. Press, 1969).

9. Jean Nabert, *Essai sur le Mal* (Paris: Presses Universitaires de France, 1955).

10. And also: "But what is this evil experienced by others, as a consequence of our own acts and faults? Suffering, death, an irreparable damage, the pain of a soul wounded by the betrayal of a friend, lost possibilities due to exhaustion and to work. We could make the list of these consequences of injustice and passion as long as you like. And it is at this point

Thus to the very extent that the unjustifiable surpasses the invalid, the demand for justification surpasses the resources of the good will least satisfied with itself. "The incertitude, the precariousness of an inner progress, the impatience for a verification or a decisive demonstration regarding the truth or the depth of our regeneration gives birth in our consciousness to the idea of absolute actions that would be their own light to themselves" (123).[11] We are thus set on the way of the testimony rendered by others, better than us, as the possibility of a justification that exceeds our own resources. However, this is spoken of in *Essai sur le mal* only in an enigmatic fashion: "There are those actions concerning which we can think that, without having been willed by me in view of his justification, they bring him, however, in return, some assurance of an actual regeneration" (124). These actions are just as contingent as are the wounds of evil. In a sense that announces Levinas's notion of substitution, in order to render the very idea of justification credible, Nabert calls on "a gratuitously willed suffering to restore the lost chances of a spiritual universe" (144).

In this way, the theme of height begins to link up with that of exteriority. "Whether it be a question of a misfortune or of guilt, evil is doubled unless, at the proper moment, the gratuitous act of another conscience occurs, a source of appeasement and a promise of justification: evil lies in the will, but evil also lies in the wrongs man inflicts on man" (145). Of course, the word "exteriority" does not belong to Nabert's vocabulary. But at least one time the word "witness" is pronounced, with its whole charge of singularity, of contingency, of otherness: "What is allowed us is to measure the difference between our own being and that of the witnesses to the absolute. In this way, and in this way alone, the inadequation of self-consciousness and pure consciousness acquires its full meaning for an individual ego, and identifies itself with the most secret imperative of his being" (149).

What remained allusive in *Essai sur le mal* becomes explicit in Part Three of *Le Désir de Dieu:* "Métaphysique du témoignage et herméneutique de l'absolu." The heart of this work, alas left only as notes and outlines, was to have been the articulation of a criteriology of the divine that would have relentlessly pursued the critique of false absolutes, or let us say of false divine names, *and* the reception of those acts and beings that, *outside of reflection,* in the actual experience of history, "tes-

---

that the examination of evil in a free will and the examination of evil that is unjustifiable in the eyes of those who undergo it cross" (125).

11. And again: "This is why an individual ego is always at the threshold to justification. He cannot break the solidarity by which he participates in the evil that touches his personnel destiny, nor can he assure himself that his own action is exempt from some secret self-complaisance, nor can he believe that his repentance is equivalent to annulling his debts, and he lacks that intellectual intuition of an act or a choice that would be the root of his being" (139).

tify to the divine."[12] A criteriology of the divine and a "hermeneutics of testimony" (328) are in truth as inseparable as are height and exteriority. Height is inseparable from exteriority to the extent that it is not human beings who make themselves God's judge, but rather it is the divine, implicated in the founding act of consciousness, that makes itself the judge of the ideas human beings make of God. This discernment turns back against us, enjoining the most extreme divestment of our particularity. Exteriority is inseparable from height to the extent that my conscience cannot by itself bring about this divestment, without the testimony of certain acts, certain lives, that, despite their radical contingency, their plain historicity, speak in the name of the absolute. Nabert does not hesitate to call them absolute testimonies to the absolute. Between criteriology and hermeneutics, the relation is reciprocal. As the ordinary usage of the term "testimony," and even more its practical use, indicates, there where an attestation is pronounced, a challenge may arise. Every testimony is produced in a trial-like process. There are false witnesses, just as there are false gods. This is why the criteriology of the divine and the discernment of testimony go together and mutually call for each other.

We can understand why this situation is unsurpassable. On the one hand, the unjustifiable, beyond the intellectual poverty of any so-called proofs for the existence of God, brings about the ruin of all speculative demonstration, whether we mean by this the tradition of medieval ontology or the Cartesian or Hegelian forms. On the other hand, if it is true that "the desire for God gets confused with the desire for self-understanding" (21), then the adequation between empirical consciousness and the originary affirmation that dwells within it is nowhere given. So much for the tradition of reflexive philosophy from Fichte to Jules Lachelier, Jules Lagneau, and Léon Brunschvicg. Lacking, therefore, either of these kinds of verification—that is, either speculative or reflexive verification—we have no other resource than the judgment applied to those determinations and objectifications coming from the history of thought and to the testimony of certain acts, certain lives, certain sacrifices.

Where does this hermeneutics of testimony take us on the way to exteriority? Nabert is unlike Levinas in that for him height and exteriority do not coincide in one and the same instance, that is, in others. For Nabert, height remains on the side of reflection and exteriority on the side of testimony. But reflection and the welcoming of signs also remain both heterogeneous and concurrent. Their heterogeneity is all the more emphasized in that the category of testimony is distinguished from that of the example, which simply illustrates the law, and even from that of the symbol, which acts on the imagination without engaging life in any way. Testimonies are real

---

12. Nabert, *Le Désir de Dieu*, 327.

events whose depths no reflection can plumb. Testimony even divides itself, outside of reflection. There is first the testimony rendered by real acts
of devotion up to death. Next, there is the testimony rendered to this testimony by witnesses to its witnesses. The testimony of the latter is called
for this reason absolute testimony to the absolute. And regarding this first
form of testimony, we must say that it was not willed for itself, yet it needs
to be understood as testimony. This is the way, Nabert observes, that "the
painter makes everything a testimony that awaits a witness" (273). A dialogic structure of testimony is indicated here between testimony as act
and testimony as narrative. Someone gives a sign of the absolute, without intending to do so or knowing that he or she does so. Another person
interprets this as a sign. It is in taking up the second form of testimony
that reflective consciousness grants the absolute testimony of the absolute
through that movement of divestment by which the consciousness is rendered less inadequate to the desire for God, as a desire to fully comprehend
oneself. Thus it is the criteriology of the divine that governs the return from
testimony to reflection.

> The criteriology of the divine corresponds to the greatest divestment
> that a human consciousness is capable of in order to affirm an order
> exempt from those forms of bondage from which no human existence
> can deliver itself. This divestment, this affirmation, are acts. At the
> limit, we would find a pure act, dominating the whole criteriology and
> all the separate qualities. But as soon as consciousness undertakes to
> spell out, to detail, to analyze this pure act, it puts it back in qualities,
> in individual acts. (265)

Reflection, I will risk saying, thereby becomes internal testimony, testimony of the third degree, grafted to the testimony rendered of the absolute
testimony of the absolute: "[T]estimony is the act of acting" (274).

Are we so far from what Levinas speaks of as the passivity of being
summoned?

Before leaving Nabert, I would like to pose two questions that will give
a transition to Levinas. The first one has to do with the delicate problem
of the epistemological status of attestation, which is an assurance, without
being a doxic certitude, an assurance always bound to acts. Testimony is a
"phenomenon," in one sense of the term, for "the phenomenon, when it is
not the neutral data of the scholar, is always a witness to or testimony of
a meaning. We must read it, we must discover that it is testimony and to
what it testifies" (273). Finally, "the phenomenon is what attests, verifies,
proves what is of another order than itself, but that far from being an essence, noumenon, or idea is an act, an affirmation" (273). We may refer to
this second-order testimony as belief, but only in a sense that I would call
nondoxic. Belief, writes Nabert, "understood not as the adhesion that ac-

companies a judgment, whatever it may be . . . , is one with the act by which we affirm and acknowledge the absolute character of a testimony" (288).

Here to believe is to trust. With testimony, it seems to me, the problematic of truth coincides with that of veracity. It is in this sense that testimony is related to and dependent upon a hermeneutics: the believing confidence of a second-order testimony in the first, absolute testimony does not coincide with deductive knowledge or with empirical proof. It stems from the categories of understanding and interpretation. Do we not link up here with Levinas's critique of intentionality and representation?

My second question: Is it possible, apart from this hermeneutics of testimony, to take up again the problematic of *Gewissen,* of the moral conscience, of the injunction, and to do so at the point where Heidegger left it? Here the passage through the question of evil and the unjustifiable is decisive. The moral conscience is first of all the protest against the unjustifiable. Its height lies in the demand for justification apart from which evil cannot be taken as unjustifiable. Its exteriority lies in the testimony of those acts whose ethical significance results from their position on the trajectory of "approaches to justification." As a result, ethics cannot be hemmed in as it is for Heidegger; instead it constitutes, to use Nabert's vocabulary, "the focal point of reflection," where the question of the adequation of empirical consciousness to originary affirmation is not distinguished from the generation of the former. The possibility of this regeneration can be deciphered nowhere else than in those acts exterior to reflection that testify absolutely to the absolute. Therefore, the hermeneutics of testimony can no more be separated from the problematic of the unjustifiable and of justification than this problematic can be unfolded outside of a hermeneutics of testimony. The greatest proximity between Nabert and Levinas is expressed in this conjunction of ethics and the hermeneutics of testimony.[13] It remains true,

---

13. This proximity is reinforced by the criticism of Heidegger (who is never named) on pp. 130–34 of *Essai sur le mal.* Can the forgetting of being, the prevalence of the existent over being, take the place of the unjustifiable? Is the return to being equivalent to justification? "Is it so easy, then?" asks Nabert. "The optimism implied in the certitude of this presence, it cannot be denied, is the antithesis of an optimism founded on the deification of man and his powers. That light that is being itself and that, at first, illumines man about what really is, it cannot be denied, is light only to the extent that it has, in effect, to disperse the shadows. But where then is evil? In the refusal that man, that existent who only exists through being, opposes to being in positing himself as an absolute existent? The understanding of being denounces this rebellion as illusory. . . . But can evil, experienced in the depths of the fault and the truth of suffering, be so easily set aside? Is the wickedness of human action only a derived mode, far from being, whose essence would include it like some fundamental ambiguity akin to the opposition of what is pure and what goes astray? A philosophy that works to overcome the loss of the sense of the reality of being is not expected, of course, to confront evil with the perfection of the act implied in the idea of a highest being. Still, to preserve in its full strength and in its comprehension the idea of what must not be, it must understand that freedom can be guilty and that this guilt does not come down to a forgetfulness of being" (131–32).

however, that for Nabert the hermeneutics of testimony remains linked to a philosophy of reflection that Levinas breaks away from starting with the very first lines of his chapter on substitution, by breaking with the primacy of ipseity over alterity. Through this gesture, height and exteriority will be placed on the same side, that of the other.

III. Levinas

At first sight, the notion of testimony seems to occupy a marginal place in the thought of Levinas. In the chapter in *Otherwise Than Being* entitled "Substitution" the word does not appear. It comes to the fore only in the section of the following chapter entitled "The Glory of the Infinite." I would like to show that the notion of testimony, even if it is introduced late in the final version of this work, is what seals the unity of height and exteriority through which we have defined the notion of testimony. In fact, both these notions are at the heart of the chapter on substitution. What we need to demonstrate is that the notion of testimony adds what has not yet been made explicit in these glorious pages.

Levinas's break with Heidegger is clear, thoroughgoing, and explicitly stated. That with Nabert, who is named once,[14] or at least with the philosophical current to which he belongs, is less clear, although it seems to be quite evident, as I shall indicate below.

Ethics unfolds outside the field of ontology; this conviction animates this whole work, as its title alone is sufficient to indicate. The "one for the other" constitutive of my responsibility for the other is of the order of a "summons," not of manifestation. This central opposition is set forth at great length by the calling into question of Husserl's notion of intentionality, which is apparently ontologically neutral. The other whom intentional consciousness is supposed to intend is not in the first instance another person, but rather anything at all capable of being represented. But representation, when it does not express consciousness's mastery over its object, as in the idealist version of phenomenology, points us to the way of manifestation, to the laying bare of beings in terms of their way of relating to being. The notion of proximity, developed in the earlier pages of *Otherwise Than Being*, indicates the initial break with the Husserlian understanding of intentionality, as captive to representation, on the plane of the sensible. The notion of substitution consecrates the break with the Heideggerian version of intentionality as uncovering, unconcealment. But these two breaks make up one and the same fracture. It is not necessary here to recall the analyses of *Totality and Infinity* where the face is removed from the realm

---

14. Levinas, *Otherwise Than Being,* 115.

of appearance (of "appearing" before a judge or tribunal, as Levinas likes to put it).[15] Here too the face stands "in contrast with a phenomenon" (120). No ontology is required to characterize the being we are in order to distinguish it from given or manipulable things. Ontology, however fundamental it seeks to be, is even an obstacle to this fuller characterization of who we are inasmuch as it presents the self in terms of the order of the revealed world, omitting the other who removes him- or herself from the order of manifestation or revelation. For Emmanuel Levinas, ethics is its own beginning apart from any ontological preparation. This is what the phrase "assignation of responsibility," which comes to occupy exactly the place of manifestation, means. Forgetfulness of the other takes the place of the forgetfulness of being, to the point that the rediscovering of being engenders the forgetfulness of the other.

This aspect of Levinas's philosophy is too well known for us to have to spend much time on it here. I would like instead to dwell at some length upon the other break in his presentation, that with the philosophy of consciousness, insofar as it seems to take away any credibility from my suggestion that, in the range of philosophies of testimony, Nabert occupies a middle ground between Heidegger and Levinas. This shift in accent in our discussion imposes itself to the extent that the point of attack in the chapter on substitution is directed against the ambitions of a philosophy of consciousness. Indeed, it is the question of identity or of identification that is the first one posed. Identity, whether this be that of an object by way of its apparent silhouettes or that of consciousness itself by way of its temporal phases, is what consciousness posits in positing itself. However, the nonradicality of the problematic of identity consists in the fact that every procedure for identification stems from the "saying" of a "said," a saying for which this identification is the "theme." There is therefore in the positing of an identity an initial forgetting, the forgetting of the saying, lost in the said. When it is a question of consciousness itself and not of its objects, thematized identity, identified identity, is said through the proper name, the mask of true identity, which has no other origin than the assignment of responsibility by the other.

What is essential, however, has not yet been caught sight of. In the background of this primacy given to identity as a theme, as the saying of the said, lies the claim of consciousness to posit itself in principle as the beginning of all meaning. This moment of Levinas's meditation is capital for it is the one where the difference between philosophies of consciousness and ontological philosophies gets erased, without the knowledge of those who thought they could locate at this place the dividing line that defines

---

15. Emmanuel Levinas, *Totality and Infinity: An Essay on Exteriority*, trans. Alphonso Lingis (Pittsburgh: Duquesne Univ. Press, 1969).

modern philosophy. Positing a principle, an *archē,* a beginning, an origin, is what characterizes ontology. Essence—a term that for Levinas must not be confused with *eidos,* but that rather designates "being" as a verb and not as a noun—does not "bring" its train here any more than in ontological philosophies before or after idealism. In this sense, the revolution of philosophies of consciousness takes place at the very heart of ontology. It is to this primacy of consciousness as master of meaning and of itself that the assignment of responsibility by the other is opposed. But how are we to articulate a philosophy of otherwise than consciousness?

I want to point out two strategies that are employed simultaneously by Levinas to free himself of the ontological prestige of self-positing consciousness. These strategies stem from what Levinas elsewhere calls the "unsaying" by which the saying frees itself from its being captured by the said. These two strategies are particularly noteworthy for their originality as much as for the way they are woven together.

The first one could be called the step "to the hither side" (*en deçà*): to the hither side of the beginning, of the *archē,* is the idea of the "an-archy" of a demand that "is the trace of the *who knows where*" (100); the idea of a past older than any rememberable past, hence not capable of being reintegrated into a present consciousness; the idea of a passivity that would not be the contrary of activity, hence that is not an undergoing, which the philosophies of consciousness could convert into an act of assuming or of consent; the idea of a "responsibility that is justified by no prior commitment" (102); the idea of a "different freedom than that of initiative" (115), of answering "without a prior commitment" (116); the idea of "an antecedence prior to all representable antecedence: immemorial" (122); the idea of a conjunction of passivity and responsibility on the hither side of all memory ("this passivity is that of an attachment that has already been made, as something irreversibly past, prior to all memory and all recall" [104]); the idea of "the anachronism of a debt preceding the loan" (112); the idea of "an accusation preceding the fault" (113).

But why this step back toward the hither side? There is just one answer: because the theme "annuls the very anarchy of its movement" (121). The hither side par excellence is finally the saying in relation to the said. We shall see below how testimony is articulated on this basis.

I will say that it is through this first strategy that the height of what has always preceded us is attained. In several places, Levinas refers to creation and the condition of the creature as what cannot and must not be thought ontologically. I shall speak below about the sense in which the terms "infinity" and "the glory of infinity," which testimony leads to, take up this movement of withdrawing toward the hither side.

Second strategy: the accumulation of excessive, hyperbolic expressions destined to shake up ordinary thinking, as though it were necessary to bend a branch in another direction than the one it habitually takes. These expressions aim at consoling the exteriority of that occurrence that assigns responsibility to me, the exteriority of the other. The "obsession" of the other: it "undoes thematization" (101). There is reference to "persecution" by the other. The extreme, scandalous hypothesis—what I am here calling excess or hyperbole—is that the other is not the master of justice who says to me: thou shall not kill, as was the case in *Totality and Infinity,* but the offender who, as offender, requires no less of me than the gesture of pardon, of expiation. Crowning this series of excessive, hyperbolic expressions we have "substitution" of myself for the other: "For under accusation by everyone, the responsibility for everyone goes to the point of substitution. A subject is a hostage" (112). This most excessive notion of all is put forward in order to undercut any return to the self-affirmation of some "clandestine and concealed freedom" underlying the alleged passivity of the self assigned the responsibility. Responsibility, that transference through which the "by the other" of the offense passes over into the "for-the-other" of expiation: "We have to speak here of expiation as uniting identity and alterity" (118). Also: "In suffering by the fault of the other dawns suffering for the fault of others, supporting. The for-the-other keeps all the patience of undergoing imposed by the other. There is substitution for another, expiation for another. Remorse is the trope of the literal sense of the sensibility. In its passivity is effaced the distinction between being accused and accusing oneself" (126). There is also mention of the "self in the ego accused by the other to the point of persecution, and responsible for its persecutor. Subjection and elevation arise in patience above non-freedom. It is the subjection of the allegiance to the Good" (126).

I want to emphasize the hyperbolic turn of these expressions whose destabilizing function seems to win out over their inciting function. Nothing less than the hyperbole of substitution is required if the self-positing of the subject in a philosophy of consciousness is to be displaced. "Already the position of the subject is a deposition, not a *conatus essendi*. It is from the first a substitution by a hostage expiating for the violence of the persecution itself" (127).

As for the interweaving of these two strategies, that of a step back, with the negative formulas that accompany it, and that of the hyperbole of ethical discourse, this is what gives force to a number of formulations in the section on substitution. I will cite just two of them, which say it all. "The ipseity, in the passivity without *archē* characteristic of identity, is a hostage" (114). And: "The overemphasis of openness is responsibility for the other to the point of substitution, where the for-the-other proper to disclosure, to monstration to the other, turns into the for-the-other proper to responsibility. This is the thesis of the present work" (119).

The time has come to say in what sense the pages on "the glory of the infinite" and on "testimony" provide a kind of crown to the whole preceding meditation. The 1972 version of this text bore the title "Truth as Manifestation and Truth as Testimony."[16] This gives us a clue. It is within the order of truth that testimony constitutes an alternative notion in relation as much to ontological philosophies as to philosophies of consciousness. In other words, what is at stake is the epistemic status of the whole prior discourse. In the chapter on substitution the adversary was, as we have seen, more on the side of the philosophies of consciousness: "The self is the very fact of being exposed under the accusation that cannot be assumed, where the ego supports the others, unlike the certainty of the ego that rejoins itself in freedom" (118). Testimony is precisely the mode of truth of this self-exposition, the opposite of certitude. As we have seen, for Levinas, philosophies of consciousness finally fall within the circle of ontology, owing to their appeal to the intermediary of a principle or *archē*. This is why when the discussion is taken up again in this new chapter it is addressed indifferently to both schools of thought, manifestation and reflexivity stemming equally from what follows in the train of being as being. This discussion may be summed up in terms of three headings: "the subject absorbed by being," "the subject at the service of the system," and "the subject as a speaking that is absorbed in the said." In contrast to this triple occultation stands "the responsible subject that is not absorbed in being." The whole of the preceding meditation is summed up in one passage: "In responsibility the same, the ego, is me, summoned, provoked, as irreplaceable, and thus accused as unique in the supreme passivity of one that cannot slip away without fault" (135). The footnote to this passage emphasizes that the impossibility referred to here is purely "ethical"; hence it implies no ontological "slipping away"—otherwise this impossibility would become a necessity.

It is against this background, which sums up the preceding analyses, that testimony is opposed to the certitude of representation, which encompasses both self-certainty and the manifestation of every being.

That the epistemic status of the discourse that runs through this whole work is what is at issue in the notion of testimony is what I am now going to show. Let us return to my working hypothesis that height and exteriority are conjoined in philosophies of testimony. Here the name for height is the glory of infinity. The word "glory," with its biblical origin, designates the epistemic status of height. Glory is not a phenomenon. It is not a theme. It cannot be called to appear in court. It is the unsaid of the said. This is why we can talk about it only given all the resources of this prior strategy of the unsaid: an-archy without a beginning, passivity of passivity, the immemo-

---

16. "Vérité comme dévoilement et vérité comme témoignage," *Archivio di Filosofia* (1972): 25–30.

rial past, obedience that precedes any hearing of the commandment. "Glory is but the other face of the passivity of the subject. Substituting itself for the other, a responsibility ordered to the first one on the scene, a responsibility for the neighbor, inspired by the other, I, the same, am torn up from my beginning in myself, my equality with myself" (144). We rediscover all the previous formulations but with a particular concern for language. Whether we speak of "election," "inspiration," "sincerity," or "prophecy," it is always a question of expressions that bring about the unsaying of a said, without which philosophy would fall back into silence: "The saying prior to anything said bears witness to glory" (145); "witnessed, and not thematized" (148).

One important consequence comes to the fore: namely, the impossibility of a positive, speculative theology and even, it would seem, of a narrative theology. Narration and unconcealment go together. Yet do we not speak of a plot? This can only be a plot without a theme: "One is tempted to call this plot religious; it is not stated in terms of certainty or uncertainty, and does not rest on any positive theology" (147). There is no experience of responsibility and its ground. The height/glory of the infinite and the exteriority/injunction of responsibility bear witness to this but neither show themselves nor posit themselves: "Transcendence owes to itself to interrupt its own demonstration" (152). This interruption, opposed to Aristotle's *ananke sténaï* (we have to stop somewhere), is an-archy. The word "God" appears only at this point where the hypostasis in the said is suspended at the moment of getting under way. In this precious interval, the word "God" remains "the only one that does not extinguish or absorb its own saying" (151). We must always unsay it, both as a proper name and a common noun. "Thematization is then inevitable, so that signification itself show itself, but does so in the sophism with which philosophy begins, in the betrayal which philosophy is called upon to reduce" (151–52).

But at the moment when the glory of the infinite, escaping every theme, risks falling into the ineffable, ethical discourse starts up again, or rather speaks—for there is finally no other testimony rendered to height, to the glory of the infinite, than the testimony of exteriority, of the assignment of responsibility. And, on this other face of testimony, the maneuver of unsaying, which is the epistemic status of testimony, repeats itself: " 'Here am I' as a witness of the Infinite, but a witness that does not thematize what it bears witness of, and whose truth is not the truth of representation, is not evidence. There is witness...only of the Infinite" (146). Undoubtedly we can say that what elsewhere was called a trace is here what is called testimony.

Allow me to say, at the end of these comments, why, despite all these analyses, Jean Nabert seems to me to remain closer to Levinas than to Heidegger. It will have been noted that at the beginning of Levinas's chapter on substitution, ethical thought could not dispense with having to explicate itself in terms of the notion of conscience, even though it had already showed the impasse of ontology. The whole of this chapter remains a long struggle with the claims of the philosophies of consciousness; otherwise the strategies I have referred to above would not have been necessary. The truth is we are never done with the question of identity and of selfhood. The section entitled "Recurrence" and the one that follows it, "The Self," bear witness to this. The fate of subjectivity is not settled with the unsaid of the theme of identity. The condition—or noncondition—of subjection still says something about the subject. What is more, a certain kind of identity, which would no longer be thematizable, is reborn from all the preliminaries that the strategy of moving back toward the hither side brings to discourse. There is, says Levinas, "an antecedent recurrence of the oneself" (104). "The ego is in itself like a sound that would resound in its own echo" (103).

Why should it be so? Because responsibility, however passively assigned it may be, requires a "who," a self, that will not be thematically identifiable, hence that will not be the same in the sense of identity that has been set aside, but that nevertheless will be a self. In this regard, I discern in the pages on recurrences and the self the foothold for a distinction that for my part I take to be essential, between identity as *idem* and identity as *ipse*.[17] I am well aware that our text oscillates between the unsaid of ipseity, as always already ensnared in the web of the theme, the said, and a certain reassertion of ipseity and of identity as "a term in hypostasis" (106), that is, on the road to thematization, but not yet thematized. In short, what is at issue is an ipseity we need to surprise before its being is captured in identifiable and thematic identity—"an identity unjustifiable by itself," it is said (106). Even more forcefully: "The ipseity, in the passivity without *archē* characteristic of identity, is a hostage" (114). The grammar of this unthematized ipseity is the accusative, the "I" of "Here I am" (*me voici*), the oneself of "to accuse oneself, to hand oneself over" as a hostage. This, in truth, is an astonishing grammar, which puts us on the road toward the unsaid: "the accusative form, which is a modification of no nominative form" (124). No concession is made, therefore, to the idealist's primacy of the ego. The self is not the ego. Yet it remains that the place of the self is inexpugnable. "The self is a *sub-jectum*; it is under the weight of the universe, responsible for everything" (116).

We can understand why it must be so. The strategy of excess just like that of the backward move leads toward an exile, a beyond being, a refuge that, no doubt, is apprehended only in the-one-for-the-other, but that nevertheless is felt as anxiety, in the sense of a constriction. For the only one

---

17. See Paul Ricoeur, *Oneself as Another,* trans. Kathleen Blamey (Chicago: Univ. of Chicago Press, 1992), for a full discussion of what Ricoeur means by this distinction. TRANS.

who can substitute for a persecutor is one who is "one and irreplaceable" (103). Another way of putting this is: "The non-interchangeable par excellence, the I, the unique one, substitutes itself for others" (117). This is the ultimate shape of the "antecedent recurrence of the oneself" (104), antecedent to thematization in one identifiable individual. Summoned, yes, the self is summoned without having chosen this, but, to this very extent, it is summoned "as irreplaceable." And if by chance one crosses out the self in crossing out one's conscience, well then, one tumbles into the ineffable and misses that presynthetic, prelogical unity that "prevents [the self] from splitting, separating itself from itself." Levinas adds the following here: "This prevention is the positivity of the one" (107).

These positive formulations concerning ipseity indicate the place for a trajectory that would go from Levinas to Nabert and from Nabert to Levinas. I am not pleading here for any form of syncretism. Nor do I deny the abyss that separates the idea of an inadequation of the self to itself from that of an exterior assignation of responsibility. I will confine myself just to suggesting the following. Would the self be a result if it were not first a presupposition, that is, potentially capable of hearing this assignment? I am well aware that to inquire regarding any capacity, any potentiality that would not be the work of this assignment is for Levinas to pose an inadmissible question. The slightest admission of a capacity that is one's own, correlative to this assignment, would ruin everything gained from a philosophy of passivity relentlessly carried through. And this certainly would be to blunt the edge of the hyperbolic expressions of an ethics without ontology. But is it forbidden to a reader, who is a friend of both Nabert and Levinas, to puzzle over a philosophy where the attestation of self and the glory of the absolute would be co-originary? Does not the testimony rendered by other actions, by other lives, reciprocal to the divestment of the ego speak *in another way* about what testimony, according to Levinas, unsays?

Part Three

The Bible and Genre: The Polyphony of Biblical Discourses

7

On the Exegesis of Genesis 1:1—2:4a

The text of Genesis 1 will provide an excellent occasion to test out the conception of a convergence of methods of exegesis I have proposed in my essay "From a Conflict to a Convergence of Methods in Biblical Exegesis."[1]

1. Beginning from the genetic method, I want to show how and why it calls for the structural method when it is a question of proceeding to the reconstitution of the redactional levels of the text. Here I shall follow the movement that runs from the exegesis of Gerhard von Rad to that of Werner H. Schmidt.

2. Beginning from the structural method, I will try to show next in what way this method leads, by an internal necessity, to the question of the history of redaction.

3. Finally, I want to show how these methods, separately and conjointly, point toward interpretation in the sense I have given this word in "From a Conflict to a Convergence of Methods in Biblical Exegesis."

From the History of Traditions to Structural Analysis

I will begin by recalling the general hypothesis that governs all of von Rad's enterprise in *The Theology of Traditions*.[2] Three points need to be emphasized.

1. It is within the overall narrative unity that constitutes the Hexateuch that the Yahwist document of faith can be understood as a whole.

2. It is important to pick out the confessional motif (or kerygmatic intention) that unites the various materials gathered together in this overall

---

Originally published as "Sur l'exégèse de Genèse 1,1–2,4a," in *Exégèse et herméneutique: Parole de Dieu*, ed. Xavier Léon Dufour (Paris: Seuil, 1971), 67–84; printed with permission.

1. See Paul Ricoeur, "Du conflit à la convergence des méthodes en exégèse biblique," in *Exégèse et herméneutique: Parole de Dieu*, ed. Xavier Léon-Dufour (Paris: Seuil, 1971), 35–53.

2. Gerhard von Rad, *Old Testament Theology*, vol. 1: *The Theology of Traditions*, trans. D. M. G. Stalker (New York: Harper and Row, 1965).

unity. This unique motif runs through the recollection of the acts of salvation that punctuate the history of Israel, so that it is by combining the historical traditions into larger sequences that Hebraic thought elaborates its theology.

3. It is possible to retrace in a diachronic manner the work of harmonization and integration applied to distinct historical traditions, to different sagas, and in this way to take up the task of a "source history," by subordinating these traditions and sagas to the successive formulations of a *theology of traditions*. This *wiedererzählen*—this "re-recounting"—constitutes Israel's fundamental theological discourse.

It is important to begin by entering into this general hypothesis and its internal complexity in some detail before we turn to the didactic teaching that makes up Gen. 1:1—2:4a in relation to this unique theology of traditions.

The three points just listed are inseparable. The meaning of the Hexateuch appears on a fairly broad scale but only on the condition that we retain, in all the amplitude of the narrative space, the simplicity of the kerygmatic kernel and only if, moreover, we recognize the same process of integration at work on the level of narratives also at work on the non-historical materials: legislation, revelation of the Name, myths of origin, and so on.

Making sense of the Hexateuch proceeds therefore in a concentric fashion. At the center stands the *credo* of Deut. 26:5f.: "A wandering Aramean was my ancestor..." Immediately surrounding this kernel is the history of the ancestors up to the conquest; in the next circle is inserted the great pericope about Sinai; and, finally, in the outermost circle, comes the history of origins.

This concentric understanding, if I may so express it, allows us to define theologically the problem posed by the creation narratives in the following terms. What is the relation between, on the one hand, the belief in election and in redemption, implied by the "theology of traditions," and, on the other hand, the faith in Yahweh as creator that inspires the creation narratives? As we see, the question is a theological question: What is the role of the theme of creation in the context of the faith of Israel taken as a whole? Yet if the question is at bottom theological, the answer necessarily must pass through exegesis, which alone is capable of justifying the thematic linkages.

It is here that von Rad inserts the diachronic study of the texts about creation. These, in effect, can be placed in a chain based on a sequence that begins with the texts that speak of a soteriology without creation and that ends with a group of texts that celebrate the creation but do not mention the soteriological motif.

It is this diachrony that calls a theology of traditions to further thought.

Let us consider the successive moments of this sequence.

The oldest faith of Israel, according to von Rad, implies a certain relation of Israel with the gift of the land, but this land is not yet nature, or the world, or the cosmos insofar as it is a distinct historical reality. On the contrary, as Amos and the Deuteronomist attest, according to the faith of Israel, the theology of history excludes any theology of nature of a Canaanite type. The second stage: a certain doctrine of creation appears in a hymnic rather than a didactic context and in close association with the doctrine of redemption. This is the theme of Psalms 136 and 148. Other texts juxtapose the work of creation *and* the mighty acts of God in history; for example, Isa. 40:27-28 and 44:24-28. In these contexts, the theme of creation upholds and stimulates faith in God's interventions in history. It is the same divine dispensation that reigns in the act of creation and in the act of redemption. The One who opened a way in the Red Sea is the same One who cut Rahab in pieces (Isa. 51:9f.).

This way of arranging these texts in a series allows for placing the themes of creation and salvation in the same category, and the same redemptive act governs both themes. To elect Israel is to create Israel and to create the world. The miracle of creation is a miracle of redemption. This subordination of the theme of creation to the soteriological theme is quite apparent in Isa. 44:5, Psalm 89, and Psalm 74. As von Rad puts it, "We regard this soteriological interpretation of the work of creation as the most primitive expression of the Yahwistic belief concerning Yahweh as Creator of the world. This belief finds expression almost exclusively in the mythological conception of the struggle against the dragon of chaos."[3] This transition phase, therefore, includes well-determined characteristics. In the first place, the creation is articulated in terms of the archaic language of victory over the sea monster, Rahab (Psalm 89). What is more, this archaic language includes no reference to creation by the word. The narrative of creation in Gen. 1:1—2:4a is not to be understood as an independent theological narrative but instead has to be set within the concentric system centered on the relation between God and Israel. In this sense, Genesis 1 is continuous with Psalms 89 and 74. And so understood, the thought process at work in such a creation narrative consists in linking the archaic form of the myth, foreign to the faith of Israel, to the history of salvation specific to the Hebraic theological world.

In a subsequent phase, a new aspect of the creation theme emerges. Thus, in Psalms 19, 104, and 8, the cosmos bears witness to the wisdom and power of God. The doctrine of creation takes on its autonomy, but once again it is a non-Israelite source that blossoms here. Henceforth the

---

3. Gerhard von Rad, *The Problem of the Hexateuch and Other Essays,* trans. E. W. Trueman Dicken (Edinburgh and London: Oliver and Boyd, 1965), 138.

doctrine will appeal to the genre of "wisdom" (see Prov. 3:19; 8:22; 14:31; 20:12; and Job 38). According to von Rad, this tradition is Egyptian, not mythological. It has no relation to the story of the battle against the primitive dragon. It bears witness to a rational, intelligible design on the creator's part. "In my opinion," says von Rad, "what we have here is an Egyptian outlook passed on to Israel by travelling teachers of wisdom."[4] This reflective, reasoned-out theology must be distinguished from the faith concerning election and salvation. The human being measured over against the size of the cosmos becomes filled with fear and admiration. The idea of salvation, when it is present, is subordinated to a cosmic vision more or less marked by a sense of providence.

If we consider this trajectory of meanings as a whole, it seems that Israel's soteriological doctrine could constitute itself only on the condition of at first holding at a distance any kind of theology of creation and that this doctrine was ready to welcome such a theology only when this theology was no longer capable of weakening the doctrine of salvation, but rather of broadening and enriching it.

How do such reflections affect our exegesis of Genesis 1?

Essentially, by a constant movement that goes from the whole to the parts, even down to the smallest details. Therefore, Genesis 1 is to be read as a prologue, not as a meaningful text that stands by itself. This initial decision has numerous consequences. This prologue will appear at first as a didactic narrative intended to provide instruction, set as preface to the soteriological texts meant to render glory to the author of the great story of Israel. We might emphasize therefore the opposition of the didactic narrative and the hymnic texts within the overall space constituted by the Hexateuch as a whole. And in support of this opposition we could point to the concise, direct character, free of any metaphorical overtones (unlike the case with the older narrative found in Genesis 2). Von Rad, for example, notes "the intense theological concentration of the text of the Priestly document."[5] But there is a yet more important consequence of understanding Genesis 1 from the perspective of its being a prologue to the history of salvation. The creation narrative appears as a graduated narrative leading from the vision of the order of the world to a summit: the creation of humankind, God's supreme work. This graduated character bears witness to a broader cosmological interest than is found in Genesis 2. But, at the same time, this cosmological focus also raises the crowning aspect attached to the creation of humankind.

Here is another distinctive feature of Genesis 1: unlike the Ionian cosmologies of the pre-Socratic Greek philosophers, the creative principle is a

---

4. Ibid., 142.
5. Von Rad, *Old Testament Theology*, 1:150.

personal will. Whatever the mode of creation may be, it is God who creates. But the most decisive feature, and the one that most bears witness to the internal relation between the creation narrative and the Hexateuch as a whole, is the creative gesture itself. This is, in one sense, a command, which implies the idea of an effortless action as well as a distinction between word and work. Here meaning is moving from the soteriological motif in the direction of a creation motif, but it is in terms of the experience of salvation that word and work as distinct, yet continuous, are articulated. In this way, the archaic theme of the magical power of the word can be taken up and modified at the same time. (I note in passing that the opposition between the soteriological and wisdom motifs hardly applies. Indeed, von Rad's references to Isa. 48:13 and to Pss. 33:66 and 148:5 lead me to think that the didactic form attests to the quite ancient presence of the motif of wisdom—Egyptian or Hebraic—at the very heart of the instruction about the beginning.)

The various enigmas of this text also can be unknotted on the basis of this explicative model. For example, chaos, which is neither created (for only order is formally created) nor uncreated (since it is subordinated to the word), remains the great menace that human experience constantly rediscovers. It is the resurgence of chaos in the experience of salvation that is the key to the chaos in what we could call the experience of creation. And as for the successive plans that run through the work of creation, they testify to the degrees of immediacy that can exist between God and God's works. The highest form of immediacy is instituted between God and humankind. The latter appears not just as created by the word in a quite general sense, but by a solemn resolution from the depths of God's heart. Humankind is created "in the form of the Elohim," that is, according to a celestial model that uproots the human being from the realm of the visible. Hence, if God is anthropomorphic, humankind is theomorphic. This double equation is in fact the equation of salvation. Finally, the completion of the great work in "the day of rest" is to be understood starting from the same soteriological foundation. It is not so much the founding of the Sabbath that is at stake in the articulation of the specific relationship between the two "histories" of creation and salvation, for what ends the one, and in this sense completes it, opens the other, and in this sense inaugurates it.

My intention, following this brief presentation of a type of exegesis of a clearly *genetic* character, is to show in what way it calls upon, willingly or not, a more structural method. The genetic method calls for the structural method both as its counterpart and as its condition.

Let us first consider the counterpart side. Briefly stated, the constant concern to set Genesis 1 within the soteriological context of the Priestly document has to be constantly compensated for by the concern to protect the specific features of the text per se. I would like to give a few examples, which will take on their fuller significance in a moment. Unless we pay attention to the text itself, we will not be attentive to the counteraccents by which it resists any simple ordering in terms of the creation of humankind. I mean, for instance, the theme of the founding of the heavens and, within this same founding, the struggle between the old schema of battle and the new schema of separation. The creation of the heavens that is a counterweight to that of humankind is at the origin of the bipolarity heaven/humankind that prevents an overly hasty anthropocentric interpretation of the Priestly document.

Even more radically, the exegesis guided by the history of traditions draws its interpretive power from an overall understanding of the Hexateuch and from the setting into a sequence of the texts about creation on the basis of a series of prior soteriological motifs. The danger is that we may thereby be imposing in advance a thematic organization that will prevent us from making the decisive movement from the semantic surface to its underlying depths. This is a movement. This movement presupposes a greater consideration for the text in terms of its specificity and for itself.

In this regard, the work of Werner H. Schmidt is indicative of a step beyond that of von Rad.[6] Even while remaining faithful to the genetic method, Schmidt undertakes to apply this method to the text considered in and for itself. His method consists in a work of discernment applied to the redactional levels, aimed at establishing the trajectory of meaning that unfolds from one level to another. Basically, our narrative contains two types of superimposed narratives, a *Tatbericht* (event-narrative) and a *Wortbericht* (word-narrative). To understand the text is to understand the movement by which a narrative where creation proceeds from the word— "God said"—reinterprets a prior narrative that only included expressions of the form "God did." Schmidt's method, therefore, is genetic in its essence, but it is precisely as such that it presupposes a prior structural analysis. The traces of the older text in the current text are not immediately apparent, as is the case elsewhere with doublets. They consist rather of the discordances at the level of the organization of the text. Hence, the discernment of the different redactional levels assumes a prior analysis of the structure of the text; without such a prior structural analysis, the disparities in meaning at the level of a depth semantics cannot be made significant.

6. Werner H. Schmidt, *Die Schöpfungsgeschichte der Preisterschrift: Zur Überlieferungs-geschichte von Genesis 1,1–2,4a*, WMANT 17 (Neukirchen-Vluyn: Neukirchener Verlag, 1964).

From Structural Analysis to Interpretation

Paul Beauchamp's work is significant in that it has reversed the relation of this structural analysis to that of genetic reconstruction.[7] I say "reversed," for there is a moment in structural analysis where it refers to a genetic reconstruction and, in this way, to a history of meaning upon which the work of interpretation may base itself.

In order to simplify things, let us oppose Beauchamp's working hypothesis point by point to that of von Rad. First, instead of starting from the Hexateuch as a whole, Beauchamp limits himself to one clearly delimited text, and he remains within its bounds as long as necessary in order to establish the complex network of its internal relations. For Beauchamp, the structure is in the text, even if he will subsequently grant that the meaning is beyond the text. Second, in approaching our text, Beauchamp makes no presumption of a confessional motif. He limits himself to how what is said is arranged. He deliberately sticks with the level of composition. The creation narrative is thus taken for itself, with no regard for its eventual subordination to the history of salvation. Third, Beauchamp does not address himself to the redactional process in terms of its diachronic dimension, in the sense of the perspective of a progressive subordination of the earlier and more or less autonomous material to the theology of salvation expressed in other texts. He takes the text in its final form in order to see how all its terms function in relation to one another, given the synchrony of their final order. He puts off for later interpretation the question whether the cosmological motif is autonomous in relation to the soteriological one. At the same time, and fourth on our list, he will be attentive to those aspects of meaning that precisely have nothing to do with a theology of history, that are neither its extension, nor its preparation, nor its prologue. First of all, the didactic aspect, in the ways that it is most irreducible to the hymnic aspect, has to be recognized for what it is. Next, we must not rush to indicate the subordination of the different phases of creation to the creation of humankind. On the contrary, the creation of the light, that of the firmament as "separating," and that of the lights that mark day and night are to be considered for themselves. In this sense, we are to apply a less global, more analytic eye to the details of the text. And, in fact, the theme of "separation" does not really appear if we move to quickly to the end of the narrative, that is, to the creation of humankind without lingering over the prior degrees. Perhaps even the dynamic of the text will be clearer if we put off that final moment that von Rad takes as the summit of the text.

---

7. Paul Beauchamp, *Création et séparation: Étude exégètique du chapitre premier de la Genèse* (Paris: Aubier-Montaigne, 1969), 58; subsequent pages numbers given in the text refer to this edition.

For the details, I refer the reader to Beauchamp's text. Here I shall confine myself to a few words about his procedure as regards the properly structural part of his thesis.

He first outlines a structure of the narrative that consists of the sequence indicated by the framing formulas: "God said," "Let there be...," "and there was," "God made," "and God called," "it was the nth day." Note that this chain, running from the stating of an order to the act of execution, is quite comparable to the logic of action of narrative theorists, insofar as the schema command/execution provides the first cell.

Several noteworthy results follow from this initial move. First, the framework of seven days does not appear as decisive as it does for a surface reading. Indeed, the first term of this structure ("God said") appears ten times. Second, it is the "operations" that support the structure, not the "objects" or created things. The task of the structural analysis is precisely to establish the principle that apportions out the created objects: light, firmament separating the waters into above and below, dry land with its plants, stars, fishes, birds, land animals, humankind. Here, once again, a marked structure makes appear a rhythm that accentuates the first word and first day, the fifth word and the fourth day, the tenth word and the seventh day. In this way, the separation of day and night, as a temporal separation presupposed by the calendar and festivals, finds itself in a key position, which for Beauchamp is even the center of the whole composition. To his eyes, the separation of day and night provides "the clearest zone of homogeneity in the interior of the text" (48). An exegesis that would too quickly put the accent on humankind would not catch sight of this law of composition, and the interpretation that follows will take account of it. Before that, though, we see two parallel series of objects constitute themselves: a first series containing light, sky, air, water, and vegetable life; and a second series containing lights (in correlation with the light), living beings, humankind (in correlation with sky, earth, and sea), and food (in correlation with vegetable forms of life)—two series of objects and two series of places, heaven on one side, earth on the other. By making the fourth day the keystone, the time filled with many classifications, we can also account for several apparent anomalies in the text: the light created before the stars, the week preceding the alternation of day and night, and so on. "The choice to indicate another beginning in the middle of the week won out over these difficulties" (70). Furthermore, does not the theme of the fourth day refer to the double relation of light to lights and the Sabbath to the festivals? "Across this plurality of orderings, the tendency toward an architectonic unification centered on the fourth day, the beginning of a series, the end of a series, shows itself" (70).

But what most interests us here is that the structural analysis itself points toward a more genetic approach and toward an interpretation. How?

The structural method sends us back toward the genetic method by bringing to light irregularities and anomalies. The persistence of the old in the new is expressed in all that resists an exclusively structural treatment; this is why the structure refers us back to the genesis. For example, the anomaly of a doublet—"and it was" and "God made"—supports Schmidt's thesis that our text proceeds from the superimposition of a *Wortbericht* on a *Tatbericht*. This hypothesis is all the more compelling in that the biblical author does not conceal his sources but, as Paul Beauchamp says, reveals them and even calls attention to them, "like a fragment of catechetic language that indicates the step taken by a personal composition" (75). Hence we can anticipate something like an exchange of points of view. If the structure refers us to the genetic point of view, this presupposes the structure, for "it is up to exegesis to say whether there is a simple accumulation or an organization of the details" (71). But also in this way a richer concept of structure comes about. Not a static structure, but a receptive, harmonious form for those tensions that in their turn call for new solutions in a subsequent work of interpretation and reinterpretation.

Let us look, therefore, at how through certain details the structural analysis refers us to the genetic analysis in terms of redactional levels. If the fourth day is the pivot point, if the narrative therefore finds its center of gravity in the founding of the calendar through a temporal separation, the genetic analysis is shown to be correct in that we have to admit that a wholly spatial separation, one linked to the mythical account of a primordial combat (cutting open Tiamat, cleaving Rahab, opening the passage across the Red Sea), was overthrown and picked up and set up again in such a way as to produce the theme of temporal separation.

But then it is through its very coherence and also therefore its incoherences that are thereby revealed that the text reveals its tradition. It is the structure linked to the theme of separation that refers us to its history.

Taking up the question of two narratives, the *Tatbericht* and the *Wortbericht,* Beauchamp poses the following question: What traces of a "silent" previous tradition are still visible in the "word" tradition (79)? We can answer such a question only if we start from the current disposition of the execution formulas, in order next to seek the significations that proceed from the relation of the theme of execution to all the other themes. Doing this, we are led to classify the modalities of execution according to their meanings (that there be . . . , that there be made . . . , let us make . . . , create, make, make by creation, and so on). This inventory will extend over all the variants of making: to separate, dispose, dispense, fabricate; and it is in establishing this inventory that the action of creating what is separated (the celestial objects) takes on its value as a turning point and as organizing the whole structure. "Here," says Beauchamp, "the adequation is total between causing word and caused object" (86). The act of separation serves as the axis of dispersion for all the forms of execution. But at the same time, the quite subtle work of harmonization, which seems to occur on the semantic plane, makes apparent tensions and resistances that reveal a choice to preserve certain themes in spite of the language of compilation (e.g., Gen. 1:24 juxtaposes "it was done" and "he did"; a similar tension exists between the title of 1:1 and the antititle of 2:4a).

It is only when work on the text has gone this far that we can invoke the "extrabiblical parallels" (Enuma Elish, the Egyptian genesis, and so on) and the "intrabiblical parallels" (Psalm 104; Job 37–38). In the former it is the idea of a gift and of God's gifts to humankind that is dominant; in the latter, on the contrary, there appears a world without humankind. "It is Job alone who is invited to look at a world composed without him, where the role of man is... practically zero" (144).

The same structural approach allows the archaisms to appear, thanks to their contrasts with the dominant structure (word–light–stars). This is the case with the difficult theme of chaos, which bears witness to an older state of thought and to a text where separation was attached to other representations. However, it is only by beginning from the text itself that we can launch an arrow toward such bases outside the text. In the text, chaos, which bears witness to an older tradition, is submitted to the act of separating. It is not therefore the preexistence of chaos that is in question, but the displacement of the act of separating from chaos to astral time. It is the structural analysis of the text that makes the tension appear between what is conveyed by the title "when God created the heavens and the earth" and the indication of something prior and uncreated that is, in a way, annulled by the rectifying and correcting affirmation that there is no other beginning other than the creation. Verse 2, therefore, does not describe what there was before creation, but a state prior to the word in verse 3. Nor do we have some particular period of time, but rather a state that is prolonged until the sixth day. It does not seem, therefore, that the author meant to say that God created what was formless; it is the beginning of order that is of interest. This is why the author leaves the origin of chaos undetermined. The unformed is what the word presupposes and yet what the creation announced in verse 1 encompasses. How? The author does not know. "Let us note that, if the author gives some consistency to what was not yet, in the proper sense, created, this was due more to the weight of tradition than to the force of his own thinking" (158). And Beauchamp goes on to say, "If there is an inconsistency, it is an indication of the tradition blossoming here" (159). Yet even this is incorporated into the new text. The final redaction roots this flowering by making of it an incision, which creates an expectation and prepares for the novelty of the creative act. In this way, any inconsistency is incorporated into the new text.

The same kind of analysis can be applied to the *ruach elohim,* the Spirit of God. This theme, stemming from the theophanies of glory, is incorporated into the new narrative, making this element of redemption into a cosmic element. So integrated, it provides a counterweight to the theme of separation by insinuating the idea of a unifying circulation. The same procedure integrates the theme of the light that, at the origin, designates an intervention of God who, by means of an arm that separates, makes things withdraw and tremble (think of the victory over the shadows by the action of sword directed against the sea monster in Job 26:13). This aspect of light from the theophany of a warrior was once, in the context of war, joined to the theme of the pushing back of the sea. It is the act of separation indicated on the fourth day, by the attraction it exercises on the prior mythological base, that assures the cosmological reinterpretation of this warlike theme.

In all these cases, as in those of the successive "words" that call for something, the comprehension of a genesis of meaning is everywhere supported by a good structural analysis of the final meaning, as it presents itself in the received text. With Genesis 1, says Beauchamp, "the *ruach* has become the support of God, the light is just the first of his creatures, and the voice impossible to distinguish from what God says has reached its most radical laying bare. We see nothing of God, we hear what he says" (198). More generally, the interpretive reworking implied by the act of separating appears in the "accidents or scars visible in the text" (229). The received text is a witness to the interpretive history of God's primordial gesture. Thanks to the movement from the surface of the text toward its depths, the most ancient themes take on a value of persistence, of energy that becomes part of the meaning of the text as we have it. "Returning toward the origins is a regression toward the most primitive aspects of the theme that blossoms in the first two verses of Genesis. To create is to break some continuity, to deform a space, to tear it in two" (p. 230). As a result, the filtering of the earlier tradition is the counterpart of a reprise of a prior archaism. And the interpretation, as a process attributable to the author, directs the meaning but does not exhaust it. What is to be interpreted becomes part of its meaning. To create by a separating word, "this representation cannot break away from the earlier details marked by a more primitive energy" (231).

Interpretation

We have set out the pair structure/genesis essential to exegesis. Let us now see how this pair, in turn, leads to a third pole: interpretation.

Let us first, however, consider one preliminary question: Who interprets? The theologian or the philosopher? The preacher or is it already the exegete? Without a doubt there is not such thing as an innocent interpretation. It is the theologian or the philosopher who interprets inasmuch as they relate the text to some problematic coming from somewhere else: the Greek notion of causality, the problem of the origin and limit of modern philosophy, or whatever. To write "God creates in separating" is already to move well beyond the text, to categorize it, to introduce it into a speculative space that is no longer that of the text but that of our culture as a whole. As Paul Beauchamp reminds us, "To explicate a text is and always has been to say what it does not say and what we take in large part for granted" (15). Exegesis is merely the preparation for this reprise by today's reader who, in appropriating the text, overcomes the cultural distance that the structural analysis and genetic reconstruction open up.

This projection of the text into another space than its own, no one will deny. The question is rather whether there is, before the philosophical-theological interpretation, an interpretation that would not be an interpretation *of* the text or an interpretation *about* the text, but an interpretation *in* the text and *through* the text. Allow me to explain what I mean.

When von Rad and Schmidt, by their genetic approach, reconstitute the work of thought crystallized in the text, they offer us a concept of interpretation whereby the act of interpreting is the act of the text itself on itself. Each new layer, in effect, is an interpretation of the preceding one. Thus, for von Rad, the confessional kernel that constitutes the gravitational space of the Hexateuch works like an interpretant, in C. S. Peirce's sense of this term, within the mass of legends, narratives, and myths caught within this space of gravitation. Putting these sources in order is an interpretation. As a result, when exegetes interpret the narrative of creation in a kerygmatic sense, they are only repeating the work of interpretation already at work in this ordering of the sources. Schmidt is faithful to von Rad in his own usage of the concept of interpretation. Interpretation is always the counterpart to some prior tradition. The *Wortbericht* is an interpretation of the *Tatbericht*. When, in their turn, exegetes interpret, they retrace the trajectory of the tradition of interpretation in the text itself.

We thus return to the notion of interpretation proposed in my introduction. It is an act of the text insofar as the text has a direction, a dynamic "sense." To interpret is to place ourselves in "its sense."

The structural method, I believe, leads to just this conclusion. In the end, it does not eliminate interpretation; rather it articulates this interpretation in terms of the depth semantics it brings to light. "If there is a structure," Paul Beauchamp says, "this is what supports the interpretation. In the hypothesis of two stages, the structure is almost completely preexisting as regards the interpretation. For our reading, the interpretation brings about a change in the scaffolding of the text and probably in a part of the material from which this scaffolding is constructed as well.... The amplitude of an interpretation does not appear where the composition is not taken into consideration" (112).

Let us recall a few examples of this depth semantics opening onto interpretation by way of structural analysis.

For example, by emphasizing the structure 1, 4, 7 (light–star–Sabbath), and by making this structure the pivot point for the constitution of the calendar, a depth semantics comes to light, one expressed through the theme of "separation." "The dominant separation is that of time" (117). It is only structural analysis that allows us to catch sight of the fit between speaking, light, and stars: "The privileged linking of the celestial sphere to the verb 'being,' the way creation affects this verb, from the first attack of the bow, is what the author has seen" (117). The stars are the words of God because they are separating words. Before humankind, there is the heavens as "a divinely willed limitation, not as substance but as function, as positioning" (118). The light that is seen is immediately named "day" and subordinated to the separation of different times.

Another example: it is at the level of a depth semantics that the tension between the poles light/sky and earth/humankind is established. There where von Rad sees especially the crescendo of the octave of creation in the direction of humankind, structural analysis brings to light a progression at the level of meaning, from "Let there be light..." to "Let us make humankind...," thanks to the contrast with the regularity and monotony of clock time, hence as a formula of variation opposed to the recurrence of formulas. What is more, this progression from chaos toward humankind takes on its full sense only as the counterpole of the setting in place of a cosmos that, at the same time, marks humankind's limit, the setting that precedes and encompasses it, the universe that surrounds it.

For my own part, I note that this new understanding of the sense of our text allows us to take up once again the relationship between the didactic genre of the narrative and wisdom literature. Von Rad does not overlook this, but he grants only a secondary and late influence to the wisdom writings. For him, it is the Yahwist who superimposes the problematic of salvation on that of creation. So the cosmological statements are then placed in the same category as the soteriological ones. The wisdom writings only add to the autonomy of the cosmic theme in relation to the soteriological one. However, we might ask, following J.-P. Audet, whether the wisdom tradition is not much older and hence contemporary with the totality of Hebraic writings, and even whether it does not envelop their soteriology. I see several indications supporting this interpretation in Genesis 1. If Paul Beauchamp's thesis is correct, the ordering of the heavens, the stars, and time, by providing a counteraccent to the creation of humankind, announces an interest in the cosmic theme that is not exhausted by the proclamation of salvation. Another indication may be that the *ruach elohim*, a vestige of the theophanies of combat, even though subordinated to the action of creation, continues to provide, in this new context, several "signs" of the "mobile, directing presence of God" (181). We know that this theme of the cosmic peregrination of wisdom, which emerges in Proverbs and Job, is in fact an ancient theme of wisdom. Might it not then be the function of wisdom to assure the linkage between the values of salvation and cosmic values? Is it not the same *ruach* that moves over the waters and that stirs among the people? Was not the same breath that settled upon a holy people after having conquered all obstacles already at work with the first word? If this be so, we need to say that a cosmic exploration in the style of wisdom is just as ancient as is attending to the historical aspect of the *ruach*.

Here is another indication of a wisdomlike aspect to our narrative: Are not the "nomenclatures" for the created things mentioned there to be compared to the catalogs so characteristic of the wisdom of the scribes? Von Rad refers in this regard only to Job and Ecclesiastes,[8] but do not the inventories in our narrative already stem from the same genre? I am also tempted to say the same thing about the linguistic labor applied to the various expressions for the creative activity: to separate, to dispose, to dispense, to fabricate, to make, to create, to make through creation, and so on. Is not this work on the sense of the text, at the semantic level, a witness to a work of thought aimed at constituting an inventory not in this case of things but of operations? And is not the correction of a battle theme into one of the setting in order of the cosmos already of a sapiential and speculative order?

Even more fundamentally, the very interest in "separating," as a relation of saying and doing, contains within itself a large speculative potential. It might even be in this way that our theme can link up with Greek speculation on causality. It certainly relates to modern speculations about the radical origin of things. From "separate," as a violent gesture linked to the primordial waters, to "separate," as a verbal, dividing gesture, do we not have the whole trajectory from a bellicose soteriology to a kind of meditative wisdom? It is structural analysis that allows us to unearth, from *beneath* the soteriological theme that ties humankind to the sequence of acts of deliverance, the relation between the laying out of the heavens and the wisdom that emerges most clearly in Proverbs, in Job, and in Psalms 104 and 136. "Thus," writes Father Beauchamp, "from a victory over a monster attributed to wisdom, we may pass by a move of transference to this same victory as having as its effect the edification of the heavens" (217). Interpretation, here, models itself on this movement, which is the very movement of wisdom, which substitutes the differentiation of lists and catalogs for the violent separation of the elements.

Interpretation, therefore, is not a violence done to the text, the irruption of the subjectivity of the exegete within the objectivity of the text.

---

8. See Gerhard von Rad, "Job 38 and Ancient Egyptian Wisdom," in *Problem of the Hexateuch*, 281–91.

Even when the exegete admits that "in order to interpret the meaning of the theme of separation," we must "seek the meaning of the text outside the text, or rather in the relationship of the text to its exterior" (233), it is still within the movement of a text toward other texts that we seek help and assistance. Indeed, what does it mean to interpret the theme of separation? It means to seek, in the other levels of significations crossed by the same signifier—the cosmological level, the social level, the level of institutions—the same functioning of meaning. Thus the "army" constituted by the whole universe suggests seeking, within this very idea of an army, a strict division of functions, homologous with the differentiation of the universe. The act of separating is thus the act that governs both the distribution of the elements of the cosmos, the division of social roles, as well as the other mysteries of distribution having to do with social and cultural life. Between the cosmos, the army, and the cultus, functional homologies can be discerned that allow us to give the notion of a symbol a nonrhetorical and properly logical character. We may even say that the theme of separation is symbolic, in the sense that the same values of distribution affect several levels of signification, several semantic fields, several domains of reality. Here the symbol appears to be more fundamental than the metaphor in the rhetorical sense of this word. It designates an analogous organization of meaning, which governs multiple orders of reality. If the metaphor is the principle of a transfer of meaning, the symbol is the preliminary gathering together into a homology of relationships that makes possible this transfer of meaning. It is in this sense that we can call the theme of separation symbolic. It is the task of interpretation to let blossom the power of gathering together at work in this symbol.

So the structural method in no way weakens the bond established by von Rad and Schmidt between genesis and interpretation. Structural analysis plays a revelatory role in regard to the work of interpretation inscribed within the text itself. Structure appears there as an instrument of negotiation between a tradition and an interpretation at work within the text itself. The interplay of structure and genesis reveals something that we can call the intention of the text. "Every intention," says Paul Beauchamp, "when it is seen as having force, is organizing.... It is the intention that unfolds an immanent genetics inside the structure" (70). This weighty text of our exegete conveys well the interplay of structure, genesis, and intention. It is the task of a detailed theory of interpretation to preserve this interplay and to magnify it.

8

The Bible and the Imagination

I. Presuppositions

1. When Dean Joseph Kitagawa proposed the topic "The Bible and the Imagination" to me, I was first perplexed, then intrigued, and finally fascinated by this subject. The title is, indeed, baffling, even paradoxical. Is not the imagination, by common consent, a faculty of free invention, therefore something not governed by rules, something wild and untamed? What is more, is it not condemned to wandering about the internal spaces of what we conventionally call the mental kingdom, and does it not therefore lack any referential import, being entirely disconnected from what is really real? As for the Bible, is it not a closed book, one whose meaning is fixed forever and therefore the enemy of any radically original creation of meaning? Does it not claim to give rise to an existential and ontological commitment, one hostile to any imaginative drifting from here to there?

My most general goal in this essay will be to lay the groundwork for calling into question these opposed presuppositions.

On the first side, I want to plead for a concept of the imagination that will highlight two traits that are usually misconceived by philosophy. First, imagination can be described as a rule-governed form of invention or, in other terms, as a norm-governed productivity. This is how Kant conceived imagination in his *Critique of Judgment* by coordinating the free play of the imagination and the form of the understanding in a teleology that had no goal beyond itself. Next the imagination can be considered as the power of giving form to human experience or, to take up again an expression I used in *The Rule of Metaphor*,[1] as the power of redescribing reality. Fiction is my name for the imagination considered under this double point of view of rule-governed invention and a power of redescription.

Reprinted with permission from *The Bible as a Document of the University,* ed. Hans Dieter Betz (Chico, Calif.: Scholars Press, 1981), 49–75.

1. Paul Ricoeur, *The Rule of Metaphor: Multi-disciplinary Studies of the Creation of Meaning in Language,* trans. Robert Czerny with Kathleen McLaughlin and John Costello (Toronto: Univ. of Toronto Press, 1977), 216–56.

Now turning to my other pole, the Bible, I would like in this essay to begin investigating two traits of reading that correspond to the two traits of the imagination just spoken of. As one part of this investigation, I would like to consider the act of reading as a dynamic activity that is not confined to repeating significations fixed forever, but which takes place as a prolonging of the itineraries of meaning opened up by the work of interpretation. Through this first trait, the act of reading accords with the idea of a norm-governed productivity to the extent that it may be said to be guided by a productive imagination at work in the text itself. Beyond this, I would like to see in the reading of a text such as the Bible a creative operation unceasingly employed in decontextualizing its meaning and recontextualizing it in today's *Sitz-im-Leben*. Through this second trait, the act of reading realizes the union of fiction and redescription that characterizes the imagination in the most pregnant sense of this term.

So this is the first presupposition of this essay, to seek *in* reading itself the key to the heuristic functioning of the productive imagination.

This presupposition, at first glance, may seem to set aside another way of approaching our subject that would consist in exploring the work of the imagination after reading, either as a personal form of the imagination (I have in mind Dorothee Sölle's fine little book *Imagination et Obéissance*) or as a collective form of the imagination (as in works on the relations between faith, ideology, and utopia, which I consider to be equally important). By placing myself at the very heart of the act of reading, I am hoping to place myself at the starting point of the trajectory that unfolds itself into the individual and social forms of the imagination. In this sense, my approach does not exclude this other wholly different approach but leads to it.

2. Within the vast domain of the form of the imagination at work in the biblical text, I propose to limit myself to one particular category of texts, the narrative texts. My reasons for this choice are as follows.

First, beginning from the side of a theory of fiction, I observe that we possess a general theory of narratives, coming from literary semiotics, which may allow us to give a concrete meaning to the twofold idea of a rule-governed creation and a heuristic model. On the one hand, narratives may be seen as a remarkable example of rule-governed invention to the extent that their submission to narrative codes testifies to the encoded character of their invention, and where their abundance attests to the ludic character of this rule-governed generation. On the other hand, narratives offer a remarkable example of the conjunction between fiction and redescription. Narratives, in virtue of their form, are all fictions.[2] And

---

2. Christian Metz, "Remarques pour une phénoménologie du narratif," *Revue d'esthétique* 19 (1966): 333–43.

yet it is through these fictions that we give a narrative form to our experience, be it individual or communal. Stephen Crites, in a noteworthy essay, has even spoken of "the narrative quality of experience" and shown how narrative provides a discursive articulation explicitly applicable to the narrative forms of lived experience.[3]

Next, placing myself on the side of the biblical text, I can hardly be contradicted if I recall that there the narrative kernels occupy a central place and play an exceptional role from the election of Abraham to the anointing of David by way of the exodus, and from the narratives of the life and teaching of Jesus to those of the Acts of the Apostles by way of the accounts of the passion. Whatever may be the destiny of those narrative theologies that some thinkers are attempting to elaborate, these narratives may be for us a favorable occasion for making our first presupposition more precise; I mean that the act of reading should be seen as the meeting point of the itineraries of meaning offered by the text as a production of fiction (in the sense given above) and the free course (*parcours*) of meaning brought about by the reader seeking "to apply" the text to life. My second presupposition, therefore, will be that it is within the structure of the narrative itself that we can best apprehend this intersection between the text and life that engenders the imagination according to the Bible.

3. A further delimiting of my subject will follow from a third presupposition, namely, that the narrative-parables (to use the terminology of Ivan Almeida [see below]) furnished the key to an enigma that I find H. Richard Niebuhr has perfectly outlined in *The Meaning of Revelation,* the enigma of the passage from a narrative to a paradigm, which in turn governs the passage from a narrative to life, which is finally the heuristic character of narrative fiction. Alfred North Whitehead, whom Niebuhr quotes favorably, wrote in *Religion in the Making,* "Rational religion appeals to the direct intuition of special occasions, and to the elucidatory power of its concepts for all occasions."[4] Niebuhr says of this:

> The special occasion to which we appeal in the Christian Church is called Jesus Christ, in whom we see the righteousness of God, his power and wisdom. But from that special occasion we also derive the concepts which make possible the elucidation of all the events in our history. Revelation means this intelligible event which makes all other events intelligible.[5]

---

3. Stephen Crites, "The Narrative Quality of Experience," *Journal of the American Academy of Religion* 39 (1971): 291–311.

4. H. Richard Niebuhr, *The Meaning of Revelation* (New York: Macmillan, 1941), 69; quoting Alfred North Whitehead, *Religion in the Making* (Cleveland: World, 1960), 31.

5. Niebuhr, *Meaning of Revelation,* 69.

But how does one intelligible event make other events intelligible? Here, between "our history" and that "special occasion," is interpolated the "rational pattern" Niebuhr calls an image: "By revelation in our history, then, we mean that special occasion which provides us with an image of which all the occasions of personal and common life become intelligible."[6]

It is no accident that Niebuhr develops this idea in a chapter entitled "Reasons of the Heart," which he opposes to the "evil imagination" evoked by Genesis. Yet his central affirmation seems to be more the formulation of a problem than the enunciation of a solution. How does a history or story become an image, a paradigm, a symbol for... (and not just a symbol of..., to take up a distinction made by Clifford Geertz)?[7] Niebuhr does do a good job in showing us the trajectory from history become an image to life, but he short-circuits the elevating of history to an image. Here is where a third presupposition intervenes, namely, that the narrative-parable is the type most favorable to investigating the link between a narrative and an image because the metaphorization process of a simple narrative is contained in the text itself by virtue of its literary form. To put it another way, the narrative-parable is itself an itinerary of meaning, a signifying dynamism, which transforms a narrative structure into a metaphorical process, in the direction of an enigma-expression (once again this is Almeida's term), the kingdom of God, an expression that orients the whole process of transgression beyond the narrative framework while at the same time receiving in return a content of provisory meaning from the narrative structure. Here we may have, it seems to me, the most complete illustration of the biblical form of imagination, the process of parabolization working in the text and engendering in the reader a similar dynamic of interpretation through thought and action.

Someone may object, perhaps, that this third presupposition condemns us to taking as our paradigm one too narrow form of narrative, a form that we might even see as an exception rather than as exemplary. To show that the choice of narrative-parables is pertinent to our investigation of the biblical form of imagination, we would have to demonstrate that the operation of parabolization is not limited just to the narrative-parable, or that it does not appear here alone, but that it is implicitly at work everywhere else.

This is where a fourth presupposition comes in, a presupposition that will furnish the most restrictive delimitation of this inquiry but also the guiding thread of the whole study.

4. To ask what makes the narrative-parable a paradigm and not an exception is to look for what makes the metaphorization at work in this type of narrative a process capable of other applications without becoming an

---

6. Ibid., 80.
7. Clifford Geertz, *The Interpretation of Cultures* (New York: Basic Books, 1973), 118.

interpretation that does violence to its text. In this essay, I have sought a key to this new enigma in an operation that the French structural school of text semiotics has brought to light, namely, *intertextuality* or the work of meaning through which one text in referring to another text both displaces this other text and receives from it an extension of meaning.

Allow me to note that this recourse to the semiotics of texts does not imply any judgment, positive or negative, concerning the currently dominant method of historical-critical exegesis. It is a question of another technique that found its first application in the domain of fairy tales and folklore. (The historical-critical method itself is transposed from classical philology as applied to profane texts.) What is specifically different about the semiotic study of texts is that it does not ask about the history of redaction of a text or to what setting the successive authors or their respective audience might have belonged. Instead it asks how a text functions as a text in its current state. If one identifies exegesis with the historical-critical method, the semiotic analysis of texts is not a form of exegesis.

Yet in drawing upon the semiotics of texts, I find that I am not enclosing myself into structuralism's abstract combinatory devices. To the contrary, the notion of intertextuality will appear in what follows in this essay, not just as one complement to the structural analysis of narratives, but as an important corrective insofar as it dynamizes the text, makes meaning move, and gives rise to extensions and transgressions—in brief, insofar as it makes the text work.

A complete demonstration would include three steps. I shall be able to develop only the first one here.

The first step consists in showing that intertextuality is indeed the operation that assures the metaphorization of the simple narrative in the case of the parables. If this analysis is successful, I will have justified my third presupposition that the parable is not an exceptional literary genre, rather parabolization is a general procedure of the narrative form of imagination.

The second step would consist in showing that the restricted intertextuality, visibly at work in the case of the parables, works as well in the case of nonparabolic narratives. Two possible examples could be the intersection between narratives and laws in the Old Testament and the overall intersection between the Old and New Testaments. If this demonstration can be shown to be satisfactory, we shall have rejoined the conditions of the first Christian hermeneutic, which was effectively engendered by the intertextuality between "the one and the other testament," to use the title of a work by Father Paul Beauchamp. By passing in this way from the restricted intertextuality of the parables to the generalized intertextuality of the whole Bible considered as a single book, we may hope eventually to regain the level of our second presupposition that revelation is the transfer from *this* history to *our* history, as suggested by H. Richard Niebuhr.

Finally, the third step would consist in showing that this phenomenon of intertextuality, brought in this way to its highest level, is indeed the key to the rule-governed imagination that, by the privileged way of narrative, invites the reader to continue, on his or her own account, the Bible's itineraries of meaning. If this analysis can one day be carried through, we shall have recovered the level of our first presupposition that the biblical form of imagination is indivisibly a narrative and a symbolic form of imagination. By beginning this process today, while having in mind some notion of where we must go from here, we shall have begun to do justice to the second interpretation of the theme Dean Kitagawa has proposed, that of Dorothee Sölle in *Phantasie und Gehorsam*,[8] and that of those other authors who have worked on the relationships between faith, ideology, and utopia. But, as I have already indicated, the present essay is limited to showing the rootedness of the imagination (that comes after reading) in the imagination that is the very act of reading.

II. Intertextuality and Metaphorization in the Narrative-Parables

Why begin with the parables? Why not? By flattening out every text, semiotics gives me the right to begin from any fragment. This is how a *book* is made: it puts all its parts in synchrony, in a space that can be traversed in any direction, between the two covers, and beginning from any center. We shall reascend the succession of our presuppositions, therefore, by first applying ourselves to the fourth one, that intertextuality is the key—or one of the keys—to the metaphorical transfer suggested by the famous clause: "The kingdom of God is like..." I must admit that this aspect of the problem completely escaped me in my earlier work on the parables published in *Semeia*.[9] I got trapped there by the question, "What makes us interpret the narrative as a parable?" I did not see the resources for responding to this question offered by the too easily overlooked trait that the narrative-parables are narratives within a narrative, more precisely narratives recounted by the principal personage of an encompassing narrative. Therefore, I am going to try to show now by drawing on the work of Ivan Almeida, a professor at the Catholic University of Lyon, that the structure embedding one narrative in another narrative is the fundamental framework for the metaphorical transfer guided by the enigma-expression

---

8. Dorothee Sölle, *Beyond Mere Obedience: Reflections on a Christian Ethic for the Future,* trans. W. Denet (Minneapolis: Augsburg, 1970).

9. Paul Ricoeur, "Biblical Hermeneutics," *Semeia* 4 (1975): 29–148.

"kingdom of God."[10] The effect of this embedding is twofold: on the one hand, the embedded narrative borrows from the encompassing narrative the structure of interpretation that allows the metaphorization of its meaning; in return, the interpretant (to use an expression taken from C. S. Peirce) is also reinterpreted due to the feedback (*par choc en retour*) from the metaphorized narrative. Metaphorization, therefore, is a process at work between the encompassing narrative and the embedded narrative.

Therefore, there are two errors to avoid in the interpretation of a narrative-parable: first, to consider only the primary narrative, neglecting its anchorage in another narrative; then one does not understand the phenomenon of metaphorization characteristic of the parable. Second, to reduce the parable to the speech-act of the personage whose story is recounted in the encompassing narrative without taking into account the transforming action exercised by the primary narrative on the encompassing narrative. Of course we have learned from Joachim Jeremias's marvelous work on the parables that Jesus does something in telling the parables, but the parables in their turn are productive of meaning at the level of the narrative of the life of Jesus. We must understand therefore, says Almeida, not just "how this personage produces something with this narrative, but how this narrative produces something in the story of this personage."[11]

To understand this work of meaning, we must first have taken into account the structures of the narrative following the semiotic method. My analysis presumes this analysis but does not confine itself to it. Furthermore, it assumes that this analysis is done in a way that allows us to go further than ordinary structural analysis does, toward the transformation of the narrative-parable by the encompassing text. In what way? In a way that already notes the dynamism at work in the narrative in order to understand how this dynamism is transgressed by the embedding. To understand a narrative dynamically is to understand it as the operation of transforming an initial situation into a terminal situation. The most elementary function of a narrative, in this regard, is to account for this transformation. To read a narrative is to redo with the text a certain "line" or "course" (*parcours*) of meaning.

I stress this theme of a "course" that connotes the transforming dynamism of a narrative. In a way, it is the first form of imagination we encounter. A form of imagination incorporated into a transformation. A

---

10. Ivan Almeida, *L'Opérativité sémantique des récits paraboles: Sémiotique narrative et textuelle: Herméneutique du discours religieux* (Louvain: Peeters, 1978), 117. He defines a parable as follows: "A narrative-parable is a narrative recounted by a personage of another narrative that encompasses it."

11. Ibid., 130.

rule-governed form of imagination, encoded, yes, but authentically productive of meaning. It is because narrative involves such a dynamism that it can be taken into the encompassing dynamism of the text within which it is embedded.

Not just any analysis of the primary narrative, consequently, can lend something to the work of metaphorization. Only the one that puts the accent on the course of meaning brought about each time by each parable. The phenomena of intersection are subsequently grafted onto those microuniverses where something happens, where something takes place.

I am adopting here A.-J. Greimas's model of analysis as used by Almeida. This is, as I said, a semiotic approach completely distinct from the historical-critical method. It takes the text in its last state, just as it has been read by generation of believing and nonbelieving readers, and it attempts to reconstruct the codes that govern the transformations at work in the narrative. Such an analysis makes a semiotic organization appear in the narrative-parables that does not differ from the elementary grammar at work in popular folktales. This grammar is not uninteresting, however, if we know how to discern not just the paradigmatic character of these codes, as Lévi-Strauss does, but their *productivity,* that is, their aptitude for engendering transformations. In truth, the two aspects are linked, for if a code is a system of constraints—as are the phonological code, the lexical code, and the syntactical code at the level of *langue*—these constraints are at the same time the conditions for producing new narrative courses, just as the constraints of *langue* are also conditions for engendering new sentences. This is why the narrative form of imagination is both constrained and free at the same time.

I shall consider, as Almeida does, the example of two parables in Mark, the wicked husbandmen and the sower. Besides being the only parables common to the three Synoptic Gospels, their position—the one near the beginning, the other near the end of that other course of meaning that, at the overall level of the Gospel, is the Incarnate Word's march toward death—will constitute below an important indication of the intersection we are looking for between these two narrative-parables and the encompassing narrative.

A. The Narrative-Parable of the Wicked Husbandmen

Let us begin with the wicked husbandmen. The personages are few in number: the vineyard owner, the tenants, and the successive envoys, the last of which is the son. An "object-value," the vineyard, circulates among them. To this must be added its fruits, which do not circulate; though the owner sends for them, it is in vain. The actions are also few in number, involving only a few verbs: to plant, hedge, rent, go, send, kill, and so on. The actants, object-values, and segments of action make up a narrative insofar as a dynamism runs through all of them—from the planting of the vineyard to the refusal to hand over its fruits, from the departure of the owner to the murder of the son. We may represent this small drama as a conflict between two "narrative programs" (Greimas), that of the owner of the vineyard who wants to reap the fruits of the vineyard he has rented out and that of the tenants who defeat this program. This dynamism, seen from the point of view of the owner, is a dynamism of progressive defeat. In semiotic terms, it is a dysphoric course, that is, one that fails to unite its subject to its object. As we shall see, the inverse case applies in the case of the sower.

But semioticians do not stop here. They note that this narrative takes place in relation to three stable themes that they call isotopies, that is, semantic invariants.

The first isotopy is quite evident. It is the vegetation and its end-product: vines, fruit, wine. More precisely, it is a vegetation-economic isotopy: a location, a harvest, an inheritance. This vegetative course from planting to fruit and the harvest will have its counterpart in a similar course in the parable of the sower, from the sowing to the harvesting of the grain. What they have in common, and what we have called an object-value, is an object with a dynamic, not a static, value: it sprouts, grows, and does or does not bear fruit. The narrative transformation follows the potentialities of this object that Almeida characterizes as "an object with a surplus value" (objet à plus-value). What is more, it is these potentialities that release the quest that is the basis for the narrative: to go get some of the fruits. The whole narrative process may be summed up in a locution that is the theme correlative to the plot: from the initial lack created by the departure to the defeat of its redress.

The second isotopy is the one common to the actions of departing, sending, and above all fighting and killing. It concerns the life and death of a body. We shall not rediscover this isotopy in the sower, where it will have been replaced by another isotopy that stands in a significant contrast to it—this will be the isotopy of the word.

The third isotopy is the one that runs the greatest risk of passing unperceived and that only a semiotic analysis can clearly recognize. It concerns the relations among places. The semiotician is attentive to it insofar as the narrative is a course. We will call it the spatial isotopy. Indeed, it is noteworthy that the entire continuation of the narrative from the sending of the first messengers to the murder of the last one—the son of the departed man—roughly constitutes a movement toward the inside of the enclosed vineyard. It is only within the enclosed vineyard that Mark has the son die. The dramatic movement from life to death is thus staked out by a spatial movement from outside, where the owner has departed to, to inside, where the son is killed.[12]

Before turning to the second parable, let us already note the power of metaphorization initially contained in the three isotopies. Let us provisionally set aside the third isotopy, that of the places. It does not immediately reveal its metaphorical power. Particular attention must be paid to the places of Jesus' preaching and of his march toward death—from Galilee to Jerusalem, then to the temple, then to the empty tomb—to register a similarity of movements from outside to inside. Louis Marin's (1971) work on the "topic of the passion" prepares us for the idea that the places referred to in the Gospels are not geographical, that is, amenable to an empirical type of verification, but topological places, or, if one prefers, semanticized places that get their signification in relation to the dramatic course.[13] In this sense, the spatial isotopy is not purely geometric. The places are capable of signifying more than just places for bodily movements. And in this sense, they are eminently metaphorizable.[14]

As for the second isotopy, that of the body and death (Almeida's somatic isotopy), it is set in motion toward metaphorization by the text's conclusion: "And they tried to arrest him" (Mark 12:12). Here the metaphorization plays directly between the content of the narrative (what is said) and its author (the speaker), who signifies himself through what he says. In other words, the destiny of the speaker is figured in what the narrative says.[15]

As regards the first isotopy, that of the vineyard and its fruits, which we have called the vegetation-economic isotopy, the listener cannot miss

---

12. I will set aside that to which structural semiotics attaches the most importance, the possibility of representing every narrative maneuver on a semiotic square. I am somewhat doubtful about Almeida's thesis (ibid., 169) that, "through a whole series of narrative 'maneuvers' which might appear to us to be aleatory, an implacable semantic logic is expressed through the determining of the courses that the transformation algorithm will be forced to follow." I am much more attentive to the fact that it is because the narrative does follow a certain course that we can *after the fact* project the poles, the axes of contrariety, the schemes of contradiction, and the relations of implication onto an immobile figure. In any case, it is more important to note that in the series of messengers there is a progression to the inside of the vineyard than to stop with the fixed polarities of its movements. The second servant in this sense signifies *more* than the first one and the son *still more* in this twofold progression on the planes of the body and space. If it is true that the narrative course is inscribed on the figure of the semiotic square, it is on the condition that the narrative *advances* and constitutes a *course*. The course, in this sense, engenders the structure (ibid.).

13. Louis Marin, *The Semiotics of the Passion Narrative: Topics and Figures,* trans. Alfred M. Johnson, Jr. (Pittsburgh: Pickwick, 1986).

14. "As has been said, the places function in the text as a semantic element not determined by the dictionary but easily contaminated. They are impregnated with significations left to them by the transforming actions and thus serve to fix the semantic continuity of the sometimes disparate events" (Almeida, *L'Opérativité sémantique,* 178).

15. Almeida (ibid., 166) is willing to recognize that we cannot reach the end of a structural analysis here without anticipating the metaphorical effects. Conversely, he is correct to emphasize "the structural condition of this movement of metaphorization."

its metaphorization that calls to mind Isaiah 5: "My beloved had a vine-yard....For the vineyard of the Lord of Hosts is the house of Israel." We can here catch a glimpse of how a narrative-parable is embedded in an encompassing narrative by means of the quotation that is the most explicit and most remarkable effect of intertextuality. Let us note in passing that this effect corrects the structuralist notion of an isotopy as a univocal level of discourse. Plurivocity is already present on the level of the primary narrative that is capable of being metaphorized.

The two beginnings of metaphorization that we have indicated, on the side of the body and on that of the vineyard, are also tightly interlaced with each other through the progress of the narrative. Something happens, in effect, in the narrative in that the tenants not only refuse to hand over the fruits but seize the first servant, beat him, and send him away empty-handed. The beaten servant is sent back *instead of* the requisite fruits. In this way, the dying body becomes the substituted and inverted sign of the refused object-value, the fruits of the vineyard. He is not just the owner's envoy, but detained *like* the refused fruits and sent back *in place of* them. "Like," "in place of," here is the beginning of a metaphorization that is inscribed as follows: so that the fruit may increase, life must decrease. We could speak here of an inverted metaphor. This rapprochement is a creation of the narrative that, at this moment, takes an odd turn. The messenger becomes something other than and more than a messenger, the "antimetaphor" of the object-value, the fruit of the vineyard.[16] The seizing of the body occurs *in place* of the seizing of the fruits postulated by the logic of the narrative. The narrative form of imagination, which prepares the way for the metaphorical form, is already notable in this transgressing of the expectation created by the sending of the messenger who was supposed to seize some of the fruits, not be captured in his own body. The servant was sent empty-handed and returned "empty-handed"—as the text simply says—which makes an antithesis to the expected plenty from the harvest.

It is not just the isotopies in terms of which the acts are unfolded that can be metaphorized. The actants can also. Greimas distinguishes the most general actantial roles (subject, opponents, helpers) and their thematic investments—here a landlord, his sharecroppers, servants, and son. Each of these roles possesses a polysemy that makes possible, on the narrative plane, the explicit metaphorization through their context. Further, within the narrative itself, the man who planted the vineyard is revealed to be a father after having acted as the owner of the vineyard and the sharecroppers' landlord. At the same time, the vineyard goes from being simply the soil for producing fruit to an inheritance. It is the progression of the nar-

---

16. Ibid., 165.

rative that makes these successive investments of the actantial roles into their thematic roles take place. *Then* the sharecroppers posit themselves as substitute heirs: "Let us kill him, and the inheritance will be ours" (12:7). We could well speak here of the "odd logic" that guides this drama. In my earlier analysis of the parables in *Semeia,* I emphasized narrative extravagance as their common trait. It is through this narrative extravagance that the deceived landlord becomes a father who sends his son and thereby brings the narrative to its critical point, what Aristotle called the peripeteia, which is answered by the denouement. In this case it is the refusal to recognize the son, his death in the vineyard, the interior that ought to have been the place of fructification and therefore of life: "And they took him and killed him, and cast him out of the vineyard" (12:8). The inside of the vineyard instead of being just a place is qualified by the action that occurs there. It is this action that makes the equation between the interior and death.

One last remark concerning the preparation, on the simple narrative plane, for the metaphorical transformations that are the principal object of our inquiry. The narrative ends with a segment outside the narrative (*un hors-récit*) where the listener is questioned: "What will the owner of the vineyard do? He will come and destroy the tenants, and give the vineyard to others" (12:9). This segment is outside the narrative first in the sense that the dysphoric climax is annulled by an action that is not spoken of as past, but which is posited as in the future as the response to a question. This action signifies the defeat of the defeat and the liquidating of the opponent. We shall see below how, in virtue of intertextuality, this postscript corresponds to the postscript to the whole Gospel. This segment is outside the narrative in the second place in the sense that it creates a new vis-à-vis to the master: "He will give the vineyard to others." At the same time, new roles for the master are created. These are not thematized but simply suggested by the indeterminateness of these "others."

As for the vineyard object-value that circulates among these actants, we do not know what it will produce once "given to others." Here the narrative, after having been closed on a definite defeat, is reopened to indefinite possibilities, thanks to the rhetorical device of the question, "What will the owner of the vineyard do?"[17] By marking the intrusion of the narra-

---

17. It is here that structural analysis runs the greatest risk of leaving aside what is essential. By projecting all the courses on the famous semiotic square, it requires them to satisfy a logic that closes the square. The liquidating of the opponent gives the diagram "the course that the square lacked" (ibid., 188). I would emphasize instead that it is the interplay of metaphors that, by producing meaning, allows the square to be closed and that gives the semiotician the conspicuous satisfaction of having "buckled up the semantic course" (ibid.). Yet can we, within the same system, both close the square and open the narrative to something outside the narrative? The distinction borrowed from Greimas between the topical narrative and a correlated narrative conceals the difficulty rather than resolving it.

tor into the narrative through a summons addressed to the listeners, this question also marks the anchoring of the narrative-parable in the weft of the narrative that encompasses it and opens the way to the parabolization we are going to talk about. It marks this anchorage in another fashion by the allusion—which is equivalent to a quotation—to the parallel text of the "Song of the Vineyard" in Isaiah: "And now I will tell what I will do to my vineyard" (Isa. 5:5). In this way, the wicked husbandmen are again made ready to be metaphorized. If the one who "will come"—according to the postscript to the narrative—obliquely signifies the narrator himself, the wicked husbandmen begin to signify the listeners themselves: "For they perceived that he had told the parable against them" (Mark 12:12). But here we have already exited the narrative and taken the path of metaphorization. It has been helpful, I believe, to have seen how this metaphorical process is in a way woven into the narrative course.

The explicit metaphorization is further guided by the device of quotation in verses 10 and 11. At first, this quotation seems odd since it does not limit itself to evoking a defeat, or even the defeat of a defeat, but a victory with an "Easter" meaning: "This was the Lord's doing." This expression, placed at the hinge linking the narrative-parable and the encompassing narrative, designates the meaning vector of the entire metaphorical process, exactly as the enigma-expression "kingdom of God" does elsewhere. Now this quotation only functions to metaphorize what is outside the narrative if it contains symbolic resources that the quotation extracts from it. The quotation *transforms* the vineyard and its fruits (the vegetative isotopy) into a "head of the cornerstone" (or architectural isotopy), by means of, may we venture to say, the whole entourage of stones in the course of the parable: the wine press in a pit, the surrounding and enclosing hedge, the tower that is erected. All these are terms that move from plant to stone. Whatever the case may be concerning this metonymic (press, enclosure, tower, cornerstone) and metaphoric (the transfer from the vineyard to the head of the cornerstone) game, it is capital that the signification wrested from the quotation is already a fact of intertextuality. Thanks to the crisscrossing between the narrative and the other texts, the vineyard—which is at stake in all the actions—does not stop signifying something more. Having been the bearer of fruits and an inheritance, it has become, on the spatial plane, the circumference within which, on the body plane, the murdered son's destiny is fulfilled. It is the narrative that extracts all this signifying power from the vineyard.

At the end of this analysis, we understand in what sense we could have said in beginning that the codes are not inert constraints but generate a structuring dynamism that is all ready for metaphorical transformation.

B. The Parable of the Sower

For the narrative-parable of the sower I will limit myself to those traits that, in a semiotic analysis, correspond to those of the parable of the wicked husbandmen. In this sense, we are entering into the process of inter-textuality—the parables, in effect, should be read together. Together they constitute a universe of meaning in which the symbolic potentialities of one contribute, by means of their common context, to making the potentialities of another explicit.

A first inspection reveals a narrative process as euphoric as the preceding one was dysphoric. Its bearer is the very act of sowing with all its meaning potentiality that is connected with fecundity: planting, growing, yielding. This act of growing encounters three successive opponents: the birds, the sun, the thorns. The parable tells of the success of this operation despite three successive defeats. And the final success is itself drawn up in three ascending degrees: thirtyfold and sixtyfold and a hundredfold. All this is well known. The most interesting contribution of a semiotic analysis consists in the identifying of the planes of discourse or, in our vocabulary, the isotopies at play here. Here is where the most remarkable correspondences to the preceding parable spring forth.

It is clear that we again have the vegetative (or economic-vegetative) code of natural growth. The grain corresponds to the vines, eating to drinking. Do we also rediscover the spatial code? Its least significant occurrence is the progression from the periphery of the field to the good soil, which vaguely resembles the movement toward the inside of the course of the wicked husbandmen. More significant is the initial note: "Listen! A sower went out to sow." The field, understood as a whole, is the outside. It is this outside that is the place of the euphoric course.

But if we rediscover the two vegetative and spatial codes, we do not find the body and death code, represented in the preceding parable by the servants and son who are attacked and killed. What might correspond to it here? As the whole tradition has recognized, it is the word, that is, exactly the saying as projecting itself into what is said. This is what immediately makes the narrative a parable insofar as the metaphor that transports the fecundity of the grain into that of the word is inscribed in the narrative. The narrative in a way narrativized the fecundity metaphor. The text suggests this in different ways. First, through the immediate framing of the narrative: "*Listen!* A sower went out to sow" (4:3). "And he said, 'He who has ears to hear, let him hear'" (4:9). The Gospel of Mark puts this warning in Jesus' mouth, therefore in the encompassing narrative. It therefore ties it to the telling of the parable by attributing it to the speaker. The Gospel tells what Jesus tells. Several semioticians have emphasized the kinship of this procedure to that of *The Thousand and One Nights*. In the same way, the speaker signifies himself or herself as inside his or her narrative, and the same holds for the two groups designated as (1) "those who asked him concerning the parables," to whom Jesus declared, "To you has been given..."; and (2) those whom Jesus speaks about in saying "but for those outside..." (which implies that the first group is the "inside"). Through the feedback of this discourse by Jesus on the narrative, the first group, "you" (who are "inside"), is narrativized as being the actors of the euphoric process, the second group ("those outside") as the actors of the dysphoric process.

We shall return below to the complete sentence, "To you has been given the secret of the kingdom of God, but for those outside everything is in parables." It turns on the enigma-term "kingdom of God," which belongs to the encompassing text and which introduces a new opposition between "the secret is given" and "everything is in parables," where "is in parables" signifies only in parables, that is, in an opaque figure, heard but not understood. That we have here a fact of intertextuality is underlined by the quasi-quotation of the Old Testament in the following verse: "...so they may indeed see but not perceive..." (see Isa. 6:9-19). This is a segment outside the narrative that the following verse (Mark 4:13) reinserts into the narrative weft through the use of a question: "Do you not understand this parable? How then will you understand all the parables?"

We see here how semiotic analysis differs from historical-critical exegesis, which deliberately severs the explication that follows the parable from the parabolic narrative properly speaking, with the idea of isolating an original kernel that eventually would constitute the *ipsissima verba* of Jesus, and risks ascribing the added explication to the redactors (and the ecclesial community they stem from). For semiotic analysis, the incorporation of the narrative and its interpretive commentary into one text is an irrecusable textual fact. So the task of this analysis is to disclose the isomorphisms between the narrative and the interpretation that contribute to the parabolizing of the narrative. It is the resemblance between the narrative courses (thirty, sixty, one hundred grains), on the one hand, and the sequence: understand, be converted, be forgiven, on the other. It is this isomorphism that allows the narrative's fiction to cross its borders and be oriented toward the enigma-expression, "kingdom of God," that polarizes it overall. This effect is obtained through the crisscrossing of the vegetative and the verbal isotopies.

It appears, therefore, that the function of the sequence 4:10-13 is to insert into the meaning of what is said something about its being said and its reception. The destiny of the sowing that is lost three times, then that finally fructifies in abundance, is signified as the destiny of the very word (*parole*) that tells the narrative. A progression of abundance, similar to that of the grain harvest (thirtyfold, sixtyfold, a hundredfold), is indicated on the level of the diffusion of the terms "to understand," "to be converted," "to be forgiven." Thus the incomprehension of some (those "outside") and the progress in understanding of others ("you") is narrativized after the fact through the interpretation. To the extent that the destiny of the sowing is metaphorized as the destiny of the word, the destiny of the word is narrativized as the destiny of the sowing. This presupposes that what we have called the vegetative isotopy was not univocal. I mean, it was not just a question in the narrative of seeds and a harvest in the agricultural sense. A meaning potential in the language—that is, in the things already said—is liberated through the entangled twofold process of metaphorizing the narrative and narrativizing the metaphor.

Does not the same thing happen to the spatial isotopy (the outside of the field, its periphery, and its interior)? Between "those to whom the secret has been given" (a relation of intimacy) and those who remain "outside" (a relation of exteriority) the distance is no longer quantitative but qualitative. The euphoric process and the dysphoric process now depend upon these opposed values concerning proximity to the speaker of the word. Therefore, these places are more than empirical sites, and the degrees of distanciation are more than measurable distances. The spatial plane is itself also metaphorized insofar as the word is recognized as the "empty case" around which are organized the figures of this discourse.[18]

It is this whole interplay, which is narrative and symbolic at the same time, that allows us to say that the word in the narrative-parable of the sower holds the same places as does the body in the narrative-parable of the wicked husbandmen.[19] This rapprochement that is also an opposition is authorized by the fact that the two other isotopies, the vegetative and the spatial ones, are common to the two narratives. And this inclines me to say that the vineyard in the first parable is to the sowing in the second what the inside in the first is to proximity in the second, and finally what the mortal body in the first is to the living word in the second. If we allow these rapprochements, a still more striking one proposes itself that will be the source of the great metaphor exhibited by the intersection of the two parables not just with each other, but with the principal narrative. We have said, in effect, that the narrative-parable of the wicked husbandmen has a dysphoric course and the narrative-parable of the sower a euphoric one. May we not say then that if the word is to increase, the body must decrease? This would be the great metaphor encompassing these two parables.

This recourse to context is therefore inscribed in the parable itself in two

---

18. Ibid., 223.

19. I am hesitant about calling this plane of the word an isotopy in the same sense those of space and vegetation are. To the extent it is the "empty case" and only narrativized after the fact, we may not consider it an isotopy belonging to the narrative itself, something Almeida does not recognize sufficiently.

ways: on the one hand, on the side of what is said, through the metaphorical potentialities of the semantic fields that narrative semiotics encounters at the level of the narrative's large isotopies; on the other hand, on the side of the speaker, through the use of enigma-expressions such as "the secret of the kingdom of God" and "(only) in parables," which at the same time sort out the listeners and identify them respectively with the agents of the euphoric course (the fecundity of the sowing of the seeds in the outside) and the dysphoric course (the death of the body at the interior of the vineyard). The parable of the sower is exemplary in that it reunites these two processes, thanks to the exchanges between the speaking word and the spoken narrative. In this sense, it reveals the central operation by which the narrative becomes a parable.

C. Metaphorization through Intertextuality

We may now concentrate our attention on the second process, the metaphorization that occurs through the intersections of discourse within the encompassing narrative. It, more than any other, is what exercises the reader's productive imagination.

In sum, the whole meaning of my essay is contained here. A parable, the sower, contains in the perimeter of its pericope a first crisscrossing between the vegetative plane of fecundity and the more verbal one of communication of the message. This first crisscrossing produces the metaphor of a sown word or of a sowing that becomes a message. Then two parables taken together, the wicked husbandmen and the sower, created a second-degree crisscrossing, this time within the microuniverse of the parables. This crisscrossing between the euphoric process of the word and the dysphoric process of the body's march toward death in turn prepares the way for a still more fundamental intersection between the two parables taken together and the narrative, which tells of the one relating the parable, that encompasses both. Finally, it is the same process of embedding that we try to follow in writings other than the Gospels, then between the Gospels and these other writings. In this series of embeddings, the same process of metaphorization is at work to guide the reader and to engender in him or her the capacity to pursue the movement of metaphorization beyond his or her reading.

Someone may object that, by saying this, I am abusing the notion of metaphor that, in classical rhetoric, only designates a transfer of the meaning of words. But I have shown in *The Rule of Metaphor* that the thought process of a metaphor has its initial support in the sentence, that is, in the operation of predication.[20] A metaphor is first and essentially an "odd"

---

20. Ricoeur, *Rule of Metaphor,* 65–100, 125–33.

predication that transgresses the semantic and cultural codes of a speaking community. The theory of intertextuality allows us to take another step and to call not just the collision between two semantic fields in a sentence a metaphor, but also an intersection between texts, both of which carry their own semantic codes. The analysis of narrative-parables allows us to take this step and to extend the process of metaphorization to the widespread semantic conflicts instigated by the fact of intertextuality.

We may now approach by itself the phenomenon of parabolization through intertextuality that we have had to anticipate in order to account for the very dynamic of the narrative. I shall now take the two expressions "parabolization" and "metaphorization" as synonyms, it being understood that a metaphor can occur not only between words but between whole sequences of sentences. The isotopies play a role at this discursive level comparable to that of the semantic fields that enter into interaction in metaphor-sentences. *Parabolization is the metaphorization of a discourse.* In the case of the narrative-parables, it consists of the metaphorization of a narrative taken as a whole. Intertextuality thus becomes an extension and, consequently, a particular case of the interaction I have placed at the center of my theory of metaphor. In this I follow I. A. Richards, Max Black, Monroe Beardsley, and others. These authors perceived that the semantic clash between significations does not occur without an interaction between contexts. It is this interaction that we are now going to consider.

The decisive point brought to light by Ivan Almeida is that the intersection among contexts is a phenomenon of *writing*. It is an operation of the *text* considered as a living work. Because the sequences have been written down together within the limits of one text—here a Gospel—they constitute a network of intersignification, thanks to which the isolated texts signify something *else*, something *more*.

This is how I understand the transition between semiotic explication and interpretation that has its fulfillment in the thought, action, and life of interpreting individuals and communities. We are leaving the structure (or sense), but we are not yet at the application or appropriation (the reference). We are accompanying *the interpretive dynamism of the text itself.* The text interprets before having been interpreted. This is how it is itself a work of productive imagination before giving rise to an interpretive dynamism in the reader that is analogous to its own.

I will limit myself here to sketching some of the relations of intertextuality through which our narratives, in becoming parables, give rise to a certain dynamism in the semantic system of the Gospel of Mark considered as a whole. We may arrange these procedures according to an increasing scale of intimacy in textual interaction and, consequently, in the synamization of one text to another. We will begin with (*a*) structural similarities between the englobing text and the embedded text. These isomorphisms are still external similarities compared to those we shall consider under (b) and (c).

a. The structural similarities play successively (1) on the contrast between the euphoric course and the dysphoric course in the two parables analyzed (placed respectively toward the beginning and the end of the Gospel); (2) on the interplay of isotopies sometimes common to the two parables (the vegetative and spatial isotopies), sometimes peculiar to each one (the corporeal isotopy in the one, the verbal isotopy in the other); and (3) on the explicit or implicit quotations that guide the references to other texts.

Beginning with the contrast between the euphoric and dysphoric courses, we can trace two homologous inverted courses on the level of the Gospel. Moreover, we can refer one to the *word* and the other to the *body*. In effect, what progressively happens in the Gospel is the *recognition* of Jesus as being the Christ. We can say in this regard that the Gospel is not a simple account of the life, teaching, work, death, and resurrection of Jesus, but the communicating of an act of confession, a communication by means of which the reader in turn is rendered capable of performing the same recognition that occurs inside the text.[21]

This recognition, this knowledge concerning the narrator of the parables, progresses across the parables told by Jesus and about Jesus, his gestures and those ascribed to him, thereby engendering a sorting out of various groups: the crowd, adversaries, friends, and disciples who are thereby placed in variable relations of proximity to the person of Jesus. This sorting is aimed at constituting the community of those close to him who hear and understand.

This advance of the word is paralleled by a decline of the body, if we consider that the success of Jesus the miracle worker on the bodies of those he heals at the beginning of his ministry leads to the defeat of Jesus' body in death.

In this way, we see spring forth a certain parallelism between the overall narrative structure of the Gospel and that of the two parables taken together. It is this parallelism instituted by the text—by the "texture" of

---

21. We could consider as the encompassing narrative in relation to the narrative-parable the narrative of the days of Jesus' life that end in his passion and death, therefore from the calling of the disciples to the women's fear at the tomb. We could then take as adjoined narratives ("correlated" narratives in A.-J. Greimas's sense), the framing narratives throughout that the text posits and in a way proposes in advance the meaning that the narrative properly speaking must produce, the prologue (Mark 1:1-13), the epilogue (Mark 16), along with the sequence on the death of John the Baptist (Mark 6:14-29) that anticipates the meaning of Jesus' death. This is why I speak of recognition to designate the confession professed by the very personages in the Gospel's narrative, culminating in the centurion's confession. The narrative of the life and death of Jesus is organized in such a way that the knowledge unveiled right at the beginning should be appropriated by the actors themselves and, beyond them, by the reader. It is the work of the text to do this.

the text—that makes a place for the process of mutual parabolization of the encompassing narrative and the embedded ones. This is the structural similarity that results from the mirror relation between the large and small narratives, apropos principally of the contrast between the euphoric course of the word and the dysphoric course of the body. The parable of the wicked husbandmen, in effect, simulates the dissemination and growth of the word. Perhaps here we should also refer to the transfiguration, the declaration before the high priest, and the centurion's confession. The power of the metaphor is already present in this simple structural similarity where something *passes* from one text to another. A relation of intersignification is established between the large narrative and the small one. A new signification springs forth from this relation of intersignification as in the case of any live metaphor. The encompassing narrative and the embedded narratives seem to say together that the life of the word occurs through the death of the body.

The places, as we have seen, are also not foreign to this type of relation, both in the parables (the "outside" of the seeds, the "inside" of the vineyard) and in the encompassing narrative (the sending of the disciples, the empty tomb). In this regard, we must repeat again that the biblical places are eminently metaphorizable (the opposition between Galilee and Jerusalem is a semanticized space), and their metaphorization is promoted by the superimposition of relations of proximity between Jesus and another group of actors in the drama onto the properly spatial relations.[22]

The text gives rise equally to a certain affinity between the theme of eating and drinking in the large narrative (the ears of grain plucked on the Sabbath, the miraculous multiplication of bread and fish, the bread and wine of the Last Supper) and the two parables' vegetative isotopy (the vineyard and the sowing). The superabundance of bread and fish miraculously multiplied, for example, is joined to the grain in the parable by means of the parallel metaphorization of both of them as a sign of the word that, in effect, is shared without being exhausted. We ought also not forget the leaven of the Pharisees and that of Herod (Mark 8:15), which become synonyms of the vineyard within which the son is killed by the wicked husbandmen.

b. But parabolization is not reduced to an isomorphism that would leave the encompassing and embedded texts intact. The narrative-parable is not only the homologue of the large narrative; it signifies the destiny of the one who tells the parables and whose life is told by the Gospel. The exchange occurs between the personages of the embedded narrative and the person of the one who tells it. The bond between the encompassing narrative and

---

22. Let me recall again my doubt concerning the possibility of a structural analysis independent of these implicit or explicit processes of metaphorization. In effect, the isotopies are immediately and directly metaphorized. It is only through an abstraction that we constitute them as isotopies, that is, as univocal levels of discourse.

the embedded narrative is made tighter here thanks to this remarkable trait of the narrative-parable that it is told by the personage of another narrative that encompasses it. Thus Jesus himself signifies the diminution of his mortal body in telling of the wicked husbandmen, and he signifies the growth of his living word in telling of the superabundant fecundity of the grain.

In the same movement, the listeners are obliquely intended and analogously sorted out, following the models of the wicked husbandmen or the "bad" and "good" soil. (Let me remark in passing that this implication of the speaker in what is said in the narrative-parable in no way leads us back to the old discussions about Jesus' "messianic conscience." The problem is not psychological but semiotic, in the sense that it is the belonging to one text and the work of the text as such that produce this reverberation of the narrative-parable on the person who tells it.)

c. To the extent that the encompassing narrative and the embedded narrative penetrate each other, we catch sight of the role that enigma-expressions such as the "kingdom of God" may play in this work of parabolization. The bond of these enigma-expressions, introduced by the encompassing narrative, to the immanent meaning of the narrative is infinitely more intimate than any isomorphism or even than any insertion of the illocutionary force of the utterance into the very weft of the spoken narrative. We may certainly still speak of an isomorphism to designate the correspondence we may observe between the enigma-expressions that the evangelist has put into the prologue that precedes the narrative of Jesus' ministry and into the epilogue of his resurrection, expressions through which the kerygmatic meaning of the whole Gospel is anticipated (Son of God, Lord, Christ). It is a question, however, of much more than an isomorphism, for we can no longer speak here of an isotopy in such expressions, even if we speak of a religious isotopy with the semioticians.[23] It is rather a question of limit-expressions, as I said in my article in *Semeia,* or, to use an expression of Jean Ladrière's, of the horizon of structuration of the religious symbolism taken as a whole.[24] If we may still speak of parabolization with regard to such limit-expressions, it is to the extent that a

---

23. Here I disagree with Ivan Almeida, who, to remain as long as possible in accord with Greimas's structural analysis, extends the categories of that analysis into a region of meaning where we can decidedly no longer speak of an isotopy in the rigorous sense of the term. If, as the author so well puts it, these expressions are *expressions-énigmes,* they do not designate any determined object, but the horizon of structuration, the dynamizing pole, the vanishing point of the whole process of parabolization. Consequently, we may no longer speak of an isotopy, which would assume the stability of one theme running through all the relevant terms of a single semantic field. This is why I hesitate to speak of a "religious isotopy" in the sense we have spoken of a vegetative, spatial, and verbal isotopy. Indeed, we have already seen the notion of an isotopy vacillate due to the effect of metaphorization which affects almost all the terms of a narrative-parable.

24. Jean Ladrière, "Le Discours théologique et le symbole," *Revue des sciences religieuses* 49 (1975): 116–41.

limit-expression's meaning, without being signified by any action or personage in a narrative, is signified by the movement of transgression that transports the narrative outside the customary logic of narratives. In this sense, the kingdom of God is not what the parables tell about, but what happens in parables.

In my *Semeia* article, I attached this final process of parabolization to the aspect of the narrative's extravagance on the narrative plane. What landowner, in effect, would be so foolish as to send his son after his servants had been killed? What sowing could return thirtyfold, sixtyfold, a hundredfold? In this manner, the narrative metaphorizes itself by transgressing its own narrative structure through an "odd" usage of the art of narrating.

This metaphorizing relation runs in two directions. The expression "kingdom of God" is in its turn referred to its enigmatic character by the movement of transgressing the narrative. Without this movement, these expressions risk falling to the rank of frozen religious representations. In this way, the expression "kingdom of God," left to itself, could become nothing more than a dead image with some vague political content. It is the extravagance of the narrative that, by bursting out of the mundane meaning of the narrative, attests that "my kingdom is not of this world," that is, does not belong to any specific project of human action and remains, in the strong sense of the word, impractical like some utopia. The expression-enigma, under the pressure of the extravagance of the narrative, thus becomes a limit-expression that breaks open the closed representations.

We have attained the point where it is no longer intertextuality as such that is at work, but where it is carried beyond itself by the meaning vectors of the enigma-expressions. To continue our analysis, it would be necessary to change methods and to show how these enigma-expressions mobilize in the reader opaque and mute expectations concerning liberation from evil and the regeneration of the "evil imagination." These limit-expressions, in effect, would be nothing more than hollow words if, on the one hand, human beings did not have some experience of limit-situations such as evil and death and the strong desire to be freed from them. It is these fundamental experiences that the enigma-expressions come *to configure*. But they would still only be words, if, on the other hand, they were not preceded by religious representations borne (*charriées*) by an older culture that these limit-expressions come to correct. It is the task of hermeneutics to correlate what these limit-expressions intend with human experience in its religious quality and with the available representations already qualified as religious by our culture. In brief, it is in configuring the most tenacious and most dense human hope, and by rectifying traditional religious representations, that limit-expressions continue their course beyond a narrative. As Almeida says, we leave the structural analysis of isolated sequences for the interpretation that is at work in the text as a whole. We are now leaving the interpretation internal to the text for a hermeneutic of the text's *referential intentionality.* But the passage from the text to life, which governs the passage from the semiotic phase of interpretation to its existential phase, is still guided by something that takes place in the text that, with Ladrière and Almeida, I have called the text's horizon of structuration. The new configurations of people's religious experiences and the rectifications of their representations are still accompanied by the new restructuration that the expression-enigma "kingdom of God" and others similar to it impose on the signifying dynamism working in the narrative-parables. In short, it is still the parabolizing of the narrative, brought to its highest degree of incandescence, that gives rise to the transition from semiotic interpretation to existential interpretation. Here is where we pass from the work of imagination *in* the text to the work of imagination *about* the text.

And here is where our inquiry guided by the idea of intertextuality must end, at least for the moment.

- 9 -

Biblical Time

There are few problems that have given rise to so many vain polemics and have finally led to so many misunderstandings as has the comparison between the biblical conception of time and the Hellenic (or Greco-Latin) one. And yet it was only a few decades ago that there seemed to be, if not a consensus, at least a presumption in favor of the radically dichotomous thesis of the Norwegian theologian Thorlief Boman in his *Hebrew Thought Compared with Greek.*[1] Exegetes as eminent as Gerhard von Rad for the Old Testament and Rudolf Bultmann for the New, followed by most of the contributors to Gerhard Kittel's *Theological Dictionary of the New Testament,* all seemed to lend support to this thesis by opposing the historical conception of the Hebrews and the first Christians as a whole to the cosmological conception of the Greeks and, more generally, the primacy of the ear and hearing for the former as opposed to the primacy given the eye and vision by the Greeks. Oscar Cullmann, in *Christ and Time* (first published in 1946),[2] reinforced this overall opposition by opposing the Greek cyclical time of ceremonies and festivals to the linear time of the Bible, a time marked out by decisive events culminating in the incarnation, which henceforth divides time in two, with one of its arrows pointing toward the pole of creation, the other toward the pole of the apocalypse. In this way, biblical *kairos* and Greek *chronos* were radically distinguished from each other.

Why then speak here of misunderstanding and deception?

Because it has become more and more apparent that the question itself was badly posed. Was there really, people began to ask, something like a

Originally published as "Temps biblique," *Archivio di filosofia* 53 (1985): 29–35; a slightly different version of the text was included in "Time and Narrative in the Bible: Toward a Narrative Theology," unpublished manuscript, Sarum Lectures, Oxford, 1980; printed with permission.

1. Thorlief Boman, *Hebrew Thought Compared with Greek,* trans. Jules L. Moreau (London: SCM Press; Philadelphia: Westminster Press, 1960); German original: *Das Hebraische Denken im Vergleich mit dem Griechischen* (Göttingen: Vandenhoeck & Ruprecht, 1952; 2d ed. 1954).

2. Oscar Cullmann, *Christ and Time: The Primitive Christian Conception of Time and History,* rev. ed., trans. Floyd V. Filson (Philadelphia: Westminster Press, 1964).

Greek and a biblical conception of time? If we take a brief and summary look at the question as it applies to the Greek side, we see that a threefold distinction imposes itself.

First, it is necessary to make a distinction between, on the one hand, popular religion and the mystery cults, and, on the other hand, that nebulous configuration we designate by the title "Greek thought." Temporal implications may be discerned on the side of the festivals and initiatory rites that do recall the cyclical time of other great cultures, but we do not find the same thing as regards the Greek thinkers.

Second, among the Greek thinkers themselves it is necessary to respect the incredible diversity found among the poets, the historians, and the philosophers. In this regard, the great Italian scholar Arnoldo Momigliano, in his 1966 article "Time in Ancient Historiography," reprinted in his *Essays in Ancient and Modern Historiography,* has emphasized the absence of a conception of the whole of time in the historians of antiquity.[3] All of them work with a limited segment of time and on the basis of documents they think worthy of their confidence. What is more, their historical practice seems to stem from a struggle against forgetfulness, hence obliquely as against time conceived of as the great destroyer. However, these historians do not inquire thematically into the relationship between the succession of events and a universal chronology or even into the principle of synchrony between the respective histories of cities or people they tell. And the question of the relation between history as whole and the cosmos is totally foreign to them, which is all the more reason why it is vain to seek a cyclical conception of time in their work.

Third, it is important not to confuse the implicit conceptions of time that the historian of ideas may reconstruct from the epic or tragic poets or the historians through comparison with the philosophers, and the attempts at an explicit definition of time that we can read in Plato's *Timaeus,* Aristotle's *Physics,* or certain of the Stoic and Epicurean texts. It is one thing for a poetic text, for example, to imply a conception of time that is never thematized as such and another thing completely to pose the question What is time? and then answer it with a concept, whether it be a question of defining physical time or of articulating a coherent vision of progress or decadence or of proposing the answer of a personal form of wisdom to the lived experience of the past, the present, and the future.

Hence, when we speak of a Greek conception of time we must avoid the threefold error of reducing the cultural dimension to a literary factor, this literary factor to some philosophical expression, and this philosophical expression to some explicit thesis, even that of Plato or Aristotle.

---

3. Arnoldo Momigliano, *Essays in Ancient and Modern Historiography* (Oxford: Basil Blackwell, 1977), 179–204.

If such is the case on the side of Hellenism, we must undertake a parallel dismantling on the Hebraic and ancient Christian side as well, and begin by distinguishing among the different epochs, settings, and authors. This is a necessary condition if we want to compare what can really be compared. Now if we take up the three levels I have mentioned from the Greek side—religion, nonphilosophical thought, and philosophy properly speaking—resemblances and differences may appear on a level that we do not find on the other side.

For example, on the cultural level, we certainly do find, in the periodic return of the ceremonies of the Hebrew New Year, the suggestion of a cyclic conception quite comparable to the one that we encounter in all those cultures where a signification of regeneration is attached to the commemoration of the founding acts that happened *in illo tempore,* to use Mircea Eliade's categories and vocabulary. However, there is an abyss between what I have just called the suggestion of a cyclical conception and the explicit profession of such a doctrine. Moreover, on the thematic plane, there are no doubt as many differences as resemblances between reminiscence in the Hellenic sense, such as Jean-Pierre Vernant has evoked it in his *Myth and Society in Ancient Greece,* and the vehement "remember" of Deuteronomy.[4] I shall return to this later. But at least the comparison is a homogeneous one between cultural phenomena of the same order.

Undoubtedly it is on the second level, that of nonphilosophical thought, that the most significant resemblances and differences are revealed. Thus, Momigliano, in the article I referred to earlier, undertakes a term-by-term comparison between the Greek and the biblical historians, and he draws a series of differentiating features from this comparison that have little to do with the alleged opposition between cyclical and linear time. Again, I shall return to this later in an analysis of the narrative composition of the Scriptures.

But if a homogeneous comparison can be set up, first on the cultural level, then on the level of nonphilosophical thought (to use a negative characteristic that applies both to poetry and to history), the same thing no longer applies on the third level, that of philosophical formulations. We must admit that on this level there is a total dysymmetry. What we call Hebraic thought, including its wisdom literature, offers no parallel to the distinction between philosophy and nonphilosophy, so characteristic of the Greek world. And it is on this level that the problems have been most badly posed. As James Barr has shown in his *Biblical Words for Time,* it is totally improper to seek in semantics, and even more so in etymology, a Hebraic equivalent for the Greek speculation arising from the question

---

4. Jean-Pierre Vernant, *Myth and Society in Ancient Greece,* trans. Janet Lloyd (Atlantic Highlands, N.J.: Humanities Press, 1980).

ti ho chronos?[5] In this regard, the method used in Kittel's dictionary is much to be criticized, as is that of Cullmann, especially when he thinks he has found a stable opposition between the biblical and more particularly the New Testament use of *kairos* and the Greek *chronos*. We have to turn our backs resolutely on any attempt to weigh the thematic definitions applied to time such as we find them in the Greek philosophers and exegetical constructions based upon just vocabulary and the contextual values of individual words.

Now it is by taking into account these critical remarks that I should like to propose here an approach limited to just the biblical domain and based on the following methodological rules. (1) Giving up the idea of drawing from the Bible a *concept* of time capable of entering into competition with that of the Greek philosophers, I shall attempt to disengage the temporality implied by, and in a way brought about by, the Bible as Scripture. (2) For this investigation I shall take as my guide the literary genres of the Bible, and behind these literary genres the *acts of discourse* characteristic of the Bible: narrations, legislations, prophecies, wisdom sayings and literature, hymns and psalms, and I shall attempt to establish a correlation between the structure of these acts of discourse and that of the temporality implied by or brought about by the literary genre corresponding to these respective acts of discourse. (3) Beyond this correlation between the structure of acts of discourse and the structure of certain temporal qualities, I will be attentive to the "interweaving" of such acts of discourse and their corresponding temporal qualities. More precisely, I shall place the accent on the interweaving of narrative and nonnarrative texts, as is indicated by the enumeration of literary genres and their corresponding acts of discourse I have just given. I cannot overemphasize that the biblical narratives, whether it be a question of the exodus or the story of Jesus, always stand in a dialectical relation with the other literary elements that, even when they are entirely nonnarrative, as in the wisdom writings and the Psalms, do include a specifically temporal dimension. The preliminary sketch that follows is entirely devoted to the interweaving of the temporalities corresponding to this interweaving of literary genres and the acts of discourse constitutive of these genres. (4) My investigation of this interweaving brings into play a reading of the biblical writings laid out as one vast "intertext." This reading must of course take into account the historical-critical method, but it cannot be reduced to it. Where the historical-critical method focuses on the differences between the diverse literary layers brought together in the final redaction, in order to reestablish the *Sitz-im-Leben* of this or that narrative or this or that institution, the reading I am proposing begins from the fact that the meaning of the recounted events and the proclaimed institutions

---

5. James Barr, *Biblical Words for Time* (Naperville, Ill.: A. R. Allenson, 1962).

has become detached from its original *Sitz-im-Leben* by becoming part of Scripture, and this Scripture has so to speak substituted what we may call a *Sitz-im-Wort* for the original *Sitz-im-Leben*. My reading shall begin from here, from the *Sitz-im-Wort* of events, actions, and institutions that have lost their initial roots and that, as a consequence, now have a *textual* existence. It is this textual status of the narratives, laws, prophecies, wisdom sayings, and hymns that makes these texts contemporary with one another in the act of reading. This synchronic reading is called for to complete the diachronic approach of the historical-critical method. This synchronic reading is at the same time an intertextual reading, in the sense that, once they are apprehended as a whole, these texts of different origins and intentions work on one another, deplacing their respective intentions and points, and they mutually borrow their dynamism from one another. So read, the Bible becomes a great living intertext, which is the place, the space for a labor of the text on itself. My reading, in short, seeks to grasp this labor of the text upon itself through an act of reconstructive imagination.

Briefly stated, these are the most important methodological decisions that preside over my investigation of the interweaving of temporalities of different qualities, underlying the interweaving of the literary genres, or better the acts of discourse in the Bible—an interweaving constitutive of the biblical intertext. In other words, I propose to show how a time of narratives, a time of laws, a time of prophecies, a time of wisdom sayings, and a time of hymns mutually affect one another in such a way as to compose the intertextual "model" designated as "biblical time."

Narratives and Laws

That the narrative genre and the act of discourse consisting of telling a story constitute the genre and the act of discourse at the base of an inquiry into biblical time should surprise no one. The Yahwist document, since Wellhausen commonly called the J document, gives ample testimony for such a choice. What is more, the way the narratives of the Pentateuch are ordered seems to support those exegetes who emphasize linearity as the primary characteristic of narrative time. Indeed, the J writer does apportion along a single line the deliverance from Egypt, the march in the desert, the episode at Sinai, the remainder of the time in the desert, and the entry into the promised land. Within the gravitational space constituted by the major narratives of deliverance, he also includes the giving of the law, the occupation of the land, and the traditions of the patriarchs. And to this protohistory he adds a narrative preface in the form of a creation narrative, spread out over seven days, along with a history of the decadence of the human species, which is interrupted by and rebegun by the first salvific act with a historical character, the election of Abraham. In other words, the narrativization invades everything, bringing together and arranging within a single chronology narrative modes that, in the words of James Barr, have extremely varying relations of distance in relation to what the Greeks conceived of as historiography. And other writers set end to end other narratives relative to the Davidic monarchy and the preeminence of the temple at Jerusalem over all the other cultic locations and acts.

This narrative framework is not sufficient to justify contemporary attempts to establish a purely narrative theology, however. The first phenomenon of intertextuality that I must insist upon with force obliges us to temper this ambition from now on. It has to do with the intersection between the narratives and the laws in the J document. This intersection between the narrative and the prescriptive is so primitive that we do not know of any literary state of the text where the narratives would constitute a separate genre. Even the hypothesis, so strongly embraced by von Rad and since then so strongly contested, that the traditions relative to Sinai and its laws must have had a distinct origin and must have been subsequently interpolated into the narrative of deliverance, the desert, and the conquest, even for this hypothesis the decisive fact is that the Yahwist school apprehended as one indivisible whole, as one unknotable knot, the whole constituted by the laws and the narratives. And from this union results both a narrativization of ethics and an ethicization of the narratives. A narrativization of ethics in the sense that the giving of the law itself becomes a memorable event that calls for its narration, and that demands to be told and retold, as Deuteronomy loves to emphasize. Because of this, the law is not atemporal: it is marked by the circumstances of this giving and by the very places of its injunctions, the desert, the mountain, the borders of Jordan. However, the opposite is no less important. The instruction issuing from the successive legislations, unified under the emblem of Sinai and Moses, colors the narratives themselves. These narratives, under the pressure of the prescriptive, become narratives of the march of a people with God under the sign of obedience and disobedience. This inclusion of the narrative in the prescriptive, reciprocal to the inverse inclusion, is pushed so far that in the tradition of Judaism, even before the closing of the canon, the narrative does not constitute a separate genre. There is just the Torah—the instruction—to which are added the Prophets and the other books, principally the writings of the sages and the psalms. One result is that the historiography stemming from the Deuteronomic school, then from the Priestly document, and then from the Chronicler will be a history of disobedience, a history that is *ethicized* throughout.

But what is the result of this intersection of literary genres and acts of discourse for understanding biblical time? Essentially, that the law qualifies not just the event of its giving but all the narratives in which this giving is encased, in such a way that the founding events become events that do not pass away but remain. The law, in effect, brings with it the dimension of an *irrevocable anteriority,* of a past prior to every past, something that the Hebrew Bible expresses concretely in its theology of the covenant in speaking of God's faithfulness. And at the same time, this ethical anteriority affects the narrative anteriority in such a way that the narrative becomes something more than pure linearity. In *Old and New in Interpretation,* James Barr underlines this aspect of the biblical narratives, which he calls the cumulative aspect of the stories told.[6] According to this schema, the events are not simply added to one another, but in each instance they augment the meaning of the preceding events. Here is one of the keys to the Yahwist's work of composition. Yahweh is always the one who is *already* known and the one whom new encounters, new words, and new actions make differently and better known. The God of the burning bush was already the God of the Patriarchs (even if, for a historical-critical approach, the term "God of the Fathers" might once have designated different tribal divinities). By tying the Patriarchs to one another with a genealogical bond, by establishing a link of correspondence between the promises made to the Patriarchs and those made to Israel as a whole, and then by linking together the successive covenants by the same principle of correspondence, the Yahwist composes a cumulative history accompanied by a form of understanding that is itself cumulative about who Yahweh is. I emphasize this feature because it belongs to a narrative that employs a strong ethical coloration to present this structure of a cumulative history. This feature is like the mark of the irrevocable anteriority of the law on the narrative anteriority that, without the former, would dissipate into the "one time" and "never again." The community that tells (and tells itself) the narratives of deliverance and of the giving of the law and the land takes on its quite peculiar identity—an identity that we may say is indivisibly narrative and ethical at the same time—from the traditions that flow from this conjunction of ethical anteriority and narrative anteriority.

The Traditional Narratives and the Message of the Prophets

The second step in our traversal of the biblical texts brings us to the prophets, from Amos and Hosea to Zechariah. No reading of the Bible—whether historical or structural—can fail to inquire into the meaning that results from the collision between the mass of prophetic writings and the whole constituted by the narratives and the law. Here I am interested in

---

6. James Barr, *Old and New in Interpretation: A Study of the Two Testaments* (London: SCM Press, 1966).

this confrontation only from the point of view of its temporal implications, however.

I have just spoken of a confrontation. In fact the irruption of the prophetic message produces a break in the temporal structure of the tradition. We pass right by the phenomenon in question if we begin by taking up the aspect of "prediction" in prophecy. We would then be guided by the trivial idea that the tradition looks back toward the past and prophecy looks forward toward the future. But the tradition also looks toward the future. In founding the identity of the people, it projects itself toward the future in the form of an unuprootable confidence in a security that cannot fail. But it is precisely this assurance, transformed into a possession, that the prophet Amos denounces when he proclaims vehemently that the Day of Yahweh will not be a day of joy but one of terror and mourning. Hence it is in relation to this illusory projection of the tradition about the future that the prophet takes his stand. And he does so in opposing to this fallacious assurance the true reading of the present situation. It is in this sense that we can say that the first temporal structure of prophecy is not foresight but the irruption of real history, or, to put it another way, the confrontation of an ideological use of the tradition with a truthful discernment of historical actuality.[7]

This dimension of reality and actuality is revealed through a number of features. First, the prophet is present in his words, at the very moment when he says, "Thus says another." Indeed, it is in this moment that Hosea speaks of Hosea and Isaiah of Isaiah, whereas the voice that speaks of Moses in the great narrative tradition is silent—only historical criticism can reconstruct a J writer, then E, D, and so on. But all these figures are absent from the text of which they are the presumed authors, and history reaches them only as the "implied authors" of a narrative that unfolds by itself. To this first feature is linked the fact that, not content to speak for themselves, the prophets, since Amos, wrote down their prophecies. The present of prophecy is thus signed and cosigned as before a notary public. It is to this present of prophecy that the deciphering of historical actuality by the prophets is to be linked.

The shock of the collision between this deciphered actuality and the tradition lies in the fact that the prophets before the exile perceived, in a future that for them was already on its way toward the present, the *end* of the covenant and hence of the people of the covenant. What is rightly called the prophecy of misfortune, in order to oppose it to the prophecy of redemption found in the prophets of the exile and the return, consists in the fact that these prophets did not limit themselves to announcing this or that catastrophe but the end, the close of a history, of that history in

---

7. See Paul Beauchamp, *L'Un et l'autre Testament: Essai de lecture* (Paris: Seuil, 1977).

fact to which the narratives and the laws give the promise of an unbreakable duration. Let us linger a moment over the significance of this prophecy of misfortune from the point of view of temporal structures. In announcing the imminence of the end of the covenant and of the people of the covenant, prophecy has a profound effect upon the traditional narrative and transforms its intention radically. Past history is suddenly perceived, through anticipation, as already closed. And at the same time, it is divested of its founding function. What earlier I called a narrative and ethical identity is suddenly uprooted by the announcement of the close of all history engendered by the historical narratives. To my knowledge no other culture exists that has so integrated within the narrative and ethical constitution of its identity such a tragic break or interruption.

But a new reversal, a reversal of the reversal, is produced with the prophets of salvation, who gradually win out over the prophecies of misfortune, beginning already with Jeremiah and Ezekiel, at the time of the exile, and then in a decisive fashion during the period of the second temple, especially with Second Isaiah. For us, who are interested in a synchronic reading of the biblical intertext, what is most important is not this progressive replacement of one form of prophecy with another so much as this dialectic of reversal and its role in the constituting of biblical time. The clearest temporal signification of this dialectic lies in three things. First, that the promise of life is announced as being beyond a "piece of nothingness," to use a striking expression of André Neher in his wonderful book on Amos.[8] In other words, the tragedy of interruption is integrated as a necessary negative moment into the dialectic of time. Next, that the future is essentially anticipated as something new. The new covenant, Jeremiah and Ezekiel announce, is not written on stone but on hearts. A temporal logic is thereby engendered that, in the time of the early church, will expand into the temporal schema that opposes—and composes—the Old and the New Testaments. However, the third moment of this dialectic is the most surprising one of all. The new is not anticipated as radically different but as a sort of creative repetition of the old. Very concretely, the prophets of the exile and the postexile anticipated the return as a restoration, and they described this restoration in advance as a new exodus, a new desert, a new Sinai, a new Zion, a new Davidic descendance, and so on. This is why I risked using the expression "creative repetition" to describe this anticipation. This mode of thought dominates the whole work of Second Isaiah.

A few centuries later, the early church will turn this procedure into a hermeneutic and find in it the basic structures of its typological reading of the Old Testament. This development authorizes us to speak, with a certain

---

8. André Neher, *Amos: Contribution a l'étude du prophétisme* (Paris: Presses Universitaires de France, 1955).

prudence to be sure, because of the retrospective use of the term, of an interpretation of the New in terms of the Old already at work in the Old Testament.

This temporal dialectic inherent in prophecy cannot fail to affect all the writings that later tradition placed under the title Torah, which unites the narratives and the laws in that inseparable unity I described earlier. When set within the gravitational space of prophecy, the Torah itself acquires a new temporal meaning. For a reading that moves backward, prophetic discourse draws from the traditional discourse an unforeseen potential of hope. This is unexpected insofar as the promise contained in the tradition itself now appears as not saturated by prior accomplishments, whether we refer to the installation in Canaan or the establishment of the Davidic monarchy. Under the pressure of prophecy, the promise appears as essentially unfulfilled. In other words, narrative when touched by prophetic eschatology liberates a potential of hope, beyond the closure of the established tradition. And the typological recovery of figures borrowed from the traditional narrative rests upon no other principle. The past is not simply exhausted, as the prophets of misfortune say; rather, it leaves behind a storehouse of inexhaustible potentialities. But it requires prophecy and its eschatology to open this initial surplus of meaning that, so to speak, lies dreaming in the traditional narrative.

The Time of Wisdom: The Everyday and the Immemorial

Our third step brings us to a set of clearly nonnarrative writings, the wisdom writings. Commentators have not failed to underscore the independence of wisdom in relation to every narrative. One might conclude that these writings fall outside the bounds of our inquiry. But such is not the case. For, although nonnarrative, these writings nonetheless do have their own temporality. For a structural reading, the important question is therefore to understand how this specific temporality affects the temporalities of the narratives, the laws, and the prophecies, inasmuch as these different kinds of texts are brought together in the same book. Thanks to this new contrast with writings that, in one way or another, are marked with a past or a future history, we see that the wisdom writings themselves are not interested in history, but that the same thing cannot be said about time. Even if, for the history of redaction, we have to do here with heterogeneous texts, for a structural reading what is important is the interweaving of these texts in reading and therefore the intersection of their respective temporalities.

Let us follow a course that begins with Proverbs, moves on to the book of Job, and ends with Qoheleth, or the book of Ecclesiastes. This course will make us traverse quite different qualities of temporality.

I am first of all struck by the way in which the proverbs, in spite of their modesty, conjoin in a striking way the everyday and the immemorial. The everyday is the time of works and days. It is punctuated by those maxims that tell how to conjoin a righteous heart and a happy life. This time of the everyday ignores the great events that make history. It is the time of "every day." And this time without events does not get narrated. It is spoken of in proverbs. "The smallest kind of wisdom" only requires "the smallest coin of poetry," says Paul Beauchamp in an apt expression. And yet it is by way of the everyday that wisdom brings to light the immemorial, that is, what, as ageless, has "always existed."

There is nothing surprising therefore about what wisdom, apparently turning its back on narrative, takes as its beginning. We all know many texts—Prov. 8:22-32 in particular—that have allowed commentators to speak of a "hypostasis" of wisdom. At this stage, the immemorial is not just what Wisdom says but Wisdom itself when it speaks. And so conceived as one and eternal, Wisdom allowed the sages to explore the wide speculative domain that they shared with every people, thereby allowing them to share in the wisdom of the nations.

It is under the sign of this sharing in the wisdom of the ancient Orient that wisdom passes from the proverb to radical questioning. In this way, the advice that claims to regulate the good life is unavoidably thrown into question as soon as a look at the world shows that the practice of good not only does not infallibly lead to happiness but is rarely obtained. The proverb then gives way to the enigma, as soon as the question takes over from the giving of advice. Why, ask the sages, do the evil prosper and the righteous suffer? Why? For how long? complain the psalms. The book of Job, quite clearly, in our Bible is the leading example of this quarrel, of this judicial process that confronts humankind and God.

My problem here is not to examine to what point the book of Job gives an "answer" to the question that sets it in motion. Rather my problem is that of the destiny of the immemorial once wisdom is so caught up by the weight of the question and dragged toward the abyss. The immemorial here is the human condition once it is confronted with what Karl Jaspers called limit-situations: struggle, the fault, failure, suffering. However much humankind may change, these limit-situations have something of the immutable, or, to put it a better way, of the perdurable and the sempiternal about them. This is why the discourse that discusses these enigmas is itself ageless. In a certain way, here, everything has been said. This is the feature that makes this discourse foreign to narrative. Narrative founded the narrative identity of a particular people. Wisdom addresses itself to the human condition in its universal aspect. In Job it depicts a suffering hero, stripped of all historical bonds to any people. But in so doing, it addresses every one by means of and beyond this one Jew.

Wisdom may also take another course than that of the book of Job. With Qoheleth it may return toward the everyday. But this is not the same everyday as for Proverbs, which was the everyday prior to a meditation on death. The everyday of Qoheleth is the everyday as rediscovered by someone who has looked death in the face and renounced knowing. It is the everyday under the sign of not knowing. Made modest, divested of its pomp, wisdom is then tempted to an excess of humility. The wise person who does not know feels discharged of the responsibility of carrying history on his or her shoulders. Hence that person is tempted to reduce the space of life to an everyday round deprived of historicity: "There is nothing new under the sun." Here we are at the antipodes of narrative, and at the same time we have reached the limits of the Book.

Yet, although we have gone beyond narrative, we have not gone beyond time.

In the first place, the immemorial time of wisdom rejoins the ethical anteriority not only of the law or instruction but of the promise that the recounted events put to the test. In this way, this immemorial time reinforces the tendency of the traditional narratives to become archetypal, whether we think of the exodus, which the parenesis of Deuteronomy sets up as the paradigm of all deliverances, or of the giving of the successive legislations, condensed into the equally paradigmatic figure of Moses. Immemorial time in the end rejoins the deep temporality of the creation narratives, closer to myth than to saga, to the point that some exegetes have considered these narratives of creation and the fall as fragments of a narrativized wisdom or as narratives with a sapiential tone, which amounts to the same thing. It is not just the cumulative character of the narratives akin to sagas that we may take as a narrative equivalent of a wisdom apparently without events, however. We may also attribute the typological tendency, sketched out in Deutero-Isaiah and culminating in the New Testament writers, to the labor of the spirit of wisdom at the very heart of the narratives. In all these ways, the immemorial time of wisdom reinforces all the nonlinear features of the great Yahwist narrative. And this cannot fail to affect the very notion of a history of salvation as it triumphs in the work of the evangelist Luke, which Cullmann believed he could project onto the unilinear trajectory of time.

Here we attain the deep level where the narrative and the nonnarrative interweave and exchange their respective powers of temporalization.

The Hymn

I do not wish to conclude without having said at least a few words about the time of the hymn, of the psalms, which the Christian church incorporated into its own liturgy and which has accompanied so many solitary readings as well. Yes, there is a time of the psalms, which in a way envelops all the other temporalities that we have considered so far. This time is that of today *and* every day. The historical-critical method as we find it applied in Sigmund Mowinckel's still admirable *The Psalms in Israel's Worship* has taught us to recognize the cultic function of the reciting and the singing of the psalms.[9] It is the privilege of worship to reactualize salvation, to reiterate the creation, to remember the exodus and the entry into the promised land, to renew the proclamation of the law, and to repeat the promises. This function of reactualization is indicated grammatically by the use of "I" and "we," which, after having once referred to the king, have become placeholders capable of being occupied by whoever, individual or community, assumes the speaker's position. We can thus understand how praise can include the recitation of the epic history and the time of recitation can envelop the time of the narrative. The rhetorical clause, so studied by scholars, "Blessed be you, you *who* brought us out of Egypt, ... blessed be you ... *because* you have delivered us," bears witness to this. As does the phrase, "I thank you, O Yahweh, *for* you have rescued me." In this way, the psalm is a recapitulation in the present time of worship and prayer of all the specific temporalities of the narratives, the law, and the Prophets. Everything said in them is taken up again in the hymnic utterance borne by an "I" or a "we." In particular, as regards narrative, it is by making it a memory that the hymn takes up and repeats the narration. This inclusion of the narrative in the hymn marks the ultimate transfiguration of the narrative that our inquiry today can consider. And the repetition of the law in memory is no different. It is this model of a hymnic repetition of the law that we find realized in the parenesis of Deuteronomy. It is no accident that we rediscover there, driven home again and again, the word "today." Today is the day when it is important to remember the commandments, especially the first one, which contains all the others. The parenesis brings about a doubling here, not of the law in its content, to which it adds nothing, but of the offering and the proclamation of the law. Whence comes the very name Deuteronomy: the reiterated law.

This, briefly, is the "model" of temporality that a synchronic and intertextual reading of the Hebrew Bible may recompose. Narrative and the time of narrative—with their apparent linearity—constitute only its most visible framework. But the teaching of these narratives, their truth for us today, requires the mediation of all the other literary genres and all the other acts of discourse interweaving throughout the canonical texts. This is why the project of a merely narrative theology is a chimera. What it fundamentally fails to understand is first the primitive overlapping of narrative

---

9. Sigmund Mowinckel, *The Psalms in Israel's Worship,* trans. D. R. Ap-Thomas (Nashville: Abingdon, 1962).

and law in the Torah, then the dialectic between the whole of tradition as prescriptive as well as narrative with prophecy and its eschatological indication. Next, a simple narrative theology misses the deepening of the transitory character of historical accomplishments through the immemorial time of wisdom and, finally, and most important of all, the powerful recapitulation of all these figures of time in the "today" of the hymn. To put it another way, the model of biblical time rests on the polarity between narrative and hymn and on the mediation brought about between telling and praising by the law and its temporal anteriority, prophecy and its eschatological time, and by wisdom and its immemorial time.

It would be a new task to show how the Christian kerygma transforms this model of biblical time without fundamentally altering it. And it would be a further, just as complicated, task to take up again the irritating problem of the resemblances and differences between Hellenic and biblical time, from where my introductory remarks left it. But at least we have prepared the terrain for a more fruitful confrontation between them, by having shown not just their extreme complexity but also the subtle coherence of what as a form of shorthand we call "biblical time."

– 10 –

Interpretive Narrative

This chapter is devoted to a category of narratives that we may call interpretive narratives. These are narratives in which the ideological interpretation these narratives wish to convey is not superimposed on the narrative by the narrator but is, instead, incorporated into the very strategy of the narrative. I shall take as an example of such narratives the passion narratives in the Synoptic Gospels, which seem to me particularly apt for illustrating this specific literary category. In them, the kerygmatic proclamation makes specific what, a moment ago, I called, in a neutral sense, an ideological interpretation, because this interpretation results directly from the narrative configuration. Indeed, as one literary critic, Frank Kermode, has pointed out, a noteworthy feature of the Gospel of Mark is that it functions like a midrash; that is, simply as a narrative it exercises an interpretive function.[1] It is this idea that a narrative can have an interpretive function in relation to its own kerygmatic intention that will serve as a guideline for my analysis. Having developed this directing idea in the first part of my remarks, I shall then subordinate it in the second part to an inventory of the procedures and strategies brought to light by contemporary theory of narrative.

From Kerygma to Narrative

Let me begin by indicating again the guiding idea behind my remarks, namely, that the juncture between exegesis and theology, before being a work of interpretation applied *to* the text, already functions *in* the text if this text is a narrative with an interpretive function.

This type of narrative is not just limited to the Gospels. In *The Art of*

Reprinted with permission from *The Book and the Text: The Bible and Literary Theory*, ed. Regina M. Schwartz (Oxford: Basil Blackwell, 1990), 237–57.

1. Frank Kermode, *The Genesis of Secrecy: On the Interpretation of Narrative* (Cambridge, Mass.: Harvard Univ. Press, 1979).

Biblical Narrative, Robert Alter has applied a strictly literary approach, which places between parentheses the historical-critical method and any attempt to sort the text into sources, strata, borrowings, and so on, to a number of narratives taken from the Hebrew Bible, in order to set into relief the art of literary composition that presides over the redaction of the text as we now read it.[2] He notes in this regard that if literary analysis cannot ignore the history of tradition and of redaction, in return it must hold that this work of identifying sources (J, E, D, P) itself rests upon unacknowledged, and generally naive, literary criteria. For example, that the oldest text must be the shortest one, the one that presents no interruption or doubling, the one that is clearly delimited and coherent. However, these criteria slight the rich resources of what he calls "historicized prose fiction,"[3] resources that the modern novel has made us more aware of, and resources that a purely literary study of the Bible shows its astounding mastery of. The most important lesson to be gained from Alter's work—a lesson that had already been formulated with much power by Eric Auerbach in his *Mimesis*[4]—is that it is precisely the narrative composition, the organizing of the events in the narrative, that is the vehicle for, or, better, that foments, the theological interpretation. He adds that it is the fullest grasping of this literary art that proceeds to the sharpest perception of the theological intention.[5] What struck Alter in the more dramatic of these narratives is the fact that the text aims at communicating the conviction that the divine plan, although ineluctable, gets realized only by means of what he calls "the refractory nature of man."[6] These are not pious stories; they are stories of cunning and murder, stories where the right of primogeniture is scoffed at, where the election of the hero depends on the oblique maneuvers of an ambitious young man such as David. Taking this problem up from the other end, we might say that a theology that confronts the inevitability of the divine plan with the refractory nature of human actions and passions is a theology that engenders narrative; better, it is a theology that calls for the narrative mode as its major hermeneutical mode, and it does so in virtue of the paradoxical and—why not?—the aporetic character of such a theology that pays no attention to speculative dialectic. Thus the closing words of Alter's book are relevant to our investigation: "It is in the stubbornness of human individuality that each man and woman encoun-

---

2. Robert Alter, *The Art of Biblical Narrative* (New York: Basic Books, 1981).
3. Ibid., 24.
4. Eric Auerbach, *Mimesis: The Representation of Reality in Western Literature,* trans. Willard R. Trask (Princeton, N.J.: Princeton Univ. Press, 1953).
5. His most striking example is drawn from legendary narratives, such as the stories about Joseph, or from stories that come close to being chronicles, such as the story of the ascension of David to power or the well-known narratives about his succession.
6. Alter, *Art of Biblical Narrative,* 33.

ters God or ignores Him, responds to or resists Him" in "the perilously momentous realm of history."[7]

We have yet to see what narrative constraints of prose fiction these ingenious writers treated both as conventions to be respected and as norms to transgress, within the very process of figurizing these constraints. This is what Alter undertakes to discover in his book, where he emphasizes the art of reticence, the roles of the interior monologue and indirect discourse, and, above all, the position of the omniscient narrator. However, the most important thing is the appropriate character of these narrative techniques as regards the hermeneutical problem of the collusion between the inevitable divine plan and the unpredictability of human contingency.

My question is whether the passion narratives have a comparable function, as regards the close imbrication of theology within the narrative, and whether the problem is not to bring into relation the theological function and the narrative structure, whether it be a deep or a surface structure, so as to evaluate appreciatively the appropriateness of this structure for this function. Indeed, it seems to me that the most striking feature of the Gospels' narrative lies in the indissociable union of the kerygmatic and the narrative aspects. But it is not sufficient just to assert this, we have also to show by what literary procedure the form of the Gospels' narrative is obtained, that is, the form of a kerygmatized narrative or a narrativized kerygma.

Let me say something first, though, about the term "kerygmatic" and about its relation to the term "theological," applied by both Auerbach and Alter to some of the Hebraic narratives. Three features of the Gospels' narratives, which I will order in terms of an increasing difference, indicate the resemblances and the differences between these two terms.

First, the Christian kerygma prolongs the biblical message insofar as it too confronts the inevitability of the divine plan and the contingency of human action. Later, we shall see that the core of the passion narratives may be summed up in the phrase "the Son of Man had to be betrayed." This formula, which underscores the inevitability of a certain course of events, also depends upon a narrative about treason, denial, abandonment, and flight, which testifies to the refractory nature of human beings, the privileged pathway for the inevitable plan. Thus, in the passion narratives, a narrative mediation similar to the one described by Alter gets inserted between the statement that "the Son of Man had to be betrayed into the hands of sinners" and the contingency of "and Judas drew near to him." The verb "betrayed" has the double sense of something inevitable and of recalcitrance. Through this first trait, the passion narratives are inscribed within the larger biblical orbit insofar as, in the absence of any speculative

7. Ibid., 189.

mediation in a Hegelian fashion, the narrative mediation brings about the unity of the supratemporal and the intratemporal.

A second feature completes the first one at the same time that it corrects it. What is at issue is not a theology but a Christology—or, rather, a number of Christologies. In this regard, it is the history of forms—and its residues, the history of traditions and the history of redaction—that makes us attentive to the difference between the respective christological projects of the four Gospels. However, only literary analysis shows that it is across the specificity of the narrative composition of each Gospel that its corresponding christological project can be discerned, no matter what was its polemical or apologetic aspect in relation to the ecclesial disputes of the day. This tie between the narrative and its *Sitz-im-Leben* is surely the concern of the historical-critical method, but the way in which this polemic or apologetic project is brought to discourse is a matter for a literary analysis bearing on the narrativization of the kerygma. Only then does what we might call the *Sitz-im-Wort* of the reported events make sense.

If the narrative mediation characteristic of the Gospels in general and of each Gospel in particular prolongs the Hebraic theologoumen of a divine plan carried through in spite of... or thanks to... our human refractory nature (our first trait), and if, furthermore, this mediation specifies the theological project as a christological one (our second trait), we may ask in the third place whether there is not something in the christological kerygma that calls for narrative, in an absolutely specific way. Ernst Käsemann has emphasized this point with much force. The most primitive kerygma that the historical-critical method can reconstitute does not oppose the Christ of faith to the Jesus of history, but rather bears witness to their identity. The Christ who speaks to the enthusiastic believers, the charismatics of the primitive assemblies, is held to be identical with the Jesus about whom there circulate narratives having to do with his teaching, his miracles, his confrontations with this or that group, including his own disciples. In producing a narrative with a kerygmatic weight, the project of narrativizing the kerygma seems well anchored in the Christian kerygma in its most definite specificity. Do we not have one indication of this in the least narrativized proclamations, such as in 1 Cor. 15:3-8, where we read "that Christ died for our sins in accordance with the scriptures, that he was buried, that he was raised on the third day in accordance with the scriptures, and that he appeared to Cephas, then to the twelve"? That this is the same kerygma that we discern in the filigree of the Gospel of Mark, for example, is a disputed question. But that the kerygma of 1 Corinthians 15 contains a minimum of narrativization is what matters to our investigation. Let us look closer at this passage. We find four verbs in the aorist of narration, constituting the beginning of a narrative chain and punctuating the proclamation. We may see in this a call for narrative, which, without being the only provocation to narration, can be taken at least as a condition *sine qua non* of narrativization. The equation we are seeking to reconstruct between a narrativized kerygma and a kerygmatized narrative seems indeed to have its rationale in the identity proclaimed between the Christ of faith and the Jesus of history. Starting from this core, it is comprehensible that other factors of narrativization may have played a role or been drawn into the same gravitational space. I will mention a few of them.

In the first place, there is the question that Hans Frei's book about the identity of Jesus Christ centers upon: "Who do you say that I am?"[8] (After all, the Old Testament can also be summed up in the question, Who is the Lord?) It is one of the functions of the narrative art, through the combined interplay of plot and character development (as has been well known since Henry James's reflections in *The Art of Fiction*), to answer the question Who? by indicating what we may call the narrative identity of the character, that is, the identity produced by the narrative itself. Now, it is a fact that the identity of Jesus remains an acute question throughout the Gospels. And, as I shall indicate further in a moment, it is perhaps the function of some narratives to deepen the enigma of the character, while clarifying the arrangement of the plot. This identity of Jesus is essential to the equation between the Jesus of history and the Christ of faith. To say who Jesus is, is also to say who the Christ is. And this is what the Gospels do, especially the passion narratives. If it is true, for example, that Mark wanted to polemicize against a Christology of glory that wanted to do away with the humiliation of the cross, and if it is true that, through his narrative, he wanted to illustrate a Christology of the Son of Man that retains the features of the Suffering Servant from the "songs" of Second Isaiah, as well as those of the persecuted righteous person of the Psalms, it is no less true that it is through narrative means that he carries out this apologetics for his Christology. It is in narrating that he interprets the identity of Jesus. Correlatively, it is in composing his narrative with a literary art that is in no way maladroit—as has been said for a long time now—that he signifies his Christology of a suffering Son of Man.

Here is another corollary: I mentioned brief narratives about the life of Jesus that might have been drawn into the gravitational sphere of the kerygma looking for a narrative and in the course of narrativization. Some of these already indicate a trajectory capable of ending up in a passion narrative. On this point, it seems to me that Joachim Jeremias, along with my late colleague Norman Perrin in his *Rediscovering the Teaching of Jesus*,[9] was correct in discerning a deep-lying affinity between the theme of Jesus

---

8. Hans Frei, *The Identity of Jesus Christ: An Inquiry into the Hermeneutical Basis of Dogmatic Theology* (Philadelphia: Fortress Press, 1974).

9. Norman Perrin, *Rediscovering the Teaching of Jesus* (New York: Harper and Row, 1967).

betrayed, taken in its double theological and narrative signification, and those narratives that depict Jesus sharing the table of tax collectors, sinners, and prostitutes and giving discourses—parables and other forms—that generated confrontation. Between preaching, confronting, sharing sinners' food, and being betrayed, there is, if not a completely given narrative connection, at least what the Russian structuralists call a *fabula* or, let us say, occasions for narrative, which present a sort of homology among themselves, a mutual fittingness, surpassing any pure chronological arrangement. It is these occasions for narrative that must have served as a basis for the rule-governed composition of a large narrative in which the passion would be both an ineluctable continuation of earlier events and a distinct core, more narrativized than the other portions, yet capable of extending its narrative cohesion to what went before, so that the Gospel appears to us today, in the words of Martin Kahler, as a passion narrative preceded by a long introduction.

I would like to add two narrative effects to these different aspects of the call for narrative, which, when considered in themselves, give rise to a certain autonomy of the process of narrativization, to such an extent that it escapes the control of the christological intention and, in a way, begins to amplify itself on its own terms. These two effects are, moreover, in many ways the opposite of each other. What we too quickly call an embellishment has a more complex function that is a source of perplexity. If it is true that narrative interprets, one of its ways of doing so is to explain in a plausible manner, on the basis of what is reasonable, following Aristotle's rule in the *Poetics*. Every narrative explains, as soon as it tells why some character did something. As has been said, there is no narrative if one simply reports, "The king died, the queen died." There is a narrative if one says, "The king died, the queen died of grief." By introducing a motive, the narrative invites us to explore a whole set of connections with the resources and conventions of what is reasonable. Thus, to cite an example, the role of Judas swells, becomes more precise and more anecdotal from one Gospel to the next.[10] Thanks to this amplification subordinated to the rules of what is reasonable, the narrative is clothed with an aspect of what Hans Frei in his *The Eclipse of Biblical Narrative* has called being "history-like."[11] With

---

10. Let me note in passing, without being able to give it the full development it deserves, the recourse to *testimonia,* to citations from the Old Testament. Contrary to what the modern reader may tend to think, the affirmation that a recounted event fulfills an earlier prophecy—itself quite arbitrarily taken out of context—does not make the narrative suspect but rather augments its credibility, if we follow the criteria for reception of a text current among the first Christians. In this sense, it counts in the same way as does the anecdotal or material feature, which we may say reinforces what Frei has called the "history-like" aspect of the narrative. We have here two converging procedures for conveying credibility.

11. Hans Frei, *The Eclipse of Biblical Narrative: A Study in Eighteenth and Nineteenth Century Hermeneutics* (New Haven: Yale Univ. Press, 1974).

Matthew, and especially with John, this effect of quasi-historical verisimil-itude is confined to material positivity, most likely owing to a polemical intent.

However, the increasing autonomy of the narrative can also aim at a strictly opposite effect. The systematic usage of reticence, as the inverse of amplification, a usage that Robert Alter sees at work in many narratives in the Hebrew Bible—for example, Abraham and Isaac are silent on the route to the place of sacrifice—can guide a perfectly opaque narrative that aug-ments the enigma by strictly narrative means. Perhaps the distinctive feature of the Gospel of Mark is that Mark narratively produces more opacity than clarification. This feature, better than the inverse one of amplification, can be set in relation with the type of Christology that constitutes the keryg-matic intention of his narrative. A narrative that obscures things, as Mark's may in fact do, may have a profound affinity with the Christology of the suffering Son of Man that he presents. But whatever the variety of modes of narrativization, it is the task of hermeneutics to track down these homolo-gies between narrative technique and kerygmatic function. In a moment, I shall give a few examples of this.

Narrative Articulation

In the second part of my remarks, I would like to refer to some of the narrative techniques put in service of a kerygmatic narrative. I shall do so briefly, but I do want to indicate how I see the articulation of the narrative and the kerygmatic, if we limit ourselves to a literary analysis of the text that deals with it as a prose fiction.

Three levels of analysis seem to me to provide a place for forms of literary analysis distinct from those of the historical-critical method.

1. The first level is that of a semiotics of narrative, illustrated by the methods of Vladimir Propp and A.-J. Greimas, where the analysis is carried out in terms of "functions" (or abstract segments of action) or "actants" (or typical characters). This method is especially pertinent for texts close to the traditional folktale, in which a certain order is initially upset by a mis-deed or a lack, then reestablished through a series of qualifying tests that glorify a hero, who encounters the aid of helpers and the hostility of oppo-nents. Use of this perspective is not out of place inasmuch as the popular tale illustrates logical universals of narrative that function at a depth con-cealed by their being invested in individual figures (Jesus, Peter, Judas, and so on). What I have called the narrativization of the kerygma implies just such a passage through the semiotic constraints on narrativity and its most universal features. The benefit of this approach results, furthermore, from its immense respect for the text, whose details, at end of the analysis, are

justified through a mutual adjusting of the general rules of narrativity and their individual instantiations.

So I will not reproach this method for imposing too rigid a grid on its texts. Those who have practiced it are well aware of the half-steps and rectifications required by any investigation into the details of a semic reconstruction, whether discursive or figurative. Nor will I reproach it for missing the link between the narrative and the kerygmatic aspects—which would be a mortal reproach. By setting on stage of the receivers, through whom comes about the contract that qualifies the hero, we have in effect a semiotic equivalent of the kerygma of election. What is more, semiotic analysis should be praised for including, among the numerous codes and isotopies it considers, an ideological code, under which may be placed the christological titles.

Instead, I will say that the semiotics of narrative is constrained in the case of the passion narratives to working at its limits, and this calls for two complements I shall discuss in a moment. It must do so for three reasons. First, its codified roles are largely subverted by their figurization in the passion narratives. It is not correct to say that Judas is the only opponent. We shall see in a moment that everyone betrays, denies, flees, up to and including the women at the tomb. And what are we to make of the pair Judas/ Peter? Here any semiotic analysis runs into a real test. This subversion of roles, I believe, is the narrative expression of the kerygmatic project; for example, Mark's Christology. The subversion is double in the sense that the helper Peter becomes an opponent, while the opponent Judas becomes, as do the recalcitrant characters of the Hebrew Bible, the instrument of the hero's triumph. Yet perhaps it is the equation between glory and humiliation in the figure of the hero that most drives semiotic analysis to work at its limits. And this leads to my second reservation. Speaking precisely of figures and figurization, Louis Marin has shown in a convincing fashion, in his "semiotics of the traitor," that the figurative level is far from being just a plane where structured roles from a deeper level are given some specification.[12] This is the level where initiatives get taken, which not only introduces contingency into the narrative, it also governs the transformations that take place on the deeper levels. Here working at the limit leads to subversion of the model in question itself. Marin, for example, uses the occurrence of the dynamics of the narrative on its surface level to ask whether it is not this dynamism, reported on the surface plane, that engenders the transformations on the semiotic and discursive planes. What is at issue here is the question of the passage from the paradigmatic to the syntagmatic in a model where the transformation rules are themselves atemporal (for

---

12. Louis Marin, *Semiotics of the Passion Narrative,* trans. Alfred M. Johnson, Jr. (Pittsburgh: Pickwick Press, 1980).

example, conjunction, disjunction, and so on). In other words, the important question that Marin raises—which has not been sufficiently noted—is whether it is not from the figurative level, the level of figurization itself, that that semiotic model receives, through a kind of recoil-effect, its capacity for syntagmatization. With this, the distinction between depths and surface wavers, particularly if it is in fact from the figural contingency that the model draws its power for narrativization. Indeed, what we have here is the question of the functioning of the Aristotelian peripeteia, which a careful literary analysis can discern beneath the heavy weight of semiotic apparatus, but which we are better able to recognize when we come to the limits of such semiotic analysis. In my own investigations concerning narrative, I relate this aspect of concordance and discordance in narrative to a first-order understanding of narrative, and I expect the second-order rationality of semiotics to provide an ever-finer, less intuitive reconstruction of the accidents in any narrative.[13] My own belief here is that, as in historiography, to explain more is to understand better what has already been preunderstood.

This brings me to my second reason for saying that the semiotics of narrative touches its limits in the case of the passion narratives. Let us return again to the question of contingency: Jesus betrayed. This puts it on the figurative level. But "to betray" also works on a second plane, which is not one that semiotics calls the deep level, that is, the level of the codified roles on the plane of a logic of narrative. The Son of Man betrayed is both a theological statement and an event at the same time. In the first instance, the statement is transhistorical, even gnomic: the Son of Man had to be betrayed. . . . The time of this being betrayed is that time signified by the "hour" ("And he prayed that, if it were possible, the hour might pass from him" [Mark 14:35], at Gethsemane). In the second case, the event gets inscribed in the chronology that Mark indicates through the series of the three hours of the watch: "It is enough; the hour has come; the Son of Man is betrayed into the hands of sinners. Rise, let us be going; see, my betrayer is at hand" (Mark 14:41-42). The hour in the first sense of the term, the one in which the man of sorrows prays to the Father that he might be removed, and the hour in the second sense, where the one who will betray him approaches, form a pair that stem from the figure in the text, but this is no longer a question of the figurization of codified roles, but rather something more in the sense of *Figura,* so admirably exposited by Erich Auerbach in his well-known article with this same title.[14] This *Figura* assures the unity of the kerygmatic and the eventlike by giving the figure another kind of depth

---

13. Paul Ricoeur, *Time and Narrative,* 3 vols., trans. Kathleen McLaughlin and David Pellauer (Chicago: Univ. of Chicago Press, 1984–88).

14. Erich Auerbach, "Figura," in *Scenes from the Drama of European Literature* (New York: Meridian Books, 1959), 11–76.

than that dealt with by semiotics, a typological depth, which subsequently will be articulated in terms of the theory of the four senses of Scripture.

Can narrative semiotics make sense of all this? Yes, but only up to a certain point. I have said that semiotic analysis has at its disposal a whole conceptual arsenal with its categories of sender and receiver and its notion of an ideological isotopy. Its limit, however, lies in the fact that both the sender and the receiver and the isotopy constitute structural entities deprived of the plurivocity that allows for the symbolic transferences at work in the two expressions "to be betrayed" and "hour."

2. Here I see a second relay station, which, by the way, is not alien to semiotics. Do we not make better sense of the kerygmatic meaning of being betrayed and the term "hour" by assigning them to a speaker, that is, to someone who speaks the narrative and who interprets it while recounting it? The distinction here between uttering and utterance is an extremely important one, for it allows us to make sense of an "instance of discourse" that the notion of an ideological code is not able to account for. Indeed, a code is a preexisting virtual system of discourse that prescribes the inscription of appropriate isotopies in a narrative. An instance of discourse, on the contrary, is a singular operation, like *parole* or speaking in relation to *langue* or the atemporal language system. I would not deny that narrative semiotics might be developed in this direction. And it has its successes, as shown by Greimas's *Maupassant* and his essays collected in volume 2 of *Du Sens*.[15] Yet it seems to me that there is something in this notion of an instance of discourse that destabilizes the actantial model. Evidence for this is the fact that the theory of utterance, or of speech-acts, has undergone considerable development, without making use of either Greimas's semiotic square or the whole weighty apparatus of semiotics in general. I have in mind not only the work of Gérard Genette and his distinction between utterance and statement (or narrative properly speaking and the told story, the recounted events, the *fabula*) but also all the works devoted to the relation between the narrator's discourse and that of the character, an excellent example of which may be found in Dorrit Cohn's *Transparent Minds*.[16] To this work should be linked the work of the second generation of Russian structuralists, Mikhail Bakhtin, Jurij Lotman, and Boris Uspensky, who have developed a theory of "point of view" as the principle of narrative composition.[17] For literary analysis, there can be no doubt that

---

15. A.-J. Greimas, *Maupassant: La Semiotique du texte: Exercises practiques* (Paris: Seuil, 1976); idem, *Du Sens,* vol. 2 (Paris: Seuil, 1983).

16. Gérard Genette, "Frontiers of Narrative," in *Figures of Literary Discourse,* trans. Alan Sheridan (New York: Columbia Univ. Press, 1982), 127–44; idem, *Narrative Discourse: An Essay in Method,* trans. Jane E. Lewin (Ithaca, N.Y.: Cornell Univ. Press, 1980); Dorrit Cohn, *Transparent Minds: Narrative Modes for Presenting Consciousness in Fiction* (Princeton, N.J.: Princeton Univ. Press, 1978).

17. Jurij Lotman, *The Structure of the Artistic Text,* trans. Ronald Vronn (Ann Arbor:

the christological qualification given to the characters and events in the passion narratives stems from that dialogic principle of literary composition. And when Lotman and Uspensky deal with point of view, they draw upon this work, which needs to be applied in detail to the passion narratives.

3. I would like to indicate one last development in literary theory that will give us another tool even more appropriate to the problem of the narrativization of the kerygma, or of narrative with a kerygmatic intention, which we may call confessional narrative. This is the notion of narrative voice. In one sense, it is close to that of point of view, since, for Bakhtin, point of view and voice are interchangeable terms, as may be seen in his notion of a polyphonic narrative. But, however much it may be possible to depersonalize point of view, as, for instance, Genette proposes to do when he substitutes focalization for point of view in his recent *Nouveau Discours du Récit,* it is impossible to do so for the narrative voice. Someone speaks, someone speaks to me in the text, someone addresses himself or herself to me, a voice, which is of course an instance of the text, but which tells me, like the voice to which Augustine attributes the origin of his conversion, "Tolle! Lege!" (Take and read!). In this sense, if there is an *écriture,* a writing, in all speech, as Jacques Derrida puts it, there is also a speaking in the writing. This speaking in the writing is the narrative voice, the narration of the narrative, for which all the fictive or real events are in the past, in the preterit of narration.

These are some of the resources for a literary analysis of the passion narratives that allow us, if not completely to capture or, even less, to exhaust them, at least to get closer to this unique literary genre: a narrative constructed as interpreting a kerygma, which it brings to language by articulating it on the level of narrative.

Outlines of a Literary Analysis of the Passion Narratives in the Gospel of Mark

To conclude I would like to attempt to outline a literary analysis of the passion narratives in Mark, which, following Robert Alter's approach to Hebraic narrative, will show how the christological component is signified on the narrative plane by the arranging of the events, by the interplay between utterance and statement, and, finally, by the intervention of point

Univ. of Michigan Press, 1977); Mikhail Bakhtin, *Problems of Dostoevski's Poetics,* trans. R. W. Rotsel (Ann Arbor, Mich.: Ardis Publications, 1973); Boris Uspensky, *A Poetics of Composition: The Structure of the Artistic Text and a Typology of Compositional Form,* trans. Valentina Zavanin and Susan Wittig (Berkeley: Univ. of California Press, 1973).

of view and the narrative voice.[18] Jesus betrayed is the major peripeteia. This theologoumen of Jesus betrayed is given a history that, in each of its episodes, is a story of treason, denial, abandonment, and flight, oriented toward the disappearance of Jesus' body, to the point of positing the equivalence between Jesus "risen" (elsewhere) and Jesus absent: "He is not here" (Mark 16:6). We may, of course, reduce the narrative component to the benefit of the work of the concept. This is what happens in the Hegelian reinscriptions of the theology of the cross into the negativity of the absolute Spirit's return to itself. But the Gospel of Mark never goes so far as to formulate this separate theology, even in its confessions of faith, sealed by the centurion's confession in response to the dying Jesus' cry of dereliction. This confession is narrativized by the bias of a "quoted monologue," to use one of Dorrit Cohn's categories: he said, "Truly this man was the Son of God" (15:39). Beyond this procedure of using quotation, the monologue is also narrativized by the motivation the omniscient narrator assigns to him: "And when the centurion, who stood facing him, *saw that he thus breathed his last,* he said. . . . " This clause constitutes an extraordinary example of a narrative having to do with the intimate thoughts of a third person, which themselves belong to the order of interpretation. The same thing must be said of Jesus' double confession before the high priest (" 'Are you the Christ, the Son of the Blessed?' And Jesus said, 'I am' " [14:61-62]) and before Pilate ("Are you the King of the Jews?" asks the Roman. "You have said so," answers Jesus [15:2]).

What the direct confession about Jesus or of Jesus cannot produce, on either the kerygmatic or the narrative plane of signification, is the series of antagonistic relations—treason, denial, flight, and abandonment—that stakes out the theme: Jesus betrayed into the hands of sinners; in other words, the more and more violent dialogic structure that ends in the situation of dereliction. Nor is the monologic confession capable of correcting the misunderstanding that is not just confined to the relations between antagonists but that transpires throughout the whole narrative, to the point of making such an opaque narrative that the reader is finally led to identifying with the women at the empty tomb, concerning whom the narrative tells us: "And they went out and fled from the tomb; for trembling and astonishment had come upon them; and they said nothing to any one, for they were afraid." Flight, silence, fear, this is how the Gospel of Mark terminates in 16:8 according to the majority of exegetes.

If such is the case, to explicate this Gospel means looking for the indications of the equation it posits between its Christology of a suffering Son of

---

18. I shall cite the Revised Standard Version text. I must also acknowledge my dependence on the work of Xavier Léon-Dufour in his essay "Passion (Récits de la)," in *Supplément Histoire/Bible,* cols. 1419–92, and in his essay in *The Passion in Mark,* ed. Werner H. Kelber (Philadelphia: Fortress Press, 1976).

Man and the story of the betrayed Jesus. The chain that these indications constitute makes the passion narrative into a literary unit, whatever may be the history of its tradition or of its redaction, including any conjectural relation between it and a primitive narrative or between a shorter and a longer version.

1. Let us begin with the "anointing at Bethany" (14:3-9). In Mark and Matthew it comes immediately after the announcement of the chief priests' and scribes' plot against Jesus—in Luke and John it is not at this point, Luke having an anointing narrative at 7:36, while John places it six days before Easter, in the context of the resurrection of Lazarus. Why does this anointing occupy this place in Mark? Perhaps because so embedded (by 14:1-2) in the passion and resurrection narrative, it refers us in a symmetrical way to the anointing that does not take place on Easter morning. In it, the moment of absence is already indicated (cf. 14:7-8: "But you will not always have me. She has done what she could; she has anointed my body beforehand for burying"). The anticipated anointing thus counts as a burial anointing. Let us further note the interfacing of the themes developed in what follows. First, the indignation of "some" in 14:4 (who in Matthew will become the "disciples" and in John, "Judas Iscariot, one of his disciples") announces Jesus' being abandoned by his own followers, among whom Judas is just one. If the start of Judas's treason in 14:10-11 immediately follows the pericope of the anointing at Bethany and precedes the preparation of the Passover meal, is this not so as to establish the equation between the theologoumen "The Son of Man had to be betrayed" and the event of Jesus betrayed? There is still another significant indication. By calling Judas "one of the twelve" in 14:10, the narrative underscores his belonging to the group of disciples—Matthew will retain this point, as will Luke with even greater emphasis; as for John, like Luke, he would prefer to satanize Judas. We need also to ask what the exchange of Jesus' body for money signifies. It is a derisory exchange if the true exchange, the final one, is the one that exchanges the body for the word in 16:8. But let us not lose hold of our guideline, Jesus betrayed, which connects the two registers of theological necessity and narrative contingency.

2. Let us move on to the narrative of the Last Supper, which tradition history and redaction history tell us is an independent pericope. Clearly we are to take the preparation, the treason denounced at the table that all share, and the ritual meal as one articulated whole. In this respect, the preparatory episode in 14:12-16 does not emphasize Jesus' omniscience for Mark. The important thing is that the preparations be made "to eat the Passover" and that this has to be done on the first day of azymes, alluding to the leaven of the Pharisees and that of Herod. Eating the Passover meal is in essence what Mark recounts in 14:17-25. But the negative moment throughout the narrative continues to invert the basically positive meaning

of this gesture. To eat the Passover meal is an act with a wholly positive meaning, whether we emphasize the eschatological implication of the final banquet or the sacramental and ritual import of the instituting of the eucharistic meal. Yet the "negative" constantly accompanies the "positive" with its shadow. The pronouncement about treason is made right at the heart of the meal (14:18). Once again the sinister word "betray" recurs: "One of you will betray me, one who is eating with me." Psalm 41 is made use of here, to tie together "betray" and "eating with me." At the same time, the connection between Judas and the twelve announces the secret bond between Judas's treason, Peter's denial, and everyone's flight. The traitor is among the disciples at the meal. Treason is internal to the community. Perhaps we should even go further and, following structural analysis, emphasize the opposition between "eating with"—that is, to nourish a body in a relationship of conviviality—and "betray," that is, to hand over a body, by rupturing another space, that of community. In any case, Judas is not directly named: "one who is eating with me." In this way, the banquet of betrayal is the obligatory path to the eschatological banquet that breaks through the story as told. Absence is once again tied to being betrayed: "The Son of Man goes as it is written of him" (14:21). (Matthew says the same thing; Luke has: "The Son of Man goes," which attenuates the absence while increasing the manifestation of power.) As for the instituting of the Eucharist, it too is as marked by absence as by presence. "This is my body"; "This is my blood of the covenant"—indications of presence. "Truly, I say to you, I shall not drink again of the fruit of the vine until that day when I drink it new in the kingdom of God"—absence. Final fulfillment is announced, but it is accompanied by a fearful warning: "One of you will betray me,... one who is dipping bread in the same dish with me." One question marks his path: Can one really be his disciple? Is this an impossible vocation, an impossible mission?

3. Next comes the narrative about Gethsemane (14:26-42). Is there no reason, I mean no narrative reason, why in 14:26 Mark has Jesus and the twelve go out "to the Mount of Olives," thereby making this indication a resting stone in view of the episode of Gethsemane, and before the announcing of Peter's denial, symmetrical in so many ways to Judas's treason? We most likely are meant to meditate on the pair Peter/Judas, where the helper, Peter, becomes an opponent on the figurative plane, while the opponent, Judas, secretly becomes the helper in the hero's qualifying test. Once again the individual figure of the one who denies Jesus is not left in isolation: "You will all fall away" (14:27). It is this same "you all" that is signified by the disciples falling asleep. What is more, they are successively designated as the "disciples" in 14:32 then by the trio Peter, James, and John in 14:33, which anticipates the more individualized narrative of Peter's denial, the epitome of all abandoning him. All, three, one.

As for Jesus at Gethsemane, I am struck by what so many commentators have said about it when they oppose the stoic sovereignty of Jesus in Luke to his dereliction in Mark and even in Matthew: "And he . . . began to be greatly distressed and troubled" (Mark 14:33). We must not be afraid here to follow Frank Kermode's suggestion that the narrative deepens the mystery more than it clarifies the motivations. For here the theological line that ties the righteous one to death requires, on the narrative plane, an incomparable passage to the void. If it is true that the messianic mission passes through suffering and death, the anxiety and sense of horror that seize Jesus have to go so far as his plea that he be spared from such suffering; that is, that it be taken out of the messianic mission. Is this to say that for an instant Jesus wanted to avoid the cross? The text says instead that "he fell on the ground and prayed that, if it were possible, the hour might pass [far] from him" (14:35). The very word "hour" removes this agony from the chronological and narrative contingency. But it is, in fact, another hour, the one that designates the moment when the one who will betray Jesus "is at hand." For the passion to "come," the one who betrays Jesus must "come": "The hour has come" (14:41). Henceforth the eschatological hour and the chronological hour coincide. As for the flight of the disciples, readers will become less severe than they might have been when they read in 14:40 that "they did not know how to answer him." If Peter stands out from the chorus of misunderstanding, nevertheless he still belongs to it, too. At the Last Supper, everyone drinks the cup; at Gethsemane, "They all forsook him, and fled" (14:50). What the disciples and Peter do not understand, refusing it in their hearts and through their flight, is Mark's Christology of the Son of Man.

4. The arrest of Jesus is the pivotal event, the beginning of the short narrative, according to historical-critical exegesis. However, the writer of the long narrative does not lose the guiding thread, the word "betrayed": "Now the betrayer . . . " (14:44). Structural analysis uncovers a still more subtle tie between the betraying kiss, which is a contact with the body, and the anointing touch, as though the first sign of the traitor stood in a relationship of parody to the anointing. The tie between the pericope of Gethsemane and that of the arrest is less subtle. It can be summed up in one word: abandonment. Those who were sleeping during the time of agony flee at the time of arrest (14:51).[19]

All the pericopes that follow constitute so many illustrations of the notion of narrative as interpretation, that is, as contributing to a christological reading of the narratives relative to Jesus' passion. Taken together, they

---

19. I must pass over the incident of the *neaniskos* (young man), clothed with a linen cloth, who runs away naked. Frank Kermode has given us a brilliant and troubling exegesis about him, from the point of view of a hermeneutic for which the narrative in obscuring more than clarifying things, engenders and preserves the secret.

assure a perfect narrative and theological coherence with what precedes, as well as with the passion narratives. If it is legitimate from a historical-critical point of view to inquire into the suture between the pericope about the agony at Gethsemane and that of the arrest, said to inaugurate the short narrative (arrest, trial, execution), the narrative and theological continuity between Gethsemane and the arrest bear the mark of a clear literary art. This unity is assured by the theme of the "betrayed" Son of Man. The conflict he gives rise to is merely raised to a higher level by the narrative of the events that carry through this betrayal in the narrative time. The slide in the meaning of the word "hour" from the eschatological plane to the episodic plane had already prepared this tilting toward a more clearly event-based narrative, namely, the events of the short narrative. But if it is true that the disciples' rejection of the suffering Messiah is essential to the narrativization of the Markan narrative of the suffering Christ, then the episode at Gethsemane was necessary to his passion narrative.

5. Denial and trial. If this is what is kerygmatically at stake in the interpreting narrative, we can then give a more plausible explication of certain pure narrative features in the composition of the following episodes, in particular the fact that Mark interwove Peter's denial into the narrative of the double Jewish and Roman trial. (For example, 14:54 sets the continuity of the theme into the account of the trial.)

The motif of denial leads quite far back in Mark's Gospel, to the incident at Caesarea Philippi (7:27-30). From this moment on, it looks as though the confession about Christ was cut short and, in this sense, is misleading. What Peter had not accepted, beginning at this moment, was the necessity of the cross. If it is true that at the end of the episode at Gethsemane everyone had fled, Peter is the only one to flee who, remembering what Jesus had said about his denying him, becomes aware of his own distress: "And he broke down and wept" (14:73). (Matthew, followed by Luke, attenuates things: "And he went out and wept bitterly.") Peter flees, just like at Gethsemane. This is the hyper-chronological and, if I may put it this way, the homological connection that, once again, ties the narrative to the kerygmatic by means of a kind of echo phenomenon. The case of Judas has made us familiar with this kind of conjunction between two planes, that of inevitability and that of contingency. Inevitability: Jesus had told him what would happen and Peter remembers it. Contingency: the anecdotes about Peter warming himself, the servant recognizing him, and the cock who cries at just the right moment.

The embedding of the interrogation before the Sanhedrin within the narrative about Peter's denial and the cutting in two of this narrative have the striking effect of reinforcing the narrative pair questioning/denial (both episodes have the same introduction: 14:53-54).

However, the most intriguing pair is that of Peter and Judas. Peter is, of course, not the one who betrays (the body of Jesus, as Louis Marin emphasizes). He merely denies him in words. But speech is not innocent, as the incident at Caesarea Philippi just referred to made clear. His denial gets a special gravity, however, from its being interwoven with the interrogation before the high priest. In a way, Peter too is a false witness. This underlines the peril of antitestimony like a faultline in the disciple's service. It is this latter trait that makes the helper slip toward the side of the opponent. And what thereby becomes common to Judas and Peter is their comparable contribution to the righteous one's march toward death, in spite of the contingency proper to the pericope about each one of them. Inasmuch as his denial is that of the leader of the apostles, Peter can be said to be an opponent more crushed by the narrative than Judas himself. In his denial culminates the scandal that brings the disciples' blindness to its highest point.

It is here that the narrative clouds over and leads to the unsayable. For if Peter is Satan, as we are told in the episode at Caesarea Philippi, is this not so because all the figures, when confronted by the enigma of Jesus, reply to the question "Who do you say that I am?" with a comparable withdrawal. From Judas who betrays him, to the disciples who flee, to Peter who denies him, to the women who, they too, at the empty tomb are seized with horror and flee. It is against this shadowy background that Peter's denial takes on its full weight. Starting as a negative model of the condition of being a disciple, it becomes a source of uncertainty for the reader insofar as the reader is invited to proffer an affirmation of faith with such force that it will cut the ambiguity of everything that has gone before.

6. As for the *crucifixion* narrative (15:20b-41), its dramatic structure is not commanded by the polarity between the traitor and the helper but rather by the dereliction that calls for the eclipsing of both of them. Suddenly, the dramatic effect is produced by another system of opposition that will henceforth play itself out on the level of the christological signification itself and that the narrative will interpret through recourse to the narrative resources belonging to it. If it is true that two theologies confront each other here, that of the divine man and that of the suffering Son of Man, it is by strictly narrative means that Mark separates these two theologies. The tour de force, it seems, is his having placed the theology of the divine man in the months of adversaries, who here are mockers: "Save yourself and come down from the cross." "He saved others; he cannot save himself." The grotesque confusion of the cry "Elo-i" as an appeal to Elijah, who was himself treated as a divine man, contributes to this repudiation of the theology of the divine man. Even more, the great cry, which for the latter theology should have been a cry of triumph, transmuted into a cry of dereliction by borrowing from Ps. 22:1. It is true that the centurion's confession, which uses the title Son of God (Mark 15:39), seems to attenuate

this intratheological conflict, but we may note that this title is cropped of its divine-man signification by the important addition that the centurion "saw that he thus breathed his last." It is because he saw how Jesus died that the centurion could give its correct theological signification to the episode of the crucifixion.

To the dereliction of Jesus left alone corresponds the displacement of the role of the opponent from the figure of the traitor to that of the mockers, a displacement that almost seems to indicate the extinction of this function. As for Jesus' cry, it brings to a peak his abandonment at Gethsemane. The disciples have fled, there remain the mockers—and the centurion.[20]

7. Just a few words, to conclude, about the narrative of the empty tomb.[21] I offer them from the perspective of this inquiry, namely, how a narrative with an interpretive vocation functions. The formula for such a narrative will be the following. If Jesus lives and lives elsewhere, then here there has to be an empty tomb. It is in relation to this narrative structure with a kerygmatic function that we may attempt to interpret one unique feature of Mark's narrative, namely, that the only ones present at the tomb are the women, no guards (as in Matthew), no disciples (as in Luke and John), and not even the figure of Jesus himself (as in Matthew and John). This "parsimony of presence" is particularly appropriate to the general tone of the Markan passion narrative and accords quite easily with the hypothesis that the narrative of the empty tomb constituted the actual redactional conclusion of the Gospel of Mark. What I have called narrative parsimony illustrates the following formula. The Lord resurrected, according to the kerygma, has as his narrative trace only the absence of the body of Jesus. If it is true that Mark here continues to oppose a Christology that would immediately lead to a Christology of glory, short-circuiting the Master's suffering and the difficulty of being a disciple, then the narrative that

---

20. Dan O. Via, in his *Kerygma and Comedy in the New Testament* (Philadelphia: Fortress Press, 1975), points to the theme of powerless death confronted by the struggle between power and not-power that takes place through the passion narratives and in the whole Gospel. Power: the leaders of the Jews, soldiers, thieves, the centurion, Simon compelled to carry the cross. The narrative brings about a transvaluation of the images of coercion, by having the only bearer of power left on stage—the centurion—pronounce the confession of Christian faith. This dialectical reversal was anticipated in the figure of Simon of Cyrene, who, constrained to do something, is transformed into a model of service. Simon, literally, bears his cross. The reversal of the cry of triumph, if such is the case, into a cry of dereliction belongs to the same reversal. What is more, the reversal brought about by the transvaluation of images of coercion rejoins at an even deeper level the theme of the fulfilling of destiny—the Son of Man has to be betrayed—through the interplay of oppositions. It is through treason, denial, and, finally, the application of violence to the body of Jesus that the destiny of the Son of Man is accomplished. The irony of the conclusion to the crucifixion narrative is to have the Son of Man proclaimed the Son of God by the one who has the mandate of power, who saw how Jesus died a death without power.

21. See John Dominic Crossan, "Empty Tomb and Absent Lord," in *Passion in Mark*, ed. Kelber, 135–52.

best interprets this theology of the suffering Son of Man is one that does without an appearance of Jesus himself to Peter and the apostles. The only presence is the women—and a missing anointing. Even the vision of the "young man" (*neaniskos*) does not contradict this parsimony of presence. He is a messenger who represents Jesus, but who is not Jesus (his position on the right is that of Christ next to the Father, his white robe is that of the elect in heaven). In the dimension of pure presence remains the voice, the voice that says, "Do not be amazed; you seek Jesus of Nazareth, who was crucified. He has risen [from the dead], he is not here" (16:6). This negativity of presence belongs to the guiding theme of the progressive disappearance of the body throughout the passion narrative. A decrease in the body, an increase in the word. A word that is not our own designates Jesus in the third person as "risen absent" (note the anacoluthic form: "He has risen, he is not here"). A message is contained in the command that follows ("Go, tell his disciples and Peter"): "that he is going before you to Galilee; there you will see him, as he told you" (16:7). Whatever may be said from a historical-critical point of view about the way that Galilee is a place indicated throughout the Gospel of Mark, and whatever may be said about the allusions to the relationship between the community of Mark and that of Jerusalem, or about the question of the mission to the Jews and that to the Gentiles, literary analysis will underscore the future tense of this announcement: there you will see him. This advance of Jesus over the disciples that the narrative presents allows it to stop at the threshold of the future as a narrative that cannot cross this threshold owing to its very narrative constraints. These constraints mean that the narrative finds its appropriate conclusion in the conjunction between the voice of an unidentified young man, even if he is a celestial character, and an awakening elsewhere, which the voice speaks of in the third person.

Is it not the case that we must say that the narrative not so much elucidates things as obscures them, in the sense that its manner of narratively interpreting the kerygma is to reinforce the enigmatic aspect of the events themselves? If not, why did Mark end this pericope, and quite probably his Gospel, with the verse: "And they went out and fled from the tomb; for trembling and astonishment had come upon them and they said nothing to anyone, for they were afraid" (16:8)? Flight, fear, silence. We are not even told that the message conveyed by the young man was communicated. If we admit that the Gospel's narrative historicizes the kerygma of the risen Christ, must we not also say that the genius of Mark is to have placed all the resources of the narrative art for negativity and even obscurity at the service of his Christology of a suffering and crucified Son of Man?

Part Four

Theological Overtures:
God, Self, Narrative, and Evil

❈

11

Hope and the Structure
of Philosophical Systems

The aim of this essay is to explore a way that could lead to a renewal of the classical problem concerning the relation between philosophy and theology. Usually this problem is conceived as that of the relation between reason and faith. This relation between reason and faith is itself conceived as a confrontation between the object of reason and the object of faith or, that is, between the God of the philosophers and the God of Jesus Christ; and this confrontation between objects leads to another confrontation between the method of reason and the method of faith or, let us say, between proving and believing.

My presupposition in raising the problem of hope, rather than that of faith or even of love, is that a displacement of the problematics may entail a radical change in the very nature of the confrontation between philosophy and theology. Hope may concern philosophy not so much by proposing an object—let it be even an object beyond all objects, a transcendent object— but by requiring a change in the organization of philosophical systems. If there is something like an *intellectus spei* (as a parallel to the expression *intellectus fidei*), it may be that this *intellectus spei,* this intelligibility of hope, does not consist in pointing to a specific object but to a structural change within philosophical discourse. This structural change could concern what we might call the act of closing this discourse. In the same way as there is the problem of the starting point in philosophy, as was emphasized by Descartes and Husserl, there is also the problem of the closing point, or better, of the horizon of philosophical discourse.

Such is the way that I want to explore. My working hypothesis is expressed in the title of this communication: "Hope and the structure of philosophical systems."

This title means that I am seeking for a relation that has its expression in the movement and in the impulse of the discourse; in other words, I

Reprinted with permission from *Proceedings of the American Catholic Association* (1970): 55–69.

am seeking for a relation that concerns the finality of the discourse, the fulfillment of the desire that pushes it forward.

Before exploring this structural aspect of philosophical discourse, I shall say a few words concerning two previous questions: What does hope mean for biblical theology, and what kind of intelligibility does hope develop?

The Task of a Biblical Theology of Hope

What is hope? What does hope mean for biblical theology? If we want to respect the specificity of the notion, we must say first that hope does not primarily belong to philosophical discourse; the theologians of the past were right when they called it a "theological virtue"—along with faith and love. Under that title they preserved the dimension to which hope belongs. It is this dimension that we have to recognize.

I shall borrow the main idea of this first part from the German theologian Jürgen Moltmann in his *Theology of Hope*. Jürgen Moltmann is the heir of a long tradition of exegetes starting from Johannes Weiss and Albert Schweitzer; for this school the kernel of the New Testament is constituted by the preaching of the kingdom of God. If it is true that the kerygma of the primitive church, following the preaching of Jesus, was centered around the eschatological event, then the whole of theology must be reinterpreted according to the norm of eschatology; theology can no longer take as its leading thread a notion of *logos* or of manifestation that would be independent from, and prior to, the hope concerning things to come. The task of a theology of hope would be to revise all the theological concepts on the basis of an exegesis ruled by the preaching of the kingdom to come.

The revision finds a significant help in a parallel attempt by Martin Buber to oppose the God of the promise—the God of the desert, the God of wandering—to the gods of the "epiphany" religions. Those gods appear here and now—they are present in their idols or in the figure of the king. The God of Israel does not appear, is a mere name that excludes all images.

This opposition between the Name and the idol is the key to a series of oppositions:

1. The first is that to the Name corresponds a theology of history; to the idol a cosmological vision.

2. The second is that the kind of history that is coherent with a theology of the Name is not itself a given history centered on a given present; it is a history directed toward a fulfillment. In that sense history is itself the hope of history; each achievement, each fulfillment, is understood as the reinstatement of a promise—the "not yet" of the promise gives its tension to history.

Such were the ideas that a Christian theologian like Jürgen Moltmann could find in a Jewish interpretation of the Old Testament, mainly the idea of a theology of history ruled by the tension between promise and fulfillment.

The next question for this Christian theologian was whether the central preaching of the primitive church concerning the Risen Lord did not mean the fulfillment of the promise and in that sense the elimination of promise as the central concept of theology. If the kingdom of God is among us, where is the promise? It was precisely the function of a Christian theology of hope to reinterpret the resurrection itself as an eschatological event. Moltmann proceeds to this reinterpretation by showing that the resurrection is not only an event of the past, is not only a manifestation of the sacred, as was the case with pagan epiphanies; it is an event that opens a new future and reinstates the promise by confirming it. Resurrection is the sign that now the promise is for all persons; its meaning abides in the future, in the death of death, the resurrection of all from the dead. In that sense Moltmann dares to speak of the future of the resurrection of Jesus Christ; if Christ is the firstborn from among the dead, then the meaning of his resurrection is incomplete as long as its promise is not fulfilled in a new creation, in a new totality of being. It is therefore the task of a theology of hope to liberate the preaching of the "one who comes" from its falsifications through the Greek Christologies for which incarnation would be the temporal manifestation of the eternal being.

Now I am not a theologian, but a philosopher. It is not my task to say to what extent it is true to say that the main category of Christianity is promise rather than presence, that God is the "one who comes" rather than the "one who is." I do not claim that this hermeneutic of the resurrection alone is valid and orthodox. I only say that, more than any other, it gives rise to thought.

The Irrationality and Rationality of Hope

The first thought to which hope gives rise as soon as it is applied to the field of human existence is, paradoxically, the irrationality of hope itself. For an existential anthropology indeed hope develops what Kierkegaard called an "absurd logic." Shall we take this path? And if we take it, must we not renounce the project of an *intellectus fidei et spei?* I do not think so. On the contrary, the authentic rationality of hope can be grasped nowhere else than at the end of this "absurd logic."

The first expression of this "absurd logic" of hope is to be found in the anthropological conception of St. Paul. Paul is the first thinker who tried to elaborate an existential interpretation of the two central christological events: the cross and the resurrection. And this existential interpretation is fundamentally antinomic: death of the old human being, rebirth of the new one. This second birth is the eschatological event in existential terms. Now this eschatological event cannot be expressed by the means of a logic of identity. We must express it as a break, as a leap, as a new creation, as a wholly other.

The most striking expression of this antinomic anthropology may be found in the famous fifth chapter of the Epistle to the Romans: "Then as one man's trespass led to condemnation for all, so one man's act of righteousness leads to acquittal and life for all" (5:18-19).

Everyone knows the parallelism between Adam and Jesus Christ. This parallelism provides a rhetorical framework for the new logic of hope that breaks through the logic of sin:

> But the free gift is not like the trespass. For if many died through one man's trespass, much more have the grace of God and the free gift in the grace of that one man Jesus Christ abounded for many. . . . If because of one man's trespass, death reigned through that one man, much more will those who receive abundance of grace and the free gift of righteousness reign in life through the one man Jesus Christ. (Rom. 5:16-17)

Such is the absurd logic of hope, expressed by this grammatical device: much more, much more.

The logic of crime and punishment was a logic of equivalence ("the wages of sin is death"); the logic of hope is a logic of increase and of superabundance ("When sin increased, grace abounded all the more" [5:20-21]).

This absurd logic is the logic of hope as opposed to the logic of repetition. Hope means the "superabundance" of meaning as opposed to the abundance of senselessness, of failure, and of destruction.

The existential meaning of this law of superabundance is rich and complex. There are many ways of living according to this eschatological event of the new creation. Many ways: personal and collective, ethical and political. All these ways are irreducible to a mere wisdom of the eternal present: they bear the mark of the future—of the "not yet" and of the "much more"; in the terms of Kierkegaard, hope makes of freedom the passion for the possible against the sad meditation on the irrevocable. This passion for the possible is the answer of hope to all Nietzschean love of destiny, to all worship of fate, to all *amor fati.*

The passion for the possible implies no illusion; it knows that all resurrection is resurrection from among the dead, that all new creation is in spite of death. As the Reformers used to say, the resurrection is hidden under its contrary, the cross. For seen from the standpoint of hope, life is not only the contrary of but the denial of death; this denial relies on signs, not on proofs. It interprets in a creative way the signs of the superabundance of life in spite of the evidence of death.

The much more of the law of superabundance cannot go without the in spite of, the in spite of death, which gives to hope its lucidity, its seriousness, its determination.

For my part I should say that freedom is the capacity to live according to the paradoxical law of superabundance, of denying death and asserting the excess of sense over non-sense[1] in all desperate situations.

Such are the aspects of irrationality of hope. It is only in the terms of a paradox that we can speak of the passion for the possible, of the denial of death, of the much more of grace, of the excess of sense over non-sense.

The question is now whether this so-called irrationality of hope does not develop another kind of rationality. We spoke of a law of superabundance. Is it not the key of another logic, of a logic of existence for which the excess of sense over non-sense would be the rule? Only a logic of identity and equivalence—the equivalence between sin and death, crime and punishment—is overcome. Is there not another logic—which we may already call a dialectical logic? For that other logic, it is the excess of sense over non-sense that gives rise to thought.

The second part of this communication will be devoted to this dialectical logic implied by hope, or, at least, to an introduction to this dialectical logic. This second part could be put under the title *Spero ut intelligam:* I hope in order to understand. But we shall not be able to develop all the implications of this *intellectus spei,* which would imply a complete system of thought and action. We shall limit our investigation to the constitution of philosophical discourse and find the rational equivalent of hope in a structural aspect of this discourse.

As I said by anticipation in my introduction, this structural aspect concerns the act of closing this discourse. To the problem of the "starting point" in philosophy we shall oppose the problem of the "closing point," or, better said, of the horizon of philosophical discourse.

Spero ut Intelligam

In order to explain what I mean by horizon, and to explore the relation that may eventually be found between hope and the structure of the horizon of philosophical systems, I propose to consider two opposite types of philosophical systems concerning what I called the act of closing the discourse:

---

1. Under the expressions "sense" and "non-sense" I want to unite the logical, the ethical, the existential, and the religious aspects of meaning and meaninglessness in life. Perhaps St. Paul had the same broad intention when he spoke of "sin" in a more than moralistic purpose.

the Hegelian and the Kantian types. For the sake of the demonstration I do not take them as individual systems but precisely as types. As the historical order is unessential to the undertaking, I shall start with the Hegelian system.

As is known, in Hegelian thought, the horizon of the system is called absolute knowledge. What kind of horizon does absolute knowledge represent for the rest of the system? Not at all a sense to come, an unexplored field of meanings, but the philosophical repetition of antecedent mediations. There is nothing new in absolute knowledge; it merely concludes the reconciliation already at work in the successive phases of the philosophical process between certitude and truth. In the preface of the *Phenomenology of the Spirit,* Hegel asserts that the truth that was only in itself along the dialectical development of figures is for itself at the end of the process. There is now adequation between the immanent sense of the process and the sense that this process has for us, as philosophers. This adequation is absolute knowledge. Absolute knowledge is not at all a new and ultimate meaning that could be added to the previous development; it is this development itself as absolutized; or better, it is the final meaning that gives meaning to all intermediary meanings. The Hegelian system is a system written from the end toward the beginning, from the standpoint of the totality toward the partial achievements of the system.

And this end is not something that could be awaited or expected—it is the eternal present of thought that sustains the history of thought. It is not by chance that the last pages of the *Encyclopedia of Philosophical Sciences* are devoted to a commentary on the thirteenth book of the *Metaphysics* by Aristotle. Absolute knowledge is this divine thought that Aristotle called *noēsis noēseths,* the thought of thought. But for Hegel this thought of thought is identical to the system as a whole, in a kind of recapitulative summary of all the intermediary mediations. If I am correct in interpreting the concept of absolute knowledge by Hegel, we may say that the Hegelian system represents the contrary to a philosophy of hope. It is a philosophy of reminiscence, for which rationality belongs to the whole as present; this discrepancy between Hegel and the *intellectus fidei et spei* clearly appears in the famous text that ends the preface of the *Philosophy of Right.*[2]

Philosophy always comes too late! If this be true of philosophy, then what about reason? With that question we are sent back from Hegel to Kant or, better, from the Hegelian type to the Kantian type of philosophizing.

---

2. In any case, philosophy always comes on the scene too late to give instruction as to what the world ought to be. As the thought of the world, it appears only when actuality is already there cut and dried after its process of formation has been completed. The owl of Minerva "spreads its wings only with the falling of the dusk" (Hegel, *Philosophy of Right,* trans. T. M. Knox [Oxford: Clarendon Press, 1942], 13).

But before considering this Kantian type I want to make a general remark concerning the relation between Kant and Hegel. This relation is not merely an antithetic one. For us, and within us, as modern readers of Kant and Hegel, a kind of debate and of reciprocal debate has occurred, which for evident reasons could not occur between the authors themselves. Thanks to this debate, something of Hegel has overcome Kant, but something of Kant has also overcome Hegel. This exchange, this mutual amendment, was possible because we became as radically post-Hegelian as we are post-Kantian; I think that this permutation still shapes philosophical discourse today. The present discussion concerning the act of closing the philosophical discourse will help us to comment on what happens when the Kantian and the Hegelian ways of philosophizing are confronted and, so to say, exchanged within us.

The way that I want to explore is opened by the important distinction made by Kant between understanding (*Verstand*) and reason (*Vernunft*). This duality has many implications that are adequate to the *intellectus fidei et spei*. How? Mainly, thanks to the function of horizon assumed by reason in the twofold constitution of knowledge and of action. In both fields reason means, first, the requirement of a totality of meaning and, second, the impossibility and even the prohibition of achieving any given totality, hence finally the projection of a task that is the philosophical equivalent of hope and the most adequate philosophical approximation of freedom according to hope.

We are led then to oppose two philosophical styles, that of a philosophy of absolute knowledge and that of a philosophy of the limits. And we have not only to oppose them but also to think them together, not only one against the other but also one through the other.

Let us say first which part of the Kantian philosophy I consider as overcome by Hegel; then we shall be able to isolate the part of that philosophy that deserves to survive the critique.

I should say that the dead part in Kant's system is his ethics of duty; I think that Hegel correctly characterized it by saying that it is an abstract way of thinking, that is, according to the rigorous notion of abstractedness, a thought that separates, that isolates, that divides; in that case, it separates the form from its content, duty from desire, coherence from life, universality from historicity, legality from effectiveness, rationality from reality. In that sense the *Critique of Practical Reason* is only a critique of understanding, not of reason; and a critique of "judging" understanding, not of practical, effective, and real reason. Here I agree entirely with the Hegelian critique of Kantian morality, and I oppose to this abstract morality the Hegelian concept of the right, defined as the actualization of freedom. In that sense, duty, and in general all formal morality, would be a mere segment, the most abstract of all, within the whole process of history, thanks to which freedom becomes real; from that point of view the history of contract and that of penal law and the kind of rationality at work in economic and political life are more significant for the actualization of freedom than any morals of mere intention, deprived of all impact on individual desires or on collective institutions. I do not hesitate to say that a modern philosophy of the will should consider as closely the kind of concrete practical philosophy developed in Hegel's *Philosophy of Right* as the abstract philosophy of duty received from Kant. Alone, this great philosophy of the will, inspired by Hegel, could intimately unite the heritage of Aristotle and that of Kant. In a sense, this broad philosophy of the will has still to be done. It does not belong to the past but to the future. Its task is the one that Hegel conceived for it in the *Philosophy of Right;* it is the theory of the actualization of freedom within the historical reality of humankind.

Now the question comes: What is the horizon of this process of actualization of freedom? At that point precisely my disagreement with the Hegelian style of philosophizing begins and with this disagreement the possibility of a return to Kant.

The concept of actualization of freedom by which we defined the field of practical reason has two dimensions: that of fulfilled achievement and that of unfulfilled claim. And these two implications belong to the structure of actualization as such. On the one hand, human action makes sense because we may discern in some places adequation between rationality and reality; in those cases the Hegelian axiom is true: what is rational is real, what is real is rational. Among those cases we may cite, still with Hegel, the contractual law of exchange, the acquisition of penal law, the conquest of civil rights, and some aspects of the modern state. In order to understand those cases of rational reality or of real rationality, we want a kind of dialectic that, like the Hegelian dialectic, is a successful dialectic, that is, a dialectic in which negation is absorbed in mediation; for that kind of successful dialectic, for which philosophy is not prophecy but reminiscence and recapitulation, its totem animal was well chosen: that is, it is Minerva's owl, the bird that "spreads its wings only with the falling of the dusk."

But, on the other hand, do those cases cover the whole field of human action? Are they not rather sorts of islands of rationality, surrounded by irrationality? Is not the Hegelian philosophy of action a kind of extrapolation based on the limited experience of the fulfilled achievements of humankind? Thanks to this extrapolation, the sphere of rational reality or of real rationality is equated with the absolute knowledge that Hegel found in the thirteenth book of Aristotle's *Metaphysics* and in the new Platonic tradition.

Hence the question: Has not Hegel destroyed the spring of action by excluding the second dimension of action, that of unfulfilled claim, which counterbalances the first one, that of fulfilled achievement?

We have an important reason to think that a horizon of unfulfilled claim belongs to the most genuine experience of action. This reason relies on our experience of evil. All of us have some hint of this experience and of the difference between evil and failure. We understand that failure is fundamentally technical, that is, merely concerns a contingent discrepancy between ends and means and as such could be avoided or repaired; that evil affects the origin of action and not only the technical disposition of means in relation to their ends; that there is something broken in the very heart of human action that prevents our partial experience of fulfilled achievements from being equated with the whole field of human action.

It is that breach, that brokenness, that is denied by the Hegelian claim to absolute knowledge and its bold extension from partial rationality to total rationality. For Hegel, the philosopher can speak only about negations that can be mediated, that is, overcome by a negation of negation. Evil is only a case among nonmediated negations, and forgiveness of sins is merely a case of mediation in process, as we read at the end of the sixth chapter of the *Phenomenology of the Spirit.* The blindness to the reality of evil and to the specificity of the experience of humankind concerning evil cannot be separated from that other blindness that we just denounced, the blindness to the experience of unfulfilled claim that is the counterpart of that of fulfilled achievement on which the Hegelian philosophy of action relies.

As I said, with this disagreement begins our return to Kant. For me, Kant remains the philosopher who thought the limits of knowledge and of action and who linked the possibility of a philosophy of hope to this meditation about the theoretical and practical limitations of humankind.

At that point we could be tempted to go directly to the last work of Kant, *Religion within the Limits of Reason Alone,* and to reach immediately the point where the notion of radical evil leads to that of regeneration, which is another name of hope, the philosophical name of hope, if we may say so. But by this way of jumping directly to the end we should miss the target, which is not to locate somewhere the theme of hope, as an ultimate theme, but to understand how it belongs to the structure of the system. Hope is not a theme that comes after other themes, an idea that closes the system, but an impulse that opens the system, that breaks the closure of the system; it is a way of reopening what was unduly closed. In that sense it belongs to the structure of the system as such.

If such is the structural function of hope in philosophical systems, we cannot separate the third question raised by Kant in the *Opus Postumum* from the two others that precede it. The three questions read: What can we know? What must we do? What may we hope? The three questions constitute a unique pattern, an inseparable structure, and the interplay of the defective verbs "can" (*können*), "must" (*müssen*), and "may" (*dürfen*) warns us that the interconnection between knowing, doing, and hoping must be respected along with the attitudes ruled by the three expressions *können, müssen,* and *dürfen.* Knowledge is what we can, doing is what we must, hoping is what we may, or are allowed to.

This is the reason why we must not jump directly to the end and take hold of the last connection between evil and regeneration. In order precisely to understand this last connection in the Kantian work, we must follow the roundabout way that starts from the first *Critique* and goes through the dialectic of this first *Critique* and from there reaches the dialectic of the second *Critique,* and only after that reaches the level of a philosophical approach to what religion understands by sin and forgiveness, and then try to elaborate within the limits of reason alone the philosophical equivalent of hope, which is regeneration.

If we do not start with the first *Critique* and with its "Dialectic" we miss something essential to a philosophy of hope, that is, the destruction of absolute knowledge. Between hope and absolute knowledge we have to choose. We cannot have both. Either one or the other, but not both together. It is the function of the "Dialectic of Pure Reason" to destroy the absolute object, to which absolute knowledge could be equated: the metaphysical subject, a noncontradictory concept of free causality, and above all a philosophical concept of God, let us say of the God of the philosophers. A philosophy of hope has then to be confronted with what Kant called transcendental illusion, which occupies the place of the Hegelian concept of absolute knowledge. The field of hope has exactly the same extension as that of transcendental illusion. I hope at the very place where I am deceived by the so-called absolute objects: "I" as a substance, "freedom" as an object in the world, "God" as a supreme being, as the cause of all causes, as the whole of all partial reality. In that sense reason must first despair, despair of the absolute, despair of itself as claiming to reach the absolute under the form of an object of knowledge. But despair, within the *Critique of Pure Reason,* is not a feeling, an emotion; it is a process, an operation, the positive act of opposing a limit to the claim of the understanding and of the sensibility, to which the understanding is linked—the claim to grasp the absolute as an object of knowledge, submitted to the conditions of space and time. This act of despair is already an act of hope since it is not the thought of the unconditioned that is destroyed but the claim to equate to this thought of the unconditioned an objective knowledge that proceeds from condition to condition.

Transcendental illusion becomes in that way the instrument of the disjunction between *Denken* and *Erkennen*—*Denken* as the thought of the unconditional, *Erkennen* as the work of the understanding, as knowledge through objects. This disjunctive act, which Kant calls the limit, is the answer to the first of the three questions: What can I know?

Such is the first step of a philosophy of hope: it consists in an act of renunciation by which pure speculative reason gives up its claim to fulfill the thought of the unconditioned along the line of the knowledge of empirical objects; this repudiation by reason of its absolute claim is the last word of theoretical reason.

This theoretical structure encompassing the thought of the unconditioned, the theory of transcendental illusion, the critique of absolute objects, the positing of a limit, is essential to the *intellectus spei*. It provides a framework for many of the post-Hegelian critical conceptions of metaphysics and of rational theology; even atheism can be reinterpreted as an aspect of the same critique of transcendental illusion in a philosophy of the limits; through this reinterpretation, atheism may be cured from another illusion, from its own illusion, the illusion that puts humankind at the center and transforms it into a new absolute. The thought of the unconditioned prevents us from this last illusion, which we could call the anthropological illusion.

In that way we may understand that a philosophy of the limits does not close the philosophical discourse, but breaks the claim of objective knowledge to close it at the level of spatio-temporal objects. The limit is an act which opens, because it is an act which breaks the closure. In that sense, it already belongs to hope, in spite of the fact that it is merely negative, as the destruction of an illusion and of a claim.

Now what does the second *Critique,* the *Critique of Practical Reason,* add to this dialectic? Essentially, it extends to the will the same structure, the same act of ending the philosophical discourse in a way which both breaks a closure and opens an horizon.

The main theme of the "Dialectic of Practical Reason" is the concept of the supreme good. This classical idea receives in the Kantian dialectic a new meaning; it is not a second version of the absolute object that has been excluded from the sphere of theoretical reason; it is a practical requirement, that of the fulfillment of the will. The will requires a kind of unconditioned totality that is not fulfilled by the concept of duty or of moral law but only by the synthesis of virtue and happiness; this requirement opens a new antinomy since we must add to the concept of virtue a notion that we had to exclude from the definition of the moral principle. This antinomy between the integrality of the complete object of practical reason and the purity of moral life has the same kind of fecundity as the cosmological antinomies that divide reason from itself at the speculative level. This practical antinomy prevents us from introducing some kind of interest in the name of happiness. For my part, I consider this antinomy of practical reason as a significant framework for some other post-Hegelian critiques of religion, for example, for the Freudian critique that unmasks some childish need for security and protection behind the preaching of reward and of consolation. Kant teaches us that the reconciliation between purity of motives and the requirement of happiness is not at our disposal, as something that we could acquire by ourselves and possess. This connection—this *Zusammenhang*—must remain a transcendent synthesis between the work of humankind and the fulfillment of the desire that constitutes human existence.

Such is the second approximation by reason of the philosophical meaning of hope: it is the anticipation, the expectation, of a connection between the purity of heart and satisfaction of our most intimate desire. This expectation is rational in the sense that it is thought as a necessary connection, as a synthesis a priori between terms that the understanding isolates and opposes. The autonomy is not overcome by some third term that would be homogeneous to the contradicting terms but by a heterogeneous and transcendent term that lies at the horizon of rationality.

The practical synthesis does not therefore violate the rules of a philosophy of the limits. It adds nothing to our knowledge of the world: it completes our will without extending the sphere of objective knowledge.

If we take into consideration this idea of a practical synthesis that is required but not given, then the famous "postulates of practical reason" appear as a mere commentary on the practical synthesis. They express our hope in a total fulfillment of the requirements of reason. They speak of an "extension," of an "increasing," of an "opening," which can never be converted into an intellectual intuition, through which classical metaphysics and rational theology would be covertly reinstated. The postulates of practical reason speak of God, of immortality, and of freedom beyond a kind of "speculative death of God" implied by the philosophy of the limits. And they speak of God, of immortality, and of freedom only in a practical way, that is, as the existential implications of the structure of action, as the existential conditions for the actualization of freedom. They speak of the reality thanks to which freedom may exist. This reality can only be postulated; this expression means that, in the language of rationality, the modality of belief remains that of hypothesis and not that of evidence. From an epistemological point of view, hope is not apodictic but hypothetical; its necessity is not that of speculative evidence as it is for Hegel; the necessity of hope is not epistemological, but practical and existential. This necessity is immanent to a will that expects and requires the fulfillment of its desire for reconciliation; this necessity is that of practical reason, not of absolute knowledge. The God of the postulates is not an entity about which we could speculate; God is intended as the origin of a gift, the gift of this reconciliation of which we spoke earlier, between the purity of heart and the need for happiness. The meaning here implied remains that of a belief; nevertheless, it is a "rational belief" inasmuch as this connection can be understood and even thought as necessary from a practical point of view.

Such is the second step along the roundabout way that we had to take before reaching the last work of Kant, *Religion within the Limits of Reason*

Alone. If we had omitted the preparatory stages—the critique of transcendental illusion, the paradoxes and antinomies of practical reason—we should have been tempted to oppose to the Hegelian concept of absolute knowledge an empty concept of belief or of hope. Indeed the last book of Kant has too often been viewed apart from the whole structure of a philosophy of the limits. It is only against the background of the whole system that the main doctrine of this book can be understood.

As is well known, it is the problem of evil that opens the specific investigation of Kant's book. Now, evil is a problem for the philosopher only inasmuch as it belongs to the problematic of the actualization of freedom; evil makes of freedom an impossible possibility. In spite of the fact that evil proceeds from our freedom, it is no longer within our power to change this acquired nature of "bad will." We can change the maxims of our actions; we cannot change the nature of our freedom. Here we reach the bottom of the abyss. As Karl Jaspers has noticed, Kant carries to termination his philosophy of the limits; not only our knowledge but our power has limits. The theme of radical evil plays here the same role as that of transcendental illusion in the speculative philosophy; it adds a practical despair to theoretical despair. This twofold despair is the reverse side of hope. The postulate of freedom must henceforth pass through the night of understanding with the crisis of transcendental illusion, and through the night of powerlessness with the crisis of radical evil. A real liberty can only be hoped, beyond this speculative and practical Good Friday. We are nowhere so close as here to the Christian kerygma: hope is hope of resurrection, of resurrection from among the dead. In philosophical terms: evil requires a nonethical and nonpolitical transformation of our will, which Kant calls regeneration; it is the task of "religion within the limits of reason alone" to elaborate the condition of possibility of this regeneration, without alienating freedom either to a magical conception of grace and salvation or to an authoritarian organization of the religious community.

In that sense the Kantian critique of classical theology, either medieval or Lutheran, must be taken seriously and considered as a positive contribution to what we could call a critique of hope within the limits of reason alone.

I want now to conclude this essay with the following propositions:

1. The problem of hope, as compared to that of faith, is less the problem of a specific object than that of the finality of philosophical and theological discourse. Philosophy and theology are concerned with hope in the way in which both are related to their respective closing point or horizon.

2. The specific task of theology, in that respect, is to relate the preaching of hope in all fields of human experience and action—ethical or political—to the central preaching of the church, that of the Risen Lord. In other words, theology understands hope as the anticipation through history of the resurrection of all from among the dead.

3. As such hope is both irrational, as being "in spite of" death and "beyond" despair, and rational, as asserting a new law, the law of superabundance, the superabundance of sense over non-sense.

4. The philosophical equivalent of hope and of its law of superabundance is to be found in the kind of dialectic that rules the relation between freedom and its full actualization. Where the Hegelian dialectic, which is a conclusive dialectic, is the philosophical equivalent of a speculative theology centered on the eternal now of truth, the Kantian dialectic, which is a nonconclusive dialectic, has more affinity with a theology of hope, that is, with an interpretation of Christianity for which hope cannot be overcome by absolute knowledge, by gnosis, and for which therefore hope opens up what knowledge claims to close.

5. Between a philosophy of hope and this kind of nonconclusive dialectic, there is not only a relation of correspondence, which still remains a static relation, but a dynamic relation, which I call a relation of approximation. By approximation I mean the effort of thought to come closer and closer to the eschatological event that constitutes the center of a theology of hope. Thanks to this active approximation of hope by dialectic, philosophy knows something and says something of the Easter-preaching. But what it knows and what it says remain within the limits of reason alone. In this self-restraint abide both the responsibility and the modesty of philosophy.

12

Naming God

Few authors have the gift or the talent to write, "What I Believe." Yet more than one listener to Christian preaching may stand ready to describe the ways they understand what they have heard. I am one of these listeners.

I. Presupposition

To confess that one is a listener is from the very beginning to break with the project dear to many, and even perhaps all, philosophers: to begin discourse without any presuppositions. (We could speak simply of the "project of beginning," for to think without presuppositions and to begin to think are one.) Yet it is in terms of one certain presupposition that I stand in the position of a listener to Christian preaching: I assume that this speaking is meaningful, that it is worthy of consideration, and that examining it may accompany and guide the transfer from the text to life where it will verify itself fully.

Can I account for this presupposition? Alas, I stumble already. I do not know how to sort out what is here "unravelable" situation, uncriticized custom, deliberate preference, or profound unchosen choice. I can only confess that my desire to hear more is all these things, and that it defies all these distinctions.

But if what I presuppose precedes everything I can choose to think about, how do I avoid the famous circle of believing in order to understand and understanding in order to believe? I do not seek to avoid it. I boldly stay within this circle in the hope that, through the transfer from text to life, what I have risked will be returned a hundredfold as an increase in comprehension, valor, and joy.

Shall I tolerate the fact that thinking, which aims at what is universal and necessary, is linked in a contingent way to individual events and particular texts that report them? Yes, I shall assume this contingency, so scandalous

Reprinted with permission from *Union Seminary Quarterly Review* 34 (1979): 215–27.

for thinking, as one aspect of the presupposition attached to listening. For I hope that once I enter into the movement of comprehending faith, I shall discover the very reason for that contingency, if it is true that the increase in comprehension that I expect is indissolubly linked to testimonies to the truth, which are contingent in every instance and rendered through certain acts, lives, and beings.

II. Text

Naming God comes about only within the milieu of a presupposition, incapable of being rendered transparent to itself, suspected of being a vicious circle, and tormented by contingency. This is the presupposition: naming God is what has already taken place in the texts preferred by my listening's presupposition.

1. Do I therefore place texts above life? Does not religious experience come first? My presupposition does not say that nothing can be taken as religious "experience"—be it a feeling of "absolute dependence," a response to a will that precedes me, an "ultimate concern" at the horizon of all my decisions, or "an unconditional confidence" that hopes in spite of...everything. These are some of the synonyms of what has been called faith, those at least that are most familiar and closest to me. So understood, faith is certainly not an act that can be reduced to any act of speaking or any piece of writing. This act represents the limit of any hermeneutic because it is the origin of all interpretation.

But the presupposition of listening to Christian preaching is not that everything is language; it is rather that it is always within a language that religious experience is articulated, that one hears it in a cognitive, practical, or emotional sense. More precisely, what is presupposed is that faith, inasmuch as it is lived experience, is *instructed*—in the sense of being formed, clarified, and educated—within the network of texts that in each instance preaching brings back to living speech. This presupposition of the *textuality* of faith distinguishes *biblical* faith ("Bible" meaning book) from all others. In one sense, therefore, texts do precede life. I can name God in my faith because the texts preached to me have already named God.

Yet if I do not put texts above life, do I not nevertheless give writing a privilege that really belongs to speaking? Do we not call these texts the word of God? And is not preaching a speech-event? If there is an abstraction and a hypostasis of the text that I will fight against below, the contrary abstraction, that of a dialogue or an encounter between an I and a Thou, calls for similar reservations. An apologetic that is based just on dialogue tends to make us completely lose sight of what is unique to instruction through texts. Examining some specific texts below will reveal how the purely dialogic interpretation of the relation between God and humanity is too narrow and exclusive. I limit myself here to calling the dialogic scheme into question on the simple level of the communication of discourse; that is, on the plane of a text's being addressed to and received within a community of interpretation.

Someone may readily say, recalling Plato's critique of writing in his *Phaedrus*, that when living speech is given over to "external marks" such as letters and written signs, communication is irremediably cut off. Something is lost that belongs to the voice, the facial expression, and the common situation of interlocutors in a face-to-face setting. This is not false. It is even so true that the reconversion of writing into speech aims at re-creating a relation not identical to, but analogical to, the dialogic relation of communication. Yet it does so precisely beyond the "scriptuary" step of communication and with its own characters that depend on preaching's posttextual position. What the unilateral apologetic for dialogue misunderstands is the extraordinary promotion that happens to discourse in passing from speech to writing. By breaking away from the bodily presence of a reader, the text also breaks away from its author: that is, from the intention the text is supposed to express, from the psychology of the person behind the work, from the understanding that person has of himself or herself and of his or her situation, from his or her relation as author to an initial public, the original target of the text—all at the same time. This triple independence of the text with regard to its author, its context, and its initial audience explains why texts are open to innumerable "re-contextualizations" through listening and reading that are a reply to the "decontextualization" already contained in the very act of writing or, more exactly, of publication.

2. If I make believers scribes, will it be long before I make them literary critics? Taken in the closure of their own textuality, my texts will then close in upon themselves. They will be open to other texts that they cite or that they transform, but the interplay of intertextuality will only come to be more separated and closed off from the side I have called life. What I call the hermeneutical approach (or simply the theory of interpretation) is exactly the refusal of this "literary" hypostasis of the text, simply substituted for that of dialogic speaking. I would like to develop two arguments against this hypostasis.

A text is first a link in a communicative chain. To begin, one of life's experiences is brought to language. It becomes discourse. Then this discourse is differentiated into speech and writing, with the privileges and advantages of which I have spoken. Writing, in its turn, is restored to living speech by means of the various acts of discourse that reactualize the text. Reading and preaching are such actualizations of writing into speech. A text, in this regard, is like a musical score that requires execution. (Some critics, reacting against the excessive emphasis on the text-in-itself, even go so far as to say that it is "the reader in the text" who completes its meaning; for example, by filling in its lacunas or by resolving its ambiguities; that is, by straightening out its narrative or argumentative order.)

Cut away from speaking-becoming-writing and from writing-becoming-speaking, the text is no more than an artifact of critical method. This artifact may, in turn, be put in a series with other artifacts, as we place a book alongside other books in a library. Intertextuality in the proper sense of the word is such a library. And other less classificatory, more genetic operations may be applied to this constructed series. The old *Quellen-forschung* already practiced this game of referring one text to another in a genetic filiation. The quoting of the code in the theory of intertextuality, which today replaces the borrowing of a message, basically belongs to this same family of procedures: abstract a text from the communicative chain, put it near or together with another equally abstract text, then make a whole out of these texts in genetic or structural series. The illusion is the same, that of believing that one has understood a text better when one knows another text from which it arises through borrowing or through quotation.

Yet it does not suffice to replace a text in the communicative chain in order to overthrow the hypostasis of the text-in-itself. Its most central hypothesis must be attacked, namely, that writing brings about a fundamental mutation in discourse concerning the relation between "sense" and "reference." This mutation would abolish the question of reference solely to the benefit of the sense. By reference is meant discourse's character of relating itself to an extralinguistic reality, what above I called the lived experience that is brought to language, before any bifurcation within discourse into speech and writing. By sense is meant, within the perspective of abolished reference, a network of relations purely internal to the text, whether it be a question of a hierarchical relation by which units of a lower rank are integrated into units of a higher rank, a relation between the surface message and the underlying codes, a combination of various codes within the same text, or the quotation of some codes external to the text considered within the relation of intertextuality mentioned above.

The hermeneutical thesis, diametrically opposed to the structuralist thesis—not to structural method and inquiry—is that the difference between speech and writing in no way abolishes the fundamental function of discourse (which encompasses these two variations: oral and written). Discourse consists of the fact that someone says something to someone *about something*. "About something" is the inalienable referential function of discourse. Writing does not abolish it, but rather transforms it. In oral discourse, face-to-face interlocutors can, in the final analysis, refer what they are talking about to the surrounding world common to them. Only writing can, by addressing itself to anyone who knows how to read, refer to a world that is not there between the interlocutors, a world that is the world of the text and yet is not in the text. Following Gadamer, I call this "the 'thing' or issue of the text." This issue of the text is the object of hermeneutics. It is neither behind the text as the presumed author nor in the text as its structure, but unfolded in front of it.

This same consideration applies to biblical texts. God, who is named by the texts held open by my desire to listen, is, in a way still to be spoken of, the ultimate referent of these texts. God is in some manner implied by the "issue" of these texts, by the world—the biblical world—that these texts unfold.

By so orienting the hermeneutical axis of my meditation toward the issue of the text, I recognize the vanity of an inquiry oriented toward the text's author that would seek to identify God as the voice behind the narrative or prophetic voice. I am well aware that a long tradition identified revelation with inspiration, in the sense of an insufflation of meaning that made God a sort of overarching author of the texts wherein faith instructs itself. But if the word "revelation" means something, its meaning is to be sought on the side of the issue the texts tell about, as an aspect of the biblical world.

III. Poetic

How do I respond to the following objection? This defense of the referential dimension of a text only holds for discourse of a descriptive character: ordinary discourse about the things of life, scientific discourse about the world's physical entities, historical discourse about events that really happened, sociological discourse about actual instances of existing societies. Referential discourse stops at the threshold of poetic discourse. There, language celebrates itself. Or, if it does seem to refer to something, it does so to the extent that it expresses emotions that are wholly subjective and that add nothing to the description of the world. Thus naming God is, at best, a poetic activity without any bearing on description; that is, without any bearing on true knowledge of the world.

I do assume provisionally the assimilation of biblical texts to poetic texts. I will speak below about the manner in which the Bible is a poem, albeit unique and, in this sense, eccentric. I do assume this assimilation because I object to the theory that reduces the referential function to descriptive discourse in order to allow only an emotional function to poetic discourse. (I note in passing that the structuralist reduction of literary texts to their immanent sense depends largely on a theory wherein poetic discourse has already been stripped of its referential function due to the subterfuge of the opposition between descriptive and nondescriptive discourse. What is held to be essential, in effect, is that "literature" occurs in the nondescriptive zones of discourse, whether it takes the form of fictive narration, lyric, or an essay. It is a matter, therefore, of directly refuting this theory of poetic discourse, independently of its link to literary structuralism; for example, in the form it assumes in Anglo-American logical positivism.)

If some have held the poetic function of discourse to exclude its referential function, this was because, at first, the poem (again understood in a wide sense that includes narrative fiction, lyricism, and the essay) suspends a first-order referential function, whether it is a question of direct reference to familiar objects of perception or of indirect reference to physical entities that science reconstructs as underlying the former objects. In this sense, it is true that poetry is a suspension of the descriptive function. It does not add to our knowledge of objects. But this suspension is the wholly negative condition for the liberation of a more originary referential function, which may be called second-order only because discourse that has a descriptive function has usurped the first rank in daily life, assisted, in this respect, by science. Poetic discourse is also about the world, but not about the manipulable objects of our everyday environment. It refers to our many ways of belonging to the world before we oppose ourselves to things understood as "objects" that stand before a "subject." If we have become blind to these modalities of *rootedness* and *belonging-to* (*appartenance*) that precede the relation of a subject to objects, it is because we have, in an uncritical way, ratified a certain concept of truth, defined by adequation to real objects and submitted to a criterion of empirical verification and falsification. Poetic discourse precisely calls into question these uncritical concepts of adequation and verification. In so doing, it calls into question the reduction of the referential function to descriptive discourse and opens the field of a nondescriptive reference to the world.

It is this nondescriptive reference to the world that is awkwardly covered over by the traits of the emotional function of poetic language. As though emotions were simply "subjective"! What we here are calling emotions, in the wake of poetic language, are precisely modalities of our relation to the world that are not exhausted in the description of objects. Basic emotions such as fear, anger, joy, and sadness express ways of belonging to things as much as ways in which we behave in relation to them; all the more reason why feelings, temperaments, moods, and *Stimmungen,* expressed, shaped, and instructed by poetic language, should throw us into the midst of things.

I will not hesitate to say, given the rapid pace of this refutation of positivism in poetics, that it seems to me that this referential function of poetic discourse conceals a dimension of revelation in a nonreligious, nontheistic, nonbiblical sense of the word, yet a sense capable of furnishing a first approximation of what revelation in the biblical sense may signify.

To reveal is to uncover what until then remained hidden. Now, the objects of our manipulation dissimulate the world of our originary rootedness. Yet in spite of the closed-off character of our ordinary experience, and across the ruins of the intraworldly objects of everyday reality and science, the modalities of our belonging to the world trace out their way. Revelation, in this sense, designates the emergence of another concept of truth than truth as adequation, regulated by the criteria of verification and falsification: a concept of truth as manifestation, in the sense of letting be what shows itself. What shows itself is each time the proposing of a world, a world wherein I can project my ownmost possibilities.

Hence, naming God, before being an act of which I am capable, is what the texts of my predilection do when they escape from their authors, their redactional setting, and their first audience, when they deploy their world, when they poetically manifest and thereby reveal a world we might inhabit.

IV. Biblical Polyphony

It is the naming of God by the biblical texts that specifies the religious at the interior of the poetic.

1. A preliminary remark: the very word "God" primordially belongs to a level of discourse I speak of as *originary* in relation to utterances of a speculative, theological, or philosophical type, such as: "God exists," "God is immutable and omnipotent...," "God is the first cause," and so on. I put theological utterances on the same speculative side as philosophical utterances inasmuch as theology's discourse is not constituted without recourse to concepts borrowed from some speculative philosophy, be it Platonic, Aristotelian, Cartesian, Kantian, Hegelian, or whatever. For the philosopher, to listen to Christian preaching is first of all to let go (*se depouiller*) of every form of onto-theological knowledge. Even—and especially when—the word God is involved. In this regard, the amalgamation of being and God is the most subtle seduction.

Modern philosophy accomplishes this letting go of knowledge about God in a certain fashion with its own resources. I am thinking principally of Kant and his general conception of philosophy as knowing our limits. There the index of this letting go is the idea of a "transcendental illusion" that reason necessarily produces whenever it undertakes to forge a knowledge of God by way of "objects." The paralogisms and antinomies thus become for critical reason the ascetic instruments by which it is led back to itself within those boundaries where its knowledge is valid.

But this letting go of the knowledge of God through the resources of critical philosophy has no apologetic value, even in its negative form. For if a first hubris is knocked down, that of metaphysical knowledge, a second one replaces it, that of a knowledge that is no longer metaphysical but transcendental. This knowledge makes the "I think" the principle of everything that is valid. This knowledge does not stand on the side of objects to be known but on the side of the conditions of possibility of knowing, therefore on the side of the subject. The idea of a subject that posits itself thus becomes the unfounded foundation, or, better, the foundation that founds itself, in relation to which every rule of validity is derived. In this way, the subject becomes the supreme "presupposition."

Listening to Christian preaching also stands in the order of presuppositions, but in a sense where presupposition is no longer self-founding, the beginning of the self from and by the self, but rather the assumption of an antecedent meaning that has always preceded me. *Listening excludes founding oneself.* The movement toward listening requires, therefore, a second letting go, the abandoning of a more subtle and more tenacious pretension than that of onto-theological knowledge. It requires giving up (*dessaissement*) the human self in its will to mastery, sufficiency, and autonomy. The Gospels' statement that "Whoever would save his life will lose it" applies to this giving up.

This double renouncing of the absolute "object" and the absolute "subject" is the price that must be paid to enter into a radically nonspeculative and prephilosophical mode of language. It is the task of a philosophical hermeneutic to guide us from the double absolute of onto-theological speculation and transcendental reflection toward the more originary modalities of language by means of which the members of the community of faith have interpreted their experience to themselves and to others. It is here where God has been named.

2. A second remark. The naming of God, in the originary expressions of faith, is not simple but multiple. It is not a single tone, but polyphonic. The originary expressions of faith are complex forms of discourse as diverse as narratives, prophecies, laws, proverbs, prayers, hymns, liturgical formulas, and wisdom writings. As a whole, these forms of discourse name God. But they do so in various ways.

Indeed, it is worth noting that each of the forms of discourse just mentioned encompasses a particular style of confession of faith where God is named in an original fashion. This is why we miss what is unique about biblical faith if we take categories such as narrative, oracle, commandment, and so on, as rhetorical devices that are alien to the content they transmit. What is admirable, on the contrary, is that structure and kerygma accommodate each other in each form of narration. It is within this mutual accommodation of the form and the confession of faith that the naming of God diversifies itself.

The whole of contemporary exegesis has made us attentive to the primacy of the *narrative* structure in the biblical writings. The theology of the

Old Testament is first established as a "theology of traditions" around several kernel events: the call of Abraham, the exodus, the anointing of David,
and so forth. The naming of God is thus first of all a narrative naming. The
theology of traditions names God in accord with a historical drama that
recounts itself as a narrative of liberation. God is the God of Abraham,
Isaac, and Jacob and is, therefore, the Actant of the great gesture of deliverance. And God's meaning as Actant is bound up with the founding events
in which the community of interpretation recognizes itself as enrooted, set
up, and established. It is these events that name God.

In this regard, the naming of God in the resurrection narratives of the
New Testament is in accord with the naming of God in the deliverance narratives of the Old Testament: God called Christ from the dead. Here, too,
God is designated by the transcendence of the founding events in relation
to the ordinary course of history.

In this sense, we must say the naming God is first of all a moment of
the narrative confession. God is named in "the thing" recounted. This is
counter to a certain emphasis among theologies of the word that only note
word-events. To the extent that the narrative genre is primary, God's imprint is in history before being in speech. Speech comes second inasmuch as
it confesses the trace of God in the event.

But my concern here is not to deal with the problems of narrative. It is
rather to insist upon the variety of ways of naming God that the listener to
the word discovers in the texts of his or her predilection.

The well-known opposition between narration and prophecy first solicits
the listener's attention. In narration, no one seems to be speaking. It is as
though the events recounted themselves. God, then, is named in the third
person within the horizon of the recounted event. In prophecy, the prophetic voice announces itself in the *consciousness* of being called and sent:
"The word of the Lord came to me, saying 'Go and proclaim in the hearing of Jerusalem. ... ' " God is now signified as the voice of an other behind
the prophetic voice. To put it another way, God is named in a double first
person, as the word of another in my word. It is easy to understand how,
through forgetting the narrative genre and the other genres where God is
also named, a certain hypostasis of the prophetic genre could have led to
identifying revelation and inspiration and to the entire "subjectivization"
of the naming of God. God, named as the voice behind the voice, becomes
the absolute subject of discourse. We then break off the essential dialectic between the narrative and the prophetic. We first break it at the level
of grammatical persons, the prophetic "I" being always balanced by the
narrative "He." But it is also broken at the level of the events themselves,
for prophecy is not just its own voice but also what is intended by the
event as with narration. Without locking prophecy into the prediction of
the future, prophecy does bear forward toward "the Day of Yahweh," con-

cerning which the prophet says it will not be a day of joy, but of terror. This collision between an imminent threat and the remembrance of the founding events introduces a fault into the very meaning of the recounted history. The tension between narration and prophecy thus is expressed in a dialectic of the event, and it gives rise to a paradoxical understanding of history as simultaneously founded in remembrance and menaced through prophecy. In this way, even in the prophetic genre, God is named in and through the event and not just as the voice behind the voice.

All the other genres of discourse in which biblical faith has found expression must be brought together, not just in an enumeration that would juxtapose them, but in a living dialectic that will display their interferences with one another. Thus the prescriptive discourse of the Torah, separated from narrative discourse and prophetic discourse, tends to shrink to the dimensions of an imperative that Kant held to be both heteronomous, due to its origin as a commandment, and conditional, due to its conjunction with promises and threats. God is then named as the author of the law. Taken in itself, this naming is not false. It is part of the meaning of this naming that I perceive myself as designated in the second person by God: "*You* shall love the Lord your God with all your heart, and with all your soul, and with all your might." I am this "you." But the meaning of this double naming of God as the law's author and of myself as face-to-face with God is illumined only in the dialectic between prescriptive discourse and the other forms of discourse.

First, the teaching of the Torah is organically linked to the founding events recounted in the great deed for which the exodus constitutes the kernel. In this way, the promulgation of the law is organically linked to the narrative of deliverance. To this overlapping of the prescriptive and the recitative is added the concrete character of the time of apprenticeship that is attached to the idea of the covenant, concerning which the modern notion of an imperative only expresses the most abstract trace.

The concrete character of the teaching is confirmed if we also bring together the commandment and the prophetic commission. This, too, designates the prophet as a summoned second person: "(You) go proclaim." The person sent was thus personalized as "you" by the prophetic voice. Then this "you" became the "I" of the double voice of the herald. A similar dialectic of persons is produced by what we could call the ethical voice: the "you" of the summons becomes the responsible "I."

The dialectic of the ethical and the prophetic that is the counterpart of the dialectic of the ethical and the narrative extends beyond the exchange between the prophetic and the ethical voices. It is inscribed in the movement of the commandment, which, in turn, is deployed into the minutia of the innumerable commandments or compressed into the single goal of sainthood and the single commandment of love. The new law and the new covenant express, if we may put it this way, an ethic based on prophecy. God is then named as the one who says, "A new heart I will give you, and a new spirit I will put within you; and I will take out of your flesh the heart of stone and give you a heart of flesh."

The New Testament takes this interplay of exchanges to the extreme. The new commandment taken up from Deuteronomy leans on the evangelical narrative of the life of the Liberator, and it is through the remembering of the resurrection and under the sign of the promises of a universal resurrection that the kingdom of God allows itself to be understood.

Yet the naming of God in narrative, prophecy, and prescription must not be deprived of the enrichment brought by wisdom and hymns. Wisdom is not just contained in the wisdom writings. Overflowing the framework of the covenant, its meditation bears on the human condition in general. It is directly addressed to the sense and non-sense of existence. It is a struggle for sense in spite of non-sense. Unjust suffering has a central place here to the extent that suffering itself poses its enigma at the juncture between the order of things and the ethical order. This is why wisdom does not so much speak of what ought to be done as of how to endure, how to suffer suffering. The naming of God here is less personalized than in prescription or in prophecy, whether the nothingness of God be brought face-to-face with the incomprehensibility of God in terms of God's silence or absence, or if wisdom itself be celebrated as a barely personalized transcendent entity. A wholly other voice than the prophetic voice or the ethical voice may be heard, which has some traits in common with the narrative "He." At its limit, wisdom discourse encounters a hidden God who takes the anonymous and inhuman course of things as God's mask.

The relation to God is internalized in another way with the hymns of celebration, supplication, and thanksgiving. It is no longer just humanity who is a "you" for God, as in the prophetic commission or the ethical commandment. God becomes a "you" to the human you. This movement toward a double second person reaches its highest point in the psalms of recognition just as the movement toward the double first person culminates in the prophetic voice as the voice of an other.

Thus God is named in diverse ways in narration that recounts the divine acts, prophecy that speaks in the divine name, prescription that designates God as the source of the imperative, wisdom that seeks God as the meaning of meaning, and the hymn that invokes God in the second person. Because of this, the word "God" cannot be understood as a philosophical concept, not even "being" in the sense of medieval philosophy or in Heidegger's sense. The word "God" says more than the word "being" because it presupposes the entire context of narratives, prophecies, laws, wisdom writings, psalms, and so on. The referent "God" is thus intended by the convergence of all these partial discourses. It expresses the circulation of meaning among all the forms of discourse wherein God is named.

V. *Limit-Expressions*

The referent "God" is not just the index of the mutual belonging together (*appartenance*) of the originary forms of the discourse of faith. It is also the index of their incompleteness. It is their common goal, which escapes each of them.

Indeed, that God is designated at the same time as the one who communicates through the multiple modalities of discourse just discussed and who also holds back is why the dialectic of the naming of God cannot be transformed into a form of knowledge. In this regard, the episode of the burning bush (Exod. 3:13-15) has a central significance. Tradition has rightly named this episode the revelation of the divine name. This name is precisely unnameable. To the extent that to know a god's name was to have power over that god, the name confided to Moses is certainly that of the being whom humanity cannot really name, that is, hold at the mercy of our language:

> Then Moses said to God, "If I come to the people of Israel and say to them, 'The God of your fathers has sent me to you,' and they ask me, 'What is his name?' what shall I say to them?" God said to Moses, "I am who I am." And he said, "Say this to the people of Israel, 'I am has sent me to you.' "

Thus the appellative "Yahweh"—he is—is not a defining name but one that is a sign of the act of deliverance. Indeed, the text continues in these terms: "God also said to Moses, 'Thus you shall say to the Israelites, "Yahweh, the God of your ancestors, the God of Abraham, the God of Isaac, and the God of Jacob, has sent me to you": this is my name forever, and thus I am to be remembered throughout all generations.' " Far, therefore, from the declaration "I am who I am" authorizing a positive ontology capable of capping off the narrative and other namings, instead it protects the secret of the "in-itself" of God, and this secret, in turn, sends us back to the narrative naming through the names of Abraham, Isaac, and Jacob, and by degrees to the other namings.

This recession into infinity of the referent "God" is suggested by the particular structure of certain other forms of the discourse of faith that we have not yet spoken of, which especially belong to the New Testament and more particularly to Jesus' preaching about the kingdom of God. There, God is named at the same time the kingdom is named. Yet the kingdom is signified only through parables, proverbs, and paradoxes for which no literal translation can exhaust their meaning. This indirect character of the naming of God is especially noteworthy in the parables. We find in them a narrative structure that recalls that of the theology of traditions, yet there are considerable differences. The narration is unfolded less in terms of large historical frescoes of an epical style than as compressed into brief little stories of everyday life whose narrative form recalls that of tragedy or of comedy. What is more, just as drama conjoins a "plot" and a "theme" in its structure (*mythos* and *dianoia* in the vocabulary of Aristotle's *Poetics*), the parable has a "point," one signified by the plot itself, and which may easily be converted into a proverb (just as a proverb may become the "point" of a parable if the proverb is given a plot).

It is as plot and as point that the parabolic narrative undergoes a transference of meaning, a metaphorical displacement that through the crisis and the denouement of the story recounted obliquely intends the kingdom: "The kingdom of God is like a ... " In this way, the parable joins a metaphorical transfer to a narrative structure. But this is not the whole story nor even what is essential. For what carries the literal meaning toward the metaphorical meaning is a characteristic of the plot and the point that is related to a similar characteristic that may be better read from these other forms of discourse.

In the eschatological saving, it is the calculating of the times practiced by apocalypticists that is subverted. "The kingdom of God is not coming with signs to be observed; nor will they say, 'Lo, here it is!' or 'There!' for behold the kingdom of God is in the midst of you." The same transgression affects the ordinary use of the proverb, which is meant to provide guidance for living in ordinary circumstances. Paradoxes and hyperboles dissuade hearers in some way from forming a coherent project of their lives and from making their existence into a continuous whole. Paradox: "For whoever would save his life will lose it; and whoever loses his life for my sake and the gospel's will save it." Hyperbole: "But if any one strikes you on the right cheek, turn to him the other also; and if one would sue you and take your coat, let him have your cloak as well; and if any one forces you to go one mile, go with him two miles." In the same way that the proverb (submitted to the law of paradox and hyperbole) only reorients by first disorienting, the parable (submitted to what I call the law of extravagance) makes the extraordinary break forth in the ordinary. Indeed, there is no parable that does not introduce into the very structure of the plot an implausible characteristic, something insolent, disproportionate; that is, something scandalous. Thus it is the contrast between the realism of the story and the extravagance of the denouement that gives rise to the kind of drift by means of which the plot and its point are suddenly carried off toward the Wholly Other.

If we now bring together what has been said about the Unnameable Name signified in the episode of the burning bush and this kind of transgressing of the usual forms of the parable, the proverb, and the eschatological saying through the concerted use of extravagance, hyperbole, and paradox, a new category appears that we may call the category of *limit-expressions*. This is not a supplementary form of discourse, even though the parable as such does constitute an autonomous modality of the expression of faith. It is rather a question of an indication or a modification that undoubtedly affects every form of discourse through a sort of passing over to the limit. If the case of the parable is exemplary, it is because it combines a narrative structure, a metaphorical process, and a limit-expression. In this way, it constitutes a short summary of the naming of God. Through its narrative structure, it recalls the original rootedness of the language of faith in narratives. Through its metaphorical process, it makes manifest the poetic character of the language of faith as a whole. And finally, in joining metaphor and limit-expression, it furnishes the matrix for theological language inasmuch as this language conjoins analogy and negation in the way of eminence: "God is like ..., God is not ... "

VI. Poem of God or Poem of Christ?

Some will object that the preceding meditation is too "biblical"—if one may put it this way—and not "Christian" enough. I have followed the spoor of the naming of God through the Bible without insisting on the specificity of the naming of God in the New Testament. In opening my run through the various modalities of discourse, I have considered the narration of the exodus and that of the resurrection as arising from the same narrative genre. In closing it, I have placed the Unnameable Name from the episode of the burning bush face-to-face with the limit-expressions from the New Testament. As one kind of justification, I might limit myself to asserting that my topic was "God," not "Christ." But I do not want to elude the objection that holds that the poem of Christ has replaced the poem of God, following the formula of Christian atheism that God is dead in Jesus Christ, with the consequence that the referent "God" recedes to the rank of a simple cultural given that needs to be neutralized. I do not want to avoid this objection because it calls into question the very hypothesis of this meditation, namely, that the New Testament *continues* to name God. I will not hesitate to say that I resist with all my strength the displacement of the accent from God to Jesus Christ, which would be the equivalent of substituting one naming for another.

I hold that what Jesus preaches is the kingdom *of God,* which is inscribed in the naming of God by the prophets, the eschatologists, and the apocalyptics. What is the cross without the cry, "*My God, My God,* why have you forsaken me?" inscribed into the naming of God by the psalmist? And what is the resurrection if it is not an act of God homologous to that of the exodus? Hence a Christology without God seems to me as unthinkable as Israel without Yahweh. And I do not see how it could avoid becoming diluted into an individual or collective anthropology, one that would be entirely horizontal and stripped of its poetic power.

If one says that the God we ought to renounce knowing has been made known in Jesus Christ, this proposal does not make any sense unless, in confessing the initiative of Jesus' words, we name at the same time Jesus' God. Jesus' humanity is not thinkable as different from his union with God. Jesus of Nazareth cannot be understood apart from God, apart from his God, who is also the God of Moses and the prophets.

Perhaps we can no longer write a Christology beginning from above; that is, beginning from trinitarian speculation, in relation to which the event of Jesus would be contingent. Yet neither can we write a Christology beginning from below; that is, beginning from the historical figure of the man Jesus of Nazareth—unless at some point it intersects with the whole naming of God that encompasses Jesus' message and his message *about* God. This point of intersection is the place where Jesus is signified and understood by the confessing community as "the man whose existence is determined by the God he proclaimed" (Wolfhart Pannenberg). What sense would this expression have if we were not capable of understanding together—that is, under the form of the most extreme tension and conflict—God's determining the existence of Jesus *and* the naming of God by all the biblical texts? Perhaps, with Pannenberg, we need to enlarge this circle to include the whole of history, to the extent that we need to see it as the history of the question concerning God and the history of the failure of the quest for God.

Some may say that the relation between the christological ground and this mediation through the whole of history of the names of God is circular. Certainly it is circular. But this circle must itself be courageously assumed. Everything, in one sense, begins with the cross and resurrection. But the cross does not allow itself to be spoken of or understood as the relinquishment of God except in relation to all the signs of God's weakness that belong to the whole naming of God. And the resurrection may be understood only through the memory of God's liberating acts and in anticipation of the resurrection of every human being.

Hence, it is perhaps the task of Christology to maintain, in the interior of the *same* meaning space, as the two antagonistic tendencies of the *same* naming, the celebration of total power, which seems to dominate the Old Testament, and the confession of total weakness, which seems to be declared by the New. It would then be necessary to discover that, on the one side, the total power of the biblical God, once stripped of Greek ideas of immutability and impassivity, already leans toward the total weakness signified by the contestation and failure of God. But it would also be necessary to understand symmetrically that the kenosis, signified by the cross, ceases to be the simple idea that some today would like to draw toward the idea of the death of God, as soon as it is put in relation with the power expressed through Jesus' preaching of the kingdom and the Christian community's preaching of the resurrection. In this way, the New Testament announces a power of weakness that needs to be dialectically articulated along with the weakness of power that the other namings of God suggest.

In no way do I deny the difficulty of this dialectical labor. It must avoid the constraint of the logic of identity as much as the license of the logic of difference, as well as any false appeasement of the dialectic. The doctrine of the Trinity did this labor for one epoch of thought. A similar labor ought to be undertaken today, one that would take up the whole space of the naming of God and its discordant concordance.

VII. Poetics and Politics

I would like now to link my investigation of the multiple naming of God to my earlier proposal about the revelatory power of poetic language. Three remarks will demarcate the transfer from the text toward life.

1. First, a preliminary question. Shall I take up the idea that the naming of God depends on the poetic word? I will reply: in a certain sense and up to a certain point.

This sense is the one I tried to establish above, which I will summarize in three points. (a) Poetic language is language that breaks with everyday language and that is constituted in the crucible of semantic innovation. (b) Poetic language, far from celebrating language for itself, opens up a new world, which is the issue of the text, the world of the poem. (c) The world of the text is what incites the reader, or the listener, to understand himself or herself in the face of the text and to develop, in imagination and sympathy, the *self* capable of inhabiting this world by deploying his or her ownmost possibilities there. In *this* sense, religious language is a poetic language. Here, the word "poetic" does not designate a "literary genre" that could be added to narration, prophecy, and so on, but the overall functioning of all these genres as the seat of semantic innovation, as the proposition of a world, and as the instigation of a new understanding of oneself.

But religious language is not simply poetic. Or, if one prefers, it is so in a specific manner that makes the particular case a unique one, an eccentric one. What differentiates it is precisely the naming of God. All the literary genres we have referred to, from narration to parable, constitute "speaking about God." This specificity does not abolish any of the poem's character istics. Rather it adds to the common traits of the poem the circulating of an overarching referent—God—that coordinates the texts at the same time that it escapes them. Touched by God's "name," the poetic word undergoes a mutation of meaning that needs to be circumscribed.

One might be tempted to attach this mutation of meaning exclusively to the role of the limit-expressions (the Unnameable Name, paradox, hyperbole, extravagance). These limit-expressions surely do have the immense virtue of making us aware of the specificity of religious language, but they do not entirely constitute it. They only work within the milieu of a fundamentally analogical or metaphorical language, itself engendered by the narrative, prescriptive, prophetic, and finally the parabolic naming of God. These limit-expressions serve to qualify, modify, and rectify this analogical language.

This can be demonstrated in the following way. Narratives, prophecies, laws, and so on, are not established at the level of the concept but at that of the schema. As Kant says concerning the schema of a concept, these are the procedures and methods for providing images, not for the concept, nor even for the Idea—as in the theory of aesthetic ideas in the *Critique of Judgment*—but for the Name. Or, to use another vocabulary, more familiar to modern epistemology, these schemas are models; that is, rules for producing figures of the divine: models of the monarch, the judge, the father, the husband, the rabbi, the servant. These models are not just, nor even principally, models for figures of the divine, but for figures of God's accompanying God's people, human beings, all of humanity. These schemas or models remain very diversified and heterogeneous and are incapable by themselves of forming a system. After all, the only systems are conceptual systems. Yet their propensity is toward anthropomorphic representation, toward becoming an idol. The functioning of the model, therefore, must be set within a dialectic of the Name and the idol. The Name works on the schema or model by making it move, by making it dynamic, by inverting it into an opposed image. (Thus God assumes all the positions in the figures of the family: father, mother, spouse, brother, and finally "Son of Man.") Just as, according to Kant, the Idea requires the surpassing of not only the image but also the concept, in the demand to "think more," the Name subverts every model, but only through them.

The role of limit-expressions must be understood within the framework of this dialectic of the Name and the idol. They are the model's complement and corrective. They are, following a remarkable analysis by Ian Ramsey, the model's qualifiers.

We may not therefore reduce the mutation of poetic language in religious language, under the pressure of the naming of God, to the single game of limit-expressions. It is the models and their qualifiers taken together that are the seat of this mutation. The result is that the poetics of the name of

God—which is expressed principally in the models' labor—is not abolished but intensified through paradox, hyperbole, and all the primary expressions that give rise to the "negative way" at a higher degree of conceptuality (itself only conceivable in relation to the analogical way for which it is the complement and the corrective).

2. My second remark will take us a decisive step along the trajectory from poetics to politics. If I have so resisted the temptation to concentrate all my attention on the subversive character of limit-expressions in relation to the metaphorical character of models, it is in part because the combined interplay of models and their qualifiers continues in a wholly significant fashion in the *practice* that results in the transfer from texts to life.

This practice, it should not be necessary to emphasize, is not external to our understanding the texts of faith. On the one hand, these texts do not exhaust their meaning in some functioning purely internal to the text. They intend a world, which calls forth on our part a way of dwelling there. It is part of the essence of poetics to "remake" the world following the essential intention of the poem. In this sense, the *applicatio* spoken of by the older hermeneutics is indeed the terminal moment of understanding. I prefer to use another language here, but one that I maintain is rigorously synonymous: to understand oneself in front of the text. In its turn, understanding oneself in front of the text is not something that just happens in one's head or in language. It is what the gospel calls "putting the word to work." In this regard, to understand the world and to change it are fundamentally the same thing.

Now, in a hermeneutic that puts the accent exclusively on limit-expressions, the self-understanding that corresponds to the demand of the text also takes on an extreme character, the one that Kierkegaard, for example, pushed so far. The logical and practical force of the limit-expressions of Scripture will not be to recommend some type of conduct, whatever it may be, but rather to bring about within the heart of ordinary experience, be it ethical or political, a general suspension to the benefit of what we may symmetrically call life's *limit-experiences*. Of course, the consonance between these limit-experiences and the limit-expressions is not inevitably nor uniquely translated into those experiences of catastrophe that Karl Jaspers calls limit-situations: fault, failure, death, struggle. Limit-experiences can also be culminating experiences of creativity and joy. Yet they all have in common the surpassing of the ethical and the political at the expense of the positive, although always precarious and provisory, role of the analogical "models."

3. These "models" can nourish an ethical and political reflection inasmuch as they govern the anticipation of a liberated and revived humanity. On this point, I entirely follow André Dumas in his recent attempt (in his *Political Theology and the Life of the Church*) to ground the transition

from what he calls metatextual existence to political engagement on the functioning of some typical models from the Old and New Testaments. I also agree with him that the most "telling" (*parlant*) of these models is that of the "fratriarchal" struggle on the horizon of possible reunions. Still, I do not think that in order to assure this transition we may *substitute* a political theology for a hermeneutical one. Just as hermeneutical theology pays heed to the theologies of God's transcendence, to the extent that it preserves the specificity of the naming of God at the heart of the biblical poem, it also attends to political theologies. And it does so in numerous ways. First, in its textual aspect, hermeneutics does not place the accent on the dialogic relation between the author and the reader, nor even on the decision taken by the listener to the word, but rather—and essentially—on the world of the text. It models self-understanding on this world of the text. If language does not exist for itself, but in view of the world that it opens up and uncovers, then the interpretation of language is not distinct from the interpretation of the world.

Hence self-understanding in the face of the text will have the same amplitude as the world of the text. Far, therefore, from being closed in upon a person or a dialogue, this understanding will have the multidimensional character of biblical poetics. It will be cosmic, ethical, and political. I hold, therefore, that a hermeneutic that takes the world of the text as its central category does not run the risk of privileging the dialogic relation between the author and the reader, nor any personal decision in the face of the text. The amplitude of the world of the text requires an equal amplitude on the side of the *applicatio,* which will be as much political praxis as the labor of thought and language.

There is another reason for not substituting a political theology for a hermeneutical theology: if a hermeneutical theology opens in this way to political practice, as one of the dimensions of application that fulfills understanding, in turn, it does not become absorbed therein, to the extent that it is first of all precisely and fundamentally a poetics. If I have so sought to preserve the poetic qualification of the naming of God, it is to preserve the precious dialectic of poetics and politics. Certainly, human existence is political existence. Yet the texts within which Christian existence understands itself are not political to the extent that they are poetical. Thus the models for a partnership (*compagnonnage*) between God and God's people and the rest of humanity constitute what I will call a poetics of politics, which, in order to receive a properly political qualification, needs to be articulated through analyses, knowledge, interests, organizations, and so on. To use a Weberian language, I will say that these models reach the political only by nourishing an ethics of conviction that is always irreducible to one of responsibility, which, let it not be forgotten, is also the ethic of the limited use of violence.

~ 13 ~

Toward a Narrative Theology:
Its Necessity, Its Resources,
Its Difficulties

My essay is mainly about the *difficulties* that a narrative theology is doomed to face. But I would not embark on such a seemingly self-defeating enterprise if I were not convinced that rebuilding theology on a narrative basis is sound.

1. The Need for a Narrative Theology

Fundamentally I share its refusals and suspicions: the refusal of a purely *speculative* theology, which would rid its discourse of any reference to the stories about Israel, Jesus, and the early church; the refusal of a *morally* oriented theology, which would retain only the atemporal teachings of an ethical monotheism; furthermore (and of these three points, this is the most sensitive one), an antipathy to an *existential* theology indifferent to the historical dimension, which would be exclusively attentive to the irruption of the word in the instant of the decision of faith. I also accept the affirmations underlying these denials. First, theological discourse, however conceptual it can and must be, can only elaborate the horizon of meaning implicit in the narratives and symbols constitutive of the Jewish and Christian traditions. Second, if theological discourse does not consist in extracting anemic generalities from the narratives recorded in the Scriptures, it has to disentangle the intelligibility immanent in the recounted stories from our own individual and communal histories and stories. Finally, in contrast to an existential theology that exalts the instant of decision, a narrative theology takes into

Originally an unpublished paper presented at the Symposium on Narrative Theology, Haverford College, 1982. Published as "De moeilijke weg naar een narratieve theologie: Noodzaak, bronnen, problemen," in *Meedenken met Edward Schillebeeckx*, ed. H. Häring (Baarn: H. Nielissen, 1983), 80–92.

account the long duration of a history of several millennia as it has been condensed in the two Testaments.

To this general agreement with the very project of a narrative theology I want to add a more specific introductory statement that will provide an orientation to the whole essay.

To my mind the project of a narrative theology is not identical to that of a theology of history—if we mean by a theology of history an attempt to construe world-history in a Hegelian sense under the guidance of a *Heilsgeschichte,* proceeding from Genesis to Revelation, and punctuated by such saving events as the exodus and the resurrection. In this regard, I should argue that the "eclipse of biblical narrative," which Hans Frei describes in his magisterial book, applies to a pattern of thought arising from the confusion between a theology that takes into account the narrative dimension of the biblical faith and a more or less sophisticated theology of history.[1] This confusion arose very early. In fact, *the* biblical narrative has reached the shores of our culture as a grandiose but frozen one-dimensional narrative in which all the varieties of discourse are leveled off. The creation story, the fall story, and the patriarch stories are held as equally authentic accounts as, say, the story of the succession to David's throne or the story of the dramatic encounter between Jesus and his opponents. The biblical narrative that collapsed is, in fact, this flat linear account that amounts to a world-history and that competed with newly conceived world-histories from the Renaissance time down to Hegel.[2]

In that sense we should not speak of "the biblical narrative," but, with Ulrich Simon, in the second part of his wonderful book *Story and Faith,* of "the Christian pattern."[3] It is important to notice that this "Christian pattern" took shape when narrative creation had already stopped; it is typically postcanonical. We are hitting here on a paradoxical phenomenon, namely, that the same process that has *preserved* the biblical narratives that we now read, by selecting and gathering them and by putting on them the seal of authoritativeness, the same process that has made them *unalterable,* transhistorical, and capable of endless reinterpretations in always new cultural contexts—this same process has concealed and buried "the multiplex nature" (Barr) of both the Old Testament and the New Testament tradition. Henceforth, the Christian pattern claims to be the universally chronological schema of the "history of salvation" in which we are ourselves included.

---

1. See Hans W. Frei, *The Eclipse of Biblical Narrative: A Study in Eighteenth and Nineteenth Century Hermeneutics* (New Haven: Yale Univ. Press, 1974).

2. We may wonder whether the origin of the claim to universality of *the* biblical narrative has to be traced back to the Yahwist composition or to the eschatology of the prophets or to the apocalyptic movement or to Luke's first sketch of a Christian "history of salvation."

3. Ulrich Simon, *Story and Faith in the Biblical Narrative* (London: SPCK, 1975), 81f.

Furthermore, this "Christian pattern" tends to abolish the peripeties, dangers, failures, and horrors of history for the sake of a consoling overview provided by the providential schema of this grandiose narrative. Concordance finally conquers discordance. By saying that, I do not want to overlook the ambiguities pertaining to the "Christian pattern," the fragile balance between God's manifestation and God's hiddenness, between divine guidance and human responsibility, between corporate events and individual destinies—in brief, between the rationality of a providential worldview and the paradoxes of humankind's historicity. The triumphant concordance between the beginning and the end does not suppress, but enhances, the militant discordance of the middle. Nevertheless, concordance visibly prevails.

The question, then, is whether the so-called biblical narrative is not a culturally motivated reduction of the rich interplay of temporal qualities that are displayed by the different literary genres encompassed in the canonical Scriptures. If this diagnosis is true, one of the tasks of a narrative theology would be to liberate the biblical narratives from the constraints of the "Christian pattern" and ultimately the multiplex network of biblical narratives from the univocally chronological schema of the history of salvation. Then memory and hope would be delivered from the *visible* narrative that hides that which we may call, with Johann-Baptist Metz, the "dangerous memories" and the challenging expectations that together constitute the unresolved dialectic of memory and of hope.[4]

This task is all the more compelling now that the post-Enlightenment age has displayed ominous symptoms that point toward a collapse of the very capacity to tell stories and to listen to stories. The destruction of any genuine sense of tradition and authority in conjunction with the abusive prevalence of the will to dominate, exploit, and manipulate the natural environment of humankind—and consequently human beings themselves—amounts to an *increase of forgetfulness,* especially that of the past sufferings of humankind, which is the ultimate cause of the impinging death of the capacity for storytelling.[5] In that sense, the fight for a "rebirth of narrative" that Ulrich Simon is yearning for—a rebirth of narrative in general and not only of the biblical narrative—is, as such, a specifically Christian task.

---

4. Johann-Baptist Metz, "A Short Apology of Narrative," in *Concilium 9: The Crisis of Religious Language,* ed. Johann-Baptist Metz and Jean-Pierre Jossua (New York: Herder and Herder, 1973), 84–96.

5. "It is as if something that seemed inalienable to us, the securest among our possessions, were taken from us: the ability to exchange experiences" (Walter Benjamin, "The Storyteller," in *Illuminations,* ed. Hannah Arendt, trans. Harry Zohn [New York: Schocken Books, 1969], 83).

II. The Resources of a Narrative Theology

The main resources of a narrative theology are the tremendous achievements we are witnessing in the field of *narratology*. These achievements may be put under four headings.

1. First we find in the *art of emplotment* the paradigm of all the literary devices employed by narrators in order to draw an intelligible story *from* a variety of events or incidents or, reciprocally, in order to make these events or incidents *into* a story. In that way emplotment brings together such heterogeneous features as circumstances, agents, interactions, ends, means, and unintended results. It provides then heterogeneous elements with the ambiguous status of a concordant-discordant whole, to use one of Frank Kermode's expressions. This first trait has an important corollary concerning the temporality proper to poetic composition of the story.

This temporality interweaves the two temporal components: on the one hand, the pure, discrete, and interminable succession of what we may call the story's incidents and that constitute the episodic side of the story; on the other hand, the aspect of integration, culmination, and closure brought about by what Louis O. Mink calls the "configurational act of narrating." This act consists in gathering together the incidents of the story and in creating a configuration from a succession. This trait has to do with the twofold structure of human time. Time is both what passes away and what endures. The creation of a temporal whole is precisely the poetic way of mediating between time as passage and time as duration. What we try to pinpoint is the temporal identity of what is enduring in the midst of what is passing away.

2. The second field of inquiry opened by narratology concerns the *epistemological status of the intelligibility* displayed by the configurational act of emplotment. My claim here is that narrative intelligibility shows more kinship with practical wisdom or moral judgment than with theoretical reason. This thesis entails an important corollary concerning the relation between contemporary narratology and the intelligibility proper to emplotment. I see narratology as a *simulation* of narrative intelligence by means of a second-order discourse belonging to the same level of rationality as the other sciences of language.

Aristotle was the first to underscore the capacity of poetry to "teach," to convey meanings endowed with a certain kind of universality. The very act of configuring the plot makes it typical and understandable in spite of, or thanks to, the singularity of its "heroes" designated by "proper names." This typification of the story allows poetry to be connected with this other kind of intelligibility, that of ethics, which Aristotle called *phronesis*. *Phronesis* tells us that happiness is the coronation of excellence in life and in praxis, but it does not tell us in which ways this state of affairs can be made to reign. It is poetry that shows us how shifts in fortune—mainly reversals from fortune to misfortune—are nurtured by actual practice. But it shows it in the hypothetical mode of fiction. Nevertheless, it is through our acquaintance with types of emplotment that we *learn* how to link excellence and happiness.

This kinship between narrative intelligibility and *phronesis*—as opposed to *theoria*—suggests that the universals yielded by plots are not those of theoretical knowledge and science. They are universals of a "lower" order appropriate to the configurational act at work in poetic composition.

3. The third trait that a narrative theology may retain from the present state of the current discussion in the literary field concerns the *role of tradition* not only in the transmission but also in the reception and the interpretation of received stories. This phenomenon of traditionality is very complex because it relies on the flexible dialectics between innovation and sedimentation. It is sedimentation that we ascribe to paradigms that help a typology of emplotment to emerge and to get stabilized. But the opposite phenomenon of innovation is no less prominent. Why? Because paradigms generated by a previous innovation provide guidelines for further experimentation in the narrative field. In this dialectic between innovation and sedimentation a whole range of solutions is deployed between the two poles of servile repetition and calculated deviance, passively through all the degrees of *déformation réglée*.

4. The fourth trait that I want to retain for our further discussion of narrative theology concerns the *"meaning" of a narrative*. Such "meaning" is not confined to the so-called inside of the text. It occurs at the intersection between the world of the text and the world of the readers. It is mainly in the *reception* of the text by an audience that the capacity of the plot to transfigure experience is actualized.

By the world of the text I mean the world displayed by the text in front of itself, so to speak, as the horizon of possible experience in which the work displaces its readers. By the world of the reader I mean the actual world with which real action is disclosed in the midst of "a web of relationships," to use an expression of Hannah Arendt in *The Human Condition*.

For literary criticism, this world of action is the "outside" of the text, as opposed to the "inside" of the text. As the "outside" of the text, it is irrelevant to its mode of inquiry. But the "outer" world is outer only for a treatment of language that establishes it as a self-contained set of entities, all of whose relationships are immanent. But it is the methodological decision, constitutive of linguistics as a science, of dealing with language as an "inside" without an "outside" that makes all consideration of this "outside" irrelevant. For a hermeneutics that does not take this undialectical separation between the inside and the outside of the text for granted, the problem is rather to understand how language keeps mediating between humankind and world, among human beings themselves, and between the individual human being and her- or himself, even when the poetic function, as Roman Jakobson points out, increases the gap between signs and world. This threefold *mediation* of referentiality (humankind and world), of communicability (human being and human being), and of self-understanding (human being and her- or himself) constitutes the major problem of a hermeneutics of poetic texts.

Biblical narratives may be seen as having a complex set of relationships to narratives at large. At the first level they exemplify, in a way that is not too discordant, the main features common to the whole family of narratives. The successful application of narratology to biblical narratives testifies to this continuity between religious and nonreligious narratives. I shall now consider this point of agreement in order to focus on two other kinds of relations that become increasingly puzzling.

At a second level, biblical narratives *intensify* some traits that have been overlooked in the preceding characterization of narratives in general. This *intensification* is still coherent with the usual treatment of narratives in contemporary narratology. By *intensification* I mean the following: in a sense, religious, and more specifically biblical, narratives do in their own way what all narratives do—they constitute the identify of the community that tells and retells the story, and they constitute it as a narrative identity.

Harald Weinrich has no difficulty in reminding us that Jesus told and retold stories, that he is a person about whom stories are told and about whose storytelling stories are told. As concerns the Bible as a whole, "the most important texts, the ones most relevant to religion, are stories." This determines the status of the Christian tradition: "We too became part of an unbroken tradition of storytelling. Christianity is a community of storytellers" (and also a "community at table together," adds the author in terms that remind one of Norman Perrin speaking of Jesus' table-fellowship with "tax collectors and sinners").[6]

This is particularly true of the large-scale stories that encompass fragmentary stories. The work of the Yahwist has been often described as the composition of the grand story starting from the creation to the settlement in the promised land. Furthermore, the work of Luke, adding the Acts of the Apostles to the Gospel, could be seen, according to Hans Conzelmann, as the foundation of the Christian *Heilsgeschichte,* developing from the prophets of the old covenant, through the story of Jesus, to the *parousia,* and placing the church in the "midst of time." This is the beginning

---

6. Harald Weinrich, "Narrative Theology," in *Concilium 9: The Crisis of Religious Language,* ed. Johann-Baptist Metz and Jean-Pierre Jossua (New York: Herder and Herder, 1973), 45–56.

of the process that by a progressive hardening has led to the hypostasizing of the "Christian pattern" from which a narrative theology may have to disentangle itself. But before generating these potentially disastrous effects, the encompassing story generates a partnership by making our fragmentary stories converge with the encompassing story. Robert MacAfee Brown, in a fine article entitled "My Story and 'The Story,' "[7] shows in how many ways this convergence is created, from the stage of a challenging relationship that may run both ways—the liberation story of the exodus challenging my own status as Pharaoh-like, or the Auschwitz story challenging the biblical story of salvation—to a stage of reconciliation, when the story is reenacted in the liturgical celebration. Then "the story and our story become one and the same."[8]

Dietrich Ritschl summarizes this role of the encompassing story as generating partnership by describing the partnership itself as a confluence of stories (zusammenfliessen von stories). This role has its echo in Christology, to the extent that it grounds the community of sinners on the loving initiative of Christ assuming the sin of the world and therefore including our stories in his story.

But the capacity of the biblical story to *intensify* the usual function of narratives can be seen in a more concealed feature of the biblical story. We called it an all-encompassing story. And we were right to the extent that we stayed at the surface of the text and took for granted the linear arrangement of the grandiose story extended from Genesis to Revelation. But is it a story in the sense of the *closed* stories that have a beginning and an end in time? If it is true that it has been read in that way after the canon was closed and that people tried again and again to apply datation to this linear and chronological display of intervals and periods between *the* beginning and *the* end, we may doubt that the encompassing story is homogeneous to the partial stories. Ritschl does justice to this enigmatic character of the overarching story by calling it a metastory. By that he means two things: first, it does not have the structure of the self-contained stories that we tell because it is an open or ongoing story; and, second, it can be told only through the stories collected and gathered within its range. In that sense, beside the detail-stories, it is, as such, an unspeakable story. There are stories of the exodus, of the passion, and even more fragmentary stories such as the story of Joseph or that of Peter's betrayal. But the story of the partnership between God and Israel is, as such, not only open and ongoing but

---

7. Robert MacAfee Brown, "My Story and 'The Story,' " *Theology Today* 32 (1975): 171.

8. Dietrich Ritschl and Hugh O. Jones, *"Story" als Rohmaterial der Theologie,* Theologische Existenz heute 192 (Munich: Christian Kaiser Verlag, 1976). See also Hugh O. Jones, "The Concept of Story and Theological Discourse," *Scottish Journal of Theology* 29 (1976): 415–33.

unfathomable and unspeakable. At that point the character of the meta-story as that which cannot be told joins the theological theme of God's ineffability. Or rather the ineffability of the Name is the same thing as the inexhaustibility of the metastory. This close connection is clearly asserted in the episode of the burning bush, which at the same time proclaims the retreat of Yahweh in the incognito "I am who I am" and Yahweh's partner-ship with Israel's journey: "Thus you shall say to the Israelites, 'Yahweh, the God of your ancestors, the God of Abraham, the God of Isaac, and *the God of Jacob,* has sent me to you'" (Exod. 3:14-15).[9]

III. The Difficulty of Narrative Theology

Such is the sense in which the biblical narratives may be said to intensify the narrative quality of experience. But there are compelling reasons for raising doubts concerning this continuity between biblical narratives and narratives in general. I shall mention four of them.

First, these narratives belong to the class of *"sacred" stories as opposed to "mundane" stories.*[10] It is not that they use a language different from everyday language; on the contrary, these stories root theological discourse in ordinary language. It is not their language that is sacred but their *function.* Let us start from what we just said about the metastory. We have only to add a few decisive traits in order to understand the difference be-tween sacred and mundane stories. First, these stories are *traditional* in the sense that their having been told in that way in the past constitutes a rea-son for retelling them. Second, they are *authoritative* in the sense that they consist in selections and collections that separate the canonical from the apocryphal ones. And third, they are *liturgical* in the sense that they reach their full meaningfulness when reenacted in a cultic situation.

Mundane stories, by contrast, are *innovative* works that raise a specific question of authorship. They have no institutional authority beside the one that they generate by being received, approved, and circulated—hence their characterization as mundane. Once more this distinction was already ad-umbrated with that of "closed" and "open" ("ongoing" or "not able to be told") stories. But the situation of consciousness as regards each class of narratives says something more. "For the sacred story does not transpire

---

9. These exegetical remarks find support in Frank Kermode's treatment of *secrecy* in the Gospel of Mark and his general contention that the most intriguing narratives are those that conceal as much as they reveal. There is thus a hidden kinship between the idea that metastories cannot be told and the idea that narratives generate secrecy. See Frank Kermode, *The Genesis of Secrecy: On the Interpretation of Narrative* (Cambridge, Mass.: Harvard Univ. Press, 1979).

10. Stephen Crites, "The Narrative Quality of Experience," *Journal of the American Academy of Religion* 39 (1971): 291–311.

within a conscious world. It forms the very consciousness that projects a total world horizon, and therefore informs the intentions by which actions are projected into that world."[11] In other words, the sacred story creates a world of consciousness within which the self that is oriented to it creates in turn works of art that are subject to change by conscious reflection.

This first set of remarks concerns, of course, the functioning of the biblical narrative in societies where traditional, authoritative, and liturgically reenacted stories have kept their formative role. What we have called in our introductory part the "eclipse of the biblical narrative" concerns among other things this status of the biblical narrative as sacred story.

A second kind of discrepancy between biblical narratives and ordinary stories concerns the *complex relation between story and history* in biblical narratives. Advocates of narrative theology try to discard this issue by merely listing biblical narratives among stories for which the question of factual truth is irrelevant. But this apparently merely descriptive stance is a way of begging the question. For example, Harald Weinrich, speaking of the stories told by Jesus (obviously his parables), writes: "There is no trace of an historical interest in the truth of the story, in the sense of Ranke's 'as it really,' either in the disciples' question or in the Master's answers." And the author goes on: "For this reason, I cannot get away from the suspicion that the question about history in theology may be a false one."[12] The suggestion, then, would be to substitute relevance for truth, in the sense of factual truth. And relevance would mean ability to further a certain kind of action, to invite the hearers "to imitate the actions of the story." But the practical use of the biblical stories is not a substitute for an inquiry into the relation between story and history. It is an indisputable trait of the basic stories of the Bible that they are *history-like,* with the exception of intended fictions such as parables and maybe some stories in the Old Testament, Jonah and others. The perplexing problem is that this history-like feature, for those who live in the story, to return to the expression used above, ignores our distinction between fiction and history. It is not fiction because there is no such feeling of fable-invention as the one that Aristotle ascribes to poetry writing. It is not history because the purpose of history writing according to documentary evidence is also not part of the writer's intention. Therefore, the problem is only ours. But it is ours precisely as a result of a crisis generated by the *history-like* character of the biblical narratives.

We are left, therefore, with a quandary: we can neither be content with a concept of story that would elude the dialectic of story and history nor use

---

11. Ibid., 298. This situation of consciousness *between* sacred stories and the mundane stories explains why Crites can ascribe a *mediating* role to the form of the experiencing consciousness itself and to the incipient story that shapes it.

12. Weinrich, "Narrative Theology," 50.

a concept of history that would not take into account this variable curve of relationships between story and history.

A third feature adds to the strangeness of biblical narratives as regards their relation to profane or mundane stories. It is, to my mind, the decisive trait with which any narrative theology has to come to grips. No biblical narrative works merely as narrative. It receives not only its theological but even its original religious meaning from its *composition with other modes of discourse*. I have underlined elsewhere the unbreakable conjunction between narratives and laws within the Torah.[13] Laws transform narratives into instruction, and narratives transform law into gift. In this way we are also led to acknowledge that the Hebraic tradition is prevented from becoming a mystifying ideology, thanks to its dialectical relation to prophecy. Prophecy, on the one hand, reveals within the narratives themselves the potential of unfulfilled promises that reorient the story of the past toward the future; narratives, on the other hand, provide the eschatological anticipation of the "new" era with images and types. This typological use of past stories for the sake of the projection of the future gives to the narratives themselves a meaningfulness that is quite alien to ordinary storytelling. Furthermore, we have to take into account the deep impact of the wisdom literature on the narratives themselves that, henceforth, display the imprint of perpetuity characteristic of the wisdom sayings. This transfiguration of narratives through wisdom, added to the typological use of past stories for the sake of the anticipation of the era to come, put biblical narratives outside of the stream of popular storytelling. Finally, the reenactment of the narratives in the cultic situation and their recounting through the psalms of praise, of lamentation, and of penitence complete the complex intertwining between narrative and nonnarrative modes of discourse. The whole range of modes can thus be seen as distributed between the two poles of storytelling and praising.[14]

This dialectic between narrative and nonnarrative expressions of the faith is neither weakened nor simplified in the New Testament writings. On the contrary, the "new utterance"—to use Amos Wilder's phrase—generates new polarities such as the new and the old, the already there and the not yet, whose tensions give to the New Testament narratives a special style. These tensions become conspicuous when we compare the

---

13. Paul Ricoeur, "Toward a Hermeneutic of the Idea of Revelation," in *Essays in Biblical Interpretation,* ed. Lewis S. Mudge (Philadelphia: Fortress Press, 1980), 73–118; and idem, "Naming God," above.

14. Ritschl, in *"Story" als Rohmaterial,* distinguishes between *berichtende Sprache* (report) and *anrede Sprache* (address) and underlines the correspondence between this general polarity and that of story and praise (to which he adds doxology). But story itself, to the extent that it is not merely informative-descriptive, but actually creates history and reality, becomes address. Furthermore, to the extent that the story is addressed to me, narrative identity is not only an "expressed" but an "addressed" identity.

minimal narratives of the purely kerygmatic expressions of faith and the extended narratives of the Synoptic tradition. In this tradition the relation between proclamation and narrative may appear as a retrieval within the New Testament of the Old Testament polarity of praise and narration.

This complex interaction between narrative and nonnarrative modes suggests that narratives do not cover the whole range of temporal structures underlying biblical writings. Human time is shaped in many ways by the interplay between all the temporal modes displayed by all the expressions of the biblical faith. A narrative theology also has to take into account this inclusion of narrative time within the complex network of temporal qualities pertaining to the complete gamut of religious expressions.

This brief survey of the nonnarrative modes of biblical discourse brings us to the threshold of the fourth and most critical issue—namely, the *transition from narrative to explicit theological discourse*. In a sense, the nonnarrative modes already belong to this mediating process: laws, prophecies, wisdom sayings, and hymns, by contributing to the full *meaningfulness* of biblical narratives, start the transfer from mere storytelling to the grasping of the enduring signification of the stories themselves. But when we inquire into the condition of this transfer, we must acknowledge that something is still lacking in this emerging process, that is, the recognition of the *principle* of meaningfulness itself.

The problem was already apparent in the work that may be considered as the first attempt toward a *narrative* theology; I mean H. Richard Niebuhr's *The Meaning of Revelation*.[15] The author of this book, a book that is as valuable today as it was forty years ago, does not speak of narrative theology but of "historic" faith or of "revelation in our history." It is this very concept that raises the issue that we are to discuss. How may the meaning of the story told be transferred to the story of our life? A question of intelligibility if raised, which the author puts in terms borrowed from Whitehead: "Rational religion, says the author of *Religion in the Making*, appeals to the direct intuition of special occasions, and to the elucidatory power of its concepts for all occasions." Niebuhr continues and assumes for his own this reference to the *conceptuality* of Christian faith: "Revelation means for us that part of our inner history which illuminates the rest of it and which is itself intelligible.... Revelation means this intelligible event which makes all other events intelligible."[16] With the recognition of this dimension of intelligibility we have moved from "the story of our life" to "the reasons of the heart." This move, unfortunately, raises more questions than it solves, to the extent that it proceeds from pure narrative paradigmatic images (the "reasons of the heart"). It is not that the consideration of

---

15. H. Richard Niebuhr, *The Meaning of Revelation* (New York: Macmillan, 1941).
16. Ibid., 68–69.

imagination is inappropriate. On the contrary, Niebuhr makes a decisive step by recognizing the deep unity of reason and imagination in practical reason and furthermore by locating this common action of reason and imagination in the sphere of affections of the self—pain and pleasure, joy and sorrow, anger and compassion. Imagination plays here the role of an interpreter: "None of these affections remains uninterpreted."[17] This sudden introduction of imagination in the course of an analysis devoted to narrative provides us with the decisive clue, or at least the right recognition of the difficulty involved here, if not the right solution. The shift from a narrative vocabulary to an image vocabulary helps us to raise the question of the *paradigmatic* character of the image itself and, by implication, of the story that has furthered the image. The question is implied in the following assertion: "By revelation in our history, then, we mean that special occasion which provides us with an image by means of which all the occasions of personal and common life become intelligible." Niebuhr continues that the intelligibility proper to such an "image" differs from "the conceptual patterns of the observer's reason"; it is nothing else than the task of making the past intelligible, of interpreting our present according to the analogy of the life and death of Christ, and of discovering the potentialities of our future. In other words, revelation "furnishes the practical reason with a starting point for the interpretation of past, present, and future history."[18]

The question is whether the too simple oppositions between the "reasons of the heart" and "the conceptual patterns of the observer's reason" does not conceal the conditions of the intelligibility of the practical process of interpretation applied to past, present, and future. This inquiry into intelligibility may seem useless to pastoral care (although this concession may be questioned, for the dignity of pastoral care itself), but it cannot be eluded in theological thinking. In that regard, I agree entirely with Dietrich Ritschl's strong assertion concerning the conceptual duty of theology, which he defines by the following tasks: a task of clarification (for the sake of communication); a task of coherence (for the sake of both ethics and logic); a task of reflection about the limits of flexibility of traditional creeds (as regards new formulations and modern articulations); and a task of stimulation for the sake of new insights and new discoveries Only the last one may rely solely on mere "retelling." The three others require summaries, regulative propositions, and systematic patterns.

That this second-order discourse has roots in the first-order discourse cannot be disputed. The cumulative character of biblical narratives (jointly with the use of typology in the interpretation of history) yields a pat-

---

17. Ibid., 67f. This explains that faith is to a large extent a struggle with the "evil imaginations of the heart" evoked in Genesis, that is, imaginations "resulting in continued conflict, in the impoverishment and destruction of selves both as agents and as sufferers."
18. Ibid., 80, 81, 97.

tern, a style of narrative coherence that paves the way for summaries that elicit confessional formulas and doxologies (such as the exodus-credo or the resurrection-credo). These confessional formulas, in turn, are ruled by regulative assertions that govern the selection and the gathering of the narrative, prescriptive, prophetic, sapiential, and hymnic documents. It is not unlikely that wisdom is the most decisive factor in the elaboration of such regulative assertions. That would mean, considering the antiquity of wisdom, that biblical narrative was never deprived of some principles ruling the interpretation at work through narrative—in brief, that narrative never existed without embryonic theological *thinking*, just as it never existed without its polar counterpart, praise. Praise, doxology, and regulative assertions constitute a progressive series from which theologizing emerges. We may therefore lay the stress either on the discontinuity between pure "retelling" and theological thinking or on the continuity secured by the mediating sources, from the prescriptive to the hymnic, and by the summaries, confessional formulas, and doxologies grafted mainly onto the sapiential and the hymnic expression of the faith. But the question of the origin of regulative concepts remains open.[19]

---

19. I understand—if I do not assume it without reservations—the negative conclusion of Ritschl: "The expression narrative theology, strictly speaking, is a wrong designation behind which a legitimate disposition hides.... Stories, in their typical linguistic form of narration, are not the forms of expression but the raw material of theology" (*"Story" als Rohmaterial*, 41).

14

Evil, a Challenge to Philosophy and Theology

That both philosophy and theology encounter evil as a *challenge* unlike any other, the greatest thinkers in both these disciplines are willing to admit. What is important is the way in which this challenge, or this failure, is received: Do we find an invitation to think less about the problem or a provocation to think more, or to think differently about it?

What the problem of evil calls into question is a way of thinking submitted to the requirements of logical coherence, that is, one submitted to both the rule of noncontradiction and that of systematic totalization. It is this way of thinking that has prevailed in all attempts at a theodicy, in the strict sense of this term; however diverse they may be in their responses, all have agreed in defining the problem as follows. How can we affirm at the same time, without any contradiction, the following three propositions: God is all powerful; God is absolutely good; yet evil exists? Theodocies, in this sense, appear to be a battle for the sake of coherence, in response to the objection that only two of the three stated propositions are compatible, not all three at once. However, what is assumed by this way of posing the problem is never called into question, namely, the propositional form itself in which the terms of the problem are stated, along with the rule of coherence that any solution to the problem must satisfy.

In order to demonstrate the limited and relative character of this way of posing the problem, we need, first, to get some sense of the scope and the complexity of the problem with the help of a phenomenology of the experience of evil; second, we need to traverse the levels of discourse taken by speculation on the origin and the *raison d'être* of evil, so as to be able, third, to reconnect the work of thinking, arising out of the enigma of evil, to other responses stemming from action and feeling.

Reprinted with permission from *Journal of the American Academy of Religion* 53 (1985): 635–50.

I. Between Blame and Lament

The whole enigma of evil may be said to lie in the fact that, at least in the traditions of the West, we put under the same terms such different phenomena as sin, suffering, and death. However, evil as wrongdoing and evil as suffering belong to two heterogeneous categories, that of blame and that of lament.

There is blame where a human action held to be a violation of the prevailing code of conduct is declared guilty and worthy of being punished. There is lament where some suffering is undergone. We do not make it happen, it befalls us. Being an effect, it may be related to a variety of causes—the adversity of physical nature, illness, the infirmities of body or mind, or affliction produced by the death of loved ones, the perspective of our own mortality, affronts to our dignity, and so on. Lament, therefore, occurs as the opposite of blame; whereas blame make culprits of us, lament reveals us as victims.

What then invites philosophy and theology to think of evil as the common root of both sin and suffering, in spite of this undeniable polarity of blame and lament? The first motive lies in the extraordinary way in which these two phenomena are intertwined. On the one hand, punishment is a form of physical and psychical suffering, whether it involves corporal punishment, some deprivation of liberty, shame, or humiliation. This may be why we speak of guilt itself as *poena,* that is, as a "pain," a term that bridges the gap between evil committed and evil undergone. On the other hand, one principal cause of suffering is the violence human beings do to one another. In fact, to do evil is always, either directly or indirectly, to make someone else suffer. In its dialogic structure evil committed by someone finds its other half in the evil suffered by someone else. It is at this major point of intersection that the cry of lamentation is most sharp.

We are led a step further in the direction of a unique mystery of iniquity by the presentiment that sin, suffering, and death express in different ways the human condition in its deepest unity. Two indications in the experience of evil point toward this underlying unity of the human condition. On the side of moral evil, first the experience of guilt entails, as its dark side, the feeling of having been seduced by overwhelming powers and, consequently, our feeling of belonging to a history of evil, which is always already there for everyone This strange experience of passivity, at the very heart of evil-doing, makes us feel ourselves to be victims in the very act that makes us guilty. This same blurring of the boundaries between guilt and being a victim can also be observed if we start from the other pole. Since punishment is a form of suffering allegedly deserved, who knows whether all suffering is not in one way or another the punishment for some personal or collective fault, either known or unknown? It is this dark background of both guilt and suffering that makes evil such a unique enigma.

II. Levels of Discourse in Speculation on Evil

We may not turn toward theodicies properly speaking, subject to the rules of noncontradiction and systematic totality, without having first passed through a number of levels of discourse in which we may discern an increasing order of rationality. I will consider three stages of discourse—myth, wisdom, and gnosis—as leading to the level of rational theodicies.

A. The Stage of Myth

Myth constitutes the first major transition from experience to language in several ways. In the first place, the ambivalence of the sacred, as described by Rudolf Otto, confers on myth the power to assume both the dark and the luminous sides of the human condition. Next, myths incorporate our fragmentary experience of evil into those great narratives of origin, as Mircea Eliade has emphasized throughout his many works on this topic. By telling how the world began, a myth tells how the human condition came about as something generally wretched and miserable. But myth's function of providing order, thanks to its cosmological import, has as its corollary— and its corrective—the profusion of explanatory schemes it has produced over time. The realm of myth, as the literature of the ancient Near East, India, and the Far East reveals, is a vast field of experimentation, or even of playing with hypotheses in the most varied and the most fantastic forms. Within this immense laboratory, it appears as though no conceivable solution to the order of the whole cosmos, and hence to the enigma of evil, has not been essayed at some point or another. These solutions oscillate between the level of legends and folklore, close to the demonic dimension of the experience of evil, and that of metaphysical speculation, exemplified by so many Hindu and Buddhist documents. The counterpart of this tremendous contribution of mythical thought to speculation on evil is that one is ceaselessly brought back to the question of origin: *From whence comes evil?* Rational theodicies will get caught up in this search for an origin, which may finally be a blind alley.

B. The Stage of Wisdom

Can myth fully answer the expectations of acting and suffering human beings? Only partially, inasmuch as it does respond to a form of questioning that is inherent in the very form of the lamentation: How long? Why? To this interrogation, however, myth brings only the consolation of order, by situating the supplicant's complaint within a more encompassing framework. But it leaves unanswered one important part of the question, which is not just Why? but Why me? Here the lament turns into an actual complaint. It demands that divinity account for itself. In the biblical realm, for example, one of the important implications of the covenant is that it adds to the dimension of partnership that of a lawsuit or legal process. If God brings a case against God's people, the same may be said about their relation to God.

With this insight, myth has to change registers. It must not only narrate the origins, in order to explain how the original human condition reached its present state; it also has to explain why such is the case for each and every one of us. This shift leads us from myth to the stage of wisdom. Myth narrates, wisdom argues.

The first and most tenacious of the explanations offered by wisdom is, of course, that of retribution. All suffering is deserved because it is the punishment for some individual or collective sin, known or unknown. This is the stance taken, for example, by the Deuteronomist school of historiography and superimposed onto the great traditions of the preexilic times. That the sages should argue against this dogma is easy to forecast. As soon as there are judiciary systems that attempt to apportion pain in terms of degrees of guilt, the very notion of retribution loses its spell. The actual apportioning of misfortune can only appear as arbitrary, indiscriminate, and disproportionate. Why did this person die of cancer and not that one? Why do children die? Why is there *so much* suffering, *far beyond* ordinary mortals' capacity for suffering?

If the book of Job holds the place it does in world literature, it is first of all because it provides us with a "classic" of this argumentative mode of wisdom. It is also because of the enigmatic and perhaps even deliberately ambiguous character of its conclusion. The final theophany brings no direct answer to Job's personal suffering, and speculation is left to pursue more than one direction. The vision of a creator whose designs are unfathomable may suggest either consolation that has to be deferred until the eschaton, or that Job's complaint is displaced, even set aside, in God's eyes, as the master of good and evil, following Isa. 45:7 ("I form light and create darkness, I make weal and create woe, I am the Lord, who does all these things"), or that perhaps the complaint itself has to go through a purificatory test (I shall return to these in concluding) in order that Job should become able to love God "for nought" in response to Satan's wager at the beginning of the tale.

For the time being, let us leave open these questions and follow further the line of speculation begun by wisdom.

C. The Stage of Gnosis and of Antignostic Gnosis

Thinking would not have moved on from wisdom to theodicy if Gnosticism had not elevated speculation to the level of a gigantomachy, where the forces of good are engaged in a merciless struggle with the armies of evil, in order to bring about a final deliverance of all the particles of light held captive by the shadows of evil. From this perspective, we may say that Western thought is in debt to Gnosticism, broadly conceived, for having conceived the problem of evil in terms of one all-encompassing problematic: *Unde malum?* But even more important is the inclusion of philosophical categories in the speculation on evil set forth by Augustine in his fight against the tragic vision of this gnosis. From Neoplatonist philosophers Augustine takes the idea that evil cannot be held to be a *substance,* because to think of being is to think of something one, intelligible, and good. Hence it is philosophical thought that excludes every fantasy of evil as substantial. In return, a new idea of *nothingness* comes to light, that of the *ex nihilo* contained in the idea of a total and complete creation, and associated with it, the idea of an ontic distance between the creator and the creature, therefore of the "deficiency" pertaining to creatures as such. In virtue of this deficiency, it becomes comprehensible that creatures endowed with free will could "turn away" from God and "toward" what has less being, toward nothingness.

This first feature of the Augustinian doctrine should be acknowledged for what it is, namely, the conjunction of ontology and theology in a new type of discourse, that of *onto-theo-logy.*

The most important corollary of this negating of the substantiality of evil is that the confession of evil grounds an exclusively moral vision of evil. If the question *Unde malum?* loses all ontological meaning, the question that replaces it—*Unde malum faciamus?* (From whence comes wrongdoing?)—shifts the problem of evil into the sphere of action, of willing, of free will. Sin introduces a distinct case here, a *nihil privativum,* entirely brought about by the fall, whether this refers to human beings or to higher creatures such as the angels. For this form of nothingness, there is no need to search for a cause anywhere other than in a bad will. Augustine's *Contra Fortunatum* draws from this moral vision of evil the conclusion that most concerns us here, namely, that all evil is either *peccatum* or *poena,* either sin or pain considered as punishment. This purely moral vision of evil leads in turn to a penal vision of history. No soul is unjustly thrown into misfortune. Only divine grace may interrupt the curse of punishment.

The price to pay for the coherence of this doctrine is an enormous one, and its magnitude was to appear on the occasion of Augustine's anti-Pelagian quarrel. In order to make credible the idea that all suffering, however unjustly apportioned or however excessive it may be, is a retribution for sin, it was necessary to give the concept of sin a supraindividual, historical, and even generic dimension, which led to the doctrine of original sin or of a sinful nature. I shall not retrace here the stages of its constitution, which include a literal interpretation of Genesis 3 augmented by an emphasis on Rom. 5:12-19, a justification for the baptism of infants, and so forth.[1] Instead allow me to underscore the epistemological status of this dogmatic proposition about original sin. In one sense, it does take up one fundamental aspect of the experience of evil, namely, the both individual and communal sense of human impotence in the face of the demonic power of evil already there, long before any bad initiative may be assigned to some deliberate intention. However, this enigma of the power of evil already there is set within the false clarity of an apparently rational explanation. By conjoining within the concept of a sinful nature the two heterogeneous notions of a biological transmission through generation and an individual imputation of guilt, the notion of original sin appears as a quasi-concept that we may assign to an antignostic gnosis. The previous content of this gnosis is denied, but the form of its discourse is reconstituted, that of a rationalized myth. As for suffering, which remains the leading thread in my presentation, the failure of this discourse on original sin is a double one. Besides the conceptual inconsistency just referred to, it leaves unanswered the protest of unjust suffering, by condemning it to silence in the name of a massive indictment of the whole of humanity.

D. The Stage of Theodicy

We only have the right to speak of theodicy as such (1) when the *statement* of the problem of evil rests upon propositions intended to be univocal, which is the case of the three assertions usually considered: God is all-powerful; God's goodness is infinite; evil exists; (2) when the *goal* of the argumentation is clearly apologetic: God is not responsible for evil; and (3) when the *means* used are supposed to satisfy the logic of noncontradiction and of systematic totalization. These conditions were fulfilled only within the framework of onto-theology, which joined terms borrowed from religious discourse, principally "God," and terms stemming from metaphysics, whether Platonic or Cartesian, to cite only two examples, such as "being," "nothingness," "first cause," "finality," "infinite," "finite," and so on. Theodicy, in this strict sense, is the brightest jewel of onto-theology.

And in this regard, Leibniz's *Theodicy* remains the prime example of the genre. On the one hand, all the forms of evil, not just moral evil, are taken into consideration and put under the title "metaphysical evil," which is the

---

1. See Paul Ricoeur, "'Original Sin': A Study in Meaning," in *The Conflict of Interpretations* (Evanston, Ill.: Northwestern Univ. Press, 1974), 269–86. TRANS..

unavoidable defect of all created being, if it is true that God cannot create another God. On the other hand, classical logic receives an enrichment through the addition to the principle of noncontradiction of the principle of sufficient reason, which is presented as the principle of the best, as soon as we agree that creation stems from a competition in the divine understanding between a multiplicity of world models of which only one includes the maximum of perfections and the minimum of defects. This notion of the best of all possible worlds, so scoffed at by Voltaire in *Candide* following the disaster of the Lisbon earthquake, cannot be understood so long as we have not grasped its rationale, that is, the calculation of the maximum and minimum, of which *our* world is the result. It is in this way that the principle of sufficient reason can fill the gap between logical possibility (that is, what is not unthinkable) and contingency (that is, what could have happened differently).

The failure of the *Theodicy* results from the fact that a finite understanding will be unable to reach the evidence for this guaranteeing calculation, only being able to gather together the few signs for the excess of perfections over imperfections in the balance of good and evil. Therefore, a robust human optimism is required in order to affirm that the final sum is unequivocally positive. But since we only ever have the small change of this principle of the best, we have to content ourselves with its aesthetic corollary, in virtue of which the contrast between the negative and the positive works for the harmony of the whole. It is just this claim to establish a positive total for the weighing of good and bad on the basis of a quasi-aesthetics that fails as soon as we are confronted with misfortunes whose excesses cannot be compensated for by any known perfection. Once again it is the lament, the complaint of the suffering righteous person or people, that overthrows the notion of a compensation for evil by good, just as was the case with the idea of retribution.

The sharpest, although not fatal, blow to the idea of a theodicy, however, has to be the one Kant leveled against the very basis of the onto-theological discourse upon which all theodicies are constructed, from Augustine to Leibniz. Kant's implacable dismantling of rational theology in the "Dialectic" of his *Critique of Pure Reason* is well known. Once deprived of its ontological support, theodicy falls under the rubric of "transcendental illusion." This is not to say that the problem of evil disappears from the philosophical scene, however. Quite the contrary, in fact. But it now refers uniquely to the *practical* sphere, as that which ought not to be and which action must struggle against. This shift from the theoretical to the practical sphere of reason will provide us later with the needed transition to the last stage of my presentation, dealing with the connection between thought, action, and feeling.

Before reaching this last stage of our journey, however, I need to say at least a few words about a mode of thinking that claims to overcome both the shortcomings of the pre-Kantian theodicies and the Kantian critique of rational theology: the dialectical one. By a dialectical mode of thinking I mean an attempt to use negativity as the dynamic principle of a thought that would no longer be equated with knowledge, where knowledge is understood as a subject-object correlation.

I will use Hegel and Karl Barth as two exemplary exponents of such dialectical thinking; Hegel being the paradigm of a conclusive dialectic, Barth the paradigm of an inconclusive, even a broken dialectic.

With Hegel we try to think more, with Barth to think differently.

For Hegel the dialectic is that of the Spirit that makes the difference between God and the human mind irrelevant, for Barth the dialectic deepens the gap between the Wholly Other and the world of creatures. For both of them, however, the "thought-work" leads to failure, yet to a productive failure, if I may dare put it this way. I mean, their thought leads to an aporia that calls for integration into a larger dialectic, that of thought, action, and feeling.

Thinking more with Hegel means following the painful but victorious "work of the negative" from the sphere of logic to that of Nature and of Spirit, and within the sphere of Spirit from the subjective to the objective and finally to the absolute Spirit. On every level, negativity is what constrains each figure of the Spirit to invert itself into its contrary and to engender a new figure that both surpasses and preserves the preceding one, in the twofold sense of the Hegelian concept of *Aufhebung*. This conclusive dialectic makes the tragic and the logical coincide at every stage. Something must die so that something greater may be born. In this sense, misfortune is everywhere, but everywhere it is surpassed, to the extent that reconciliation always wins out over what is torn apart.

The question is whether this triumphant dialectic does not reconstitute, with logical resources unavailable to Leibniz, another form of optimism issuing from the same audacity, with perhaps an even greater rational hubris. Indeed, what fate is reserved for the suffering of victims in a worldwiew where the pan-tragic is constantly covered over by a pan-logicism? We may say that the scandal of suffering is overlooked in two ways. First, it is diluted and defused by the very expansion of negativity beyond the human predicament. Second, it is silenced by the substitution of reconciliation (of contradictions) for consolation addressed to human beings as victims. The famous motto of the "cunning of reason" in the introduction to the *Lectures on the Philosophy of History* is the well-known stumbling block of this post-Kantian theodicy.

The irony of the Hegelian philosophy of history lies in the fact that, assuming that it does give a meaning to the great currents of history, an assumption that is not at issue here, it does so to the extent that it abolishes the question of happiness and unhappiness. History, it is said, is not "the soil in which happiness grows."[2] But if the great actors in history are frustrated as concerns happiness by history, which makes use of them, what are we to say about its anonymous victims? For we who read Hegel after the catastrophes and the sufferings beyond number of our century, the dissociation that his philosophy of history brings about between consolation and reconciliation has become, to say the least, a source of great perplexity. The more the system flourishes, the more its victims are marginalized. The success of the system is its failure. Suffering, as what is expressed by the voices of lamentation, is what the system excludes.

Will a broken dialectic—that of Karl Barth—do better justice to the phenomenon of victimization than the victorious dialectic of Hegel? Up to a certain point, yes. But beyond it, no. Up to what point? To the point when it acknowledges its broken condition as irretrievable.

The famous section of *Church Dogmatics* entitled "God and Nothingness"[3]—translating the strong German "Gott und das Nichtige"—may be assigned to a "broken" theology, to the extent that it sees in evil a reality that is not commensurate with the goodness of God and of creation, and furthermore a reality that is not reducible to the negative side of human experience, which was the only one taken into account by Leibniz and Hegel. Instead we are to think of a nothingness hostile to God, not just a nothingness of deficiency and privation, but one of corruption and destruction. In this way we do justice to the protest of suffering humanity that refuses to allow itself to be included within the cycle of moral evil in terms of the doctrine of retribution, or even to allow itself to be enrolled under the banner of providence, another name for the goodness of creation. Nevertheless, we may say that we "know" the reality of evil, to the extent that we confess that nothingness is what Christ has vanquished by "nihilating" himself on the cross, and also that God met and struggled with this nothingness in Jesus the Christ. This "christological turn" given to the problem of evil is one of the paradigmatic ways of thinking more about evil by thinking differently. I would not say that the christological turn as such constitutes a breach of the pledge no longer to return to the conciliatory mood of pre-Kantian and post-Kantian theodicies, although I would feel more comfortable with the method of correlation applied to both Christian symbols *and* human experience by Paul Tillich, Langdon Gilkey, and David Tracy. The breach, to my mind, occurs when Barth relates the reality of nothingness to the "left hand of God," the one that rejects when the right

---

2. G. W. F. Hegel, *Lectures on the Philosophy of World History, Introductions: Reason in History,* trans. H. B. Nisbet (Cambridge: Cambridge Univ. Press, 1975), 79.

3. Karl Barth, *Church Dogmatics* (Edinburgh: T and T Clark, 1958), 3/3:289–369.

hand elects: "As God is Lord on the left hand as well, He is the basis and Lord of nothingness too."[4]

Can this coordination without conciliation between God's left and right hands make sense? If it is not a covert concession to the failed theodicies of the past and accordingly a weak compromise substituted for a broken dialectic, does it not reopen the way to speculations such as those of Giordano Bruno and Schelling on the demonic aspect of the deity? Paul Tillich was not afraid to take up this issue that Barth both so encouraged and so refused. But how then does thinking guard itself against the drunken excesses that Kant denounced with the term *Schwärmerei,* which includes both the sense of enthusiasm and mystical madness?

Did not wisdom already encounter this *aporetic* aspect of thinking about evil, an aporetic aspect opened up by the very effort of thinking more and differently? With this open question my second part comes to an end.

III. Thinking, Acting, and Feeling with Regard to Evil

On the level of theoretical thinking the problem of evil remains a challenge that is never completely overcome. In this sense, we may speak of a failure of pure speculation. Yet this failure has never led to a sheer capitulation of thought, but rather to untiring refinement in speculative logic, under the prodding of the question Why?—Why me?—raised by the lament of victims. Hegel's triumphant dialectic and Barth's broken one are both instructive in this regard. The initial enigma is elevated to the rank of a terminal aporia by the very work of thinking that finally fails.

It is to this aporia that action and the catharsis of feelings and emotions are called upon not to give a solution but a response, a response able to render the aporia productive.

A turn from theory to practice was already initiated by Kant, as I have said. But this turn is not a turning away from thought. Instead it is the continuation on another plane of thought's interminable work. One symptom of this may be found in the meditation on radical evil with which Kant's *Religion within the Bounds of Reason Alone* opens. This meditation by itself is sufficient to prove that practical reason has its own way of failing and of bordering on mystery when it comes to the question of evil. If we may think in conceptual terms of radical evil as the supreme maxim that grounds all the bad maxims of our free will, then the *raison d'être* of this radical evil is inscrutable (*unerforschbar*): "There is then for us," Kant says, "no conceivable ground from which the moral evil in us could originally

---

4. Ibid., 3/3:351.

have come."[5] Along with Karl Jaspers, I admire this ultimate avowal on Kant's part. Like Augustine, and also perhaps like mythical thought, Kant caught sight of the demonic aspect of the ground of human freedom, yet he did so with the sobriety of a thinking always careful not to transgress the limits of knowledge.

Keeping in mind this transfer of the aporia from the sphere of theory to that of practice, we may nevertheless speak of the response of action to the challenge of evil.

For action, evil is above all what ought not to be, but what must be fought against. In this sense, action inverts the orientation of looking at the world. Myth tends to pull speculative thought back toward the origin of things. From whence comes evil? it asks. The response, not the solution, of action is to act against evil. Our vision is thus turned toward the future, by the idea of a *task* to be accomplished, which corresponds to that of an origin to be discovered.

But we should not assume that by placing the accent on the practical struggle against evil we have once again lost sight of suffering. To the contrary. All evil committed by one person, we have seen, is evil undergone by another person. To do evil is to make another person suffer. Violence, in this sense, constantly re-creates the unity of moral evil and suffering. Hence, any action, whether ethical or political, that diminishes the quantity of violence exercised by some human beings over against other human beings diminishes the amount of suffering in the world. If we were to remove the suffering inflicted by people on other people, we would see what remained of suffering in the world, but to tell the truth, we have no idea of what this would be, to such an extent does human violence impregnate suffering.

But I readily concede that action alone is not enough. The arbitrary and indiscriminate way in which suffering is apportioned whether by violence or by the ultimate part of suffering that cannot be ascribed to human interaction—illness, old age, or death—keeps rekindling the old questions: not just Why? but Why me? Why my beloved child?

The emotional response that the practical one calls forth as its necessary complement cannot be anything other than a catharsis of the emotions that nourish the lament and that transform it into complaint. I will take as my model for this transmutation of the lament the "work of mourning," as Freud describes it in his famous essay "Mourning and Melancholia." Mourning, Freud tells us, is a step-by-step letting go of all the attachments, cathexses, and investments that make us feel the loss of a loved object as

---

5. Immanuel Kant, *Religion within the Limits of Reason Alone,* trans. Theodore M. Greene and Hoyt H. Hudson (New York: Harper Torchbooks, 1960), 38.

a loss of our very own self. This detachment that Freud calls the work of mourning makes us free again for new affective attachments or investments.

What I should like to do is to consider wisdom, with its philosophical and theological prolongations, as a spiritual help in this work of mourning, aimed at a qualitative change in the lament and the complaint. The itinerary I will briefly describe in no way claims to be exemplary in all regards. It represents only one of the possible paths by which thought, action, and feeling may venture forth together.

The first way of making the intellectual aporia productive is to integrate the ignorance it gives rise to, the *docta ignorantia,* into the work of mourning. To the tendency of survivors to feel guilt about the death of someone they loved, as well as to the tendency of victims to blame themselves and to enter into the cruel game of the expiatory victim, we must reply: "No, God did not want that, even less did God want to punish you. I don't know why things happened as they did, chance and accident are part of the world."[6] This would be the zero degree, so to speak, in the catharsis of the complaint.

A second stage in the catharsis of the lament is to allow it to develop into a complaint against God. This is the way taken by the work of Elie Wiesel. The very relationship of the covenant, to the extent that it is a mutual action that God and human beings bring against one another, invites us to pursue this course, even to the point of articulating a "theology of protest," such as that suggested by John K. Roth in his *Encountering Evil.*[7] What one protests against is the idea of divine "permission," which remains the expedient of every theodicy and which Barth himself tried to rethink when he distinguished between the victory already won over evil and the full manifestation of this victory. Our accusation against God is here the impatience of hope. It has its origin in the cry of the Psalmist, "How long O Lord?"

A third stage in the catharsis of the lament is to discover that the reasons for believing in God have nothing in common with the need to explain the origin of suffering. Suffering is only a scandal for the person who understands God to be the source of everything that is good in creation, including our indignation against evil, our courage to bear it, and our feeling of sympathy toward victims. In other words, we believe in God *in spite of* evil. To believe in God *in spite of* ... is one of the ways in which we can integrate the speculative aporia into the work of mourning.

Beyond this threshold, a few sages advance along the path that leads to a complete renouncing of any and all complaint about evil. Some even reach the point of discerning in suffering some educative and purgative value. But

---

6. In this regard, the little book by Rabbi Harold S. Kushner, *When Bad Things Happen to Good People* (New York: Schocken Books, 1981), can be a useful pastoral aid in some cases.

7. John K. Roth, *Encountering Evil* (Richmond: John Knox Press, 1981).

we should immediately add that this meaning should not become the object of a specific teaching; it can be found or rediscovered only in each specific case. And there is a legitimate pastoral concern that this meaning taken up by a victim not lead him or her back along the route of self-accusation or self-destruction.

Some people, still more advanced as regards this path of renouncing complaining, find a consolation without any parallel in the idea that God too suffers and that the covenant, beyond its conflictual aspects, for Christians, culminates in a partnership in the suffering of Christ. But the theology of the cross, that is, the theology that holds that God died in Christ, remains meaningless without a corresponding transformation of our lament. The horizon toward which this wisdom is directed seems to me to be a renouncement of those very desires the wounding of which engenders our complaint. This is a renouncement, first of all, of the desire to be spared of all suffering. Next it is a renouncement of the infantile component of the desire for immortality, one that allows us to accept our own death as one aspect of that part of the negative that Karl Barth so carefully distinguished from aggressive nothingness, *das Nichtige*. A similar wisdom is perhaps indicated at the end of the book of Job when it is said that Job came to love God for nought, thereby making Satan lose his bet. To love God for nought is to escape completely the cycle of retribution to which the lamentation still remains captive, so long as the victim bemoans the injustice of his or her fate.

Perhaps this horizon of wisdom, at least as it appears in the West under the influence of Judaism and Christianity, overlaps the horizon of Buddhist wisdom at a significant crossing point that only a long dialogue between them could make more conspicuous....

However, I do not want to separate these individual experiences of wisdom from the ethical and political struggle against evil that may bring together all people of goodwill. In relation to this struggle, these experiences are, like all acts of nonviolent resistance, anticipations in the form of parables of a human condition where, such violence having been suppressed, the enigma of real violence will be revealed.

15

The Summoned Subject
in the School of the Narratives
of the Prophetic Vocation

This lecture has to be understood and read as the counterpart of the lecture that preceded it in my Gifford Lectures. In that lecture I spoke of the symbolic grid—including the narrative dimension—by means of which the subject understands itself in the Jewish and Christian tradition.[1]

What I would like to try to do here is to say what self understands itself in this way. In so doing I am not looking for an end point but for a point from which to suspend my whole series of investigations. To do this, I have picked out a discontinuous series of figures of the self, relative to different cultural contexts of interpretation, which only have among themselves what Wittgenstein called a "family resemblance," one that we might broadly characterize by the phrase the "summoned subject." Here the self is constituted and defined by its position as respondent to propositions of meaning issuing from the symbolic network I have previously described. Before any explication or interpretation, this phrase diametrically opposes itself to the philosophical hubris of a self that absolutely names itself. However, it does not substitute itself for this philosophical ideal inasmuch as a self that responds is a self in relation, without being an absolute self—that is, outside any relatedness and in this sense the foundation of every relation. What is more, this phrase "summoned self" indicates the place of a certain congruence with the self described in a hermeneutics of the "I am," which in its broad outlines is already a self in relation and, in this way, a self in the position of respondent. However, I do not want to insinuate that the self, formed and informed by the biblical paradigms, crowns the self of our

---

Originally published as "Le Sujet convoqué: A l'École des récits de vocation prophétique," *Revue de l'Institut Catholique de Paris* 28 (1988): 83–99; reprinted with permission.

1. The lecture referred to—"The Self in the Mirror of Scripture"—is unpublished. Readers are directed, however, to a related essay, "Pastoral Praxeology, Hermeneutics, and Identity," below. ED.

philosophical hermeneutics. This would be to betray our unambiguous affirmation that the mode of Christian life is a wage and a destiny, and those
who take it up are not led by their confession either to assume a defen-
sive position or to presume a superiority in relation to every other form of
life, because we lack criteria of comparison capable of dividing among rival claims. The self that here responds, responds precisely to that symbolic
ensemble delimited by the biblical canon and developed by one or another
of the historical traditions that have grafted themselves to the Scriptures to
which these traditions claim allegiance.

The Prophetic Call

I have chosen as my first figure of a responding self the one that is con-
figured by the so-called narratives of the prophetic call or vocation in the
Old Testament. This first figure gives the notion of the responding self a
specific determination that is expressed by the very title of this lecture: the
summoned self. In fact, all my other figures refer to it, not in the mode of
repetitive imitation but in that of a development that, however discontinuous it may be, does not break the cord that attaches these later figures to
the first one.

It goes without saying that my choice of these narratives in no way implies that I am going back on my earlier refusal to give one theological
center to the Old Testament or even that I am falling back in to that old
exegetical and theological rut that opposes prophecy to legalism in the Old
Testament. It suffices that the narratives of the prophets' vocation have
a relation of paroxysmic homology with the structure common to all the
Old Testament writings, by which I mean their dialogic structure that confronts the words and acts of God with the response human beings give
to them.

How are the narratives about the prophets' vocation, which we are now
going to examine, attached to this overall dialogic structure? They constitute clearly delimited narrative sequences and, as we shall see, structures
of a certain type within still broader narratives, those that Claus Westermann calls "stories of mediators." These may apply to cultic mediators,
the priests; heros of justice and conquest, the judges; or the prophets of
judgment, the ones I am considering here. These latter, unlike the former
cases, are mediators of history, of an ongoing history, an imminent history,
that they "see" coming about (Paul Beauchamp) and that they interpret
for their people as the carrying out of a judgment brought against them.
It is this mission that makes them mediators, not conquerors, but suffering
mediators, whose painful word is inscribed on the trajectory of the lamentation, as we see in Jeremiah. In this, their destiny announces that of the

Suffering Servant, concerning whom Second Isaiah has assembled the sorrowful songs. As in the case of this nameless servant, suffering has taken the place of action (Westermann).

If the narratives of vocation, which inaugurate the sorrowful career of the prophet, merit being detached from their context, so as to provide our first type of responding self, it is first of all because the prophet's response in them is strictly personal. In them, we do not see "I" and "we" alternate, as in the Psalms. Here the individual is no longer the member of the community of the people, even though he remains so to an extreme degree, as I shall indicate below. He is the exception, in Karl Jaspers's sense of this term, uprooted from his condition, his place, his desire. What is more, the subjective face of his response is the object of a distinct narrative, in the form of a confession in the first person. And when the narrative is in the third person, his thoughts, feelings, and emotions are reported in a form that is close to the modern "quoted" or "recounted monologue," which brings the third person narrative close to the first person of autobiography.[2]

A final reason for making these narratives a particular case is that by setting these quasi-autobiographical narratives down in writing, often on the basis of the prophets themselves, who were reported to have confided their words to writing, the later scribes gave a literary life (*survie*) to these eminently circumstantial words. A *Sitz-im-Wort* thus succeeds a *Sitz-im-Leben*, at the price of a certain dramatic stylization I shall speak of, but to the benefit of the "type" these narratives give rise to.[3] It is given this latter condition of stylization that these narratives could give birth to what, for an investigation into the responding self, constitutes the absolutely original paradigm I am giving the name the "summoned subject."

We now have to say in what sense this sent, mandated, commanded subject satisfies what I have risked calling a relationship of paroxysmic homology with the generally dialogic structure of the relation between the act of God's word and humans' recalcitrant response to it.

---

2. Robert Alter, *The Art of Biblical Narrative* (New York: Basic Books, 1981), has demonstrated the important place quotation (or the "reported" monologue) and the narrative of thoughts (the "recounted" monologue) hold in the biblical art of narration. In a similar sense, following Elizabeth Anscombe, we can use the biblical formula: "God said in his heart, I will..." to illustrate in the third person the attribution of the power to designate oneself.

3. This is undoubtedly why, after the exile, the scribes preserved these often frightful and condemnatory words, despite the paradox of a prophecy heard and received *post eventum.* Gerhard von Rad notes: "Ought we not also to remember that when a prophecy came into the hands of those who transmitted the traditions, this itself meant that the time when the prophecy could be taken in the strict sense which it had when it was originally delivered was already a thing of the past?" (*Old Testament Theology,* vol. 2: *The Theology of Israel's Prophetic Traditions,* trans. D. M. G. Stalker [New York: Harper and Row, 1965], 49). Von Rad is not wrong to underscore the scope of the hermeneutic problem raised in this way. But this is not the place to discuss that problem, except to indicate that writing transforms the exception into a paradigm.

I shall take as a reference, even if our topic requires broadening it a bit, the *Gattungsstruktur* that some exegetes have drawn from the comparison of different stylized vocational narratives.[4]

The first phase of this structure is the confrontation with God. In some narratives it takes on a quite broad scope. The burning bush for Moses, the theophany in the temple for Isaiah, the vision of Yahweh's "chariot," then the book offered as to be devoured—in the literal sense of the word— in Ezekiel. This breadth given to the confrontation scene expresses the strongly asymmetrical structure of the dialogic relation between the I of the prophet and the divine I who sends him on his mission. This initial disproportion is further emphasized by the sort of interruption the calls brings about in the life of the prophet. The prophetic ego is so radically decentered that it is at first uprooted from its initial setting. Amos is taken from his flock, as was Moses, "who was keeping the flock of his father-in-law Jethro."

Next comes the introductory speech that presents itself as an immemorial word, antedating that of the prophet and capable of designating itself in the first person as the very source of the foundation and authentication of the prophetic ego. God makes a self-announcement before calling the prophet: "I am the God of your father, the God of Abraham, the God of Isaac, and the God of Jacob" (Exod. 3:6). In this narrative from Exodus, the self-presentation of the Lord is developed in a distinct sequence, the one called the revelation of God's name: "I am who I am," a formula that must not be separated from the one that follows, where "I am" becomes a name, the Name: "I am has sent me to you." Exegetes have studied numerous variants of the formula of self-presentation, whose core can be summed up as: "It's me," "God with you," a formula taken up again forcefully in the phrase of reassurance.[5]

---

4. See N. Habel, "The Form and Significance of the Call Narratives," *Zeitschrift für die alttestamentliche Wissenschaft* (1965): 297–329. Habel examines six stylized narratives: the call of Gideon in Judg. 6:11-17, that of Moses in Exod. 3:1-12, that of Jeremiah in Jer. 1:4-10, that of Isaiah in Isa. 6:1-13, that of Ezekiel in Ezek. 1:1—3:15, and that of Second Isaiah in Isa. 40:1-11. From these he outlines a *Gattungsstruktur* with six episodes: confrontation with God, introductory speech, mission properly speaking, the envoy's objection, reassurance with an oath, giving of a sign. This overly rigid presentation is tempered by Walther Zimmerli, in his commentary on the Book of Jeremiah, in the section "Zur Form und Traditionsgeschichte der Prophetischen Berufungserzählungen," in *Biblischer Kommentar: Altes Testament* 13/1:16–21. A typology with four variants has been proposed by W. Vogels, "Les Récits des vocations de prophètes," *La Nouvelle Revue Théologique* 95 (1973): 3–24.

5. It is true that the sense of divine transcendence leads to the counterbalancing of this self-presentation of the Lord by the interposition of a messenger or by the effacing of the subject of the action, as in the case of Ezekiel, crushed by his vision: "I heard the voice of someone speaking" (1:28); then "a hand was stretched out to me, and a written scroll was in it" (2:9). However, Ezekiel had been able to say at the beginning of his narrative: "And the hand of the Lord was on him there" (1:3).

Third phase: the decisive word can then be pronounced: "I send you," "go and say to them..." This speech lays out the very identity of the one sent, often called by his name, but always individually designated.

This identity, however, is immediately perceived as torn between the greatness of the mission and the smallness of the one sent. This is the fourth phase of our *Gattungsstruktur,* the one called the "objection." "Who am I that I should go...?" says Moses, who had, however, said, "Here I am," as did Abraham according to Gen. 22:1. The same Moses, after a new protest—"I am slow of speech and slow of tongue"—will even be struck dumb. Isaiah too responded, "Here I am; send me." But, under the insupportable burden of unhappiness and condemnation, he muttered, "How long, O Lord?" Jeremiah, always torn, cried out, "I am only a boy." Ezekiel does not object; the word overcomes him. Nevertheless, we read at the end of this episode: "The spirit lifted me up and bore me away: I went in bitterness in the heat of my spirit, the hand of the Lord being strong upon me" (3:14).

The dialogic structure—dialogic although asymmetric—of the commissioning is sealed by the word of "reassurance": "I will be with you in truth"; "Go, I am with you"; "I will open your mouth." The prophet is henceforth "established," "commanded," but he must continue to listen in order to speak.[6]

Such is the schema of the "prophetic I," singularized by the prophet's call, his response, even by his recalcitrance.[7] Unlike the I (or more exactly the I/we) of the lament or praise in the Psalms, this I is constituted by a pair—by call and commission. The call distinguishes the prophet from the community of his people and constitutes him as an exception, in the sense indicated above; the commission attaches him once again to his people: "Go, and say to them..." The call isolates; the commission binds. This communal aspect of the commission cannot be blocked out by the solitude of the call. If just one is called, a whole people is intended. The people, in fact, do not stop being the setting for the word. It is, at first, in a situation of distress that the prophet is called: captivity in Egypt, the threat of destruction, captivity in Babylon. The prophet is the figure of crisis. Through this crisis, he belongs to the people from whom he is withdrawn so as to be

---

6. I will not discuss here the much-disputed question of the relation between vision and hearing, which is particularly sharp in the case of Ezekiel. I an inclined to agree with Zimmerli in saying that the vision has the function of removing someone from that person's usual surroundings, of a transfer to an absolute elsewhere, thereby interrupting the ordinary course of life of the one called.

7. Vogels is correct to modulate Habel's schema for this *Berufungsgattung* into several different types. Thus he distinguishes the officer/soldier type (Jonah, Amos), the master/servant/confident plenipotentiary type (Jeremiah, Ezekiel 2), the king/counselor type with its three subtypes (Micah, Isaiah, Ezekiel 1), and the master/disciple type (Samuel).

sent to them. Next, his words, especially when they convey a prophecy of misfortune, presuppose an instruction, a torah, that has been transgressed. This torah, even if it is in part the work of the prophetic circles, is the charter of a liberated people, whom the prophet recalls to their collective vocation. Finally, the more or less stereotyped form in which these narratives of a vocation have been confided to writing attests to the willingness of the prophet/writer to inscribe himself in a prophetic tradition, from Moses to the last prophet who speaks. However singular each call may be, it does not begin unless it is followed by something. Thus it belongs to the essence of prophetic speech in its pain to conjoin an exceptional ipseity to a traditional community. Through this conjunction, the prophetic I is "established" and "commanded."

To conclude my analysis of this first type, I see, for my part, in this figure of a "summoned subject" a paradigm that the Christian community, following the Jewish community, could make use of to interpret itself. This enterprise was made possible by the passage referred to earlier of the prophetic word from a *Sitz-im-Leben* to a *Sitz-im-Word*. Having become writing, the living word was in effect opened to a history of interpretation. The understanding of the Christ-event in light of prophetic speech belongs in this regard to this history of the interpretation of the commissioned self.

Transformed into the Christ Image

New paradigms of the responding self, capable of exemplifying the dialogic relation that structures the meaning space delimited by the biblical canon, spring up along this trajectory of interpretation.

The paradigm closest to that of the mandated self of the Old Testament is that of conformity to the Christ figure, which seems to have appeared for the first time, according to the written testimony of the ancient church, in Paul's letters.

Recall the dense yet luminous text from the Second Letter to the Corinthians where Paul says: "And all of us, with unveiled faces, seeing the glory of the Lord as though reflected in a mirror, are being transformed into the same image from one degree of glory to another; for this comes from the Lord, the Spirit" (2 Cor. 3:18). This text takes on its full relief if we set it against the background of the Mosaic prohibition of images, not just those of false gods, or idols, but also of Yahweh. Is an icon that is not an idol possible?

However, it is not on the side of the figure of Adam, created in "the image" of God, according to the creation narrative in Gen. 1:26, that Paul seeks a handhold in the Hebraic tradition, but rather on the side of the theme of "glory"—the glory of Yahweh—in which the epiphany of majesty and holiness of the Lord, his shining forth, is summed up. "The glory of the Lord settled on Mount Sinai" (Exod. 24:15-16; see Deut. 5:22). But, already in the Old Testament, the metaphor of power had been inverted with the figure of the "Suffering Servant" of Second Isaiah: a figure "with no form or majesty" (Isa. 53:2). Yet it is this figure that will make the divine glory radiate to the ends of the earth: "You are my servant, Israel, in whom I shall be glorified" (Isa. 49:3). The early church confessed the life and death, the death and resurrection of Jesus the Christ as the manifestation of God's glory, by prolonging this figure.

And it is to this reinterpretation of the glory of God figured through the person of Christ that Paul grafted the extraordinary theme of the transformation of the Christian into this same image. In this way he forged the central metaphor of the Christian self as christomorphic, that is, the image of the image par excellence. A chain of glory, if we may put it this way—of descending glory, it must be added—is created in this way: God's glory, that of Christ, that of the Christian. At the far end of this chain, if the mediation goes back to the origin, the christomorphic self is both fully dependent and fully upstanding: an image "always more glorious," according to the apostle.

We could follow the destiny of this foundational metaphor in the tradition of books about spirituality, among which *The Imitation of Christ* plays the role of the central melody. However, I would like instead to take the risk of discerning an even more concealed filiation in the figure of the christomorphic self, as an heir of the prophetic "mandated" self, in two quite well-determined cultural contexts, in each instance a bit more removed from the purely Hebraic setting. In this way, I hope to verify this originally biblical figure's capacity for renewal, as faithful to both the Old and the New Testaments.

The Figure of the "Inner Teacher"

If I have chosen at this stage of our inquiry Augustine's figure of the "inner teacher," it is because it forms a significant advance in Western thought along the way of internalizing the relation of correspondence between the divine pole of a call and the human pole of a response. If it cannot be doubted that Platonism and Neoplatonism played a major role in this process of internalization, it is still true that the biblical component of this Christian Neoplatonism remains dominant and that the Greek component undergoes a decisive transformation by being integrated into this new figure of a "mandated" self.

Augustine's *The Teacher* constitutes the basic text as regards this figure.[8] However powerful is the attraction exercised by the theme of illumination (by which Augustine's thought is rightly characterized), the relation of teaching, constitutive of the relation between master and disciple, is not transformed to the point of being no longer recognizable, even insignificant, in entering this new space of gravitation. On the contrary, it is what assures the Christian specificity of the very theme of illumination, so close in other ways to the Platonic idea of reminiscence. The relation master/ disciple remains, in effect, the central thread of this moving dialogue between Augustine and Adeodatus (the son of his "sin," according to the more humble than self-punitive expression of the recently converted rhetor, in *Confessions* 1.9), a dialogue that quite opportunely recalls that between Socrates and the young slave in the *Meno*. In the relation of interlocution proper to teaching and learning, as it was practiced in particular in the schools where language itself was the object of discourse, two features are noteworthy. First, the roles of the master and the disciple were not interchangeable. The one is superior to the other, even if this first feature will be sublimated although not abolished by the figure of the inner teacher. Second, the teacher seems to be external to the student. The one teaches and the other is taught. It is this second feature that will be completely effaced by Augustine. In fact, however, the process of internalization begins already with profane knowledge. It is complete with the intelligible truths. At this level, no one learns anything from the outside; better, one never learns anything (*nusquam igitur discere* [12.40; p. 96]). It is the inner person that discovers the truth in oneself, simply aided by the teacher. As for the signs of language, they merely serve to "alert" this person in the moment they are "consulted." It is, however, the truth of things that "presides" and thus "governs the mind itself from within."

It may seem that we have plunged back into Platonism and into Platonic reminiscence. The similarity to book 10 of the *Confessions,* devoted to memory, reinforces this impression.[9] Does not memory appear there as the store of eternal truths even more than as the trace left by the events of our personal past? Yes, but with Augustine the theory of reminiscence is separated from that of the preexistence of the soul and in this way can be given a still more important inflection. This inflection comes to it from the identification of all internal and higher truth with Christ, who alone is

8. *The Teacher,* in *Augustine: Earlier Writings,* ed. J. H. S. Burleigh (Philadelphia: Westminster Press, 1953), 69–101.

9. Memory is considered in 12.39 of *The Teacher,* but still as the faculty of the past. However, it is images of past things—not the things themselves—that we carry "in the halls of memory," as documenting past sensations, and that "we can contemplate mentally and can speak of with a good conscience [*bonna conscientia*] and without lying" (*The Teacher,* p. 96.

not just a teacher but who also, as Paul says in Eph. 3:16-17, can "dwell in your hearts."[10]

It cannot to be denied that the Christ figure is itself assimilated to eternal wisdom, following a tradition that, however Hellenistic we may consider it to be, is also incorporated into Scripture, in fact into the Hebrew Scripture (Prov. 8:22-31). Thus, it is the internal teacher that we "consult" when we discover within ourselves the truth of an intelligible order. Hence, to "consult the inner truth" does not mean to be "taught" by words: it is not "apprehended" from the outside; it is known through contemplation "in the inner light of truth which illumines the inner man and is inwardly enjoyed" (*The Teacher* 12.40; p. 96). This theme of illumination seems to have absorbed that of teaching, to the point of abolishing it, at least to the extent that contemplation has broken free of any mediation through language or words. Yet if this absorption and this breaking free were as complete as they are in Platonism, would not the designation of intelligible truth and wisdom as an inner teacher become completely superfluous, and would not the expression the "disciple of truth" (13.41; p. 98) and even more so the characterization of what is taught as "disciplines"—a word derived from "disciple"—be emptied of all significance? In fact, contemplation remains a kind of teaching because the discovery of truth is the reading within oneself of innate ideas and therefore of something always already there, but still requiring an inward discovery. This discovery still merits the name "inward learning" (14.45; p. 100), however. To this degree the figure of the inner teacher is not abolished but rather exalted over against the condition of a soul that continues on the way, because it is created, to the point of contemplating intelligible truths.[11] The metaphor of light cannot therefore be substituted for the figure of the teacher, for the simple reason that the light and the word are the same.

---

10. Augustine refers to another text of Scripture: "But you are not to be called rabbi, for you have one teacher, and you are all students. And call no one your father on earth, for you have one Father—the one in heaven" (Matt. 23:8-10). Augustine summarizes it: "We are to call no one on earth our teacher, for One is our teacher who is in heaven" (*The Teacher,* p. 100).

11. Commentators have emphasized the difference that separates Augustine here from those Neoplatonists for whom the soul, being of a divine nature, has no need of learning, even in the sublime sense intended by Augustine. See, above all, Etienne Gilson, *The Christian Philosophy of Saint Augustine,* trans. L. E. M. Lynch (New York: Vintage Books, 1967), 66–76. According to this well-known interpreter, Augustine's break with Neoplatonism begins with the distinction between reminiscence and preexistence, owing to the thesis of the creation of the soul. Memory, as a result, is memory of the present, not of the past, of the soul. Next, the illumination of a creature distinct from God does not exclude either discovery or progress. The theory of illumination is not a theory about innateness. It is this gap, I believe, that leaves a space for the figure of the teacher. Even as internal, even more internal to myself than myself, the teacher remains the other of the soul.

The Testimony of Conscience

I would like to end this overview of figures of the self—in its aspect of responding to the symbolic structure of what Northrop Frye, following William Blake, has called the Great Code of the Bible—with the theme of conscience. This is surely the most internalized expression of the responding self, which is internalized to the point of constituting itself as an autonomous instance in the ethical tradition issuing from the Enlightenment, principally with Kant's *Critique of Practical Reason* and Hegel's *Phenomenology of Spirit*. Far from undertaking a polemic against this conquered autonomy won by the conscience, I would like to show that it opens new possibilities of interpretation for the dialogic structure of Christian existence, without for all that breaking the cord that ties this figure of the responsive self to the first figure we have considered, that of the "mandated" self of the narratives about the prophetic call.

These new possibilities of interpretation have been preserved by the phenomenological analysis of the phenomenon of conscience I have presented elsewhere.[12] Two features of this interpretation are especially noteworthy: first, the structure of calling that makes conscience a voice that care addresses to itself; second, the priority of the phenomenon of testimony over that of accusation: through the conscience, the self bears witness to its ownmost power of being before measuring and in order to measure the inadequation of its action to its most profound being.

In this sense, we can note the neutral character of the phenomenon of conscience as regards its religious interpretation. It is the self that calls the self and bears witness to its ownmost power of being. It is good that things should be so. If a theological interpretation of conscience is to be possible, it will precisely presuppose this intimacy of self and conscience. It is to the dialogue of the self with itself that the response of the prophetic and the christomorphic self is grafted. In this graft, the two living organs are changed into each other: on the one side, the call of the self to itself is intensified and transformed by the figure that serves as its model and archetype; on the other side, the transcendent figure is internalized by the moment of appropriation that transmutes it into an inner voice.

Saint Paul was undoubtedly the first to have caught sight of this connection between a nonspecifically religious phenomenon (or, at least, a nonspecifically Christian phenomenon), which he called *suneidesis*—knowledge shared with oneself—and the kerygma about Christ that he interpreted in terms of "justification by faith." It is essential that this "justification," which does not come from us, should be able to be re-

---

12. See, for example, Paul Ricoeur, *Oneself as Another*, trans. Kathleen Blamey (Chicago: Univ. of Chicago Press, 1992), 203–39.

ceived within the intimacy of a conscience that already offers by itself the dual structure of a voice that calls and a self that responds, and that moreover is already constituted as an instance of testimony and of judgment. Conscience is thus the anthropological presupposition without which "justification by faith" would remain an event marked by a radical extrinsicness. In this sense, conscience becomes the organ of the reception of the kerygma, in a perspective that remains profoundly Pauline.[13]

In short, for Paul himself, the preacher of salvation by faith apart from any works, conscience is an inalienable structure of existence. It belongs to human beings—pagan or not, Greek or Jew—to have a conscience, that is, a self-knowledge that includes the minimal relational aspect of relating oneself to some instance qualified by the difference between good and evil.

A theology of conscience requires a simultaneous reinterpretation of the phenomenon of conscience and of the Christian kerygma. In *Oneself as Another,* I have indicated how the first part may be carried out through a critical appropriation of the Heideggerian analysis of conscience. In this appropriation, the autonomy of the Kantian conscience is tempered by the confession of nonmastery over oneself that characterizes what is however a radical instance properly speaking, one that, to use Heidegger's powerful expression, is always mine. The kerygma may also be reinterpreted in such a way that its transcendence is symmetrically tempered by the process of ongoing interpretation of the symbolic space opened and delimited by the

---

13. Rudolph Bultmann, in his *Theology of the New Testament,* trans. Kendrick Grobel (New York: Charles Scribner's Sons, 1951), does not hesitate in situating conscience within the constellation of "anthropological concepts" that outline the formal structures of human existence and that, in this sense, describe "man prior to faith" (see 1:206–20). The same status applies to such concepts as body (*soma*), soul (*psukhe*), mind (*nous*), heart (*kardia*), flesh (*sarx*), world (*cosmos*), and even law (*nomos*); with the last concept, the boundary between anthropology and soteriology is reached but not yet crossed. All these concepts, Bultmann emphasizes, do not designate parts or faculties but the whole of human being in terms of a certain aspect. Conscience is the knowledge shared with oneself that, unlike *nous,* is not directed toward this or that thought but rather reflects upon, examines, and judges. Therefore, conscience characterizes the relation of the human person with him- or herself, but always in relation with some demand marked with the distinction between good and evil. This demand can be very concrete, or more general, or even universal. For example, good and bad conscience express the conviction of acting in conformity or disaccord with what one takes to be the thing to do in some particular circumstance. Think, for example, of the case of whether a Christian invited by a pagan should eat meat sacrificed to idols (see 1 Cor. 8:7-12; 10:25-30). A second example: a citizen submits to authority not just "because of wrath" but "also because of conscience" (Rom. 13:5). A third example: conscience designates in depth the testimony rendered by the law inscribed in one's heart, as can be seen among pagans who do not know the law of Moses: "When Gentiles, who do not possess the law, do instinctively what the law requires, these, though not having the law, are a law to themselves. They show that what the law requires is written on their hearts, to which their own conscience also bears witness; and their conflicting thoughts will accuse or perhaps excuse them" (Rom. 2:14-15). Paul himself calls upon such testimony, which has nothing specifically Christian about it, when he protests concerning the sincerity of his words and of his way of life (1 Cor. 4:4; Rom. 9:1; 2 Cor. 1:12).

biblical canon. Frye's Great Code is inscribed in this space that we interpret insofar as it interprets us.[14]

In fact, this theology of conscience remains largely yet to be done. Few contemporary theologians have undertaken to reinterpret the phenomenon of conscience, despite the place it occupies in Luther's thought. For this reason, Gerhard Ebeling's "theological reflections on conscience" are all the more valuable.[15] He formulates his reflections in terms of a theological framework dominated by the notion of a word-event (*Wort-Ereignis*): the event of salvation is par excellence a word-event. In this perspective, conscience appears as a theme worthy of theological interest insofar as it is itself a word-event in virtue of its call structure. "The conscience could now be the point where the nature of man's linguisticality comes to light" (409). Ebeling emphasizes the unconditional character of the judgment of conscience rather than its autonomy or its solitude. Faith, too, is an ultimate and unconditional decision. Therefore, it is as "ultimate concern" that faith encounters conscience. But this unconditional character common to faith and conscience does not isolate the individual within him- or herself. Ebeling's most noteworthy suggestion concerns what he calls the triadic structure of conscience. In the conscience, care for oneself, attention to the world, and hearing God intersect: "Only where God is encountered as a question of conscience are man and the world perceived to be a question of conscience" (412). What is more, each of the poles of this triadic realization is open to the future. God is not at humankind's disposition inasmuch as God is the one who "comes" in the promise. As for the world, conscience reaches it as the creation that sighs for deliverance (Rom. 8:19). And, finally, the human being is not given to her- or himself but is questioned and thereby "opened" by the challenge to respond. With these three features, Ebeling nicely echoes Heidegger's attempt not to confine the phenomenon of conscience on the plane of morality. Conscience is fundamentally a principle of individuation rather than an instance of accusation and judgment. However, Ebeling does not go as far as Heidegger does in his interpretation of *Schuld* (guilt) beyond good and evil, if we may put it this way. Instead, he proposes to situate this phenomenon at the point of articulation between dogmatics (for him, essentially soteriology) and ethics. In this way, he believes he can fulfill the semantic intention contained in the New Testament term *suneidesis*, according to which the relation of self to self that determines human existence is that of "joint cognizance" (417). And in this way he thinks he can reconcile Paul's and Heidegger's analyses inasmuch as for both of them the call of conscience is a call of the self to itself,

---

14. Northrop Frye, *The Great Code: The Bible and Literature* (New York: Harcourt Brace Jovanovich, 1982).

15. Gerhard Ebeling, "Theological Reflections on Conscience," in *Word and Faith*, trans. James W. Leitch (Philadelphia: Fortress Press, 1963), 407–23.

where the identity belonging to ipseity proceeds from a cleavage, a *Distanz,* rather than from an *Instanz,* more radical than any "bad" conscience. Conscience reveals the problematic character of personal identity at the very moment when this identity is recalled to its condition of "ultimate concern." "Bad" conscience is, before any moral characterization, the painful sense of nonidentity from which ipseity emerges; "good" conscience is the joy that stems from the coming to expression of this self beyond the "pangs of conscience."

For my part, I would try to be more careful to indicate the dialectical aspect of the *coram seipso* and the *coram Deo,* between which Ebeling seems to see a much greater continuity than I do. He is certainly correct to say that, in the *bona conscientia,* the Christian rejoices that the gospel is effectively communicated as word-event, that the Christian is thereby as much protected against despair as warned against presumptuousness, that the "true self" lies in this reconciliation. He is equally correct to affirm that the true opposition between law and gospel, so dear to Paul and to Luther, is realized in this communication. This, in fact, is where I would place even more of the accent. If salvation is a word-event, the communication of this word-event does not take place without an interpretation of the whole symbolic network that makes up the biblical inheritance, an interpretation in which the self is both interpreter and interpreted.

For us, who live after the Enlightenment, within this dialogic structure the tension has become acute between the pole of "autonomous" conscience and that of the obedience of faith. This tension within the responding self explains the following paradox. It is to the extent that the self is capable of judging itself "in conscience" that it can respond in a responsible way to the word that comes to it through Scripture. Christian faith does not simply consist in saying that it is God who speaks in our conscience. This immediateness professed by Rousseau in his "The Profession of Faith of a Savoyard Priest" ("conscience! conscience! divine voice...") misconstrues the mediation of interpretation between the autonomy of conscience and the obedience of faith. In fact, it is already an interpretation we find in Paul when he gives "justification by faith" as the key to his message. He in no way claims to identify the conscience common to all human beings and the justification by faith that takes place through the confession of Jesus as Christ. Therefore, it is regarding this articulation that we need to reflect further, between a conscience in which, in the spirit of the Enlightenment, we have discovered autonomy, and a confession of faith in which, in the spirit of hermeneutics, we have discovered a mediate and symbolic structure. This articulation of the autonomy of conscience and the symbolics of faith constitutes, I believe, the modern condition of the "summoned self." The Christian is someone who discerns "conformity to the image of Christ" in the call of conscience. This discernment is an interpretation. And this interpretation is the outcome of a struggle for veracity and intellectual honesty. A "synthesis" is not given and never attained between the verdict of conscience and the christomorphism of faith. Any synthesis remains a risk, a "lovely risk" (Plato). To the extent that the Christian reading of the phenomenon of conscience moves from being a wager to being a destiny, Christians can say with the apostle Paul that it is in "good" conscience that they stake their lives on this risk.[16] It is in this sense, after a long journey, that he could place himself in the line of descent leading from the "summoned subject" and could cry out, amid torments that make him a brother of Hamlet, "O my prophetic soul!"

---

16. "Indeed, this is our boast, the testimony of our conscience: we have behaved in the world with frankness and godly sincerity, not by earthly wisdom but by the grace of God" (2 Cor. 1:12).

Part Five

Practical Theology:
Ethics and Homiletics

❈

~ 16 ~

The Logic of Jesus, the Logic of God

<hr>

In the extraordinary fifth chapter of Romans, Paul has found a rhetorical procedure of rare eloquence in order forcefully to express what I here call the logic of Jesus, the logic of God. Paul's procedure is this: four times he repeats, "how much more" (Rom. 5:9, 10, 15, 17). I would like here to try to understand something about the divine logic that lies behind the rhetoric of Paul.

First, let us speak of human logic, of our logic. We can do this on the same ground, that of penal law and punishment, to which Paul introduces another logic. It is the virtue of penal law to fit, by always very exact proportions, the punishment to the crime. The ideal, according to the spirit of the law, would be that the penalty equal the mistake. In this admirable effort is summarized human logic; human logic is a logic of equality, of equivalence. But the logic of God, the logic of Jesus, the logic of Paul is quite another matter. This other logic is one of excess, of superabundance.

If we are to understand this other logic, I suggest that we not go immediately to Paul's text. It is too dense and presupposes too many things. Let us first, therefore, begin elsewhere, and by a circuitous route through Genesis and Matthew, come again to Paul.

Something of this other logic can be heard in the story of the flood—or, rather, in the way in which the old Babylonian myth has been *rewritten* by the biblical writer. The story begins as a myth of punishment (Gen. 6:5-7). The whole logic of punishment is contained here and in some way divinized. This is the logic of equivalence. A crime has offended the divinity. Only death, which is to say another crime, can efface it. But there, through the logic of punishment, another logic clears a path. It is expressed in the most simple and naive way, in the manner of a repentance of God. At the end of the story, Yahweh is not afraid to engage in self-contradiction (Gen. 8:21-22). This is suggested by another logic, the logic of superabundance. It is this logic that one hears in the voices of the prophets, in Jeremiah, in Ezekiel, and in the Psalms.

<hr>

Reprinted with permission from *Criterion* 18 (1979): 4–6.

But it is in the sayings of Jesus that this other logic speaks loud and clear. Let us read Matt. 5:39b-42.

"You have heard it said...." That is the ancient law. And it says: "An eye for an eye and a tooth for a tooth." Let us pay attention here. This famous law of the talion appears barbarous to us today. Ethnology teaches us, however, that it represents the first conquest over endless vengeance, the first measuring of the penalty to the size of the crime. But what impresses us is that this conquest of limited penalty is the imposition of the old logic of equivalence. And it is this logic that Jesus reverses. How? By giving, four times in a row, an extreme commandment that each time intrigues, perhaps revolts, and in any case distresses. Let us look closely at the astonishing rhetoric of the text. Jesus does not proceed as moralists would do by giving a general rule. He begins each time with a limited situation, undoubtedly rare, surely improbable, and each time the act illuminates by what we would tend to call an overreaction.

A blow on the cheek? As Robert Tannehill remarks in his admirable little book *The Sword of His Mouth,* where I have learned to study and understand the paradoxes of Jesus, "This involves a surprising narrowing of focus."[1] As for turning the other cheek, how would one apply this order literally, without betraying in the strongest sense minority groups throughout the world? The second extreme commandment refers to a lawsuit involving a poor person with no valuable property other than the clothes on his back. Thus losing both his coat (tunic) and his cloak would probably leave the man not only penniless but naked. The third situation—"And if anyone forces you to go one mile"—probably refers to forced labor, most likely involving the carrying of a burden, perhaps under the rule of some foreign invader. But the command continues: "go with him *two* miles." Does this not simply double the chains and aggravate the alienation? The last commandment is no less extreme, if one considers that the imprudent lender, indefinitely "touched," would surely be without money to live on and reduced to the condition of the birds of the air and the lilies of the field.

Therefore, these commandments evoke from us the exclamation: we would not do that! As Tannehill puts it: "In each case an action is commanded, and this action is the precise opposite of our natural tendency in the situation. Our tendency when hit is to hit back, etc.... I would suggest that these almost absurd commands were conceived by the simple device of reversing man's natural tendency.... In this way the command... stands in deliberate *tension* with the way in which men live and think" (70–71).

We thus understand that the purpose of this accumulation of extreme cases is to call for a response that is extreme. It is not to give us a rule

---

1. Robert Tannehill, *The Sword of His Mouth* (Missoula, Mont.: Scholars Press, 1975), 68; text references in the following paragraphs are to this book.

of prudence, literally and immediately applicable, but to suggest, through the convergence of some "focal instances" (67), a kind of *pattern* in direct conflict not only with some particular acts "but with the whole pattern of behavior which pervades [the hearer's] life" (71). A commandment that is not in accordance with the logic of our ordinary ethic calls this logic into question. The narrowness of the "focal instance" prevents us from behaving as casuists and from construing some classes of situations that would call for some typical solutions of a legal, moral, social, or political character. No rule is stated that could be enforced by teachers or officers of the law. In all four situations evoked by Jesus, it would be a mistake to expect legal clarity. Jesus instructs not by means of the rule but by means of the exception.

Does this mean that we are left without direction? It seems to me that the situation here is the same as it is in other usages by Jesus of an extreme language, such as the extravagance of a parable or the hyperbole of a proverb: a log in the eye or a camel through the eye of a needle. Parables, paradoxes, hyperboles, and extreme commandments all *dis*orient only in order to *re*orient us. But what is reoriented in us? and in what direction? I would say that what is reoriented by these extreme sayings is less our will than our imagination. Our will is our capacity to follow without hesitation the once-chosen way, to obey without resistance the once-known law. Our imagination is the power to open us to new possibilities, to discover another way of seeing, or acceding to a new rule in receiving the instruction of the exception. As Ray Hart suggests in *Unfinished Man and the Imagination*,[2] while the will is the intention to a specific project, the imagination is the intention of dominant direction. It is at the level of dominant direction that we are overtaken by the disorienting logic of Jesus.

And what direction do the sayings of Jesus imprint upon our ethical imagination? It seems that it is suggested by the series, in itself open-ended, of the extreme responses demanded by the no less extreme situations. Certainly no rule emerges. But something like a pattern does. And this pattern is that of a sort of excess of response in relation to the response that is normally expected. Yes, each response *gives more* than that asked by ordinary prudence. The right cheek? The other one also! The coat? The cloak as well! One mile? One mile more! Not just this, but even that! It is this *giving more* that appears to me to constitute the point of these extreme commands. And beyond this *giving more* is manifested the same logic of Jesus that can be found in his parables, proverbs, and eschatological sayings. This logic of generosity clashes head on with the logic of equivalence that orders our everyday exchanges, our commerce, and our penal law and that

2. Ray Hart, *Unfinished Man and the Imagination* (New York: Herder and Herder, 1968).

we have seen magnified in the terrible cosmic talion of the very old myth of the flood. The logic of generosity is undoubtedly adumbrated in Yahweh's promise to humanity resuscitated from the waters. Now it occupies the whole room, a place throughout the sayings of Jesus.

Again, it is this same logic that animates the tense, contrasted, paradoxical prose of the apostle Paul in the fragment of the Epistle to the Romans that we read above: "For if, by the fault of one, many died, *how much more* the grace of God and the gift conferred by the grace of one man Jesus Christ have abounded."

It was good not to begin with this text but arrive here at last, recognizing the logic of Jesus in the logic of Paul. Because it is here again that the logic of superabundance bursts the logic of equivalence. Paul, in order to stress this, does not hesitate to repeat the same rhetorical turn, "how much more," four times, as if the abundance of the expression comes to mimic that of the gift that the apostle celebrates. But this logic, which had been expressed in the popular discourse of the parable, the proverbs, and the exhortation, is now extended to another discourse, from which will emerge the whole theology of an Augustine and a Luther. It is the dialectic of human destiny that is now depicted in terms of perdition and justification, of enmity and reconciliation with God, of law and grace, of death and life. On the side of the logic of equivalence: sin, law, and death; on the side of the logic of superabundance: justification, grace, and life. The battle of the giants intimidates us perhaps. No doubt this is expressed in a language that our culture has made strange to us. In order to decipher it, let us find the key in the very simple language of a Gospel. And let us read, behind the great words of justification and reconciliation, exactly what was meant in the small admirable text in Matthew. The Epistle to the Romans, read in the light of the Sermon on the Mount, will begin to speak to us, and we will begin to discover that Paul says the same thing as Jesus but at another level of language. Moreover, the only new thing that Paul adds will become, in contrast, all the more valuable.

This new thing is that Jesus Christ is himself the "how much more of God." For the Gospel, Jesus was at first the one who spoke and spread the good news. Now he is announced as the one who, by the folly of the cross, breaks the moral equivalence of sin and death: "*how much more*, now justified in his blood, are we *by him* saved from the wrath." The battle of giants that we just evoked—condemnation/justification, law/grace, death/life—is embodied in two figures. On the one hand, the first man: "If by the fault of one . . ."; on the other hand, the veritable man: "*how much more* the grace of God and the gift conferred by the grace of one man Jesus Christ have abounded." It is in this way that the church, through the mouth of Paul, gives a *name,* the name of Jesus Christ, to the law of superabundance. But even then, this proclamation of the church would remain an exclusive saying if we could not attach this supreme "how much more" to the enlightening paradoxes of the rabbi Jesus.

In conclusion, let us return to ourselves.

Perhaps you will ask how it possible for us, in our day, to live according to this logic of superabundance. We have said that nothing is more foreign to the spirit of the gospel than the pretension of deducing a fixed morality from the paradoxical precepts of Jesus. In return, what we can do is give some *signs* of this new economy. Allow me to suggest some, which have no other value than to arouse a similar—or different—reflection.

In the penal domain from which we began, are we not placed on guard against our natural tendency to gain satisfaction with the logic of equivalence that pervades our penal law? In other words, are we not invited to discern even in the most just punishment, the disquieting countenance of wrath and vengeance? It is good that, goaded by the paradoxes of Jesus, we would distrust our better works. But it is not only a question of distrust. Does not the more positive way become for us deliberately to orient punishment to improvement rather than expiation? Because on which side is the gospel? Is it on the side of the vengeance of society or on the side of the rehabilitation of the culpable?

Let us enlarge our field of inquiry and ask ourselves if our whole market-economy is not founded on the law of exchange, of equivalence. And is not this law of exchange, like penal law, a hidden form of constraint, especially when it dissembles a simple relationship of forces beneath a juridical form? Distrust on the basis of our economics is the same as that which obtains on the basis of our law, because it is the same rationality that regulates both. But there is demanded of us some positive signs. The law of exchange is not eternal. Ethnology tells us of an economy of the gift more ancient than that of exchange; it tells us of festive events on which human beings competed against one another with their generosity and munificence. Is not our task at the national level, and even more at the international level, to bring about the economy of the gift within a modern context? Is not our task to rectify by some positive interventions, the inequality that results precisely from our application to all our economic and commercial relations of the logic of equivalence?

It cannot be doubted. Putting into practice the sayings discussed above means searching for concrete signs that it is asked of us to give today according to the logic of Jesus.

17

"Whoever Loses Their Life for My Sake Will Find It"

In Matt. 16:25 we read, "For whoever would save their life will lose it, and whoever loses their life for my sake will find it." If we are to understand this verse, it is very important that we take note of the fact that the pericope to which it belongs was placed in all three Synoptic Gospels immediately after Peter's confession: to Jesus' question, " 'But who do you say that I am?' Simon Peter replied, 'You are the Christ, the Son of the living God.' " It is this same Peter who immediately afterward is scandalized by Jesus' announcement of his impending suffering and passion. "God forbid, Lord!" Peter cries. "This shall never happen to you," a response that calls forth Jesus' surprising, almost violent, rebuke, "Get behind me, Satan! You are a hindrance to me, for you are not on the side of God, but of men." That these two pericopes are placed in succession is not fortuitous but deliberately chosen by the three Synoptic evangelists, for this succession suggests that the price we have to pay to follow Jesus is not unrelated to the question of his identity. Peter seeks a glorious Christ and cannot accept the fact that Christ is the Suffering Servant, must be the Suffering Servant, sung of by Second Isaiah.

However, if we isolate our verse from this christological context, it is tempting to take it as a paradoxical proverb, one that belongs to the family of paradoxes typical of ancient Near Eastern wisdom sayings, or perhaps it is even a universal saying, such as the evangelists sometimes report Jesus himself as using. For example, that "the first shall be last" or that "many are called but few are chosen."

I would like to take up our text from this point of view of wisdom in order better to see what kind of radical reorientation our text within its larger context imposes on such a nonchristological, wisdom-oriented reading.

Previously unpublished sermon given at the Rockefeller Chapel at the University of Chicago, 25 November 1984.

This way of approaching the text that I am calling "wisdom-oriented" is in fact instructive, and the remainder of the passage invites us to draw some of its lessons: "For what will it profit someone if they gain the whole world and forfeit their life? Or what shall anyone give in return for their life?" Now we may well ask what is at stake in this game where one loses what one gains and gains what one loses. Wisdom seems here to aim at, beyond local or time-bound customs or misunderstandings, a basic form of miscalculation that orients the whole of life to the point of constituting our everyday existence. There is no need to dwell upon the two major symptoms of this error in calculation, which are the ones most often cited and most akin to each other, without being any less superficial for all that. I mean that "gaining the world" means having possessions and power. It is difficult indeed not to be upset by the vicious spiral brought about by the furious exploitation of the earth and the sumptuous consumption of the industrialized countries. Yet to "become the master and possessor of nature" is the very motto of modernity announced by Descartes. Nor is it any less difficult not to be worried by another spiral, that of nuclear weapons. Here to gain the world seems to imply domination without limits at the risk of physically destroying the world. It is not enough to be content to curse the superpowers for this situation. We need to admit that the dream of hegemony is the secret dream of every one of us, which we only lack the strength to carry out.

I do not want to linger over these two cases of the will to mastery over the world because I have in mind a third form of the will to power, one that concerns those of us not so devoted to possessions or power as to knowledge. As scholars, scientists, humanists, and philosophers, do we not seek to put into practice what it says, written in bronze, at the entrance to our magnificent library: "Where knowledge increases, life itself is enlarged, clarified, and improved"?[1] In what way does a wisdom-oriented reading of our text call into question this motto, our motto? Not certainly for the sake of obscurantism, ignorance, or inertia. The way in which all our knowledge is called into question by the paradox of this proverb is both more hidden and more profound than that. Rather our knowledge is called into question as soon as it turns from humility to its own will to power, a will to power that is driven by the very force of ideas and objective knowledge. Is there any of us who is innocent of this dream of mastering the world through science? Hence what the proverb brings to light is the elevation of humanity, as the bearer of knowledge, beyond everything else, even when it is situated, as the subject of this knowledge, in the world of material objects, living beings, and supraindividual social forces.

If we follow out to its limit this suspicion that a subtle form of the will

---

1. The reference is to the Regenstein Library at the University of Chicago. ED.

to power is concealed by the most sincere form of the humility of what we call the will to truth, what do we find? My own suggestion would be that it is not only profane knowledge that is called into question but also, and perhaps even more so, religious knowledge. If Christianity has so obstinately sought to construct rigorous proofs for the existence of God, is this not because we seek in God the supreme guarantee upon which to found our claim to mastery over the world, a mastery founded upon knowledge backed up by the guarantee of our scientific proofs? The height of the mastery of knowledge may well be the will to include God in our enterprise of intellectual domination, by demanding of God that God guarantee our obstinate search for a guarantee.

Have I gone too far in my interpretation of the meaning of wisdom by having it say that "whoever would save their life will lose it"? The danger would be not to go far enough. For the farther we go along the road of common wisdom, the more we are struck by Jesus' invitation in the next part of verse 25: "And whoever loses their life *for my sake* will find it."

This invitation of the Gospel to lose one's life "for the sake of Jesus" has been interpreted in many different ways across the centuries, of course, and all these ways are valuable to us because they constitute the treasure of the universal church's tradition. The early church, for example, put the emphasis on the tribulations that accompanied bearing witness during a time of persecution. The parallel passage in the Gospel of Mark directly ties the call to "discipleship" to this question of bearing witness: "For whoever is ashamed of me and of my words in this adulterous and sinful generation, of that one will the Son of Man also be ashamed, when he comes in the glory of his Father with the holy angels." And is this not what Peter himself was the first to do at Gethsemane ("Simon, are you asleep? Could you not watch one hour?" [Mark 14:37]), then again in the courtyard when he dared say to the servant, "I do not know this man of whom you speak" (Mark 14:71)? The passion narratives give this denial by Peter such a prominent place, among other reasons, just to underscore how difficult it is, even how almost impossible it is, to follow Jesus to the end.

This first interpretation of the saying "Whoever loses their life for my sake will find it" is not the only one possible, but neither has it lost its pertinence today. In many parts of the world, men and women do actually lose their lives because they are not ashamed of Jesus or of his words in front of other human beings. But what are we to make of this saying in a pluralistic society where persecution is no longer practiced? In such a society as our own, being ashamed of Jesus and his words takes on the more subtle forms of abstention and silence. I admit that the answer to the question of Christian witness in a liberal society is an extremely difficult one to formulate. Most of us, myself included, feel repugnance when confronted with the advertising-like quality much Christian witnessing has taken on in the media. Between the arrogance, the indiscretion, and the vulgarity of such testimony, on the one hand, and the flight into polite and prudent silence in the name of the private character of belief and respect for others, on the other, the most honest and courageous form of testimony, where it is needed and required by both the situation and our fellow human beings, is neither easy to discover nor to formulate. On both the individual and the communal planes, the question remains open what such honest and courageous testimony would look like in a liberal society.

However, the question of verbal testimony does not exhaust the question of discipleship. We must not overlook those interpretations of Jesus' call to follow him that we can call "practical" or those we can call "spiritual." If we turn again to the question of possessions and power I spoke of earlier in thinking about a wisdom-oriented interpretation, we may recall the example of those, such as St. Francis of Assisi, who have actually divested themselves of all their possessions. We have nothing to fear in using Francis as the example of all those "fools for God" over the centuries, along with their brothers and sisters in the faith (or out of it) today, too, who have chosen a life of frugality, at the price of marginality. The "antieconomic" character of their experiments may seem laughable to us from the exclusive perspective of "gaining the whole world." Yet their testimony cannot be ignored—or denied. It is because they overturn the underlying hypothesis of the modern world that they so irritate—and frighten—us. It remains for us who stay in the world, as we say, however, to learn what lessons we are to draw from their testimony, what internal limit we are to apply to our desires, given the lack of a quantitative limit that constrains us from outside.

As for the spiritual interpretations, I can only touch lightly upon them here, but placed under the sign of the *Imitatio Christi,* they all seek in one way or another to make us participate as believers in Christ's sufferings, through a life of sacrifice and letting go of self. I can only touch upon them, but I cannot ignore them given the way, particularly within the Reformed tradition, we feel repelled by anything that smacks of mysticism. What we must do is to recall that the tradition of the universal church is broader than the limited experience in space and time of our current denominations.

So, to conclude, let us return to the particular condition of the intellectual, the scholar, to which I devoted the most problematic part of my meditation on the aspect of wisdom in today's Gospel text. To gain the world, I said, for the learned person is to seek absolute mastery by means of knowledge and scholarly techniques. It is also, I added, for the theologian in the believer, to expect God to be the supreme guarantee for the security of our knowledge.

It is just this attempt to make use of God as the guarantee for our desire to have a guarantee that seems to me most called into question by the expression "letting go of self." Faith, Eberhard Jüngel, a theologian at Tübingen, has said is the overthrowing of the guarantee, it is the risk of a life placed under the sign of the suffering Christ. Our passage adds to this "letting go of self," "taking up one's cross." This powerful expression brings us back to the context deliberately chosen by the Synoptic authors for the verses we are considering, namely, the announcement by Jesus of his imminent passion. What bond is there between the invitation addressed to Christians to take up their cross and Jesus' announcement of the necessity of the passion? What bond is there for the Christian intellectual, for the faithful person who adopts Anselm's motto *fides querens intellectum* (faith seeking understanding)? To take up my cross is to renounce the representation of God as the locus of absolute knowledge, the guarantee of all my knowledge. It is to accept knowing just one thing about God, that God was present in and is to be identified with Jesus crucified. God took up the cross. This is the meaning of the christological hymn from Philippians: he "emptied himself, taking the form of a servant, being born in the likeness of humanity.... He humbled himself and became obedient unto death, even death on a cross."

To take up the cross of Jesus, for me, a member of the university, the community of knowledge, means not to overevaluate my knowledge, caught up as it is in questions of proof and guarantees, before this necessity—higher than any logical necessity: "It was necessary that the Son of Man should suffer and be crucified." For all God's power, God only gives Christians the sign of divine weakness, which is the sign of God's love. To allow myself to be helped by the weakness of this love is, for the question of making sense of my faith, to accept that God can be thought of only by means of the symbol of the Suffering Servant and by the incarnation of this symbol in the eminently contingent event of the cross of Jesus.

18

The Memory of Suffering

Rabbi Joseph A. Edelheit invited me a few months ago to join your congregational memorial to "the six million" on this Shabbat evening. I am eager to express my deep gratitude for this very moving invitation. I take it as a testimony that, beyond authentic friendship, your rabbi knew quite well that I consider myself as one of the innumerable recipients of the promise bestowed upon Abraham: "I will bless those who bless you and him who curses you, I will curse; and by you all the families of the earth shall bless themselves."

It is a *memorial* that I join tonight. What is the meaning of this determination not to forget that gathers us here?

The Bible usually refers memory to a quite different circumstance, that of the gift of the Torah to the people through Moses. Deuteronomy, with a striking insistence, keeps warning against the danger of forgetting: "Only take heed, and keep your soul diligently, lest you forget the things which your eyes have seen, and lest they depart from your hearts all the days of your life; make them known to your children and your children's children." Ultimately, what should not be forgotten is the deliverance from "the land of Egypt, from the house of bondage"—the very liberation that is *remembered* during the Passover week. Is it with the same memory that we want to remember "the six million"? Was not the kind of memory that Moses required a glorious memory of a release and of a gift? What about the memory of the Holocaust and its victims? Has this memory anything to do with the memory called upon by Moses?

Allow me to elaborate step-by-step the fragments of an answer, one that will certainly fall short of the expected response.

To the question of why we should remember the victims at least as much as the ancient blessings, a first answer seems to address itself to everyone (or, at least, to *nearly* everyone, to the extent that there still exist throughout the world some declared or undeclared friends of the executioners who

Reprinted with permission from *Criterion* 28 (1989): 2–4. The address was delivered on Yom Ha-Shoah, 1989, at the Interfaith Memorial Service held annually at Emanuel Congregation in Chicago.

expect our forgetfulness). This answer is simple and transparent: we must remember because remembering is a *moral duty*. We owe a *debt* to the victims. And the tiniest way of paying our debt is to tell and retell what happened at Auschwitz. This is what the great writer Elie Wiesel, recipient of the Nobel Peace Prize, keeps crying out: the most elementary compensation that we may offer to them is to give them a voice, the voice that was denied to them. In one of Elie Wiesel's latest books, one of the characters, searching for one of the survivors lost in a New York psychiatric institution, says: "Perhaps it is not given to humans to efface evil, but they may become the consciousness of evil." To remember, to recount, is a way of becoming such consciousness, such conscience. We have learned from the Greek storytellers and historians that the admirable deeds of the heroes needed to be remembered and thus called for narration. We learn from a Jewish storyteller like Wiesel that the *horrible*—the inverted image of the admirable—needs to be rescued still more from forgetfulness by the means of memory and narration.

Let us take a step further: by remembering and telling, we not only prevent forgetfulness from killing the victims twice; we also prevent their life stories from becoming banal. This danger of banality may be greater today than the danger of sheer forgetfulness. Historians, sociologists, and economists may claim to explain the tragedy so thoroughly that it becomes merely one case of barbarism among others. Even worse, an alleged full explanation may make the event appear as *necessary*, to the extent that the causes—whether economic, political, psychological, or religious—would be held to exhaust the meaning of the event. The task of memory is to preserve the scandalous dimension of the event, to leave that which is monstrous inexhaustible by explanation. Thanks to the memory and to the narratives that preserve this memory, the uniqueness of the horrible—the unique uniqueness, if I dare say so—is prevented from being leveled off by explanation.

This last remark suggests that we try to take one more step, a more hazardous one perhaps, because it touches upon some of the most deeply rooted convictions of our forefathers. In addition to the explanations that level off and make banal the murderous event to which this memorial is devoted, there are explanations that justify and make the sufferings of the victims appear as if they were *deserved*. At first sight, this concern to justify suffering does not seem to apply to the biblical faith but only to the archaic mythical background of the other religions. Is it not the purpose of the myths to explain how the whole of reality was brought into existence and, among other things, how evil started? Is it not the basic trend of all myths to look backward toward the immemorial past of the beginning, toward the time of the origin? And is it not one of the tasks of these myths to explain why humans are in such a miserable condition, to explain *why they suffer?* In this respect the Hebrew Bible keeps fighting against this regressive stance of mythical thought to the extent that the Torah is above all a forward-oriented instruction, an ethical call addressed to the action to be done tomorrow or right now. This is beyond doubt. Nevertheless, the conflict is not merely between biblical faith and mythical religion, but to a certain extent *within* this faith, the faith of both Jews and Christians. Is it not the case that some of the prophets of Israel—and accordingly a whole school of Hebrew historiography—did not hesitate to interpret the Babylonian exile and the destruction of the first temple as a punishment inflicted upon the children *because* of the sins of the fathers? With this so-called theory of retribution, a theological explanation runs the risk of weakening a certain quality of the remembrance of past suffering. But it is also the case that some other voices may be heard, as a counterpoint to the previous ones. Let us listen to Jeremiah's proclamation: "Behold, the days are coming, says the Lord, when...they shall no longer say, 'The fathers have eaten sour grapes, and the children's teeth are set on edge.' But every one shall die for his own sin; each man who eats sour grapes, his teeth shall be on edge." Still more forceful is the voice of the sages who, like the author of Job, dismantle stone by stone the pious edifice of the theology of retribution or theodicy.

In what way, someone will ask, does this theological dispute affect our duty to remember? In the following way: when the complaint of the innocent victims is no longer covered by justificatory arguments, this naked complaint is brought back to the stage of sheer outcry. Once more, the movement back and forth from lament to praise and from praise to lament—this dramatic alternation that underlies the book of Psalms—is revived. Whereas the theory of retribution makes victims and murderers equally guilty, the lamentation reveals the murderers as murderers and the victims as victims. Then we may remember the victims for what they are: namely, the bearers of a lamentation that no explanation is able to mitigate.

Should we dare take a further step? This cannot be done without fear and trembling. Is it possible that a complaint, now inexhaustible by explanation, stops questioning, "Why *my* people? Why *my* parents? Why *my* child?" Is not a cry, to the extent that it is human, already an interrogation? And is not an interrogation concerning evil already a protest—if not an accusation—no longer of humans by God, *but of God by humans?* After all, the covenant between the Lord and the Lord's people was able to generate a trial held by God against that people. Does not the same covenant provide the opportunity for a reversal of the suit? This step, I know, has been taken by several respectable thinkers. Elie Wiesel, to evoke him once more, is one of these prosecutors.

I have no authority whatsoever to censure such boldness.

Allow me to say only two things. First, those among the survivors thrown by pain and anger into the midst of this awful fight—reminiscent of Jacob's fight with the angel—may be labeled by any name except that of "atheists." Whoever accuses God is far less godless than the one who does not care at all about God. Such accusation, perhaps, expresses in its own way the impatience of hope, the prototype of which may be found in the cry of the Psalmist: "How long, O Lord?" Second, should we not go so far as to say that unjust suffering is a scandal only for those who expect from God that God be only the source of all good? In this sense, it is the very faith in God that generates indignation. Consequently, it is in spite of evil that we believe in God, rather than that we believe in God in order to explain evil. Evil—and by evil I mean exactly unjust, undeserved suffering—remains what is and ought not to be. And what says that it ought not to be, if not the Torah?

We wondered at the beginning whether the call of Moses to remembrance—which is related to the gift of the Torah and to the liberation from "the house of bondage"—and our pious commemoration of the victims of the Shoah were two radically different expressions of *memory.* The answer, it seems to me, is *no.* Lamentation needs memory as much as praise does. We remember "the six million" with all the more dedication if we acknowledge that God, whose blessing we remembered at Passover, is not the cause of suffering but rather the author of the Torah, which says: "Thou shall not kill."

19

Ethical and Theological Considerations on the Golden Rule

The problem I would like to submit to our attention can be formulated in the following terms. If we admit that the golden rule constitutes the supreme moral principle that thoughtful people will agree upon, what happens to this principle when it is set in a religious perspective or, more precisely, in the perspective delimited by the symbolic order underlying the Jewish and Christian Scriptures?

I shall proceed in the following way. In the first section, I shall justify the hypothesis just mentioned, namely, that the golden rule can legitimately be held to be the supreme principle of morality. I shall do this by comparing it to the Kantian categorical imperative. Next, in the second section, I shall explain what I mean by a religious perspective. Once again, I shall do this by referring to the Kantian philosophy of religion. The central theme of my inquiry will thereby be formulated, namely, the place of the *economy of the gift* in this religious perspective. Finally, in the third section, I shall attempt to answer the question posed above, the question about what new interpretation the golden rule receives from being set once again in the framework of this economy of the gift.

The Golden Rule and the Kantian Imperative

I agree with those philosophers who think that the task of moral philosophy is not to construct morality but rather to start from norms and rules recognized or adopted by most people, or at least by those taken to be thoughtful and wise, and then to return reflectively to the supreme maxim or principle, reserving for a subsequent task any inquiry into the

Originally published as "Considerations éthiques et théologiques sur le Régle d'Or," in *L'Interprétation, un défi de l'action pastorale* (Actes du colloque 1987 du groupe de recherche in études pastorales avec la collaboration de Paul Ricoeur), Cahiers d'études pastorales 6, ed. Jean-Guy Nadeau (Montreal: Fides, 1989), 125–35; printed with permission.

ground (*Grund*) of this maxim or principle. This point of view, which was already that of Aristotle and Kant, is forcefully presented by Alan Donagan in *The Theory of Morality*.[1] Following him, I propose identifying the principle (*Prinzip*) of morality with the golden rule as it is formulated by Hillel ("Do not do to your neighbor what you would hate to have done to you") and by Jesus in the Sermon on the Mount ("In everything do to others as you would have them do to you; for this is the law and the prophets" [Matt. 7:12]) and in the Sermon on the Plain ("Do to others as you would have them do to you" [Luke 6:31]). (I shall return below to the exegetical problems raised by the difference between these two Gospels.) Donagan correctly notes, "Although one of these formulations is negative and the other positive, they are in fact equivalent; for to forbid an action of a certain kind, and to command one of its contradictory kind, are equivalent."[2] More important than the question of the primacy of one or the other of these formulations is their relation to the Kantian categorical imperative. Why should we prefer the golden rule to a formula whose rational and universal character is so obvious: "Act only according to that maxim by which you can at the same time will that it should become a universal law."

The first reason is that the golden rule is addressed directly to the intersubjective aspect of action. Kant, of course, does this as well in the second formulation of the categorical imperative: "Act so that you treat humanity, whether in your own person or in that of another, always as an end, and never as a means only." We might think this second formulation equivalent to the golden rule. But this is not entirely true. In the first place, the golden rule sets the relation between persons in the first rank, whereas Kant subordinates this relation to the principle of autonomy, which states in a monological way the rule for the universalization of maxims cited above. So it looks as though this criterion does not thematically imply a plurality of subjects. Furthermore, the second formulation of the imperative is addressed to the humanity that is identical in each person, not to persons as in fact multiple and different, as we shall now see.

Indeed, the second reason for preferring the golden rule is not just that it places the emphasis on interaction but that within this interaction it emphasizes the fundamental asymmetry between what someone *does* and what *is done* to another. In this sense, it does not bring one agent face-to-face with another agent but rather brings together an agent and a "patient" of the action, a patient being someone to whom something is done. To dramatize this initial asymmetry, I will say that the other is potentially the victim of my action as much as its adversary. Owing to this, the golden rule recalls

---

1. Alan Donagan, *The Theory of Morality* (Chicago: Univ. of Chicago Press, 1977).
2. Ibid., 57–58.

to us that the moral problem is contemporary with the problem of violence. There are morals because there is violence, which is itself multiform: physical coercion, psychic seduction, intimidation, extortion, exploitation, manipulation, to say nothing of the nightmare that makes violence the situation of all communication by undercutting any confidence in language. This central place of violence, of course, has not been ignored by moral philosophers. Still, in the political philosophy of natural rights, the other is seen as a potential assailant, someone who may interfere with my rights. But here, the potential aggressor to whom the golden rule is addressed is me. Underlying this rule is the presupposition that to act is already to begin to exercise a *power over* others, with the risk of treating them at best as docile and at worst as nonconsenting victims. Hence the moral principle is equivalent to saying, as Alan Gewirth does in his *Reason and Morality,* "The receiver of your action is also an agent."[3] This is what the golden rule says in positing the equivalence between an action done and one undergone, between an agent and a patient. (In the third section, I shall return to this question of equivalence in discussing the relation between the golden rule and *Vergeltung.*) Returning to my comparison to Kant, someone may object that Kant did not ignore this dimension of the problem, since he presupposes, in the second formulation of the categorical imperative, that the spontaneous tendency of the agent is to treat the other as a means, which is precisely what does violence to him or her. I agree, but the difference with Kant comes back again with my third reason for preferring the golden rule.

This reason has to do with the degree of formalism of the principle of morality. In one sense, the golden rule is just as formal as the Kantian categorical imperative. It does not define actions in terms of what must or must not be done. However, unlike the Kantian formulation, it is formal without being empty, a charge that has often been leveled against Kant, particularly by Hegel. It will have been noted that Hillel's and Jesus' formulations of the golden rule refer to what might be "hated" or "wished." This reference to fear and desire, in the very formulation of the golden rule, invites moral philosophy to undertake fundamental reflection on what Donagan, Gewirth, and also John Rawls in his *A Theory of Justice* call "basic human goods," that is, goods that are not posited arbitrarily, but rather implied by the very exercise of the action of a rational and responsible agent.[4] Kant, on the contrary, forbade himself taking this route by excluding any empirical content from the sphere of the moral a priori, due to the tie between such contents and the sphere of desire and pleasure, which threatened to corrupt the principle of autonomy through a return to heteronomy. Here is

---

3. Alan Gewirth, *Reason and Morality* (Chicago: Univ. of Chicago Press, 1982), 134.
4. John Rawls, *A Theory of Justice* (Cambridge, Mass.: Harvard Univ. Press, 1971).

where the major difference between Kant and the golden rule lies. By setting violence in the very same place that Kant put desire, the golden rule
incorporates a fundamental aspect of human action, the *power* exercised
on or *over* another, and thereby refuses to draw a line between the a priori
and the empirical. The golden rule takes into account the whole of action
and interaction, of acting and suffering. It is addressed to acting and suffering human beings, with all the fragility and vulnerability included in this
fundamental condition of action.[5]

Rational Foundation, Religious Perspective

It is once again in relation to Kant that I will situate myself in order to define what I am calling a "perspective." I shall do so through a comparison
with what Kant called "foundation" (*Grundlegung*).

If we were to stop with the "Analytic of Pure Practical Reason," a
foundation is nothing other than the positing by the self of the rational
core of autonomy. In this sense, the second *Critique* does not mark any
progress over the *Groundwork of the Metaphysic of Morals,* which limits
itself to repeating the principle of morality in an indicative mode according to its second formulation: "The ground of this principle [therefore
we pass from principle to ground] is: Rational nature exists as an end in
itself." However, this proposition with an existential structure already announces another problematic, one that is unfolded in the "Dialectic" of
the *Critique of Practical Reason* and in *Religion within the Limits of Reason Alone.* This is the question of the practical *possibility* of freedom. The
question is no longer, What is the synthetic tie between freedom and the
law? but What makes the will *capable* of effectively exercising its principle of autonomy? Kant does not hesitate in characterizing what is sought
here by the term "interest." This, he says, is "that in virtue of which reason becomes practical—that is, becomes a cause determining the will." The
much-debated theory of the postulates of pure practical reason has to be
understood starting from this problematic of the practical possibility of
freedom. How can a will *exist* freely? How can it become *capable* of exercising its freedom? This is the existential question at the center of Kant's
philosophy of religion. As is well known, it is his meditation on radical
evil that inaugurates this philosophy of religion. For what is evil, if not

---

5. Elsewhere I have addressed the general question of praxis. In "The Teleological
and Deontological Structures of Action: Aristotle and/or Kant?" *Archivio di filosofia* 55
(1987): 205–17, I show that a broad concept of praxis can incorporate something like an
Aristotelian teleological moment along with a Kantian deontological moment. This teleological moment is represented precisely by the concept of basic human goods, and a
modern rethinking of the golden rule presides over this reconciliation between the two
major tendencies of Western moral philosophy.

the incapacity of the will? To restore to concrete freedom its fundamental power, what Kant calls regeneration, is the object par excellence of religion. And that this restoration should actually be possible is what it is reasonable to hope. Concrete, effective freedom thus becomes an object of hope.

But does this belong to the power of reason itself? With this question, two paths diverge, the one Kant follows and the one that recognizes a transcendent source of this power. Certainly, for Kant, humankind by itself could not have engendered "the idea of humanity agreeable to God," that is, the Christ symbol. Kant even goes so far as to say, "And it is because we are not the author of this idea, but because we find it in the nature of man, that it has the power to render us capable of effectively exercising this idea. And this is why it is better to say that this archetype came from heaven." But once this *archetype,* this *Urbild,* this *Idee* has been inscribed in what we might call the imagination of practical reason, the schematism of practical reason, it depends on us to work toward our improvement under the guidance of this idea.

It is at this point that a religious *perspective* and more precisely a theocentric one separates itself from Kant. If the origin of religious symbols remains inscrutable to us, as Kant says of the rational origin of evil and as he might have said about the coming about of the archetype of humanity agreeable to God, the reception of this symbolism falls entirely under the control of practical reason. This is why religion for Kant remains within the limits of pure reason. But what about the origin of these symbols, or their structure of meaningfulness, or their entry into the human heart, in short, their *Ereignis?* Indeed, this difficulty is not the only one to invite us to a radical change of perspective, to a theocentric and no longer an anthropological one. A second motive also proposes itself. Kant submitted to the critique of reason only one part of the symbolism of the Jewish and Christian Scriptures, the symbolism relative to sin and the forgiveness of sin, as is confirmed by his taking up the religious problematic only through the question of radical evil. It is the part overshadowed by this symbolism that brings to the fore what I am going to call the economy of the gift, an economy that fundamentally *decenters* the origin of religious symbolism in its entirety.

In order to introduce this major theme, the economy of the gift, I would like to emphasize, following James Gustafson, the polycentrism of Judeo-Christian symbolism in relation to any moralizing reduction. In so doing, we set in the foremost place the sense of our radical dependence on a power that precedes us, envelops us, and supports us. This sense is supraethical par excellence. And the symbol that articulates this experience and confers a sense on it—that is, both a meaning and a direction—is that of an original but always ongoing creation. No doubt, this symbol sets human beings in the place of honor, but within a cosmos created before them and that continues to shelter them. Each of us is not left face-to-face with another human being, as the principle of morality taken in isolation seems to imply. Rather nature is between us, around us—not just as something to exploit but as an object of solicitude, respect, and admiration. The sense of our radical dependence on a higher power thus may be reflected in a love for the creature, for every creature, in every creature—and the love of neighbor can become an expression of this supramoral love for all creatures.

However, as supramoral as it may be, this symbol of creation is not amoral inasmuch as the idea of power is immediately joined with that of goodness: "God saw everything that he had made, and indeed, it was very good" (Gen. 1:31). What it is important to emphasize here is that the predicate "good" is assigned to the state of the creature as such, and not yet to some act of the human will or to some human disposition. At the same time, this highly affirmative qualification extends to every creative activity, as creative, inasmuch as God, to use Bergson's phrase in *The Two Sources of Morality and Religion,* is a creator of creatures. It is thanks only to an invincible anthropomorphism that we project the equivalent of a human psychology in God and link the predicate "good" to a divine project. However, the notion of power has also been charged with being anthropomorphic. One way to get beyond the weaknesses of our representations is to conceive of this power in terms of its project and the project in terms of this power. This conjunction between power and project at the level of basic symbolism is reflected on the level of the *sense* of religious experience in the conjunction between a reverential humility and a compassion without limits in the benevolence of the all-powerful. It is from this latter conjunction that proceeds the economy of the gift under whose aegis I shall in a moment place the principle of morality formulated in the golden rule.

But, first, I want to consider one objection. It may be said that this tableau of the religious symbolism of Judaism and Christianity does not take into account the representation of God as legislator and judge. Is not the proclamation of the Torah as important in Judaism as is the narrative of creation? And, on the Christian side, is not the sacrifice of Christ interpreted, according to a long and important tradition, as a "satisfaction" to the justice, if not the anger, of God? And do not all the representations of a last judgment include the idea of a God who repays and punishes? Do not all these representations taken together reinforce the image of that "moral God" concerning whom Nietzsche said that he had been refuted?

I want to say two things about the representation of God as legislator and judge. First, the sense that is attached to it must not be separated from all the many senses set forth by religious symbolism. Correlatively, obedience must not be separated from that humility and that confidence we may experience in regard to the giver of life. Next, the symbolism of the proclamation of the Torah must be understood itself as a gift, as the gift of the Torah. As I shall say below, it is the gift that engenders obligation. The gift of the Torah is recounted narratively as a founding event, as we read in Exod. 20:1: "I am the Lord your God, who brought you out of the land of Egypt, out of the house of slavery." In this way, the law becomes an integral part of a history of liberation and becomes the expression of a gift. As for the Christian doctrine of "satisfaction," to the extent that it is accepted, it must not eclipse the giftlike character attached to the symbols of the cross. The apostle John opposes to the abuse of this narrow Christology of satisfaction, the sovereign proclamation: "No one can take my life from me, but I lay down my life in order to take it up again" (John 10:18).

The representation of God as legislator and judge is, therefore, neither the first nor the last of the representations that make up religious symbolism. It is preceded, as has been said, by the sense of originary creation. And at the other extremity of the symbolic keyboard is found the eschatological symbol that gives rise to the representation of God as the source of *unknown* possibilities. The symbol of the creator is "repeated," but from the angle of anticipation and not just from that of rememoration. The God of beginnings is the God of hope. And because God is the God of hope, the goodness of creation becomes the sense of a direction. The predicate "good" attached to the process of creation returns enriched by the symbols of the gift of the Torah and the gift of the remission of sins. As Clifford Geertz emphasizes in one of his essays, all religious symbolism aims at joining the two ideas of a cosmic order and an ethical order. And not just at joining them, but at reconciling them in the face of the menace of their breakup that evil represents. So it is the task, the heavy task, of the hope engendered by the symbol of God of unknown possibilities to preserve the sense of directionality in spite of . . . in spite of evil.

Such, in terms of its major articulations, is the economy of the gift: gift of creation, gift of the Torah, gift of pardon, gift of hope.

The Golden Rule "Revisited"

In this final part of my essay, I propose to test this supraethical aspect of the religious symbolism characteristic of Judaism and Christianity by confronting it with the golden rule, understood as the actual principle of morality.

In one sense, this status is confirmed by the place the golden rule occupies in the Sermon on the Mount in Matthew 7, where it seems to be taken as something established in Jewish culture, and in the Sermon on the Plain in Luke 6, where it seems rather to be recognized as a commonplace of Hellenistic wisdom. However, it is not the simple citation of the golden rule that raises a problem for interpretation but rather the effect on it of a context that seems to disavow it. This context, we know, is dominated by the commandment to love one's enemies. It is this commandment, not the golden rule, that seems to constitute the expression closest, on the ethical plane, to what I have called the economy of the gift. This expression approximating the economy of the gift can be placed under the title of a logic of superabundance, which is opposed as an opposite pole to the logic of equivalence that governs everyday morality. This logic of superabundance is expressed in several ways in the New Testament. It governs the extravagant twist of many of Jesus' parables, as is clearly seen in those called the parables of growth. A grain of wheat that produces thirty-, sixty-, one hundredfold; a grain of mustard that becomes a tree where the birds of the sky come to make their nests. In another context, Paul interprets the history of salvation in terms of this logic of superabundance. "If, because of the fault of one man's trespass, death exercised dominion through that one, much more surely will those who receive the abundance of grace and the free gift of righteousness exercise dominion in life; ... where sin increased, grace abounded all the more" (Rom. 5:17, 20). How can we not, then, fail to oppose the logic of superabundance, which flows directly from the economy of the gift, to the logic of equivalence, which seems to culminate in the golden rule?

A very strong argument in favor of this thesis that the golden rule is surpassed, if not abolished, but the commandment to love is that the golden rule, through its demand for *reciprocity,* remains within the parameters of the *lex talionis:* an eye for an eye, a tooth for a tooth. Understood this way, the golden rule just says, "I give *so that* you give" (*do ut des*). But is it not against this perverse interpretation of the golden rule that Jesus warns us in Luke: "If you love those who love you, what credit is that to you? For even sinners love those who love them.... But love your enemies, do good, and lend, expecting nothing in return" (Luke 6:32-35).

Is there then an incompatibility between the golden rule and the commandment to love? No, if we see in the commandment to love a corrective to rather than a replacement for the golden rule. The commandment to love, according to this interpretation, brings about a *conversion* of the golden rule from its penchant toward self-interest to a welcoming attitude toward the other. It substitutes for the "in order that" of the *do ut des* the *because* of the economy of the gift: "Because it has been given to you, you give in turn."

What may confirm this interpretation is the help the new commandment can receive from the golden rule as regards its own possible perversion. Taken by itself, the commandment to love indicates the suspension of the ethical, in the Kierkegaardian sense of this phrase. And from this perspective, we might interpret the deliberately excessive and paradoxical consequences that Jesus draws from this commandment as lazy or cowardly: "If anyone strikes you on the cheek, offer the other also; and from anyone who takes away your coat do not withhold even your shirt. Give to everyone who begs from you; and if anyone takes away your goods, do not ask for them again" (Luke 6:29-30).

In fact, what penal law and in general what rule of justice could apply directly, *without the detour of the golden rule,* the bare commandment to love one's enemies? What distribution of tasks, roles, advantages, obligations, and duties—following the Rawlsian schema of the "idea of justice"—could result from a commandment from which reciprocity appears to have been excluded? What equity, on the economic plane, could be drawn from the commandment to "lend, expecting nothing in return"? Detached from the golden rule, the commandment to love one's enemies is not ethical but supraethical, as is the whole economy of the gift to which it belongs. If it is not to swerve over to the nonmoral, or even to the immoral, the commandment to love must reinterpret the golden rule and, in so doing, be itself reinterpreted by this rule.

This, in my opinion, is the fundamental reason why the new commandment does not and cannot eliminate the golden rule or substitute for it. What is called "Christian ethics," or, as I would prefer to say, "communal ethics in a religious perspective," consists, I believe, in the tension between unilateral love and bilateral justice, and in the interpretation of each of these in terms of the other.

This work of mutual reinterpretation does not leave thinking at rest. We are never finished with such reinterpretations. But it is also a practical work, if I may put it this way. The applications of this dialectic in everyday life, on the individual plane, the juridical plane, the social and political planes, are innumerable and perfectly *practicable.* I will even say that the tenacious incorporation, step by step, of a supplementary degree of compassion and generosity into all our codes—penal codes and social justice codes—constitutes a perfectly reasonable task, however difficult and interminable it may be.

The golden rule is set in this way, in a *concrete* fashion, at the heart of an incessant conflict between self-interest and self-sacrifice. The same rule may tip toward either direction, depending on the practical interpretation it is given.

Allow me to cite as a kind of conclusion an astonishing verse from the Sermon on the Plain. It condenses together like a kind of oxymoron the absence of measure proper to love and the sense of measure proper to justice:

"Give and it will be given to you. A good measure, pressed down, shaken together, running over, will be put into your lap; for the measure you give will be the measure you get back" (Luke 6:38). The lack of measure is the "good measure." This is, using the tone of gnomic poetry, a transposition of the rhetorical paradox. Superabundance becomes the truth hidden in equivalence. The rule is "repeated." But "repetition" henceforth signifies transfiguration.

Pastoral Praxeology, Hermeneutics, and Identity

These comments ending a conference, made on the spot, were announced as a "return/synthesis," but I thought that this title was a kind of pitfall, for it seemed absurd to me to attempt to make a synthesis under these conditions. In the first place, the colloquy in question was one way station on a trajectory for which I knew just one segment. What is more, I was struck by the richness of the presentations, which excluded any synotopical view. It was, in fact, more a matter of a movement I tried to enter into than of some synthesis that could simply be produced on the spot.

I saw one more reason not to attempt such a synthesis in the fact that the field of ministry, while not foreign to me, was not my profession. Rather it was familiar to me as a listener to the word and therefore as one of the actors in this practical field. Being one of these actors, I have no claim to give a survey of it from some higher point of view. Therefore, I shall set aside any concern for "synthesis" and take up "return," and I shall do so in several different senses. This will come down, as you shall see, principally to a return to oneself, a return to myself: What happened to me in participating in this conference?

The Dangers of Hermeneutics

I will begin with several methodological remarks about what seems to me to have been taken for granted in the work presented at this conference, starting with what seems to me to be the danger of hermeneutics, the danger that it runs and also the danger that makes it run, the danger of a certain banalization, something like what happened in the past with existentialism. Thirty years ago, everything was existentialism. Now, everything

Originally published as "Praxéologie pastorale, herméneutique et identité," in *L'Interprétation, un défi de l'action pastorale* (Actes du colloque 1987 du groupe de recherche in études pastorales avec la collaboration de Paul Ricoeur), Cahiers d'études pastorales 6, ed. Jean-Guy Nadeau (Montreal: Fides, 1989), 125–35; printed with permission.

that isn't positivism tends to becomes hermeneutics. There is a grave danger here that involves two aspects. On one side, there is the danger of an academic hermeneutics that would become one philosophy among others, one rival philosophy occupying the same place as all the others, the pretentious place of fundamental philosophy with, moreover, the vice of being a discourse about discourse, and therefore of being, I would say, redundant. This is the current peril facing hermeneutics, to become this kind of discourse about discourse. This danger is balanced by an opposite one, that of breaking into "hermeneutics of . . . ": hermeneutics of this or of that, where finally the fields of application will become absolutely fragmented in the manner of the divisions among disciplines or of the division of labor.

I think that one cannot struggle against both these dangers at the same time. What seems most important to me, however, in the struggle against that kind of self-complacency of hermeneutics imperturbably reflecting upon itself is to recall, however banal it may seem, that application is not some supplement to hermeneutics. Application (*Anwendung*), as Gadamer says following Schleiermacher, is one body with "understanding" and "explication." Indeed, one object of this colloquy was to distinguish the steps of the process—observation, diagnosis, interpretation, and so on—but another object was to tie together these phases. Understanding and explication without application are not interpretation.

Conversely, if the self-referential tendency of hermeneutics must be combatted by the recognition of the role of application, we need also to acknowledge that every application must reflect upon its status as interpretation because, as several of our speakers said, a domain of application always has its limits. It is circumscribed. It is not self-evident that there is something called ministry, any more than there is this or that, whatever the case may be. In fact, to delimit a domain of application is a hermeneutical act that calls for reflection in terms of a general theory of interpretation. Let me recall two of the themes presented at this conference: the limitation of understanding and the existence of unutilized possibilities; the latter reopen the field, reopen what I call the *world horizon,* which always produces an effect of withdrawal. There is, therefore, a dialectic of limitation and opening, which I shall return to below.

Before leaving the methodological plane, I want to indicate one more danger that is not a corollary of the two preceding ones: the danger that we will turn hermeneutics into some sort of alternative to objective science. Under the pretext of a critique of positivism, everything that is not positivist is said to be hermeneutical. Joined to this is the danger of a vicious use of the sciences, an instrumental use, one that is denounced when we are reminded to respect the agnosticism of the objective sciences. We must be on guard, therefore, against confusing the critique of positivism with a reflective usage of the objective sciences with their segments of observation, explanation, and meaning, out of the recognition that hermeneutics does not give us the right to say just anything whatsoever. One talks, but has nothing to say; we must be careful not just to talk about talking. I believe, therefore, that we need to be quite vigilant when it comes to the dangers that court hermeneutics.

Discourse, Practice, and Interpretation

To get beyond these methodological remarks and to a more substantial plane, I think we are at a moment that I would qualify as being beyond the linguistic turn. We took this turn over the past twenty years: everything is language, we must pass through language, from logic to rhetoric, to tropes, to argumentation, and so on. In the title of my collection of essays *From Text to Action,*[1] I tried to point to a movement posterior to the linguistic turn, which would be to return in a certain sense to the things themselves. Two factors, I believe, have facilitated this surpassing of the linguistic turn: on the one hand, the recognition that discourse is an action; on the other hand, and in a contrary sense, the recognition that human action is a speaking action.

I have the impression that this is taken for granted today and that we are no longer caught in the quarrel between praxis and discourse. We know that every form of practice is discursive and that, conversely, practices are always articulated by norms, symbols, signs, not to speak of the unsaid (prejudices, for example), which is still a kind of discourse in action.

Having said this, I offer an initial proposition for discussion. To master an inflation of the hermeneutic field and to preserve a relatively technical usage of the word "interpretation," are we not brought to say that there is interpretation when we can articulate the field to be interpreted in terms of at least four large categories? What do we finally interpret? Texts, certainly, since hermeneutics arose from exegesis, juridical practice, and the practice of historical investigation. But also events, above all when it is a question of founding events—events that are not just events that pass away, but events that in some way endure. There is hermeneutics when we attempt to unfold the potential for irradiation of these events. In our Jewish and Christian traditions, we may think of the exodus, the passion of Christ, the resurrection, but also of models of conversion that are cumulative and that form systems. Therefore, texts, events—and also institutions. It is very important to see that institutions, as encodings of interactions, call for interpretations. I have attempted something like this in my essay in this volume on the golden

---

1. Paul Ricoeur, *From Text to Action: Essays in Hermeneutics, II,* trans. John B. Thompson and Kathleen Blamey (Evanston, Ill.: Northwestern Univ. Press, 1991).

rule by showing that the golden rule as instituting an ethical realm of inter-action is susceptible to several interpretations—some perverse (give in order to get), others generous (love your enemies for no reward)—and that a field is opened where it is readers who have to say how they will get out of the contradiction among love without reciprocity, the love of enemies, and the reciprocity demanded by the golden rule. In the broad sense of the word "institution," an institution is thus also a theme for interpretation. Finally, there are personages; and here I use the word "personages" rather than "persons" so as to leave a place for what I shall say below about fictional personages or characters as well as about real personages and social roles.

I do not claim that the hermeneutic field is saturated by these four cat-egories, but it seems to me that the privileged objects of interpretation are texts, events, institutions, and personages. It follows that one of the aspects of interpretation is to establish the relations of intersignification among these objects, to understand texts in terms of events, events in terms of institutions, institutions in terms of personages, by adding to them their parallels, intersections, and intersignifications.

The Problem of Identity (between the Same and the Self)

The Who and the What

Following these two initial series of comments, the first of which was more methodological, the second more substantial, here is the contribution to our discussion I would like to submit for consideration. It has to do with a problematic that came to me after having completed *Time and Narrative* and after having finished preparing for publication the texts collected in *From Text to Action*.[2] It is the problem of *identity*. It seems to me that this is also a problem for those concerned with pastoral ministry inasmuch as there is always the problem of the "who": *Who* is the actor? *Who* inter-venes? One intervenes in relation to *whom*? A reflection on this question of "who," therefore, will be my contribution to this discussion. It is in such reflection that the word "return" takes on meaning, as when I speak of re-turning to myself, that is, of a return to what I am doing, but also to my self, to the self.

It has seemed to me, these past two or three years, after having finished *Time and Narrative,* that the problematic of identity is not really best ex-pressed in terms of one or the other of our usual personal pronouns—I, you, and so on—but rather in terms of what I will call a pronoun outside pronouns, "self." This term has become perhaps a bit banal in English,

---

2. Paul Ricoeur, *Time and Narrative,* 3 vols., trans. Kathleen McLaughlin and David Pellauer (Chicago: Univ. of Chicago Press, 1984–88).

where one says "self" instead of "person." But still it is perhaps possible to rediscover the force of the word "self" in its reflexive aspect and its use as a complement to other terms. I am struck in this regard by the title of a book by Michel Foucault: *The Care of the Self.*[3] Self is always reflexive, and it is in a certain way what is reflected in all the personal pronouns. In French, the word *même* (same) expresses something equivalent to what I mean: *moi-même, toi-même, soi-même;* in English: myself, yourself, his/her/itself. My working hypothesis will aim at trying to distinguish between two senses of identity whose confusion seems to me the source of much misunderstanding and even of a number of false problems. These two senses are those of identity as *idem* and as *ipse.*

Their difference is quite clear in Latin. The word "same" in both French and English resists this clarity inasmuch as we sometimes speak of "sameness" and sometimes of "selfhood." One critical task is to liberate the problematic of selfhood from that of sameness when considering the question of the "same." Many of the difficulties, the aporias, and the paradoxes concerning this concept stem from confusing these two different meanings, and this confusion is not easy to sort out because in fact the two problematics do overlap in one region of reflection, and also in one having to do with action—I mean the question of permanence over time. This has been a problematic that has haunted philosophy ever since Locke. Locke says: permanence is memory. Hume says: I look for it but I do not find it; I find only a bundle of experiences, a bundle of impressions. And Kant exiles the identical into a transcendental subject who is no one, the "I think" that can accompany all my representations. We see further evidence of this problematic in Husserl's fourth and fifth Cartesian meditations, where the sphere of ownness (*Eigenheit, le propre*) designates both the identical that remains immutable over time and the reflexive self. This problematic is a serious one because there is a sense of anxiety that goes with the sense of losing one's identity, understood as losing one's "sameness." What are the consequences if one changes so much as to become so different that one is no longer "the same"? In concluding, below, I would like to refer to the limit-experience that is the supreme test of selfhood that comes about when the self loses the support of the same and the question of "who" is, so to speak, laid bare.

I must say that, for my part, I have been greatly helped in thinking about these issues by one aspect of Heidegger's *Being and Time* that has not been much commented upon even though these were pages that Heidegger himself held to be important. I mean those paragraphs entitled *Selbstheit* (selfhood). In French, Emmanuel Martineau translates this as *ipséité.* As

---

3. Michel Foucault, *The Care of the Self,* trans. Robert Hurley, vol. 3 of *The History of Sexuality* (New York: Vintage Books, 1986).

Heidegger notes, the difficulty about selfhood, about "ipseity," is that it is in fact a question: Who? Who did this? Who did that?

I found the same reflection in Hannah Arendt when she considers the hierarchy of human activities successively as labor, work, and, finally, action. She then asks how we are to distinguish action. Her answer is: through the stories and histories we tell about it! And what is the function of these stories and histories? It is to tell us "the who of action." Someone may say: "This is too quick; the questions of who and what separate here." But, in effect, the question "What?" leads to an inquiry into identity in the sense of what is immutable, hence to a return to substantialism. The pitfall of substance lies in this direction, a pitfall we can find up to Kant, since his first "analogy of experience," which is the first judgment corresponding to the first category of relation, namely, *Substanz*, defines substance as permanence over time, the unchanging. If we cling to the need for identity in this sense, we are anxious if it escapes us. In this regard, I see a therapeutic value to critiques of identity as sameness, as *idem*, whether they come from Hume or from Nietzsche. In the latter's last writings, which have been collected under the title *The Will to Power*, we find a vigorous expression of such a critique, one that goes too far, to be sure, when it says that there is no soul, that there is only the body, and this is just a mass of muscles; but this is Nietzschean excess, a tonic excess if I may put it that way. Still, it is good to pass through this critique, to say that, in a certain fashion, identity in these sense of *idem* cannot be found. In this way, we are sent back to the problematic of the *who*.

Identity and Narrativity

In this section of my remarks I would like to indicate how narrativity contributes if not to unraveling this problematic at least to clarifying in what way it is problematic. In my earlier work, I was interested in narrativity from the point of view of the intelligibility brought about by the plot of a narrative. I took this on in terms of two fronts: on the one hand, against that structuralism that sets up an instrumental type of rationality; on the other, against irrationalism. Today I have turned to the problem of the narrative unity of a life. What is this narrative unity of a life? Do not the identity of an actor and the objects/subjects of his or her intervention consist in such a unity? That is the question, you may say.

As can be seen, I have been brought in this way to displace a bit my older problematic where I took narrative largely as a literary activity. It was necessary to begin there, and this is why I focused on the notion of plot. From these earlier analyses I would like to retain the idea that what makes the unity of a plot is its incorporation of concordant and discordant elements; I would like now to apply this idea to the problematic of self-identity. I borrowed this idea of concordant discordance from the work of Frank Kermode. And this, I now think, is what we mean by the identity of someone; this too is a discordant concordance. Sometimes discordance prevails; other times concordance does. This idea escapes the problematic of *idem,* without falling, if we may put it this way, into the void of absurdity.

The peripeteia, the changes and reversals of fortune, in a narrative, which threaten concordance, are made significant by the plot. And if we apply this to the characters, something I did not do in my previous work, we recognize, I believe, in ourselves and in others this work of the plot. We might term this the "emplotment of character." There is thus not just an emplotment of actions; there is also an emplotment of characters. And an emplotted character is someone seeking his or her or its identity.

I think there is something important here for the practice of ministry because we add something important in this manner to the merely literary analysis. In the first place, in narratives with a literary character, we know the end. This is quite important: in some way or another, a narrative ought to have an ending. This does not mean that the action stops, but rather that the books ends. There is a last page, even if that last page remains open. In the second volume of *Time and Narrative,* I looked at Thomas Mann's *The Magic Mountain.* At the end of this novel the hero disappears into the trenches of Flanders. We do not know if he gets killed there or if he survives. We do not know whether he draws any lesson from his experience. Yet the book ends.

The books ends, but life is open-ended. This remark introduces an interesting dialectic, a dialectic of closure and opening. To make a narrative of one's own life is, in a certain way, to posit a beginning, or several beginnings, a middle, with its highs and lows, and also an ending: one has completed a course of study, a project, a book. There is a kind of apprenticeship of beginning and ending and of beginning and continuing whose model is essentially narrative. But unlike a closed literary narrative, life is open at both ends—whether we think of the obscurity of our birth, which sends us back to the jungle of our ancestors, or that something that is not an ending but an interruption, our death, which is a kind of violence. This open-endedness places us in a situation where we can bring ourselves together narratively only by superimposing in some way a configuration with a beginning, a middle, and an ending. But at the same time, we are always in the process of revising the text, the narrative of our lives. In this sense, we may construct several narratives about ourselves, told from several points of view.

Following from this, I would like to draw attention to one kind of aporia that, I recognize, I have not resolved. In this narrative we make from our lives, or from segments of our lives, many narratives or a single narrative, who are we? Are we a character in this narrative? Are we the narrator? Or we the author? I think that this ambiguity creates another type of opening, not in the sense of extension but in the sense of the uncertainty of our position. We are capable of occupying each of these three positions, character, narrator, author, in turn. We cannot rest with any one of them. Surely we are a character, but it is we who tell the story; therefore, we are its author. But we cannot simply be the author because we are already caught up in the stories of other lives. This, I believe, is one key characteristic of a lived narrativity, of what may be called in English "enacted narratives." We are also a character in others' stories and histories, in that story that others set forth and write, that they write in setting it out, and that they set out in writing it. In short, being caught up in others' stories is what creates an inextricable aspect to our lives.

Above, I spoke of birth: we are part of our parents' story. That we were born is something that happened to them, something that they did or did not make sense of, and we do not really know which is the case. We are also caught up in the stories of our friends. This morning I heard Pierre Pelletier talk about the anxiety of dying people who do not wish to upset other people. But perhaps what we have here is in fact the difficulty for such people to know how their deaths will be inscribed in others' stories, to know what stories others will make of their deaths. My dying is a part of others' history; it is even that moment when we may say I simply fall over into others' history. Pierre Pelletier said something similar this morning: "I am set in the world in a history that is not my own." Yes, we are caught up in stories, in history, and in large-scale narratives, those narratives of salvation where one is a partner, a character who is also partially a narrator and partially the author.

As you can see, I am leaving this problem of the place, in the narrative of a life, of the one who is the hero or antihero, but certainly not fully the author, an open question. The Stoics tried to resolve this problem by saying that we play a role in a history that has been written by the gods. But this is too simple and univocal a distinction, which we cannot take up again today, between author and characters, even if in this way we do come upon the questions of the relation between freedom and destiny.

The idea of *revising a life narrative* seems to me closely bound to this enigma. The term "revision" stands in a way on the boundary between the closure necessary if one is to be able to recount a life (in the same sense as I above said that we must "close" a field of study in order to work in it) and the reopening that is always possible because one can tell the story in another way. In this sense, the old Socratic notion of examining a life—that the unexamined life is not worth living—stands on this boundary between the closed and the open.

"Puzzling Cases":
Limit-Situations of the Question of Identity

I want to end by turning to a theme that at first sight may appear discordant with what I have just said, but that nevertheless does belong to our concern for the practice of ministry. This theme stems from reflection on the problem of personal identity if we begin from what are called "puzzling cases" in the English-language literature on this topic. Puzzling cases are odd; they upset our usual ways of thinking. Referring to them may seem discordant at first glance in light of what has been said again and again at this conference: we have to link all our reflection to experience, to experience taken sometimes in the sense of empirical observation, sometimes in the Gadamerian sense of *Erfahrung;* in either case, we need to stick close to people's actual lives. And here I am now asking you to consider fictions. But I do not think such an orientation is discordant because one notion has arisen again and again in our sessions: imagination as structuring and destructuring. It is structuring in that it brings about closure, destructuring in that it reopens things. It is upon the imagination that I would now like to reflect, because identity as a self and not as *idem* is perhaps itself a puzzling case.

The study of puzzling cases is well known in the literature of analytic philosophy. I have in mind here the work of Sydney Shoemaker, Bernard Williams, Thomas Nagel, and especially Derek Parfit in his *Reasons and Persons,* which is entirely built on puzzling cases arising from the possibilities of technology.[4] These cases are presented as thought experiments that may be actually carried out one day, but that, even if they are never actually carried out, are conceivable. That they are conceivable is sufficient to make us think. In *Reasons and Persons,* we find three types of such puzzling cases where identity vacillates because we end up at an undecidable situation. In such cases, we cannot say whether the subject submitted to the experiments in question remains the same or not, precisely in the sense of "sameness." This question was also raised by Locke with his well-known image of a prince and a cobbler. If we put the prince's consciousness in the shoemaker's body, will this latter be the prince or the cobbler? In fact, religious traditions, too, present such puzzling cases of identity. Think of those religions that believe in preexistence. Is it the same individual in two different lives or not? Or what about Christianity when it speaks of the resurrection as St. Paul does: "It is sown a physical body, it is raised a spiritual body" (1 Cor. 15:44)? Will these bodies be the same or different? These are the kinds of problems Parfit raises with his own examples.

---

4. Derek Parfit, *Reasons and Persons* (New York: Oxford Univ. Press, 1986).

Puzzling cases, therefore, are part of the question of identity: they are not marginal; they are constitutive of it. And the analytic philosophers using a method of counterexamples have constructed three kinds of difficult cases: brain transplants, brain bisections (one side of one person's brain being joined to one side of another person's, or one side of a brain taking over functions of what had been a whole brain), and duplicate copies. Do I survive in or as two different people, or is there no question of my survival whatsoever? Since every answer is implausible, the question of personal identity is left unanswered. Consider the third type of case, that of a perfect replica, at least as regards all relevant information. Suppose that one day we can make a perfect copy of all the constitutive information, in the sense of information theory, of me, not just of my brain, but of my hormonal system, through something like an extrapolation of our fingerprints. Next suppose that this copy undergoes teleportation and I have then to rejoin this copy. There are several possibilities. If in fact we are rejoined, are there two persons or just one? And what if I die on the way, but my copy comes to my deathbed and says, "I will take care of your wife and children; I'll even finish that book you're working on"? Can I say that I will survive in my copy? If the answer is undecidable, says Parfit, the question is "empty."

A Moral and Pastoral Consequence

What is especially interesting about Parfit's work is that he draws from this thought experiment a moral consequence that applies directly to our concern for ministry. He ends by saying, "Identity is not what matters." And he makes use of this conclusion to undermine the great Anglo-American moral tradition that is utilitarianism, understood as a "self-interest theory." Since there is no longer a self, there is no longer any self-interest. Hence, Parfit says, we can be less preoccupied with survival, in this or in some other life, and more concerned with helping others.

I interpret this argument not as a negation of the person so much as a laying bare of the question of the self, once deprived of the support of the same. If we say, "Identity is not what matters," *for whom* does it not matter? After all, there still must be someone who poses the question, "What does matter?" And I think Parfit completely contradicts himself when he says he can give an impersonal description of what identity is, which comes down to simple connectedness, physical or psychological connectedness. If there is connectedness, it is my being connected to my copy and therefore I continue in my copy. But when Parfit draws the conclusion that this is unimportant, I ask, For whom? At this moment of posing the question of importance there is someone who is interested. What is more, the victim in spite of him- or herself is submitted to an experiment where there is no other person. Indeed, I was quite struck to see in these puzzling cases that one stands alone before the surgeon, who is a bit of an executioner. Here we are at the limit of violence, of experimental torture, if you will, where the only other person involved is this disturbing character who is all-powerful in a way, since he can change my brain, change me, even.

What seems most interesting to me at this level of the problem is to compare the science fiction at work in these puzzling cases with the puzzling cases created in literature. Literature, in fact, is filled with investigations of slippery, disappearing identities. We need only to think of the works of Kafka, Joyce, Musil. I am especially interested in the example of Robert Musil's *The Man without Qualities* (*ohne Eigenschaften* = without "properties," without identity).[5] The hero has nothing that is just him; he lacks properties, and being without properties, in every sense of the word, there is nothing for him to appropriate of himself.

Now the last hypothesis I would like to present is the following: Is it not the function of the imagination, which may be perverse, even subversive, to separate the self from the same, that is, not to nullify the question Who? but to lay it bare? I ask, "Who am I?" Someone answers, "Nothing, or almost nothing." But it is not nothing to answer "nothing." And here I rejoin Pierre Pelletier once again in his comments on a dialogue with Buddhism. What we learn from this dialogue is to renounce "sameness." But the self does not thereby disappear. The Buddhist, through meditation, enters a liberated field of selfhood, freed of avarice, of the search for guarantees. In a similar way, I am reminded of the work of Eberhard Jüngel, *God as the Mystery of the World*,[6] which begins with a long critique of the search for guarantees, be they the Cartesian *cogito* or the existence of God as the guarantee of the *cogito*. Philosophers want a guarantee, even a guarantee for the guarantee. In Buddhism, the self renounces all such guarantees.

I will end by saying that if we can say that identity is not what matters, this is perhaps to be understood in the sense of what I will call the Buddhist side of a statement in the Gospel of Matthew: "Whoever would save their life will lose it, and whoever loses their life...will find it." There is certainly something profoundly enigmatic here: Have we saved our lives when we have lost them?

In this way, we can take up Parfit's conclusion, but, I think, without his contradiction of suppressing the self along with the same. I can be open

---

5. Robert Musil, *The Man without Qualities* (New York: Putnam, 1985).

6. Eberhard Jüngel, *God as the Mystery of the World*, trans. Darrell L. Guder (Grand Rapids: William B. Eerdmans, 1983).

to the story, the history of others, each of whom is in question as a self. Then the question arises of my participation in the stories and histories of others, which themselves are open/closed stories/histories. Is not this kind of mutual exchange and mutual aid in the dialectic of openness and closure the essence of the pastoral act?

Love and Justice

Talking about love may be too easy, or rather too difficult. How can we avoid simply praising it or falling into sentimental platitudes? One way of finding a way between these two extremes may be to take as our guide an attempt to think about the dialectic between love and justice. Here by dialectic I mean, on the one hand, the acknowledgment of the initial disproportionality between our two terms and, on the other hand, the search for practical mediations between them—mediations, let us quickly say, that are always fragile and provisory.

The insight promised by such a dialectical approach seems to me to have been overlooked by the method of conceptual analysis that seeks to extract from some selection of texts by ethicists or theologians who talk about love the most systematic recurrent themes. This, of course, is the approach used by many of our colleagues in philosophy and theology influenced by the discipline of analytic philosophy. To cite just one example of such a work, and it is a noteworthy one, in Gene Outka's *Agape* the subtitle, *An Ethical Analysis,* is indicative of the general orientation.[1] For this author defining love is a matter of isolating the "basic normative content" that Christian love or *agapē* "has been said to possess irrespective of circumstances."[2] By using what method? His answer is what my own approach would like to call into question: "Such an inquiry is formally similar to the one philosophers have pursued in discussing, e.g., utilitarianism as an ultimate normative standard, criterion, or principle for judgments of value and obligation."[3] The whole issue for me is contained in this response: Does love in our ethical discourse have a normative status comparable to that of utilitarianism or even of the Kantian categorical imperative?

I shall provisionally set aside the three fundamental features of *agapē*

Reprinted with permission from *Radical Pluralism and Truth: David Tracy and the Hermeneutics of Religion,* ed. Werner G. Jeanrond and Jennifer L. Rike (New York: Crossroad, 1991), 187–202.

1. Gene Outka, *Agape: An Ethical Analysis* (New Haven: Yale Univ. Press, 1972).
2. Ibid., 7.
3. Ibid.

that Outka sees as being the most systematic and the most recurrent ones in the literature he considers. Far from neglecting them completely, however, we shall return to them below in some closing remarks devoted to the practical mediations between love and justice linked to the exercise of moral judgment in a particular situation. For the moment, though, I will limit myself to listing these features without commenting on them, in order to give some idea of the ultimate end of our own investigation: first, an equal "regard for the neighbor which in crucial respects is independent and unalterable"; then, self-sacrifice, "the inevitable historical manifestation of agape insofar as agape was not accommodated to self-interest"; and, finally, the mutuality characteristic of those actions "which establish or enhance some sort of exchange between the parties, developing a sense of community and perhaps friendship."[4]

We cannot reproach Outka for not having caught sight of the conceptual incoherencies that such a typology seeks to lay bare. In fact, each of his basic features is constructed at the expense of setting aside variations, disagreements, and confusions that he deplores more than once throughout his study. What is more, it is obvious that his third feature, the one that in fact seems most decisive to him, is highly discordant with the second one. Yet these deceptions encountered in the process of an ethical analysis devoted to isolating a "basic normative content" are, to me, an indication that such a direct method is, in fact, inappropriate to our making sense of the relationship between love and justice, and that we should instead start from what in the *topos* of love resists such treatment of love as "an ultimate normative standard, criterion, or principle for judgments of value and obligation."

I would like to put this first part of my own remarks on our topic, dedicated to the disproportionality between justice and love, under the emblem of a quotation from Pascal:

All bodies together and all minds together and all their products are not worth the least impulse of charity. This is of an infinitely superior order. Out of all bodies together we could not succeed in creating one little thought. It is impossible, and of a different order. Out of all bodies and minds we could not extract one impulse of true charity. It is impossible, and of a different, supernatural order.[5]

I will not conceal the fact that this harsh judgment of Pascal will make it more difficult subsequently to find the mediations required by moral judgment in a particular situation, provoked by the question, What ought I to

---

4. Ibid., 9, 24, 36.
5. Pascal, *Pensées*, trans. A. J. Krailsheimer (Harmondsworth, England: Penguin, 1966), 125.

do here and now? For the moment, however, my question is the following: If we begin by acknowledging disproportionality, how can we avoid falling into one or the other of the dangers mentioned above, exaltation or emotional platitudes (in other words, unthinking sentimentality)?

It seems to me that one possible way presents itself that would consist in looking for those forms of discourse—which are sometimes quite complicated—that resist the kind of leveling down brought about by the kind of conceptual analysis carried out by analytic philosophy. For love does speak, but it does so in a kind of language other than that of justice, as I shall phrase it at the end of my remarks.

I would like to focus on three aspects of such language as it is shaped by the biblical tradition that are indicative of what I shall call the strangeness or oddness of the discourse of love.

The first of these aspects has to do with the link between love and praise. Indeed, we may say that the discourse of love is initially a discourse of praise, where in praising, one rejoices over the view of one object set above all the other objects of one's concern. In this abbreviated formula, the three elements—rejoicing, seeing, and setting above all else—are equally important. By saying this, do we fall once again into a kind of conceptual analysis or into sentimentality? Neither, I suggest, if we are attentive to those original features of praise for which such verbal forms as the hymn are particularly appropriate. For example, the glorification of love by Paul in 1 Corinthians 13 is akin to those "songs of praise" indicated by the Hebrew title of the book of Psalms: *mizmôrê těhillîm*. Beyond this, we should also bring together the hymn and the discourse of benediction: "Blessed is the man who walks not in the counsel of the wicked. . . . He is like a tree planted by streams of water" (Ps. 1:1, 3). "O Lord of hosts, blessed is the man who trusts in thee!" (Ps. 84:12). In this way we are brought to the literary form of the macarism, familiar to readers of the Beatitudes: "Blessed are the poor in spirit, for theirs is the kingdom of heaven" (Matt. 5:3). Hymn, benediction, macarism—in these forms of discourse we find a complex interweaving of literary expressions that we can link together in terms of the central aspect of "praise."

In turn, such praise refers us back to the more general, broader domain of biblical poetry, which Robert Alter has shown functions discordantly in relation to the rules of a discourse that would seek univocity at the level of principles.[6] In such poetry the key words undergo amplifications of meaning, unexpected assimilations, hitherto unseen interconnections, which cannot be reduced to a single meaning.

As an example, we may consider the rhetorical strategies at work in 1 Corinthians 13. The initial strophe exalts the greatness of love by a kind

---

6. Robert Alter, *The Art of Biblical Poetry* (New York: Basic Books, 1985).

of negative hyperbole, announcing the annihilation of everything that is not love: "If I speak in the tongues of men and of angels, but have not love, I am a noisy gong or a clanging cymbal." The same formula recurs a number of times: "And if I have...but have not love...I am nothing." The second strophe then develops the vision of the eminence of love in the indicative mode, as though everything were already consummated: "Love is patient and kind, love is not jealous or boastful, it is not arrogant or rude. Love does not insist on its own way, it is not irritable or resentful, it does not rejoice at wrong, but rejoices in the right. Love bears all things, believes all things, hopes all things, endures all things." The reader will have noted the interplay of assertion and denial, as well as the playful use of synonyms that makes akin quite distinct virtues, all of which run counter to our legitimate concern to isolate individual meanings. Finally, in the third strophe, a movement of transcendence beyond all limits carries the day: "Love never ends; as for prophecy, it will pass away; as for tongues, they will cease; as for knowledge, it will pass away...." And, as a final passing to the limit: "So faith, hope, love abide, these three, but the greatest of these is love."

This is the first kind of resistance that love opposes to "ethical analysis," in the strong sense of the term "analysis," that is, as conceptual clarification.

The second oddity of the discourse of love has to do with the disturbing imperative form in such well-known expressions as: "You shall love the Lord your God,...and you shall love your neighbor as yourself." If we take the imperative in the usual sense of obligation, whose case is so powerfully stated by Kantian ethics, there seems to be something scandalous about commanding love, that is, about ordering a feeling. Kant diminishes this difficulty by distinguishing "practical" love, which is nothing but respect for persons as ends in themselves, from "pathological" love, which has no place in the sphere of ethics. Freud is more obviously indignant over what is at stake here. If so-called spiritual love is just a sublimated erotic love, the commandment to love can only be the expression of the tyranny of the superego over the affective sphere. At this point in our reflections, the difficulty, however, does not have to do with the status of love within the realm of feelings (to which I shall return below), but rather with the status of the commandment, particularly as a commandment to love. Does this commandment, on the plane of acts of discourse, have the same illocutionary force as, let us say, those ordinary commands that call for obedience, such as closing a door or opening a window? And, on the ethical plane, is this commandment comparable to moral principles, that is, to those first propositions that govern subordinate maxims, as do the utilitarian principle or the Kantian categorical imperative?

I found an unanticipated source of help in responding to this question in Franz Rosenzweig's *Star of Redemption*.[7] It may be recalled that this work, which itself is far from the commonplace, is divided into three sections, corresponding respectively to the idea of creation (or the eternal before), revelation (or the eternal present of encounter), and redemption (or the eternal not yet of messianic expectation). Coming to the second section, revelation, the reader may expect to be instructed concerning the Torah, and in a sense this is what happens, but the Torah, at this stage of Rosenzweig's meditation, is not yet a set of rules. Rather, it becomes so because it is preceded by the solemn act that situates all human experience in terms of the paradigmatic language of Scripture. And what is the most apt symbol for this imposing of a primordial language on the human sphere of communication? It is the commandment to love. Yet, contrary to our expectation, the formula for this commandment for Rosenzweig is not that of Exodus, nor that of Leviticus, nor that of Deuteronomy, but rather that of the Song of Solomon, which is read at every Passover celebration. Love, says the Song of Solomon, "is as strong as death."[8] Why does Rosenzweig refer to the Song of Solomon at this place? And with what imperative connotation? At the beginning of his section on revelation, he considers just the intimate colloquy between God and an individual soul, before any "third" person comes on the scene, which is taken up in the section on redemption.[9] His insight is to show in this way how the commandment to love springs from the bond of love between God and the individual soul. The commandment that precedes every law is the word that the lover addresses to the beloved: Love me! This unexpected distinction between commandment and law makes sense only if we admit that the commandment to love is love itself, commending itself, as though the genitive in the "commandment of love" were subjective and objective at the same time. Or, to put it another way, this is a commandment that contains the conditions for its being obeyed in the very tenderness of its objurgation: Love me!

If anyone should doubt the validity of this ever-so-subtle distinction Rosenzweig makes between commandment and law, I would reply by adding that we need to relate this deviant use of the imperative to the forms

---

7. Franz Rosenzweig, *The Star of Redemption*, trans. William W. Hallo (New York: Holt, Rinehart and Winston, 1971).

8. Ibid., 202.

9. If anyone is surprised to see all reference to the neighbor put off until the third category, redemption, it should be recalled that Rosenzweig's three categories are contemporaneous with one another even though the third also develops the second one. Thus the historical dimension unfolds beyond the solitary I-Thou conversation. From here on there are laws and not just the commandment: "Love me, at the same time as there are others." In other words, the second great commandment proceeds from the first, insofar as the always imminent future of a history of redemption, with all its historical and communal implications, proceeds from the today of the commandment to love. In this sense, there is not just a lover and a beloved, but a self and an other than oneself—a neighbor.

of discourse referred to earlier—praise, hymn, benediction, macarism—and thereby dare to speak of a poetic use of the imperative. This poetic use of the imperative has its own connotations within the broad range of expressions extending from the amorous invitation, through pressing supplication, to the summons, to the sharp command accompanied by the threat of punishment.[10] Thanks to this kinship between the command "Love me!" and the song of praise, the commandment of love is revealed as being irreducible, in its ethical overtones, to the moral imperative, so legitimately equated by Kant to obligation, or duty, with reference to the recalcitrance of human inclinations.

It is from this gap between what I have called the poetic use of the commandment and the commandment in the properly ethical sense of the term that I shall undertake my attempt below at a dialectic centered on the economy of the gift.

But before attempting this dialectic, I should like to add a third feature to our canvassing of the strange and odd expressions of love. This time, I should like to consider those expressions that have to do with love as a feeling. I have held off until this point any consideration of such expressions so as not to give in to the sirens of sentimentality. But now it is under the sign of the poetics of the hymn and the commandment that we can place this third feature, which I will sum up in terms of the power of metaphorization linked to the expressions of love. We may take up this theme beginning where we left off the preceding one: the pressing appeal (Love me!) that the lover addresses to the beloved confers on love the dynamism thanks to which it becomes capable of mobilizing a wide variety of affects that we designate by their end states—pleasure versus pain, satisfaction versus discontent, rejoicing versus distress, beatitude versus melancholy, and so on. What is more, love is not limited just to deploying this wide variety of affects around itself like some vast field of gravitation. It also creates a kind of ascending and descending spiral out of them, which it traverses in both directions.

And what I have just described in the psychological terms of affects and end states has its linguistic counterpart in the production of a vast field of analogies among all of the affective modes of love, thanks to which they mutually signify one another. Thus it is thanks to what I have called the process of metaphorization on this linguistic plane that erotic love is capable of signifying more than itself and of indirectly intending other qualities of love. But it is the underlying analogy between an affect and the linguistic process of metaphorization that we must emphasize. This is what Anders Nygren and all those who have followed him in setting up a dichotomy

---

10. There is here a broad semantic field whose exploration calls for the insightfulness and subtleness of a second J. L. Austin.

between *eros* and *agapē* have underestimated.[11] Analogy on the level of feelings and metaphorization on the linguistic plane refer to a single phenomenon, which implies that here metaphor is more than just a trope, or rhetorical ornament. To put it another way, in this instance the trope expresses what we might call the substantive tropology of love: that is, both the real analogy between feelings and the power of *eros* to signify *agapē* and to put it into words.

I want to end these initial remarks by considering those features of the discourse of justice that most obviously are opposed to these aspects of the discourse of love. I shall consider justice first on the level of social practice (where it is identified with the judicial structure of a society and characterizes a state based on law), then on the level of those principles of justice that govern our use of the predicate "just" as applied to such institutions.

Beginning with justice as a kind of social practice, I would like rapidly to recall the circumstances or occasions where justice arises, how it is applied, and what arguments it makes use of. As regards the circumstances of justice, taken as judicial practices, they form one part of the activities of communication in a society. More specifically, justice is at issue when a higher court is asked to decide between the claims of parties with opposed interests or rights. How this is carried out depends on a judicial structure that itself includes a number of aspects: for example, a body of written laws, courts of justice invested with the function of passing judgment, judges—that is, individuals like us, held to be independent, and charged with passing a just sentence for a particular situation. To this we must add that these structures are held to have the monopoly of power, that is, the power to impose their decision regarding what is just by using the public means of force.

As we can see, neither the circumstances nor the means of justice are those of love. Still less are the arguments of justice those of love. In fact, love does not argue, if we take the hymn from 1 Corinthians 13 as our model. Justice does argue. And it does so in a quite specific way, by confronting reasons for and against some position, which are taken as plausible, capable of being communicated, and worth discussing by all parties involved. Thus to say, as I suggested earlier, that justice is one part of the communicational activity of a society takes on its full meaning here. A confrontation between arguments before a tribunal is a noteworthy example of the dialogic use of language, and this kind of communication even has its own ethics: *audi alteram partem* (Listen to the other side).[12]

There is one aspect of this argumentative structure of justice that we

---

11. See Anders Nygren, *Agape and Eros*, trans. Philip S. Watson (Philadelphia: Westminster Press, 1953).

12. In the case of a crime and the pronouncing of a guilty verdict that the accused does not accept, the passing of sentence is still a form of communication. As J. R. Lucas puts it,

must not overlook in our comparison between justice and love. The clash of arguments is in a sense infinite, inasmuch as there is always the possibility of a "but...," for example, through recourse to a higher court of appeal. Yet it is also finite inasmuch as the conflict ends with the rendering of a decision. So the exercising of justice is not just a case of arguments; it also involves a decision, and this is the responsibility of the judge, as the last link in the chain of procedures, wherever this may occur. And when the judge's words are those of condemnation, we recall that statutes of justice carry a sword as well as a balance scale. Taken together, all these characteristics of judicial practice allow us for the first time to define the formalism of justice—not as a fault, but as a sign of force.

However, I do not want to take up the too easy task of reducing justice to that judicial apparatus that makes it a part of social practice. We have also to take into consideration the idea or ideal of justice, whose borderline with love is less easy to trace. Nevertheless, taken even at the quasi-reflective level of social practice, justice can be opposed to love in terms of some well-marked features that will bring us to the threshold of our reflections devoted to the dialectic between love and justice.

These distinctive features result from the almost complete identification of justice with distributive justice. This has been the case from Aristotle's *Nicomachean Ethics* right up to John Rawls's *A Theory of Justice,* and it is the significance of this identification that we now have to consider.[13] It presupposes that we give the idea of distribution an amplitude that surpasses the realm of economics. It is society as a whole, seen from the angle of justice, that appears as an assigning of roles, tasks, rights, and duties, of advantages or disadvantages, of goods and costs. The strength of this representation of society as a system of distribution is that it avoids the double trap of holism (which makes society an entity distinct from the members who compose it) and individualism (which makes society an additive sum of individuals and their interactions). In a distributive conception of society, society does not exist apart from the individuals among whom the "parts" are distributed and who thus "take part" in the whole. These individuals have no social existence apart from the distribution rule that confers on them a place within the whole. This is where justice comes in as the undergirding virtue of the institutions presiding over this division. To render each his or her due—*suum cuique tribuere*—is, in some particular situation of distribution, the most general formula of justice.

But in what way is there a virtue involved here? With this question, we raise the question of the status of the predicate "just" in our moral

---

"Punishment is a language. It translates the disesteem of society into the value system of the recalcitrant individual" (*On Justice* [Oxford: Clarendon, 1980], 134).

13. John Rawls, *A Theory of Justice* (Cambridge, Mass.: Harvard Univ. Press, 1971).

discourse. Since Aristotle, ethicists have sought an answer in the tie that binds justice and equality. On the judicial plane, this equation is easy to justify: treat similar cases in similar ways is the very principle of equality before the law. But how does this apply to those notoriously unequal distributions of wealth and property, of authority and responsibility, of honor and status that have characterized human society? Aristotle was the first who, when he found himself confronted with this difficulty, distinguished between proportional equality and mathematical equality. A division is just if it is proportional to the social importance of the parties involved. At the other end of history, we rediscover the same attempt to preserve the equation between justice and equality in the aforementioned work of John Rawls, when he argues that the increase in the advantages of the most favored is compensated for by a decrease in the disadvantages of the least favored. This is his second principle of justice, which completes the first principle of equality before the law. To maximize the smallest portion, this is the modern version of the concept of proportional justice stemming from Aristotle. With it, we have in a second manner characterized the legitimate formalism of justice, this time not just as judicial practice but as the ideal of an equitable division of rights and goods to the benefit of everyone.

What are the consequences for our reflections? Let us consider further the concepts of distribution and equality, which are the pillars of the idea of justice. The concept of distribution, taken in its broadest extension, confers a moral basis on the social practice of justice, in the sense we have given it, as the regulation of conflicts. Here society is seen, in effect, as the space of a confrontation between rivals. The idea of distributive justice covers all the operations of the judicial apparatus by giving them the end of upholding the claims of each person within the limit that the freedom of the one does not infringe on that of the other. As for equality, as the mathematical equality of rights and the proportional equality of advantages and responsibilities within an unequal division, this idea indicates both the strength and the limits of the very idea of the highest form of justice. The equality of rights, completed by that of chances, is certainly a source of social cohesion. Rawls even expects his principles of justice to reinforce social cooperation. But what kind of bond is thereby instituted between social partners? My own suggestion would be that the highest point the ideal of justice can envision is that of a society in which the feeling of mutual dependence—even of mutual indebtedness—remains subordinate to the idea of mutual disinterest.

We may in this regard recall Rawls's striking formula of a "disinterested interest," by means of which he characterizes the basic attitude of the parties in the hypothetical situation of the original social contract. The idea of mutuality is by no means absent from this formula, but the juxtaposition of interests prevents the idea of justice from attaining the level of a true recognition and a solidarity such that each person feels indebted to every other person. I shall attempt to show below that these ideas of recognition, of solidarity, and of mutual indebtedness can be seen as the unstable equilibrium point on the horizon of the dialectic of love and justice.

In the next part of my essay I would like to build a bridge between the poetics of love and what we might now call the prose of justice, between the hymn and the formal rule. We cannot avoid this confrontation once one or the other of these terms makes some claim concerning individual or social practice. In our reflections on the hymn, this relation to praxis was not considered. As we saw, love was simply praised for itself, for its elevation and its moral beauty. And in the rule of justice, no explicit reference was made to love, this latter if anything being left to the realm of possible motives. Yet both love and justice are addressed to action, each in its own fashion, for each makes a claim on action. Our dialectic must therefore move beyond our separate examination of love and justice to consider their interaction.

Rather than just confusing them or setting up a pure and simple dichotomy between love and justice, I think a third, difficult way has to be explored, one in which the tension between two distinct and sometimes opposed claims may be maintained and may even be the occasion for the invention of responsible forms of behavior. Where might we find the paradigm of such a living tension? Perhaps we can find it in the fragment of the Sermon on the Mount in Matthew and the Sermon on the Plain in Luke or, in what is a single context, in the new commandment, where love of one's enemies and the golden rule are brought into juxtaposition. These two commandments are stated in the greatest proximity in Luke 6: "But I say to you that hear, Love your enemies, do good to those who hate you, bless those who curse you, pray for those who abuse you" (6:27-28). And just a bit further on: "And as you wish that men would do to you, do so to them" (6:31). Before trying to make sense of this strange contiguity, let us ask two preliminary questions: How, on the one hand, is the commandment to love one's enemies linked to the hymn of love? In what way, on the other hand, does the golden rule announce the rule of justice?

Our first question is equivalent to asking how the poetic quality of the hymn gets converted into an obligation. What was said above regarding Rosenzweig's discussion of the commandment "Love me!" points us in the direction of an answer. To put it briefly, the commandment to love one's enemies is not sufficient by itself; rather, it is the hyperethical expression of a broader economy of the gift, which has many other modes of expression besides this claim on us to act. This economy of the gift touches every part of ethics, and a whole range of significations confers a specific articulation on it. At one extreme, we find the symbolism, which itself is quite complex, of creation, in the most basic sense of an originary giving of existence. The first use of the predicate "good" applied to all created things in Genesis 1 belongs to this symbolism: "And God saw everything that he had made, and behold it was very good" (1:31). The hyperethical dimension of this predicate extended to all creatures is what we must emphasize, for the result is that it is as a creature that we find ourselves summoned. The sense of radical dependence that is at stake here, insofar as it is attached to the symbolism of creation, does not leave us face-to-face with God; rather, it situates us within nature considered not as something to exploit but as an object of solicitude, of respect and admiration, as we hear in St. Francis's "Canto de Sole." The love of neighbor, in its extreme form of love for one's enemies, thus finds its first link to the economy of the gift in this hyperethical feeling of the dependence of the human creature, and our relation to the law and to justification stems from this same economy. These two relations even constitute the core of the recital of this economy, for, on the one hand, the law is a gift inasmuch as it is bound to the history of liberation, as told, for example, in Exod. 20:2—"I am the Lord, your God, who brought you out of the land of Egypt, out of the house of bondage." Justification, on the other hand, is also a gift inasmuch as it is a free pardon.

At the other end of the range of significations that articulate the economy of the gift we find the symbolism, symmetrical to creation and no less complex, of the final end, where God appears as the source of *unknown* possibilities. In this way, the God of hope and the God of creation are one and the same God at both extremes of the economy of the gift. At the same time, our relation both to the law and to salvation is shown to belong to this economy by being placed "between" creation and the eschaton.

Now it is from its reference to this economy of the gift that the "new" commandment draws the signification we have termed hyperethical. Why "hyperethical"? It is ethical owing to its imperative form, akin to what we considered above in discussing the commandment "Love me!" However, the commandment here is more determinate inasmuch as it is linked to a structure of praxis, the distinction between friends and enemies, which this new commandment abolishes. It is ethical, therefore, but also hyperethical in that this new commandment constitutes in a way the most adequate ethical projection of what transcends ethics, the economy of the gift. In this sense, an ethical approximation of this economy is set forth that may be summed up in the expression, "*Since* it has been given you, give . . ." According to this formula, and through the force of the "since," the gift turns out to be a source of obligation.

Yet this approximation is not without its paradoxes. By entering into the practical field, the economy of the gift develops a logic of superabundance that, at first glance at least, opposes itself to the logic of equivalence that governs everyday ethics.[14] If we consider the other pole of the opposition, it appears as though it is from the logic of equivalence, which we have just opposed to the logic of superabundance of the "new" commandment, that the golden rule stems, the rule that the Sermon on the Mount and, even more so, the Sermon on the Plain juxtapose in great contextual proximity with the commandment to love one's enemies. That the golden rule does stem from a logic of equivalence of some kind is indicated by the reciprocity, or the reversibility, that this rule establishes between what one person does and what is done to another, between acting and being acted upon—hence by implication between the agent and the patient, who, although irreplaceable, are proclaimed as being able to substitute for each other.

A reconciliation between this logic of equivalence, illustrated by the golden rule, and the logic of superabundance, incarnated in the new commandment, is made almost impossible if, following certain exegetes such as Albrecht Dihle in *Die Goldene Regel,* we link the golden rule to the law of retribution, the *jus talionis,* which is the most rudimentary expression of the logic of equivalence and its corollary, the rule of reciprocity.[15] Yet this incompatibility between our two logics even seems to be sanctioned by the declaration of Jesus that, in Luke 6:32-34, somehow leads to the statement of the golden rule:

> If you love those who love you, what credit is that to you? For even sinners love those who love them. And if you do good to those who do good to you, what credit is that to you? For even sinners do the same. And if you lend to those from whom you hope to receive, what credit is that to you? Even sinners lend to sinners, to receive as much again. But love your enemies, and do good, and lend, expecting nothing in return.

Is not the golden rule retracted by these harsh words?

This apparent condemnation of the golden rule has to disturb us inasmuch as the rule of justice can be taken as a reformulation of the golden

---

14. This logic of superabundance finds a great variety of expression in the New Testament. It governs the extravagant twist of many of Jesus' parables, as is evident in those called parables of growth: one seed that produces thirty, sixty, a hundred grains, a tiny mustard seed that becomes a tree where birds may nest, and so on. In a different context, Paul interprets the whole history of salvation following the same law of superabundance: "If because of one man's trespass, death reigned through that one man, much more will those who receive the abundance of grace and the free gift of righteousness reign in life through the one man Jesus Christ" (Rom. 5:17). The extravagance of the parables, the hyperbole of the eschatological sayings, the logic of superabundance in ethics are all different expressions of what I am calling the logic of superabundance.

15. Albrecht Dihle, *Die Goldene Regel* (Heidelberg: C. Winter, 1989).

rule in formal terms.[16] This formalization is already visible in justice considered as a social practice, as the precept *audi alteram partem* bears witness, and as does the rule to treat similar cases in similar ways. It is given a more complete statement in the principles of justice referred to earlier with reference to the work of John Rawls. This does not, however, prevent our recognizing the spirit of the golden rule in even the quasi-algebraic form of Rawls's second principle: maximize the smallest portion. This formula is equivalent in effect to equalizing portions as much as permitted by the inequalities imposed by economic and social efficiency. Therefore it is legitimate for us to extend to the social practice of justice and to the principles of justice themselves the suspicion that strikes the golden rule through the logic of superabundance underlying the hyperethical commandment to love one's enemies. The rule of justice, the expression par excellence of the logic of equivalence and reciprocity, thus seems to suffer the same fate as the golden rule when put under the judgment of the new commandment.

But must we remain with this assertion of incompatibility? Let us return to our paradigm, the Sermon on the Mount (or the Plain). If the difference between our two logics were merely as we have stated it, how are we to explain the presence in one and the same context of the commandment to love one's enemies and the golden rule? Another interpretation is possible, wherein the commandment of love does not abolish the golden rule but instead reinterprets it in terms of generosity, and thereby makes not just possible but necessary an application of the commandment whereby, owing to its hyperethical status, it does not accede to the ethical sphere except at the price of paradoxical and extreme forms of behavior, those forms that are in fact recommended in the wake of the new commandment:

> Love your enemies, do good to those who hate you, bless those who curse you, pray for those who abuse you. To him who strikes you on the cheek, offer the other also; and from him who takes away your cloak do not withhold your coat as well. Give to every one who begs from you; and of him who takes away your goods, do not ask them again. (Luke 6:27-30)

These are those unique and extreme forms of commitment taken up by St. Francis, Gandhi, and Martin Luther King Jr. Yet from what penal law and, in general, from what rule of justice can we deduce a maxim of action that would set up nonequivalence as a general rule? What distribution of tasks, roles, or advantages and obligations could be established, in the spirit of distributive justice, if the maxim of lending while expecting nothing in

---

16. In truth, a certain formalism already appears in the golden rule. We are not told what it is that we are to love or hate if it is done to us; however, this formalism is imperfect inasmuch as it still appeals to emotions, to love and hate, which Kant will put on the side of "pathological" desires.

return were set up as a universal rule? If the hypermoral is not to turn into the nonmoral—not to say the immoral, for example, cowardice—it has to pass through the principle of morality, summed up in the golden rule and formalized by the rule of justice.

Yet the opposite is no less true. In this relation of living tension between the logic of superabundance and the logic of equivalence, the latter receives from its confrontation with the former the capacity of raising itself above its perverse interpretations. Without the corrective of the commandment to love, the golden rule would be constantly drawn in the direction of a utilitarian maxim whose formula is *do ut des* (I give *in order that* you will give). The rule "Give *because* it has been given you" corrects the "in order that" of the utilitarian maxim and saves the golden rule from an always possible perverse interpretation. It is in this sense that we may interpret the harsh words of Luke 6:32-39, just after the reaffirmation of the golden rule in 6:31 and just before the reaffirmation of the new commandment in 6:35. In these intermediary verses the critical point of the logic of superabundance is directed not so much at the logic of equivalence of the golden rule as against its perverse interpretation. The same rule is capable of two readings, of two interpretations, one of which is based on interest, the other of which is disinterested. Only the commandment can decide the case in favor of the second against the first.

Having said this, can we not extend to the rule of justice the same test and the same critical interpretation? We have already referred to the dissimulated ambiguity of the rule of justice. We saw the rule of justice oscillate between the disinterested interest of parties concerned to increase their own advantage as far as the accepted rule will allow, and a true feeling of cooperation going as far as the confession of being mutual debtors to one another. In the same way that the golden rule, given over to itself, sinks to the rank of a utilitarian maxim, the rule of justice, given over to itself, tends to subordinate cooperation to competition, or rather to expect from the equilibrium of rival interests the simulacrum of cooperation.

If such is the spontaneous tendency of our sense of justice, must we not admit that if it were not touched and secretly guarded by the poetics of love, even up to its most abstract formulation, it would become merely a subtly sublimated variety of utilitarianism? After all, does not even the Rawlsian calculation of the maximum run the risk in the final analysis of appearing as the dissimulated form of a utilitarian calculation?[17] What saves Rawls's second principle of justice from falling into this subtle form

---

17. This calculation would run as follows. If, once the veil of ignorance were lifted, the worst portion were to fall to me, would it not be better to choose behind the veil of ignorance the rule of distribution that, undoubtedly, would deprive me of the highest gains I might attain under a less equitable division, but which would also protect me from the greater possible disadvantages of another form of division?

of utilitarianism is finally its secret kinship with the commandment to love, inasmuch as this latter is directed against the process of victimization that utilitarianism sanctions when it proposes as its ideal the maximization of the average advantage of the greatest number at the price of the sacrifice of a small number, a sinister implication that utilitarianism tries to conceal. This kinship between Rawls's second principle of justice and the commandment to love is finally one of the unspoken presuppositions of the well-known reflective equilibrium that this theory warrants in the last resort between its abstract theory and our well-considered convictions.

The tension we have discerned in place of our initial antinomy is not equivalent to the suppression of the contrast between our two logics. Nevertheless, it does make justice the necessary medium of love; precisely because love is hypermoral, it enters the practical and ethical sphere only under the aegis of justice. As I have said elsewhere about the parables of Jesus, which reorient by disorienting, this effect is obtained on the ethical plane only through the conjugation of the new commandment with the golden rule and, in a more general way, through the synergistic action of love and justice. To disorient without reorienting is, in Kierkegaardian terms, to suspend the ethical. In one sense, the commandment to love, as hyperethical, is a way of suspending the ethical, which is reoriented only at the price of a reprise and a rectification of the rule of justice that runs counter to its utilitarian tendency.

Allow me to say in conclusion that the formulas we find in reading analytical philosophers concerned, as is Outka, with disengaging the normative content of love are formulas that describe those figures of love that have already been mediated by justice, in a culture marked by our Jewish, Greek, and Christian heritages. In this sense, we come back once again to Outka's three definitions: equal regard, self-sacrifice, and mutuality.

It is the task of both philosophy and theology to discern, beneath the reflective equilibrium expressed in these compromise formulas, the secret discordance between the logic of superabundance and the logic of equivalence. It is also their task to say that it is only in the moral judgment made within some particular situation that this unstable equilibrium can be assured and protected. Thus we may affirm in good faith and with a good conscience that the enterprise of expressing this equilibrium in everyday life, on the individual, judicial, social, and political planes, is perfectly practicable. I would even say that the tenacious incorporation, step by step, of a supplementary degree of compassion and generosity in all of our codes—including our penal codes and our codes of social justice—constitutes a perfectly reasonable task, however difficult and interminable it may be.

Bibliographical Note

The standard bibliography of Paul Ricoeur, including writings by Ricoeur and writings about him, is Frans D. Vansina, *A Primary and Secondary Systematic Bibliography of Paul Ricoeur 1935–1984* (Louvain-la-Neuve: Editions Peeters, 1985). An updated listing of Ricoeur's works by Vansina can be found in *The Philosophy of Paul Ricoeur,* ed. Lewis Edwin Hahn, Library of Living Philosophers 22 (Chicago: Open Court, 1995), 604–815.

Index of Biblical Passages

Index of Names

Index of Subjects